THE ART OF LOOKING UP

THE ART OF LOOKING UP

CATHERINE McCORMACK

WHITE
LION
PUBLISHING

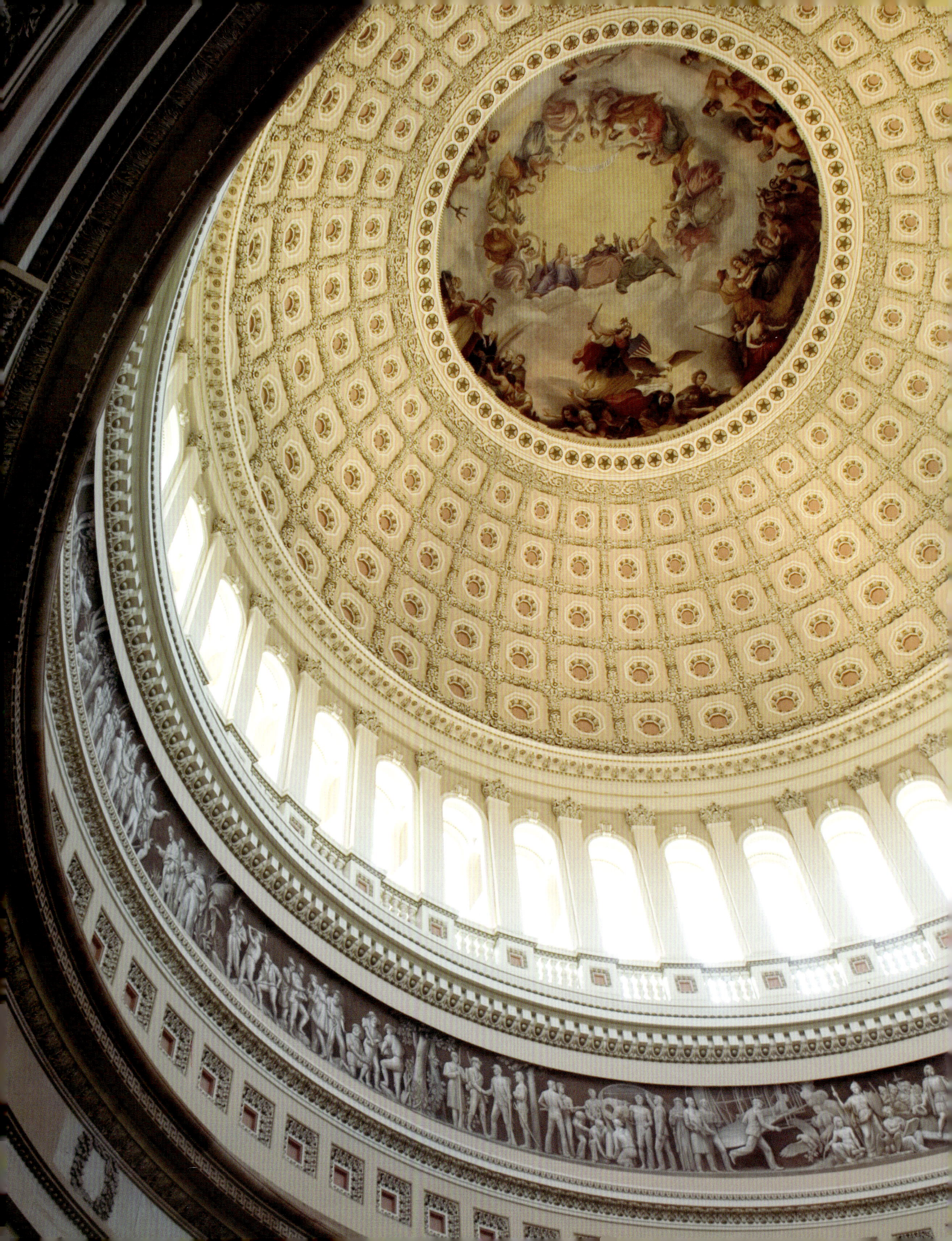

1

2

3

4

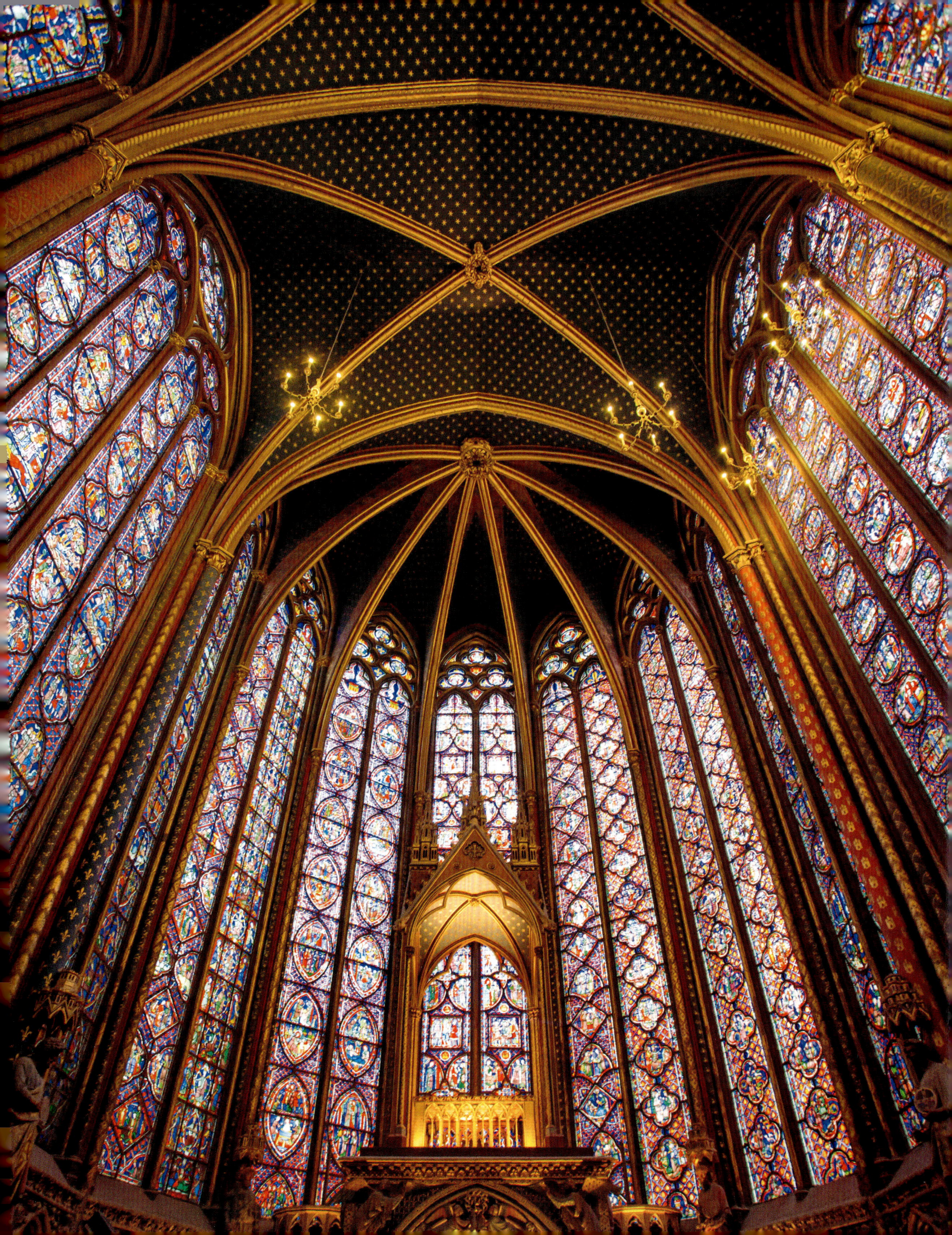

Left: The starry vault of Sainte-Chapelle, the royal chapel within the Palais de la Cité, consecrated in 1248. Soaring Gothic architecture draws the gaze and mind upwards to an imagined divine firmament, while light filters through the radiant polychromatic stained glass to create an experience of heaven on earth.

Introduction

Why do we look up? In childhood we look up for reassurance, guidance and a model of the future that awaits us. As humans we are hierarchical and believe that the higher up something is, the greater its importance, and we consequently tend to desire things that are tantalizingly out of reach. As humanity we have looked up at the sky above us to understand our place in the universe, using the constellations of the stars to chart our voyages. In looking up we reflect on our gods and construct the stories of our creation. In looking up we encounter the frontiers of our knowledge in the firmament of sky and stars that we have tried so hard to conquer and inhabit, first with air travel, then through space. For the sky binds us to our planet but also presents a boundary that we long to break through. Looking up was led by a desire for transcendence beyond ourselves and this is, perhaps, why it is here that we have long projected our religious, cultural and social beliefs and philosophies.

This might also explain why the blank spaces of our buildings – the domes, the vaults, the ceilings – have proved irresistible to emblazon and decorate; they act as a version of the sky that we can control and occupy to our own design. The words are linked linguistically, after all. The English word 'ceiling' is influenced by the Latin term *caelum* meaning 'sky' or 'heaven'.

This must be why we have designated the sky as the source of all that we revere, to the abandonment of the ground beneath us. In the early 1500s, Leonardo da Vinci said that we knew more about the movement of the celestial bodies above than we do about the soil underfoot. But it has not always been so. Before the end of the Neolithic period (c. 3000 BCE), we looked into the earth for our spirits and gods. The great sky-god cults emerged at the beginning of the Indo-European age and their dominance has not waned. They are all present in the works selected for this book – from Jupiter, the king of the pagan gods hurling his thunderbolts, Hindu's Krishna, Shiva and Vishnu and the spiritual deities of Buddhism, to the Christian god of judgment and creation and the divinity of Islam, conveyed not in pictorial form, but sublimated into pattern, colour and light.

The architecture of our religious buildings leads our gaze upwards, both in the soaring vaults of early medieval European cathedrals, and the dome, its circular shape a symbol of heaven and a metaphor for eternity from Islam to Christianity. And because we have placed our gods in the sky, looking up fosters aspirations of immortality. The ceiling is an aggrandizing space for those who have the means to occupy it in visual form, whether in the story of Christian saints or the apotheosis of popes and prince-bishops, or even artists, as in the case of Salvador Dalí's Palace of the Wind ceiling, which depicts his apotheosis into the subconscious mind.

This relationship with the sky leads to the prevalence of the colour blue in many examples of ceiling art, from the mosaics of Ravenna to Cy Twombly's ocean of azure in the Louvre Museum, known only as *The Ceiling*, or the inimitable blue of Gladys Deacon's eyes as they glare down imposingly from the North Portico of Blenheim Palace with an otherworldliness that is firmly secular. It is worth remembering that, in painting the blue of the sky, we have had to mine the ground for the precious lapis lazuli pigment that in fifteenth-century Florence produced the colour considered to be the most perfect, illustrious and beautiful (according to Italian artist Cennino Cennini). Although the story of painting the sky is a story of blue, this is not the only colour to be found here, rendered in materials that range from glass to mosaic and stone and even the wing cases of scarab beetles. Let's not forget that, while we are looking up, figures in the images above are looking down on us. The techniques of *sotto in su* (from below to above) and *trompe l'oeil* (trick of the eye) are intended to terrify, inspire and entertain, making spectators flinch as they anticipate the overspill of the illusory world of the painting into their own space. This relationship between looking up and what is below plays out in Giulio Romano's *Sala dei Giganti* in Palazzo del Te, Mantua, in which the sky gods of Mount Olympus battle with the mysterious forces of the primordial earth in the form of the giants.

There is a conspicuous absence of women artists in the book. This does not reflect a lack of capability among women, but rather a dearth of opportunity throughout the history of art. For women across all continents and cultures were prohibited from the art-academy training that typically led to commissions in the public and private spaces that feature in this book – from the grand contracts to embellish the palaces of the wealthy and powerful to the religious buildings that defined the state, or the political halls of the establishment order. And there is no way of knowing the gender of the anonymous artisans of mosaic and stonework whose work is their silent testimony in places such as the Neonian Baptistery or at the Alhambra and Topkapı palaces.

Painting as an art in itself, and also one that combined poetry and intellect, was considered a male profession. Indeed, there was even a taxonomy of masculinity within painting in Italian art theory of the fifteenth and sixteenth centuries – one in which fresco was considered the most 'virile' painting technique, reserved for such spaces as the vaulted ceiling of the Sistine Chapel in Rome, or the smaller vault of the Palazzo Farnese in the same city, or the triumphalist all-encompassing world view of Tiepolo's staircase in the Würzburg Residence.

There are a few exceptions to this gendered rule, examples that fell through the gaps, but that history has not devoted enough attention to until recently. For example, Artemisia Gentileschi (1593–1653) was born into a family of male painters and learnt her profession with her brothers in her father's studio. A successful artist in her own right, she joined her father in London to paint the nine canvases of the *Allegory of Peace* for the ceiling of the Queen's House in Greenwich, a work that is now installed in Marlborough House, London. But her contribution has been squabbled over in the scholarly archive, with the voices that dispute her hand as vocal as those who attest her presence. Founding member of the Royal Academy in Britain, in 1768, Angelica Kauffman (1741–1807) was a self-professed history painter. The most illustrious category an artist could identify as, this was almost exclusively reserved for male painters by virtue of the fact that women were prohibited from studying nude models – fundamental to painting in the academic style. Kauffman painted four images known as the *Elements of Art* for the ceiling of the Royal Academy in London in the 1780s. Each image depicts an

Right: England's only 'history painter', Angelica Kauffman's personification of 'Colour' (1778–80) depicts art as a woman who reaches with her paintbrush to a rainbow in order to take inspiration from the natural world. At her feet a chameleon also symbolizes the diversity of colour in nature.

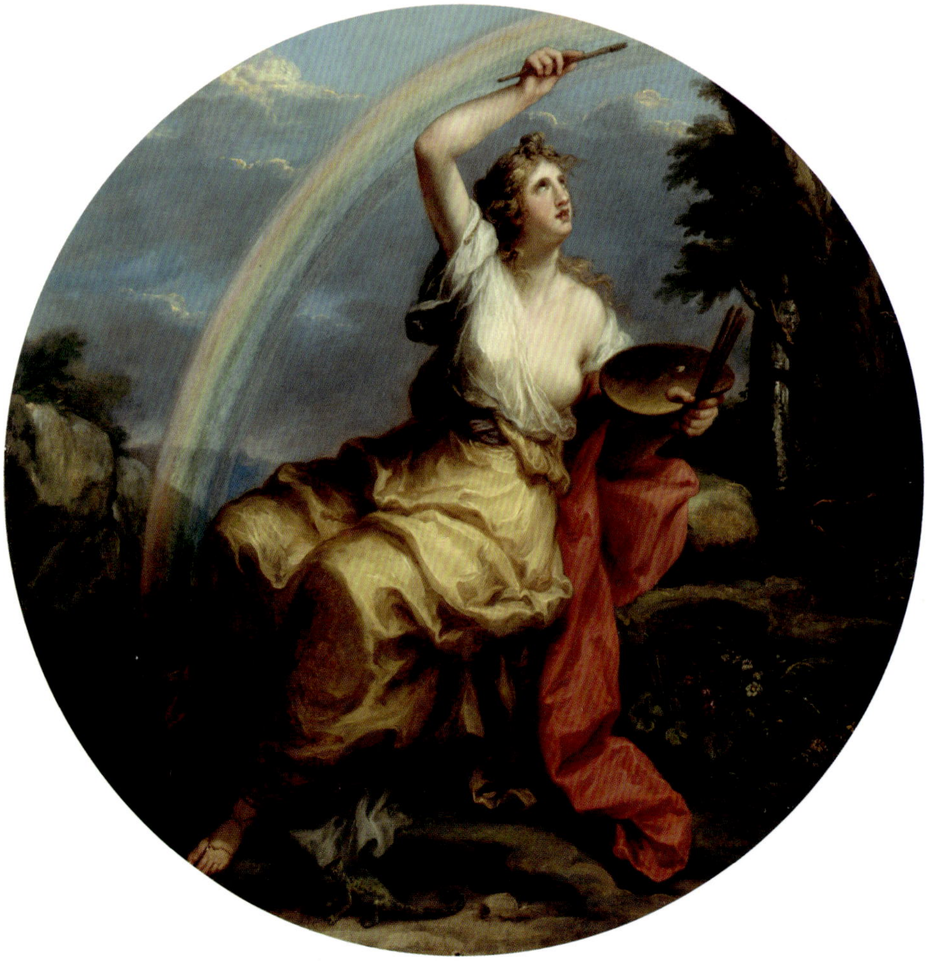

allegorical female figure representing a foundational principle of artistic practice: *Invention, Composition, Design and Colour.*

In simple terms, Kauffman represents 'art' as embodied in the form of woman. In doing so, she bucked the convention for using male figures to symbolize the intellectual act of painting and design, making a statement that was clearly intended to rethink the gender limitations on artistic practice. The works can currently be seen in the entrance hall of Burlington House, London.

The absence of these women from this book – in spite of their contemporaneous cultural prominence – raises an interesting question about art history – about how it has occluded and obscured the artistic contributions of women. The consequence of this is that archives contain far fewer images than are needed to fill the pages of a book of this nature. At least we can honour them in some way here in the space of the introduction.

All that remains to be said is that looking up does strange things to us. The body becomes vertical, the feet, hands and ground disappear. We become human columns, using only our eyes. Looking up takes us out of our heads, into star time, Krishna time, towards transcendence and freedom from our mortal bonds. But we also mustn't forget that looking up can be a form of agony; with necks crooked it becomes hard to swallow, our throats constricted and exposed. Michelangelo knew this when he described the torture of four years spent painting the ceiling of the Sistine Chapel trapped in a living hell of his own description. It seems perhaps, that we cannot always have our heads in the stars.

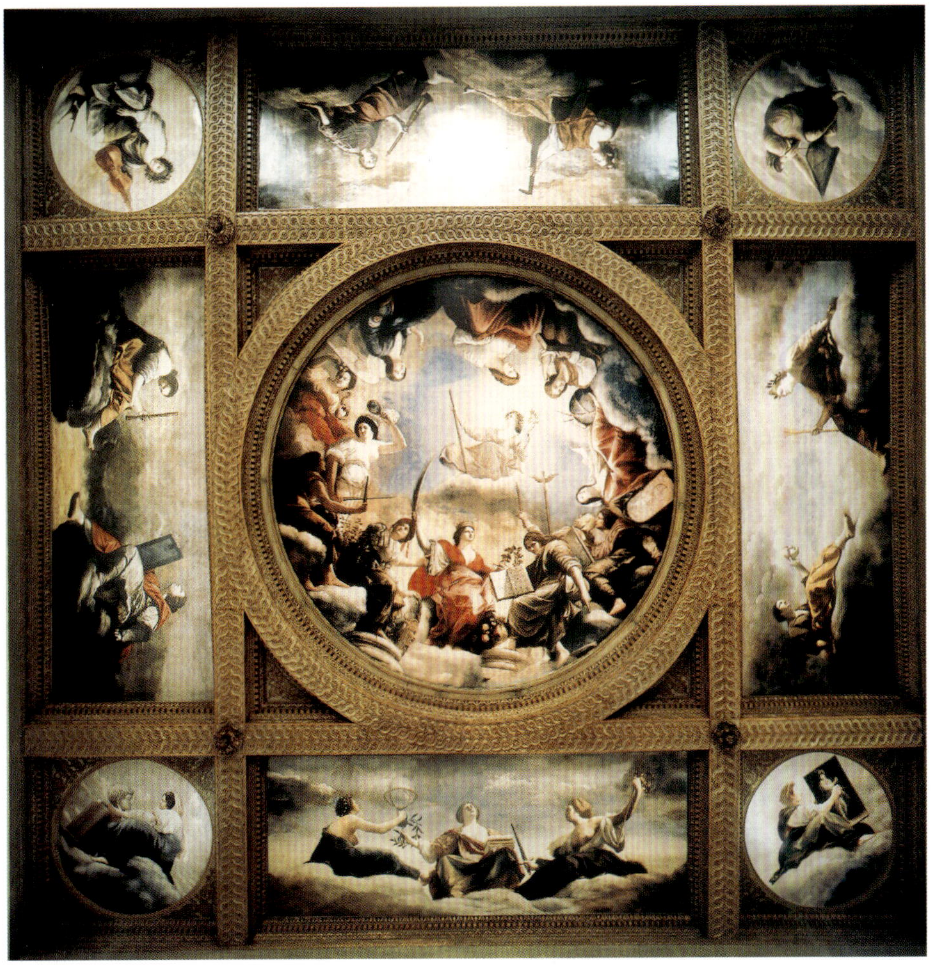

Left: Artemisia Gentileschi's nine panels depicting an *Allegory of Peace*, originally intended for the ceiling of the Queen's House in Greenwich, London. The building was designed for Queen Anne of Denmark and became the royal residence for Queen Henrietta Maria, wife of Charles I.

Overleaf: Cy Twombly's mesmerizingly oceanic *The Ceiling* in the Louvre Museum.

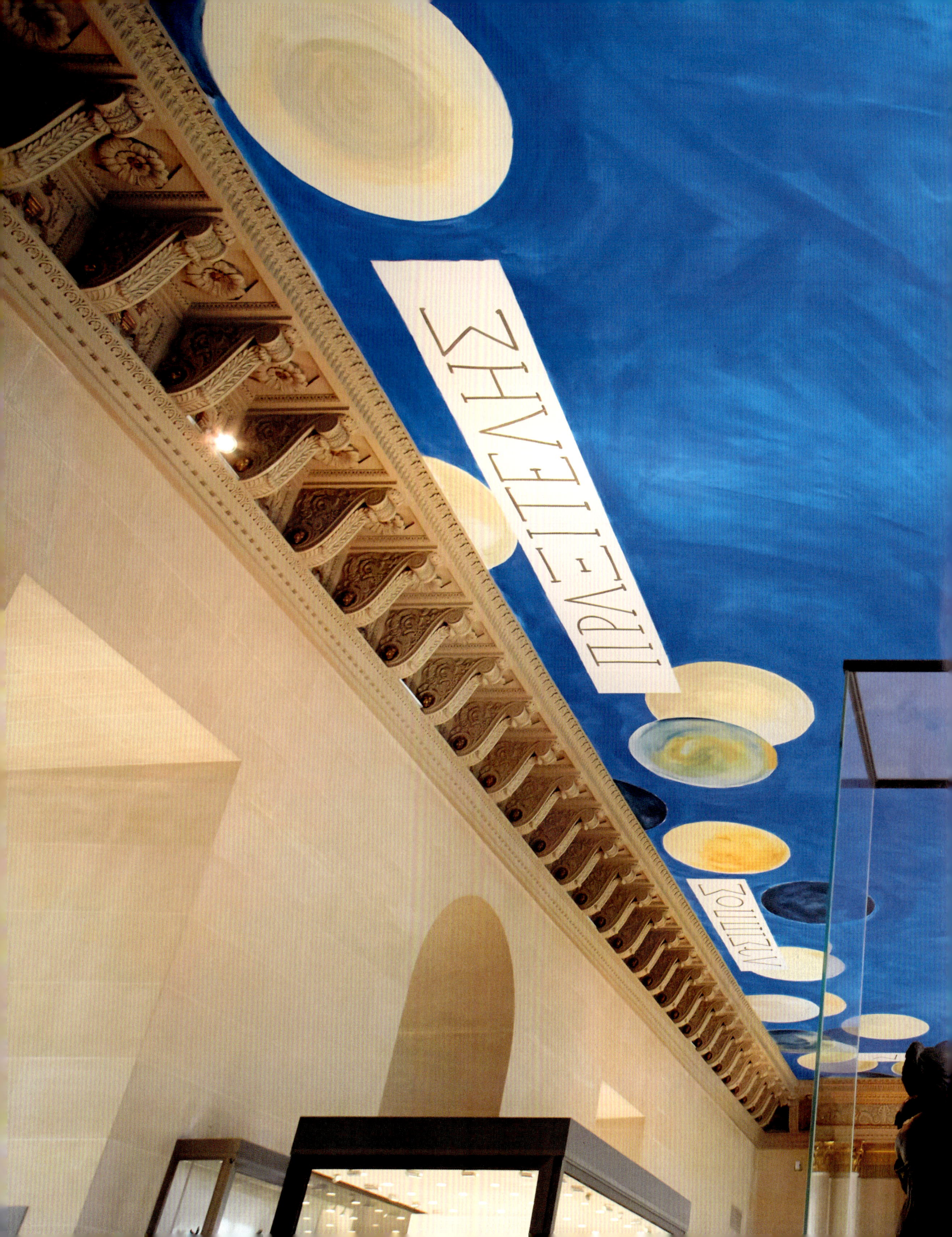
ΠΡΑΞΙΤΕΛΗΣ
ΛΥΣΙΠΠΟΣ

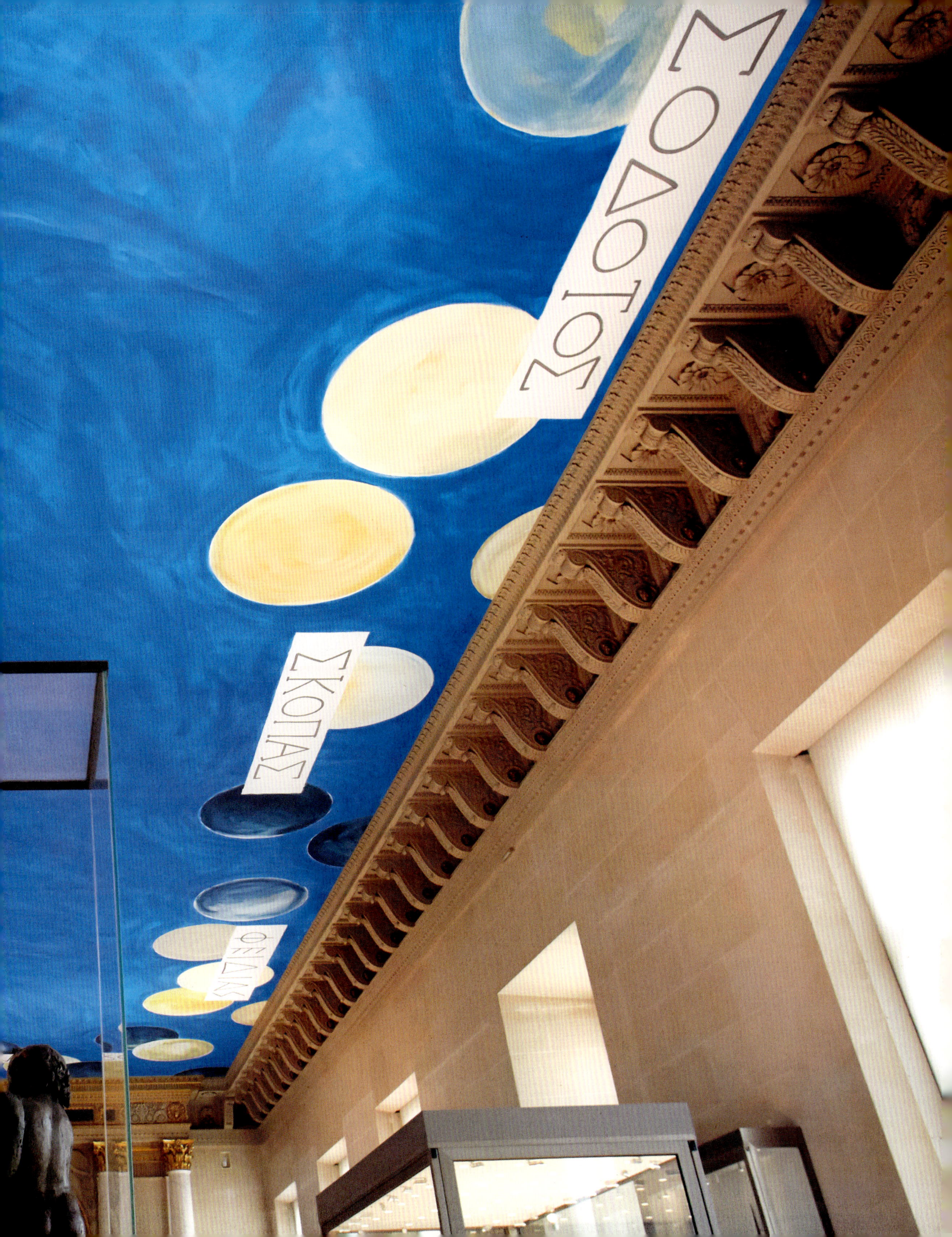
ΣΚΟΠΑΣ

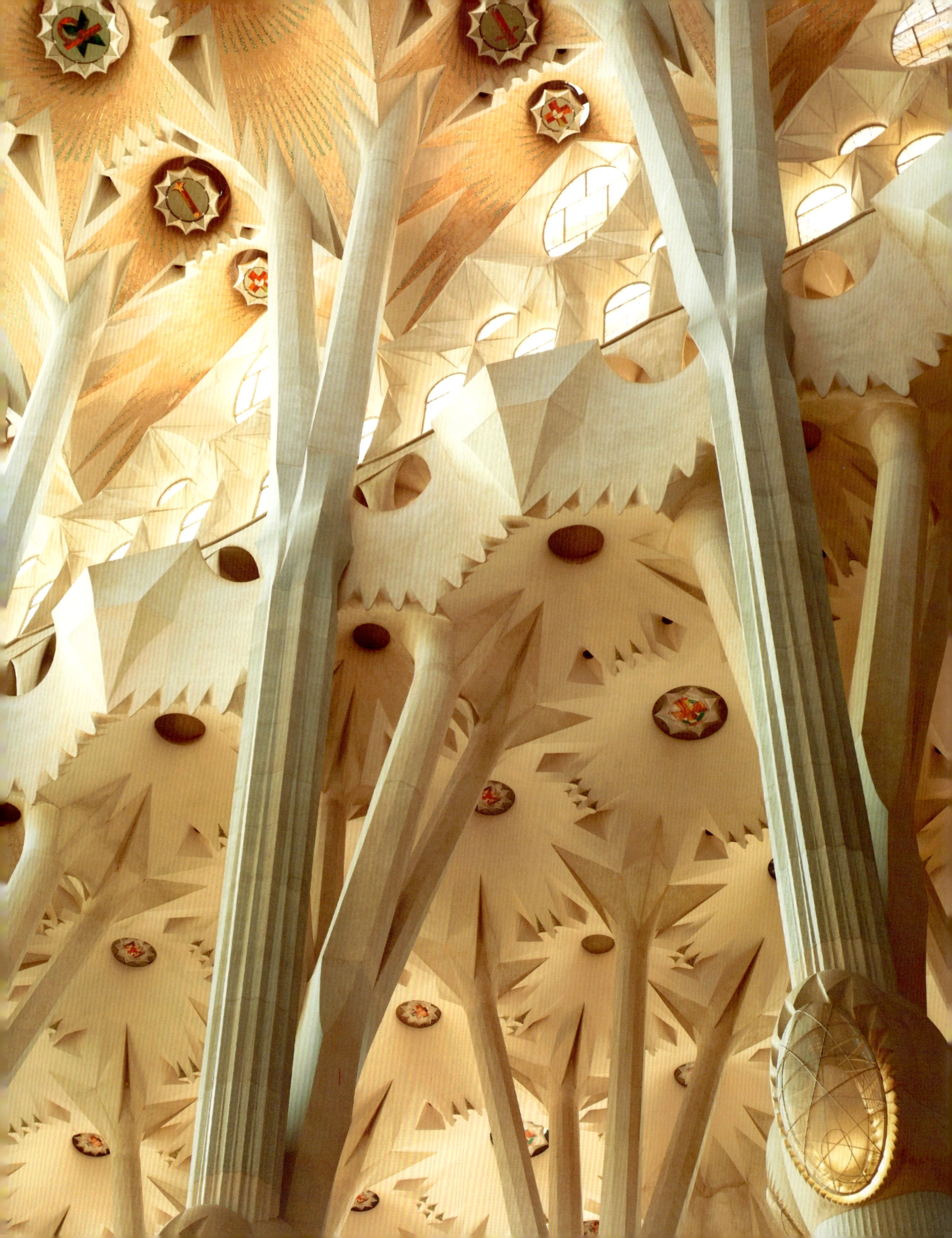

1

Religion

Regardless of race, geography or creed, all gods occupy the sky. The close of the Neolithic period (before 3000 BCE) saw the transformation of religious beliefs as they shifted from a focus on the power, fertility and spirituality of the earth to the introduction of the sky-god cults. These include the Abrahamic religions and, before those, the gods of ancient Egyptian and then ancient Greek and Roman pagan theology, who occupied Mount Olympus in the sky. In short, from the Indo-European period, we started to look up to see God. It was at this time that humanity began to design sacred spaces with versions of heaven to bridge the gap between that intangible godly place and our own mortal realms harnessed to the earth. But the depiction of gods in art has proven a perpetually divisive topic across world religions.

Christianity sees humankind as a reflection of a form of creator god that made man in his own likeness, a central creed that has motivated an avalanche of images that, themselves, have caused factional strife between different groups. Elsewhere, Islam denies picturing God or any form of life, preferring instead to meditate on the spiritual mysteries of creation through abstracted and geometric repeating patterns. Examples of both approaches can be found in the following pages, from Michelangelo's Sistine Chapel ceiling, which eulogizes the sky-bound father god giving life to the figures of the first woman and the first man, to the Imam Mosque in Isfahan, which almost levitates with colour, light and hypnotic repeated pattern to express a state of transcendent godliness outside of the material realm. Interestingly, these seemingly opposing ideologies come together in Antonio Gaudí's Sagrada Família in Barcelona, the unfinished Christian temple that suggests, with its columns and configurations of complex geometrical architecture and decorative design, that an abstract notion of heaven has its roots deep in the material earth.

Ceilings and domes were frequently used for the telling of religious narratives to those who could not read it in words, and so early images of Christianity provided an education in the scriptures and lives of the saints through more easily assimilated visual means. Such images tend to focus on transcendence and sublimation, but also judgment, sacrifice and punishment.

Religious ceilings also inevitably reflect the climate in which they were produced, for example the interest in classical humanism and the sculptures of ancient Greece and Rome, whose impact is felt in the Sistine Chapel, the revivalist fanfare of Byzantium and the Eastern Christian church celebrated in the nineteenth-century Church of the Resurrection of Jesus Christ in St Petersburg, and the reclaiming of historical techniques, styles and spiritual heritage in the face of the contamination of Western art history at Sensō-ji temple in Tokyo.

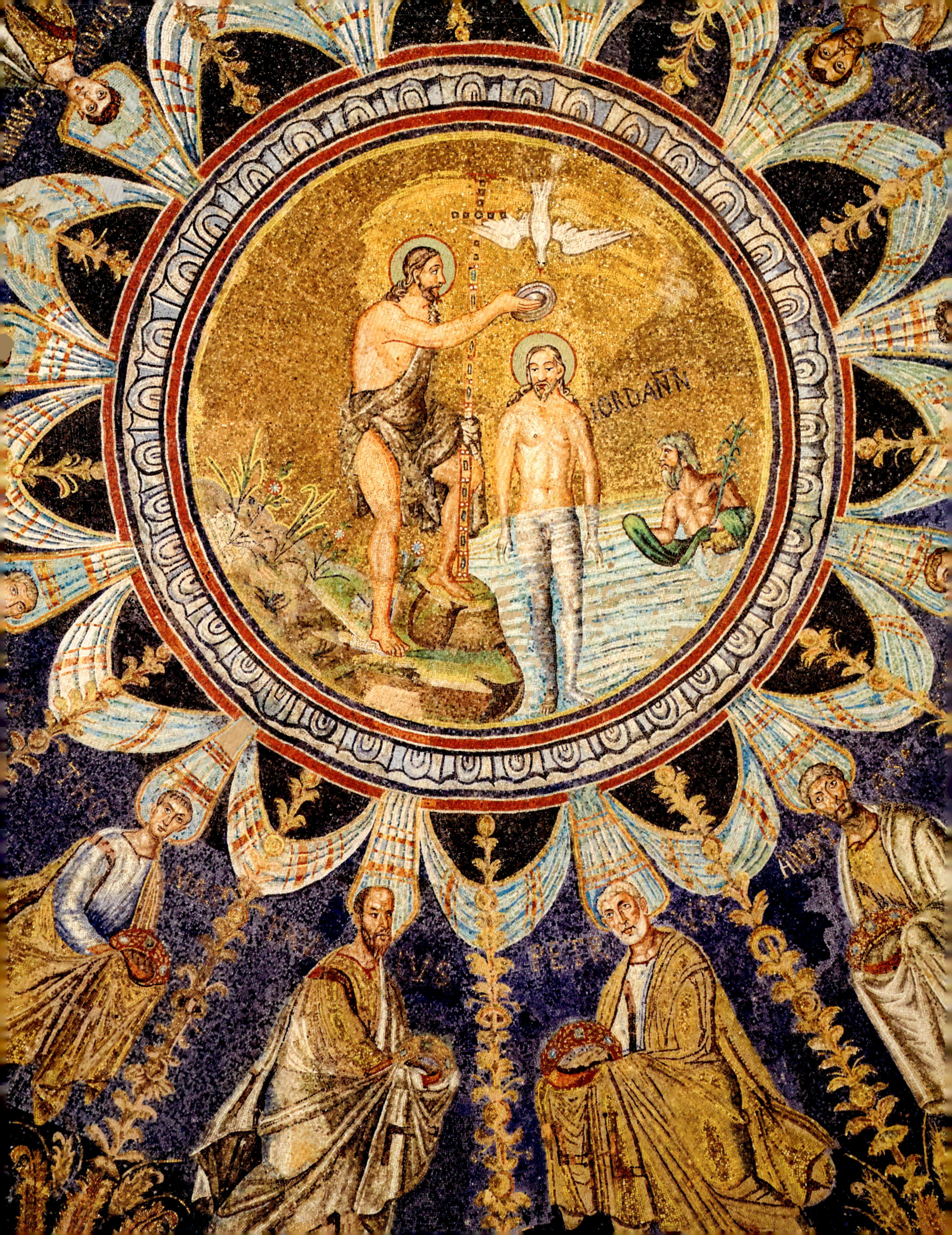
IORDANN

Neonian Baptistery
4th Century
Ravenna, Italy

Left: Central medallion of the dome (cupola) depicting John the Baptist baptizing Jesus Christ, who is submerged in the water of the River Jordan. The river itself is also personified in the figure of an old man wrapped in a green cloth, potentially drawing on earlier pagan depictions of river gods. In the outer circle, twelve attendant apostles hold crowns.

Overleaf: The blue and gold of the mosaic dome are used to reflect the splendour and beauty of Christ.

Neonian Baptistery, Italy

Looking up at the glinting mosaic dome of the Neonian Baptistery in Ravenna connects the viewer with a special point in art's early history. These tesserae of coloured stone, mineral, glass and shell take us to an era of images that predates what we now call 'art', a time when the early followers of the cult of Christianity asked themselves how they might picture God. How should they depict the invisible realms of spirituality and what symbols and tools would they use to create a language of religious beliefs that could speak in images rather than words?

At Ravenna, the answers to these questions resulted in a majestic display amid a sea of tessellated blue and gold. The two colours are symbolic. They reflect the splendour and beauty of an imagined majestic god in a celestial field of heaven, and represent the very earliest depictions of Christ as a type of sun deity emanating golden light, which emerged in the decoration of sacred spaces as early as the third century [CE].

The building of this baptistery was instigated by the Bishop Ursus and dates to the very closing years of the fourth century. It is an early example of the type of architecture that was created as Christianity took root as the official religion of the Roman Empire during the reign of the Emperor Constantine, who famously converted from paganism to the Christian faith. Built on an octagonal plan, the building had a unique function as the site for the initiation rite of baptism – a ritual that took place only once a year, on the eve of Easter Sunday. It was a place where early Christians went to be reborn and to commune with God, and this is the theme of the interior mosaic decorating the cupola, commissioned by Bishop Neon (451–473) several decades later.

The central medallion of the cupola is directly above the huge baptismal font at ground level and shows a gargantuan figure of John the Baptist baptizing a nude Christ, who is submerged up to the waist in transparent rippling water while God descends as the Holy Spirit in the form of a dove. It is a visual depiction of the words of the New Testament gospel of Mark 1: 9–11: 'Jesus was baptized by John in the Jordan. And when he came up out of the water, immediately he saw the heavens open and the Spirit descending upon him like a dove; and a voice came from heaven, "Thou art my beloved Son; with thee I am well pleased."' Much of this image has been crudely restored during postmedieval alterations, including John's head and arm, Christ's head and shoulders, and the dove. The most significant change is that, originally, Christ was depicted as beardless, in keeping with fourth- and fifth-century early Christian depictions in which the figure of God-made man resembled the youthful and clean-shaven Apollo, the pagan god of sun, enlightenment and creativity. A smaller figure of an elderly man looks on and is a personification of the River Jordan. The picturing of the river as a figure is doubly significant. Firstly, this was a solution to the conundrum of how to depict the idea of 'living water' – a concept that was central to the sacrament of baptism. Secondly, it was a way of recycling the already familiar visual tradition in earlier pagan Roman and Greek art of depicting river deities in human form.

Framing the central scene is a procession of Christ's twelve apostles led by Sts Peter and Paul. According to early Christian bishop Gregory of Nyssa (335–394), the apostles had been anticipated in scripture as 'the ministers of baptism'. They carry

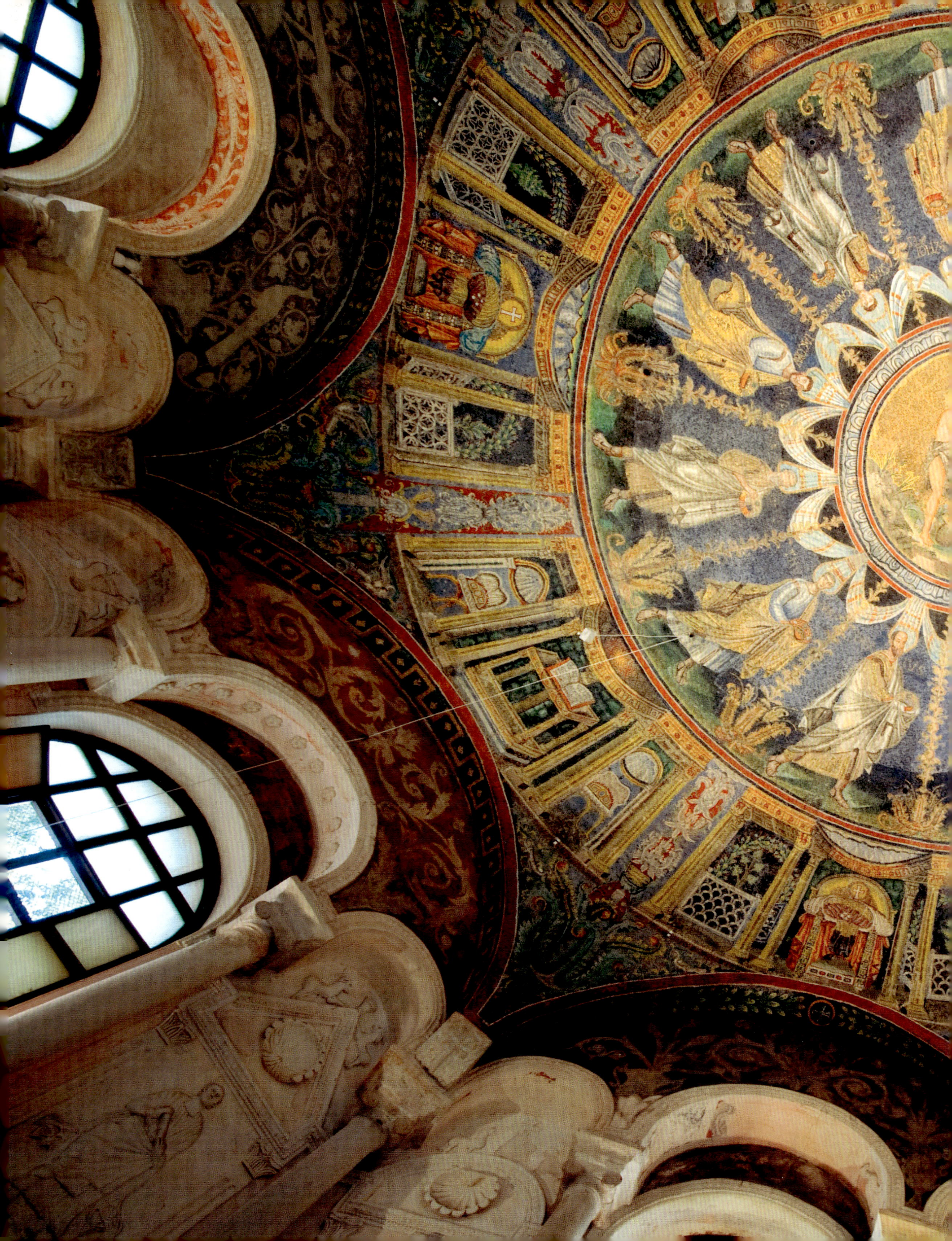

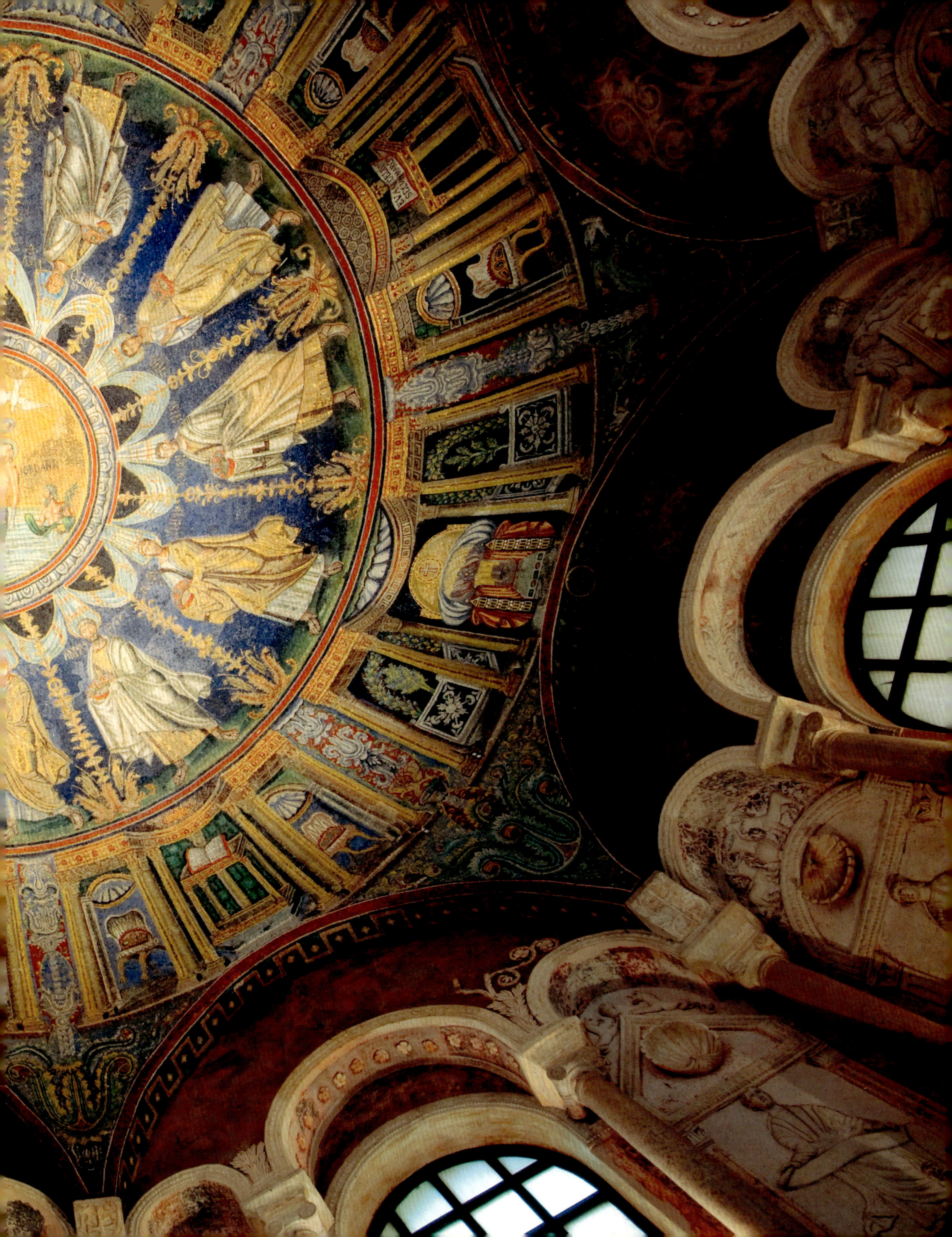

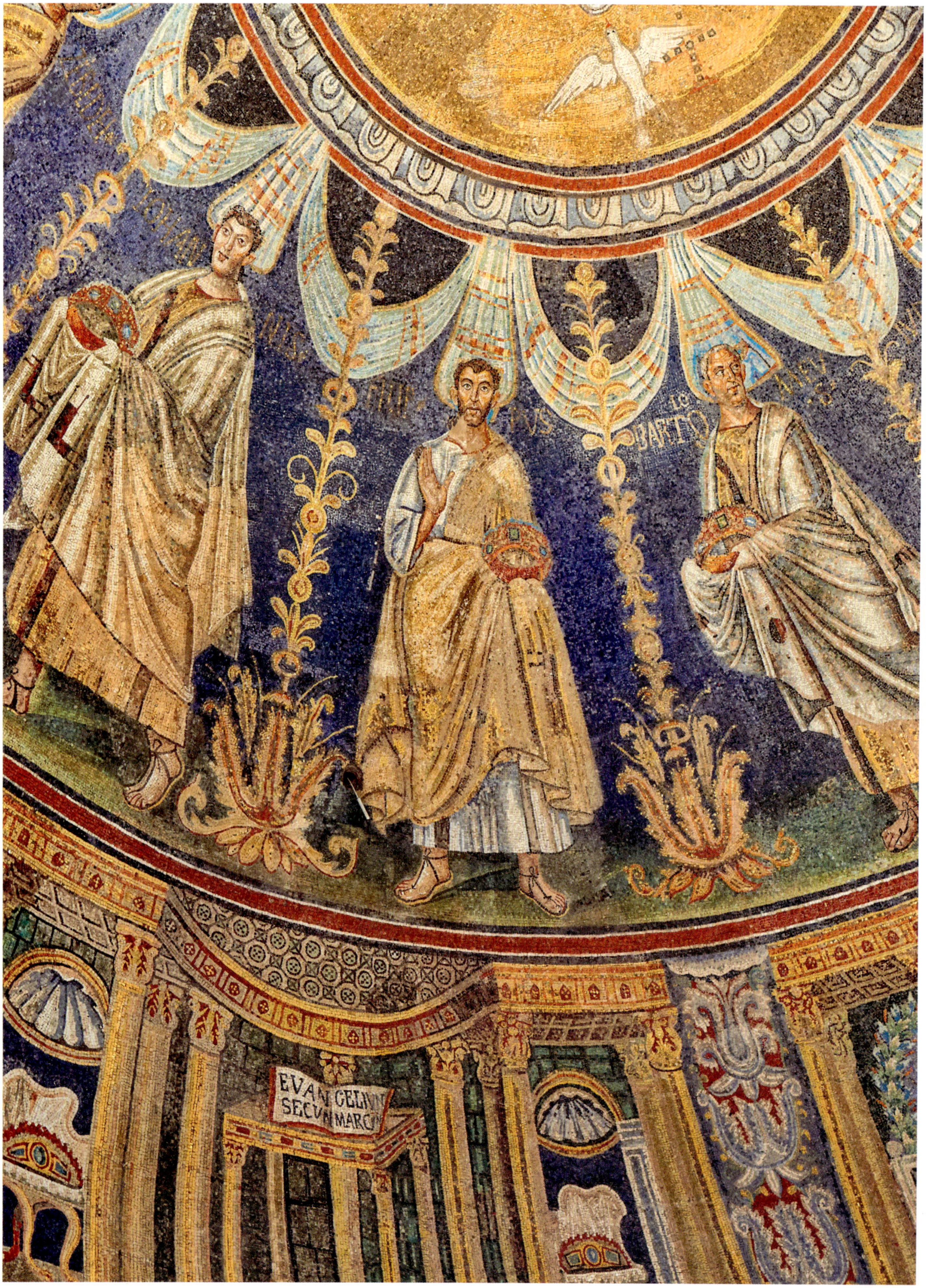
EVANGELIV
SECVNMARC
BARTO

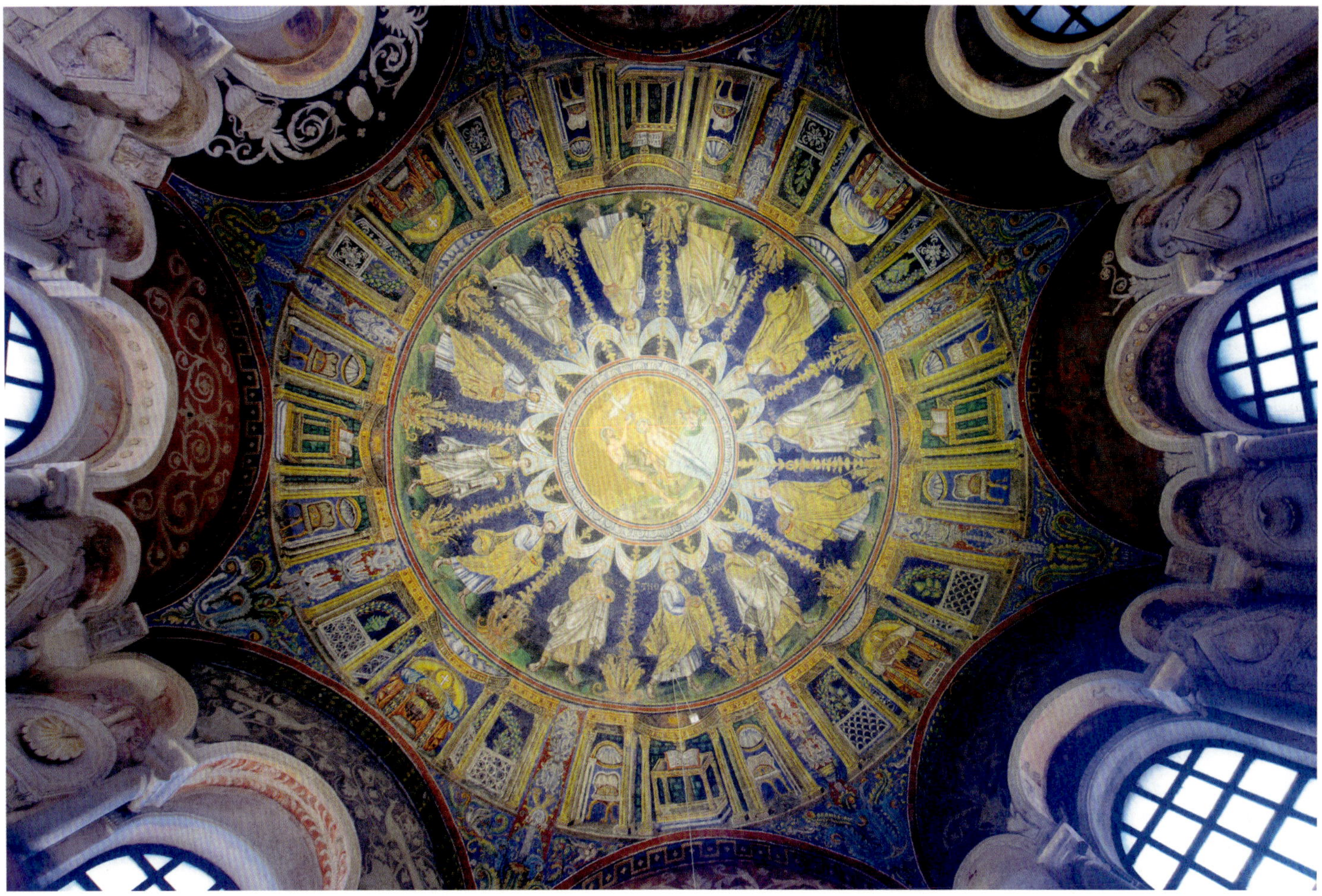

crowns, and these have been the subject of much discussion by theological scholars. Some suggest they are symbolic of a reward for the struggles that an initiate into Christianity endures, others see them as emblems of the earthly king who resided in Ravenna during the period in which it was the capital of the Ostrogothic Kingdom (493–553). In fact, the golden dome itself has also been associated with the *aurum coronarium*, the golden wreath that was bestowed on the emperors of the ancient world at their investiture. The Neonian mosaics can therefore be interpreted as a blending of symbolic associations between the imperial, pagan and Christian worlds of the early first millennium.

A third band, framing the apostles, represents the heavenly night garden, which is set against a deep, nocturnal blue, complete with identifiable flora and an array of paradisiacal birds as well as four empty thrones. These empty seats are known by the Greek word *heitomasia*, meaning 'prepared throne', and symbolize the anticipated second coming of Christ. The mosaics have not only served a community of spiritual or art-loving pilgrims, but also beguiled the psychoanalyst Carl Jung who visited the Neonian Baptistery in the 1930s, an experience that influenced his ruminations on the subconscious and conscious mind and the archetypal experiences of death and rebirth.

Left: Three of the twelve apostles who encircle the central scene of the dome. To the right is St Bartholomew, and central is St Mark the Evangelist, whose throne in heaven's court awaits him beneath.

Above: The empty seats framing the twelve apostles symbolize the anticipated second coming of Christ.

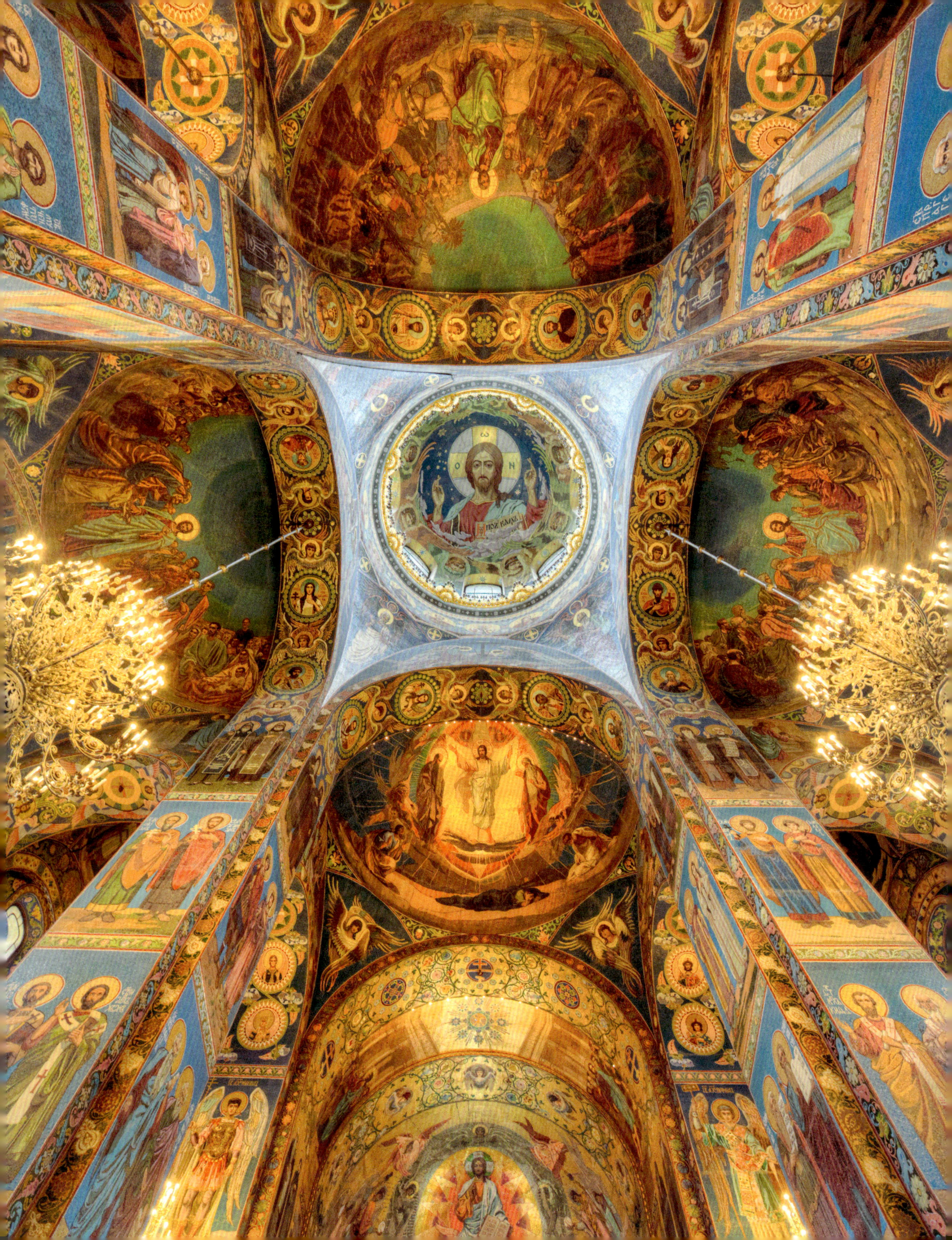

Left: View from beneath the 81 m (266 ft) high central dome on which is pictured a mosaic of God as Christ Pantocrator – all powerful and holding his hands in a gesture of either blessing or instruction.

Overleaf: A vibrant blue hue surrounds the image of Christ Pantocrator.

Church of the Resurrection of Jesus Christ, Russia

On 1st March 1881, Russian Emperor Alexander II lay bleeding on the snow-lined embankment of the canal in St Petersburg, his legs shattered and his stomach torn open. He had been on his way to the Mikhailovsky Riding School when social revolutionaries from the militant group Naradnaya Volya (People's Will) threw a bomb at his carriage and then at the emperor himself. Two years later, a dazzling church with five domes would rise in colourful bloom on the very spot where he fell, as if nourished by the spilled blood of the martyred emperor. The church took the name of the Resurrection of Jesus, to draw emphatic parallels between Christ and the slain emperor commemorated with a lavish shrine inside the church. The building, with its sumptuous decoration, served to deify the assassinated emperor, but is also a demonstration of a last gasp of national religious hyberbole. Seized and ransacked by Bolsheviks in 1917, it is no longer a consecrated church, and became known colloquially as the 'Saviour on Spilled Blood' in reference to the details of its foundation. The church has never shaken off this moribund reputation and served as a morgue during the Second World War. It has even gone by the name 'Saviour on the Potatoes' for its use as a warehouse for crop storage in the mid-twentieth century.

The outward appearance of the building references Russian church design of much earlier periods, such as St Basil's Cathedral in Moscow (consecrated 1561), and is symptomatic of a widespread revival of nationalism during the reign of Alexander II, which continued after his death as the official style of his heir Alexander III. Alexander's assassination prompted an upsurge in organized religion and the Spilled Blood was one part of an invigorated programme of church building that saw the construction of 695 major cathedrals across the country. This nostalgia for old Russia had informed the visual rhetoric of emperor Nicholas I, the father of the assassinated Alexander II. During his reign he promoted public interest and academic studies in Byzantine history to illicit an increased reverence for the historical past, perhaps in response to the perceived threat of more Western influences on St Petersburg.

Emphasis was placed on the heritage of the early Christian church in the Byzantine world and the continuation of that lineage into late-nineteenth-century Russia. This theme continues inside the church, with a radiant mosaic decoration that spans over 7,000 sq m (75,350 sq ft) of walls and ceiling and is made from twenty types of stone, including semi-precious jasper and topaz. These glistening patchworks, with heavily outlined and hieratically depicted figures, imitate the interiors of churches from the Eastern part of the Roman Empire, the territory known as Byzantium, which was the seat of imperial power from the late fourth century to 1453. The region that eventually became Russia was linked to the Byzantine capital of Constantinople (now Istanbul) through trade and the acceptance of the Greek Orthodox religion. Even the Russian language evolved from Byzantine monks, with the name of the imperial Russian ruler – the tsar – a derivative of the Roman title caesar. And when the power of Byzantium began to wane, Russia saw herself as the natural inheritor of cultural and imperial Christian power as Moscow (the former capital) declared itself to be a 'Third Rome', with all the associated glory and military prowess that had immortalized its ancient predecessor.

On the interior of the central dome, a whirlpool of violet and blue and sea green settles around the image of Christ Pantocrator –

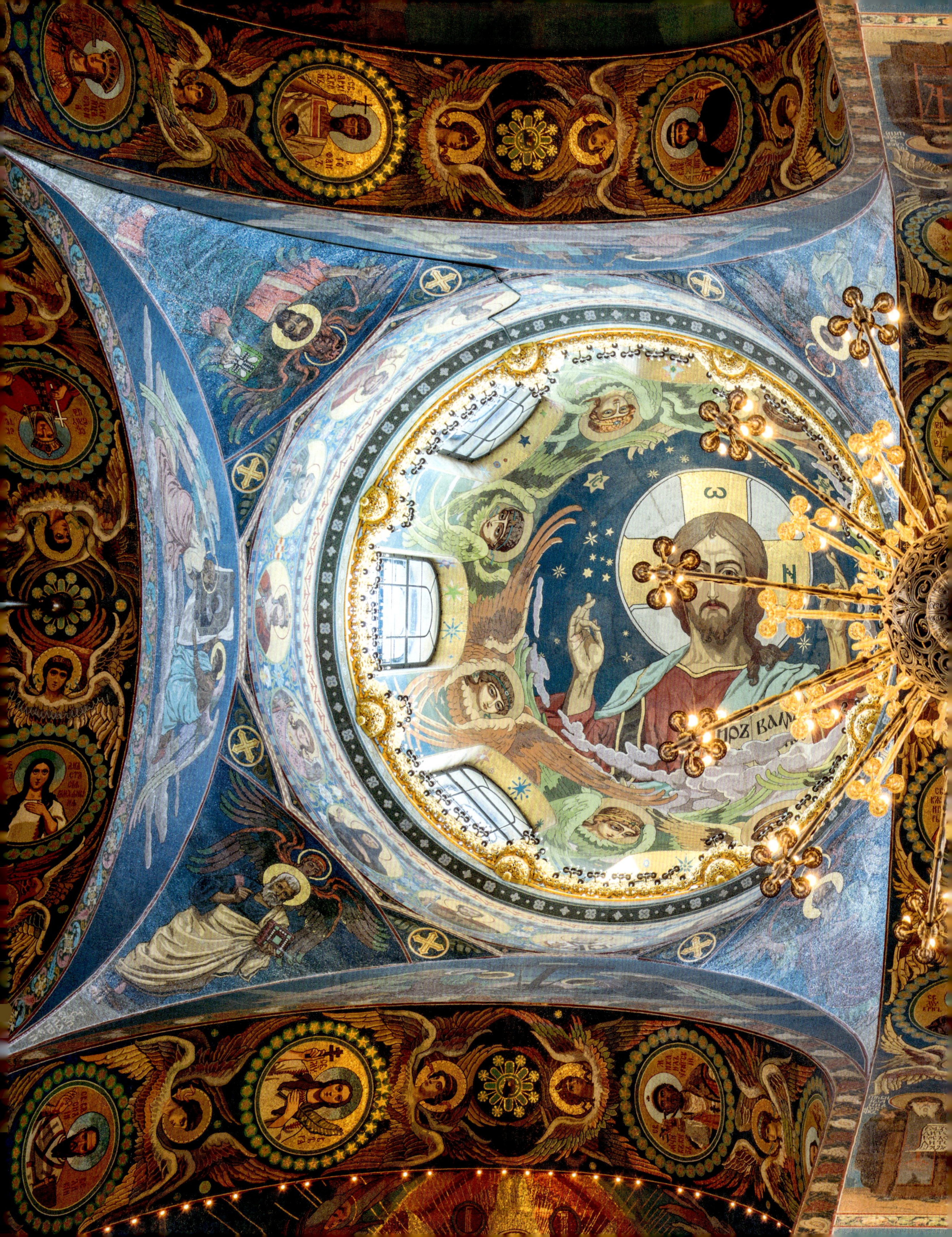

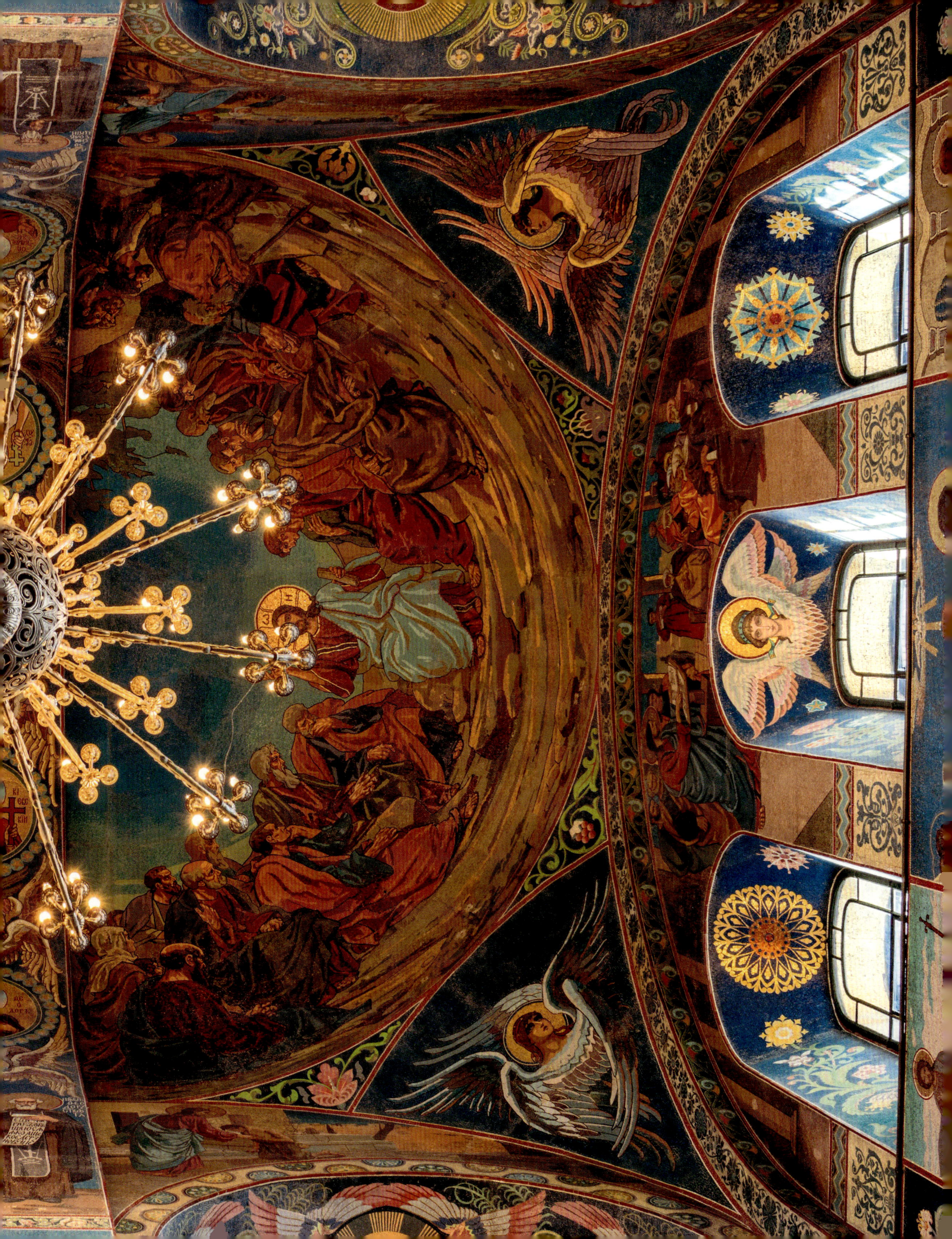

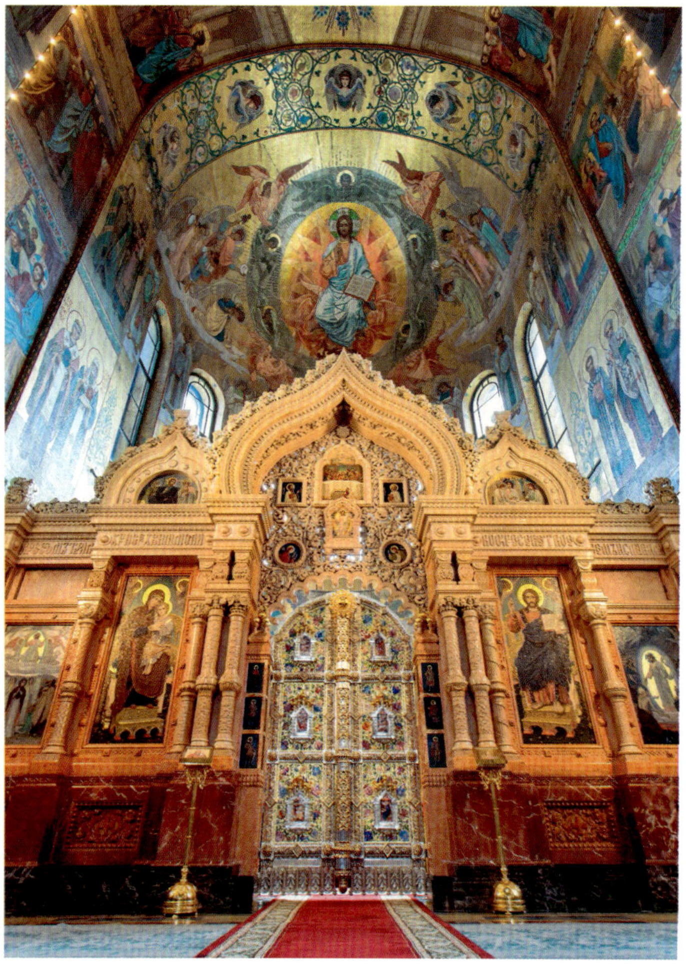

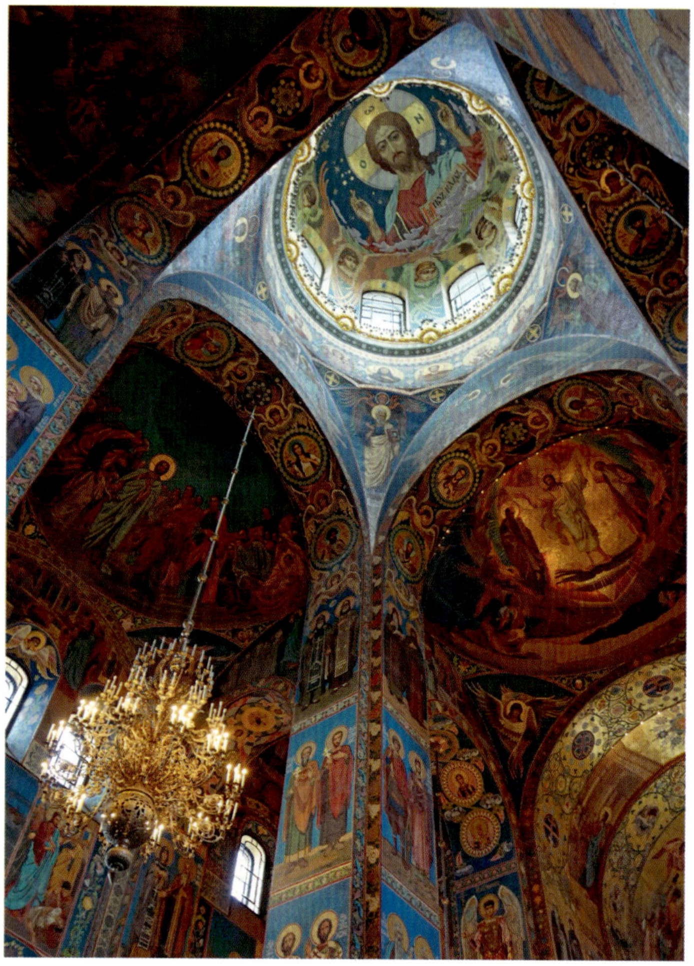

Above left: The central iconostasis that separates the sanctuary from the nave. Various shades of Italian marble give the effect that it is carved out of wood and encrusted with semi-precious stones.

Below: Detail of Christ Pantocrator, with the Greek characters 'OΩN', meaning 'the one who is', visible on Christ's halo.

Above right and opposite top: Light floods in from the central dome, ensuring it remains the focal point of the entire room.

Opposite bottom: Detail of one of the intricately mosaiced arches.

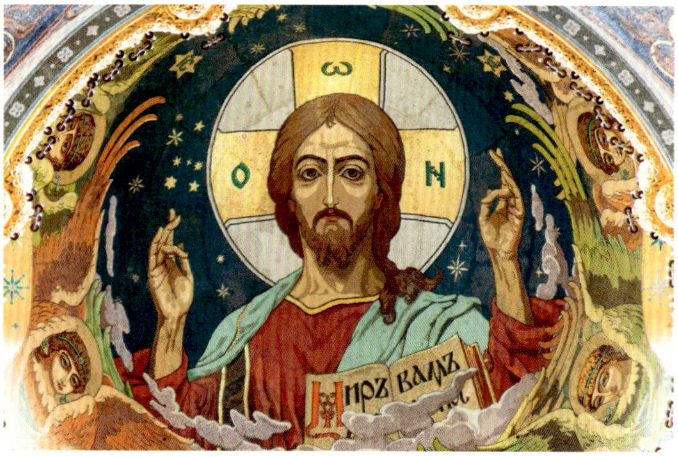

a theological presentational format of Christ that is particular to the Eastern church. Here he is, a stern judge and all-powerful God, hands raised in a rhetorical gesture of teaching or blessing. Eight dark, doe-eyed angels attend him in a circle around the base of the dome. The Greek characters 'OΩN' appear in Christ's cruciform halo; while a literal translation is 'the being one', it makes more sense if read as 'the one who is'. These are the words that were received by Moses in the Old Testament when he stood on Mount Sinai and asked to whom he was speaking when he heard the words of God. The inclusion of these symbols seems to be distinctive to Russian and Slavic religious images dating as far back as the twelfth century, and their inclusion here, in this church, in the very late nineteenth century, forges a symbolic link between Jesus Christ of the New Testament, and the awesome god of the Old Testament, as well as with the unbreakable secession of Russian religious heritage as expressed through icons and image-making in churches.

While the mosaic designs take their inspiration from church decoration dating back as far as the sixth century [CE], the images here are also informed by the stylistic techniques of the popular and successful nineteenth-century painters whose works provided a template for the mosaic decoration. For example, there is an attention to contouring of the bodies and faces and a three-dimensionality that is absent from early Christian mosaic design, such as that seen in the Neonian Baptistery in Ravenna (see p. 14), while many of the figures would not look out of place in the European and Russian salons of romantic and mythological academic painting with whom the commissioned artists were professionally involved.

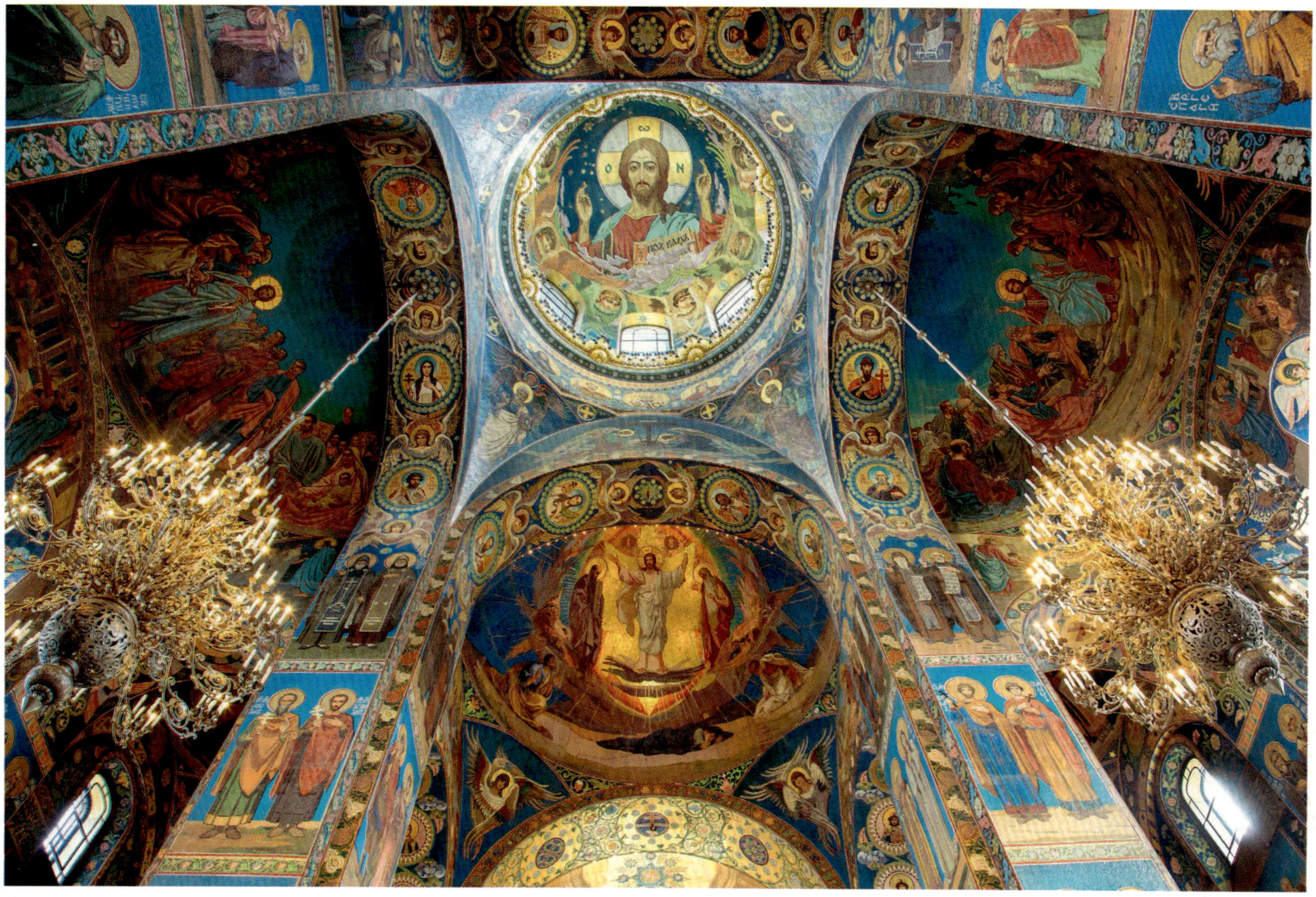

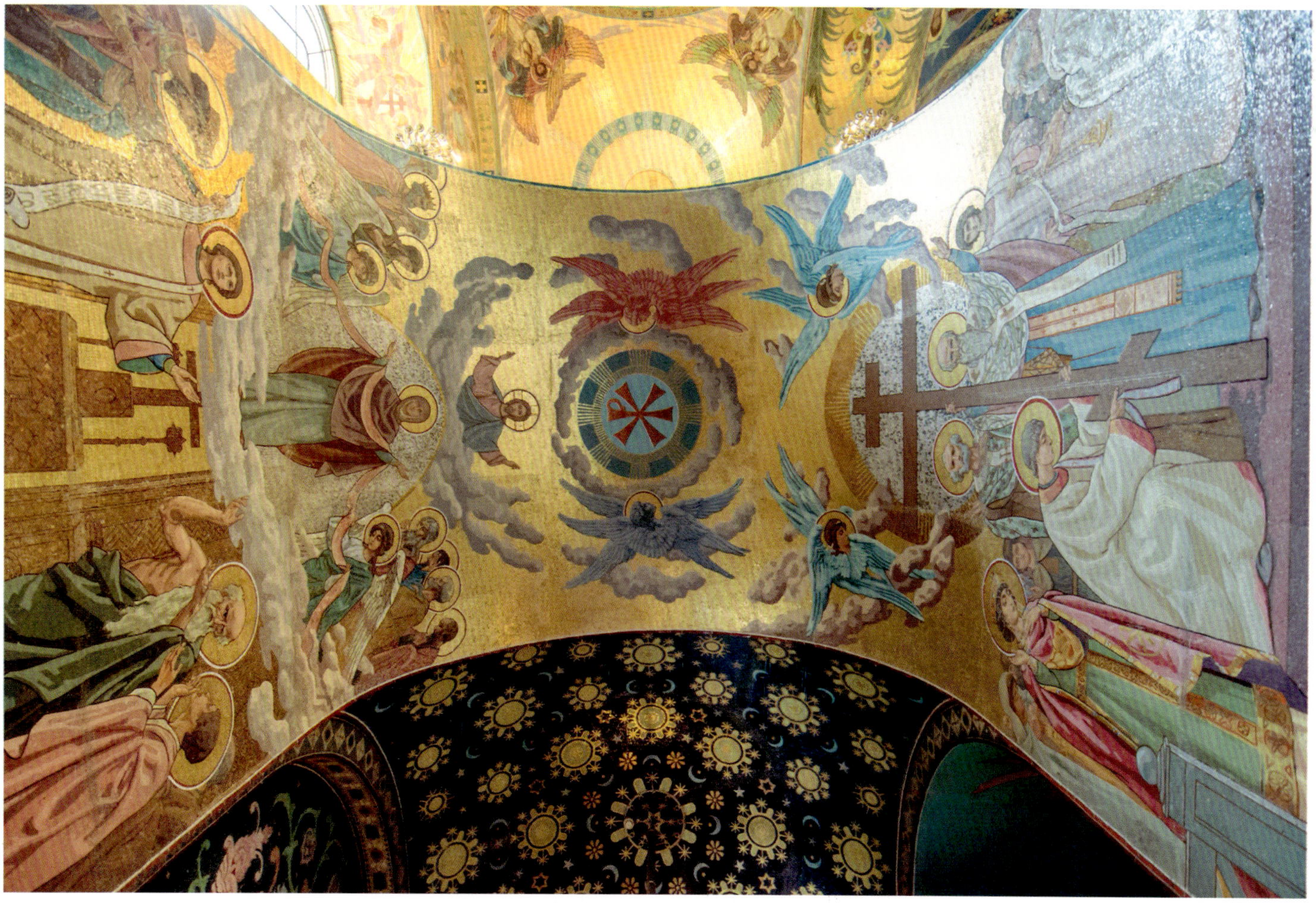

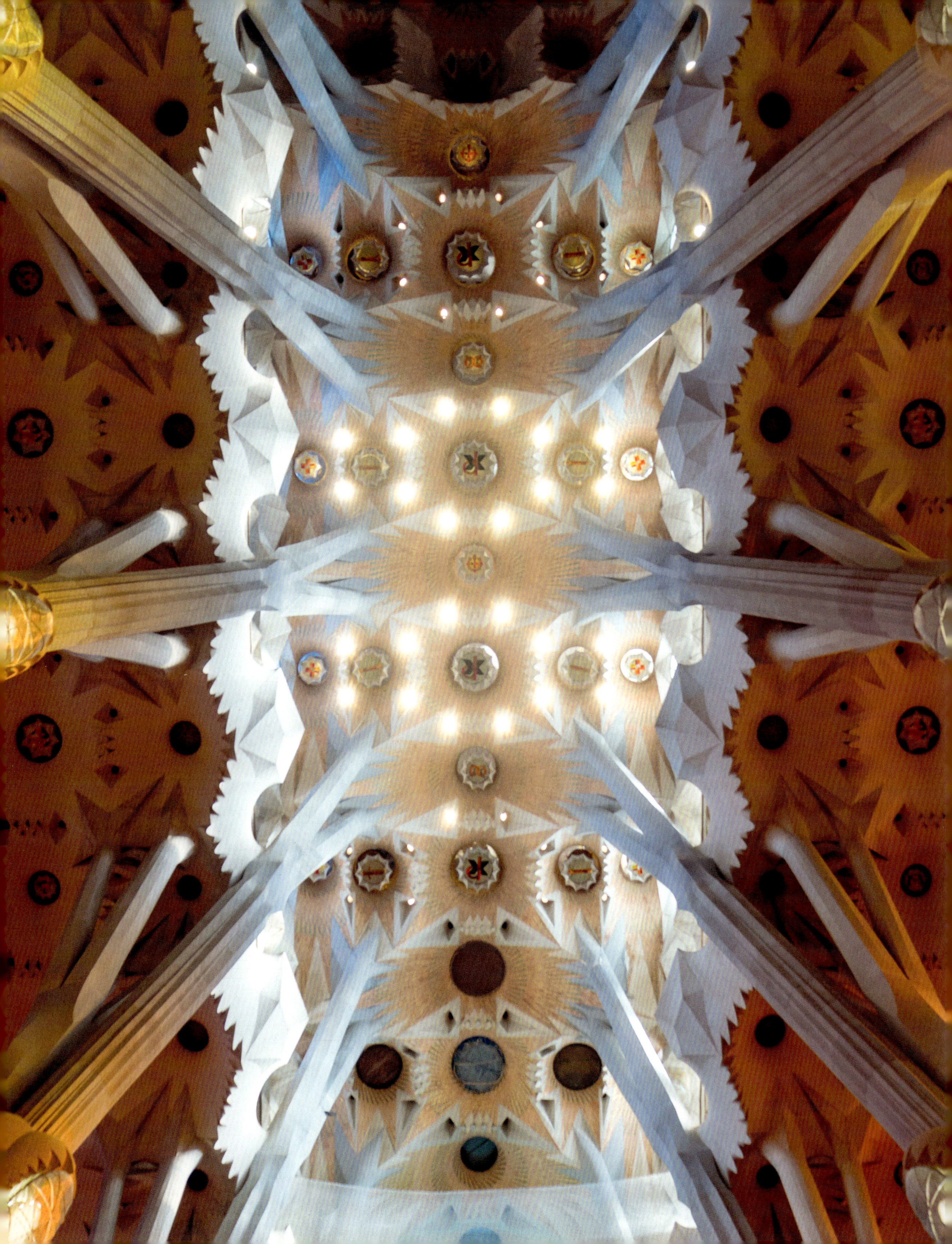

Antoni Gaudí

Sagrada Família

1883–present

Barcelona, Spain

Left: The spectacular ceiling inside Barcelona's Sagrada Família.

Overleaf: Light floods in through the stained glass windows to illuminate the Sagrada Família's intricate structure.

Sagrada Família, Spain

The Catalan architect Antoni Gaudí was hit by a tram and killed in Barcelona in 1926, two weeks shy of his seventy-fourth birthday. He left behind him the unfinished project of the Basílica i Temple Expiatori de la Sagrada Família, a gargantuan project that had occupied him for the majority of his career. The church was consecrated in 2010 by Pope Benedict XVI, despite still being in the process of construction. Now an unmistakable landmark of the city, it rises above the Barcelona skyline fusing the heritage of medieval Gothic cathedral architecture with the architect's own idiosyncratic strain of Catalan modernism.

Stepping inside the building is like entering an enchanted forest, as twisting helicoidal columns seemingly grow out of the ground, splitting into branches that support a weighty vaulted ceiling of tessellated sunflower shapes, while a rainbow haze filters through the coloured glass windows. Like giant beanstalks these columns form a solid vertical bridge between the mortal world at ground level and the celestial space above, and seem to suggest that heaven has its roots deep inside the earth. It was Gaudí's intention that anyone entering the church should gain a simultaneous view of the vaults of the nave, transept and apse – a spectacular vision, given that the central vault of the nave reaches 45 m (145 ft) in height, while the apse climbs to a vertiginous 75 m (245 ft).

The Sagrada Família revisits the overpoweringly majestic architectural language of the French Gothic style from the twelfth and thirteenth centuries, as seen in cathedrals such as Chartres, Amiens and Rouen. These buildings used amplified scale and proportions to draw the eye up towards an imagined celestial realm. The resulting space between the heads of congregants and the lofty vaults that towered over them was filled with prayer, song and chanting, while a diffused coloured light permeated through stained glass to give the sensory effect of an otherworldly paradise. In Barcelona, Gaudí eschewed the traditional engineering solutions that supported such masonry, replacing flying buttresses with unique solutions found in the mathematical complexity of the natural world. This manifested in weight-bearing columns modelled on the hyperbolic paraboloids of tree trunks and their branches, along with conoids, fractals and spirals. As such, the church is a harmonious synthesis of the built and natural environments, all underpinned by Gaudí's devout belief in God as the supreme architect of nature. As he himself suggested: 'Those who look for the laws of Nature as a support for their new works collaborate with God.'

Mathematical, philosophical and theological symbolism underpin all of Gaudí's work at the Sagrada Família. For example, eighteen towers ornament the horizon: one for each of the twelve apostles of Christ, one for each of the four evangelists and one each for the Virgin Mary and for Christ. But the architect's design also reflects the intellectual currents of the late nineteenth and early twentieth centuries, and their impact on the plastic arts and architecture. His vision can be interpreted, for example, as a synthesis of his belief in the presence of God manifest in all nature with the biological concept of the universe proposed by writer Ernst Haeckel. Haeckel's book *General Morphology of Organisms* purports that matter is integrated in thought rather than life; it had a definitive influence on Gaudí. Further

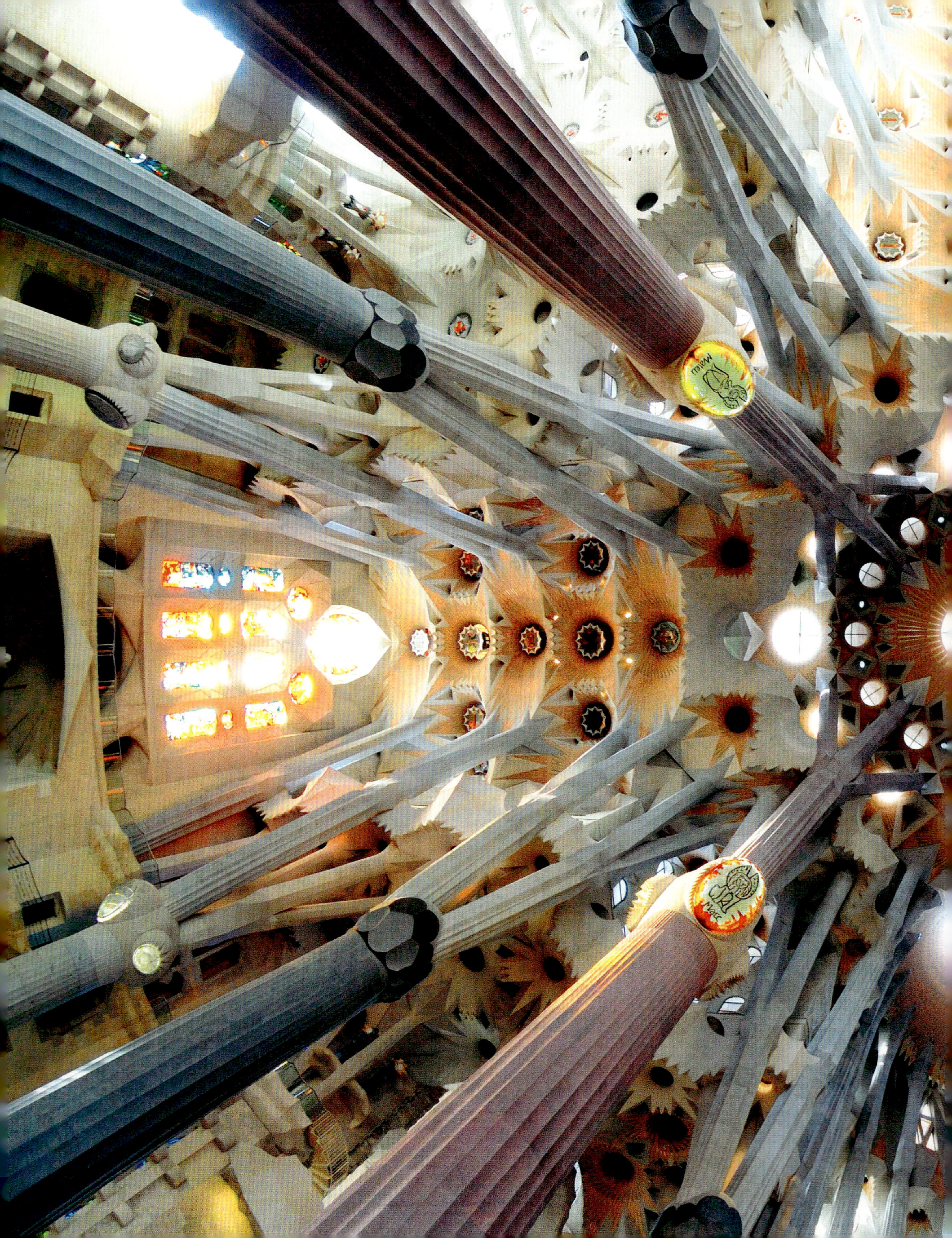
Mateu
Marc

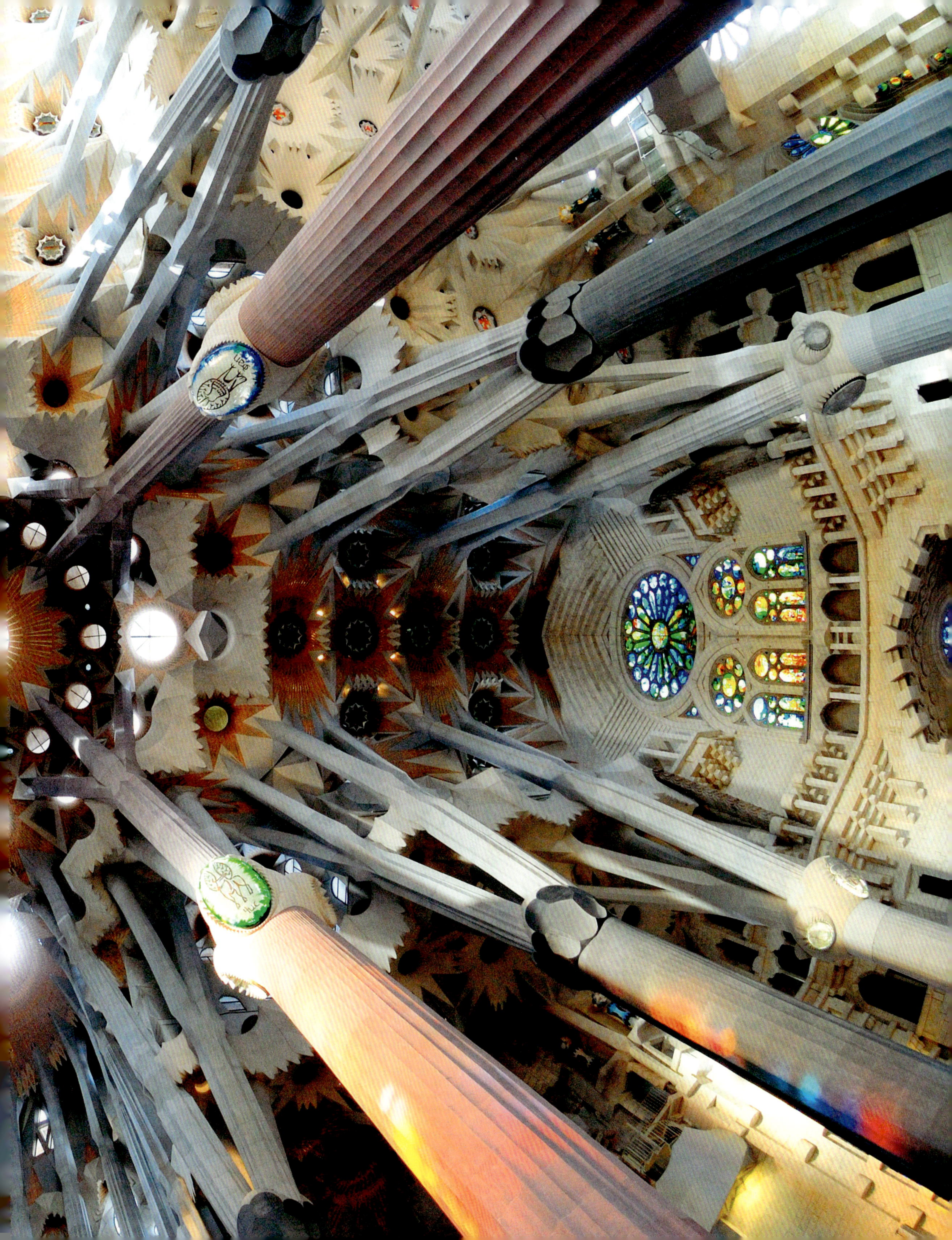

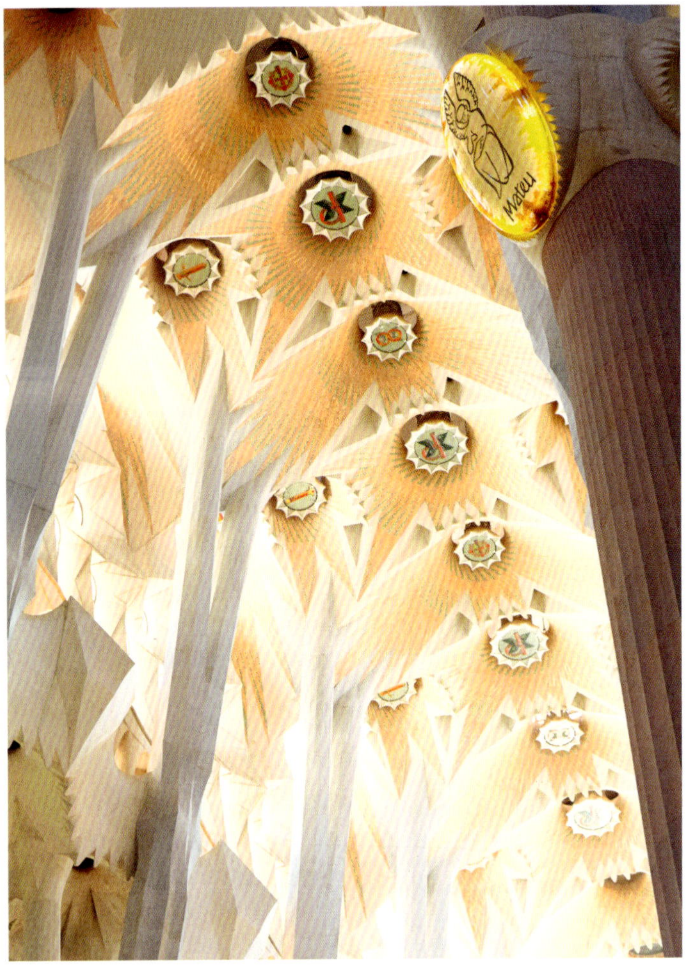

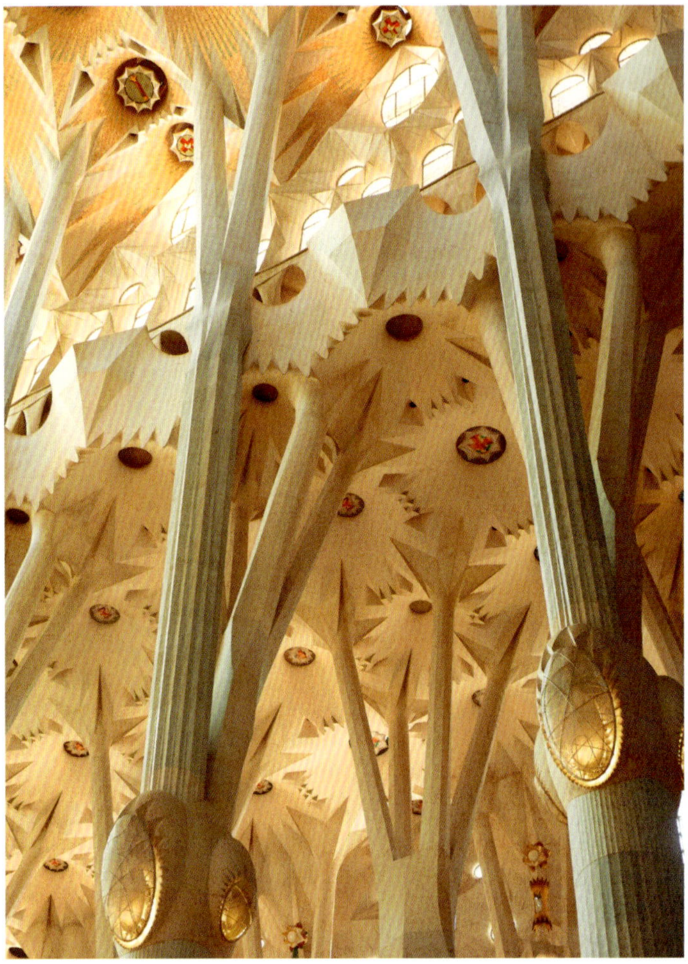

Above left and right: The columns at the Sagrada Família are modelled on the hyperbolic paraboloids of tree trunks and their branches, along with conoids, fractals and spirals.

Opposite top and bottom: Diffused coloured light permeates through stained glass, colliding to give the sensory effect of an otherworldly paradise.

developments in the field of mathematics, such as the move from flat forms to manifoldness, and Einstein's theories of relativity introduced groundbreaking concepts of space and time and a realization that Euclidian geometry was not the only way to measure physical reality. These developments nourished the evolution of a new style in architecture, which became known as the International Style or Liberty Style and drew on the form and engineering of plants and flowers for inspiration. Buildings became interpretations of space and time as well as constructions, and embraced non-traditional concepts of movement and flow. Gaudí's application of curvilinear geometrical forms in architecture anticipated the later styles of architects Le Corbusier and Frank Lloyd Wright.

Gaudí inherited the Sagrada Família project in 1883, from Francisco del Villar, who had resigned after only a year's work on the building. Intended as an expiatory church by its founders The Spiritual Association of Devotees of Saint Joseph, the Sagrada Família is dedicated to Joseph as the head of the Holy Family. This devotional choice reflects the late-nineteenth-century efforts to reassert perceived family values that were being eroded by the rampant materialism of an expanding capitalist industrial society. Building on a new site in a working-class district of Barcelona prompted Gaudí to give the building an alternative name as the 'Cathedral for the Poor'. The critical reception of the church has been particularly divisive; while many have praised it as a fitting rendering of spirituality in stone, others have found it vulgar, pretentious and even, in the words of the English author George Orwell, 'hideous'.

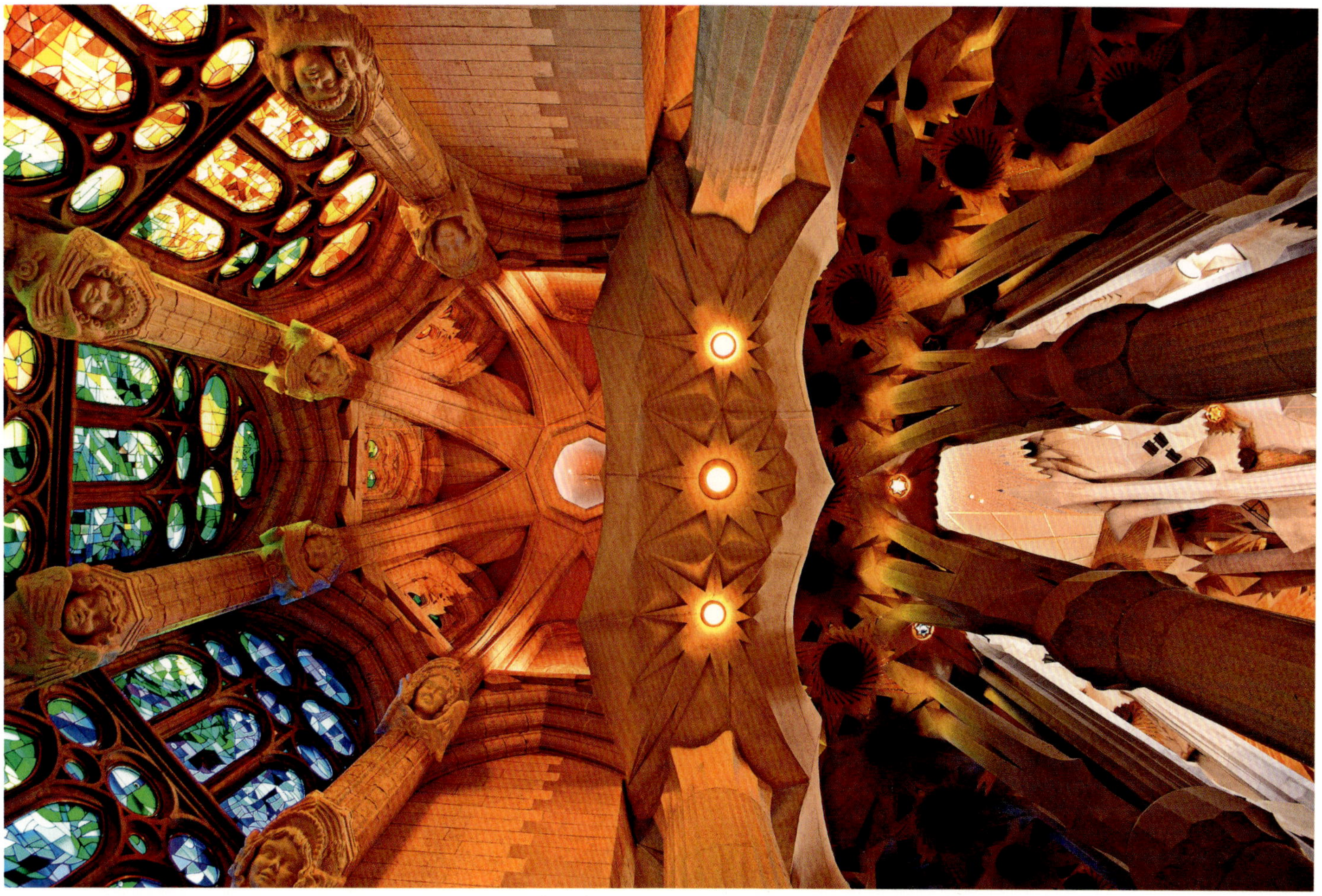

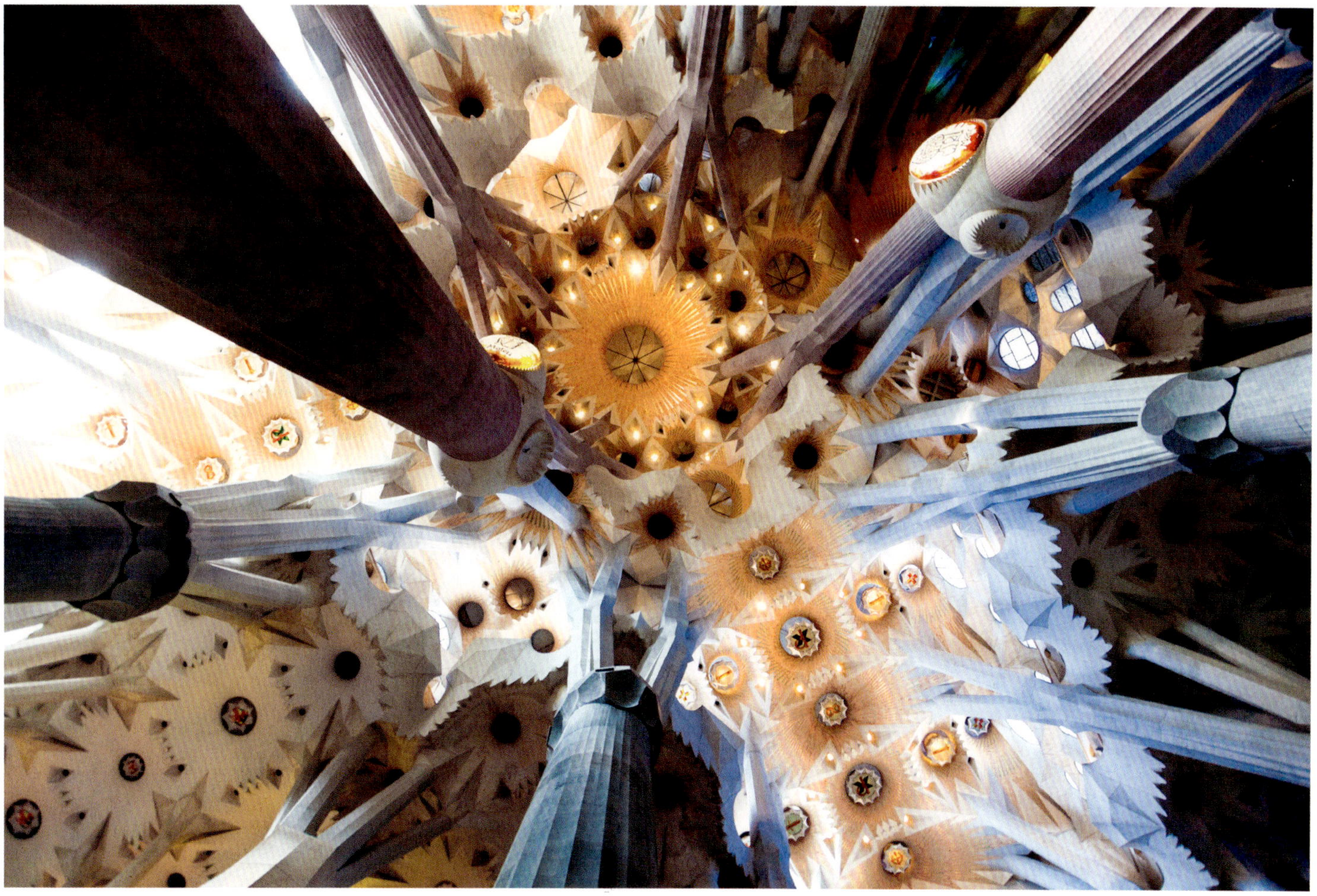

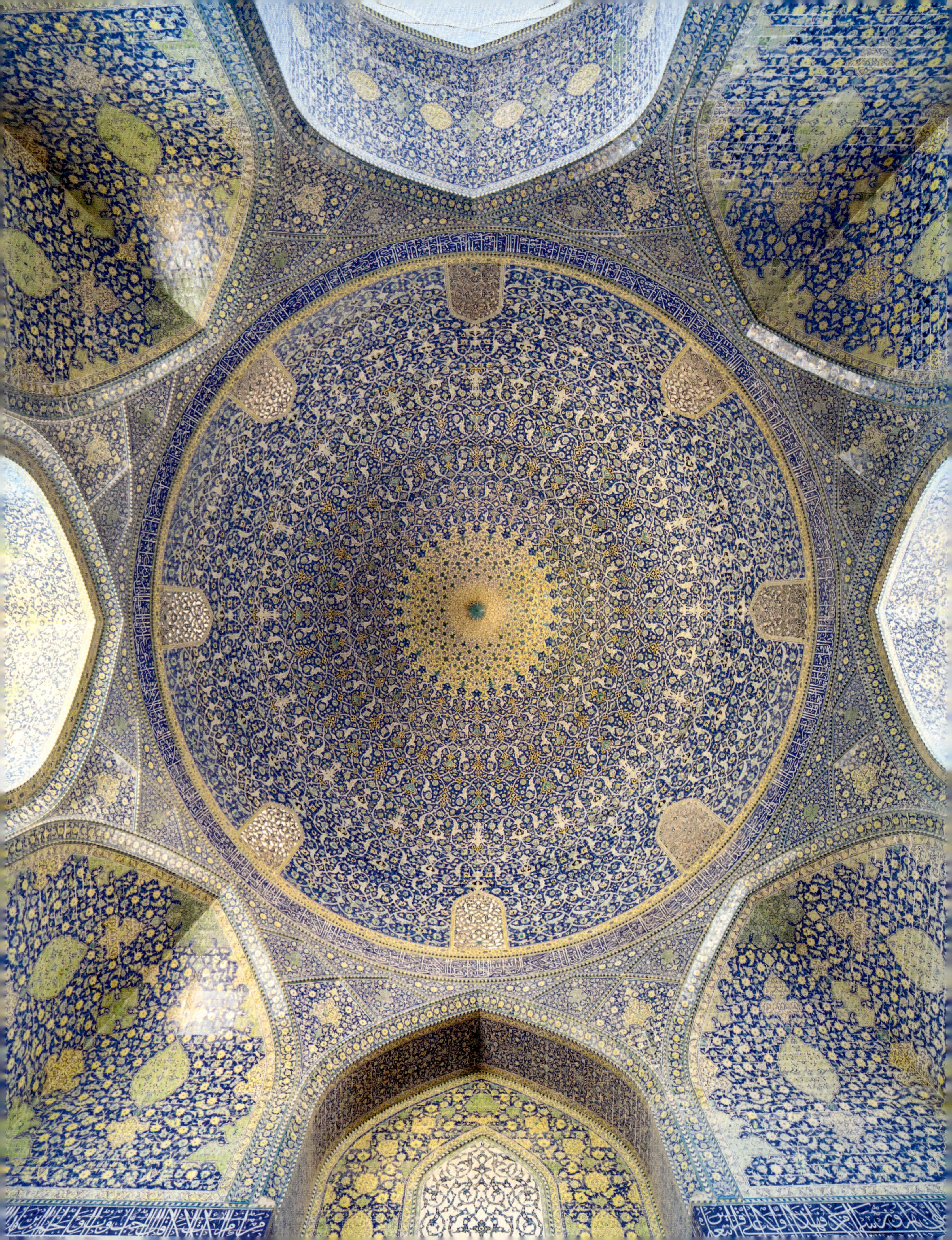

Imam Mosque
1611–66
Isfahan, Iran

Left: The hypnotic domed ceiling of Imam Mosque.

Overleaf: Almost half a million coloured ceramic tiles cover the Imam Mosque.

Imam Mosque, Iran

Much of Western art history is concerned with the interpretation of imagery, and assumes authority through deciphering symbols, unravelling complex narratives and querying authorial intent. The same practice cannot be applied when looking at the artistic language of Islam, which can be found on every available surface within what was originally called the Shah Mosque in Isfahan, Iran. The construction of the mosque took place between 1611 and 1666, as part of an intensive building programme carried out by Shah 'Abbas I, who embellished the new Iranian capital of Isfahan with glorious architecture in the name of the Safavid dynasty. Appearing on the back of the 20,000 rial banknote today, the building has been known as the Imam Mosque since the 1979 Iranian Revolution.

Beyond the threshold of the imposing entrance, or *iwan*, almost half a million coloured tiles of geometric and floral decoration lead the eye around the different spaces of the mosque in an enveloping flow of shimmering colour, creating a mirage-like impression that conjures up visions of the golden hour of dawn, a calm sunlit sea or the constellations of celestial heaven. Each of the ceramic tiles was fired using a sophisticated technique of underglazing known as *haft-rangi*, in which up to seven colours were applied to each individual tile.

The hypnotic repetition of lines, rosettes, intertwining vines and interweaving curves is characteristic of Islamic mosque decoration. There is a stark absence of anything figurative here – there are no people, animals, living things or recognizable objects from the physical world. Even the motifs that draw inspiration from nature, such as vines and floral patterns, are produced in a stylized rather than lifelike way. This was a way of warding off the risk of idolatry (when the image is worshipped or desired more than the god who is the creator of everything). As a consequence, this is a religious art in which there is no judgment (unlike Michelangelo's Sistine Chapel, see p. 38), no gender, no archetypes of good or evil, no hierarchy (see Debre Berhan, p. 54) and, some might say, no vanity. Unlike the symbolism we are accustomed to seeing in Western religious art, which might associate botanical images with the concept of paradise and the biblical Garden of Eden, these motifs strike a more metaphysical note and operate as elements of colour and form. When repeated, as they are here in seemingly infinite patterns, they evoke something akin to a flow of pure perception that lifts the viewer out of the ordered and finite world to experience something transcendental. It is through this silent theology of colour, light, repetition and order that God appears, therefore, and not through a figurative image.

Despite efforts to understand this concept, traditional Western art historians struggle to describe elements of Islamic art. For example, the curvilinear shapes are termed 'arabesques', which is simply French for 'Arab style'. Historians of the 1920s also wrongly interpreted the stylized nature of floral and vegetal motifs as symptomatic of a fleeting spring season in the Middle East, which didn't allow for the observation and accurate depiction of plant life. What these appraisals failed to realize is that this art doesn't seek to imitate the world, but rather looks for ways of seeing divine immanence in the ordered and infinite language of the material world, and so transcend its concrete bonds.

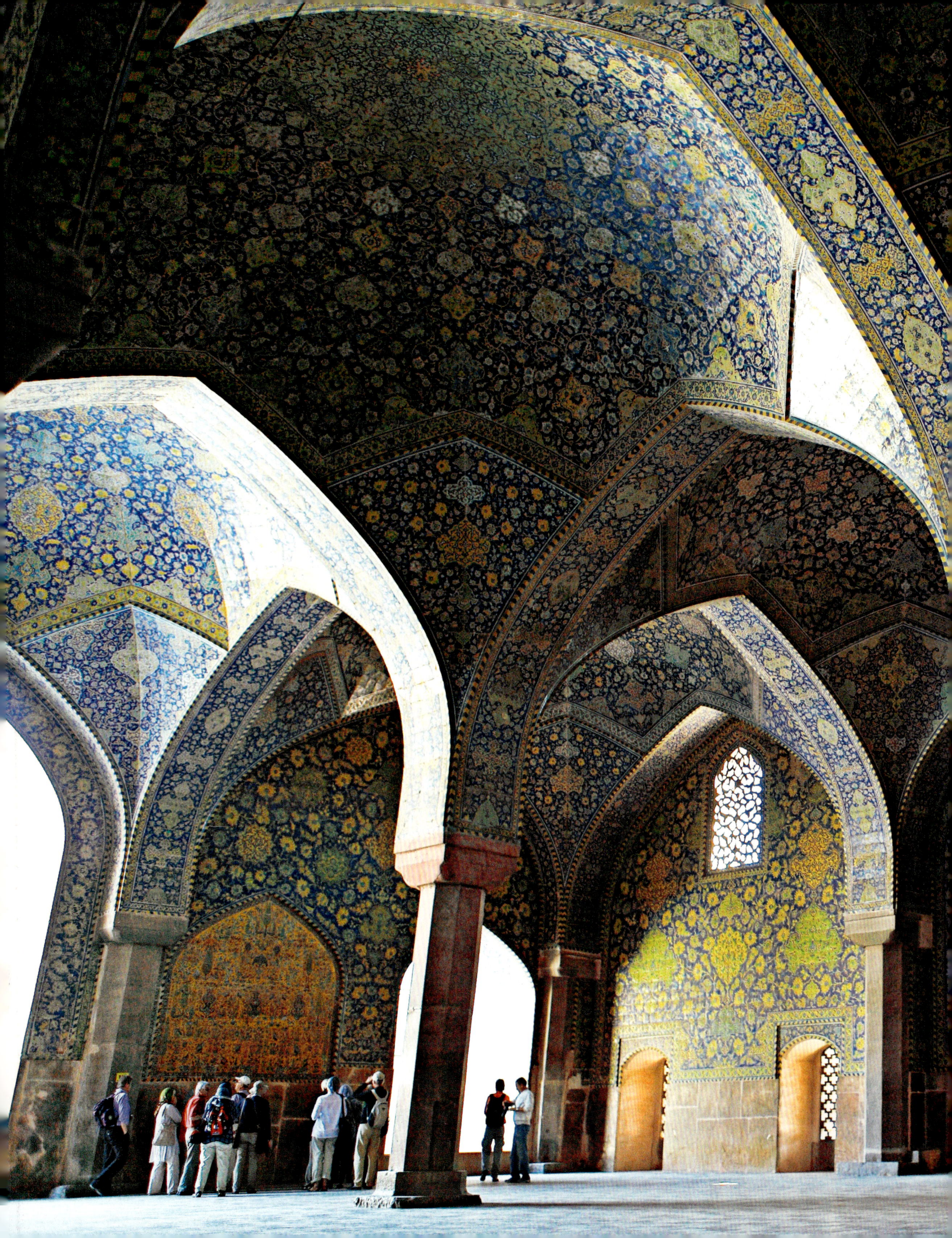

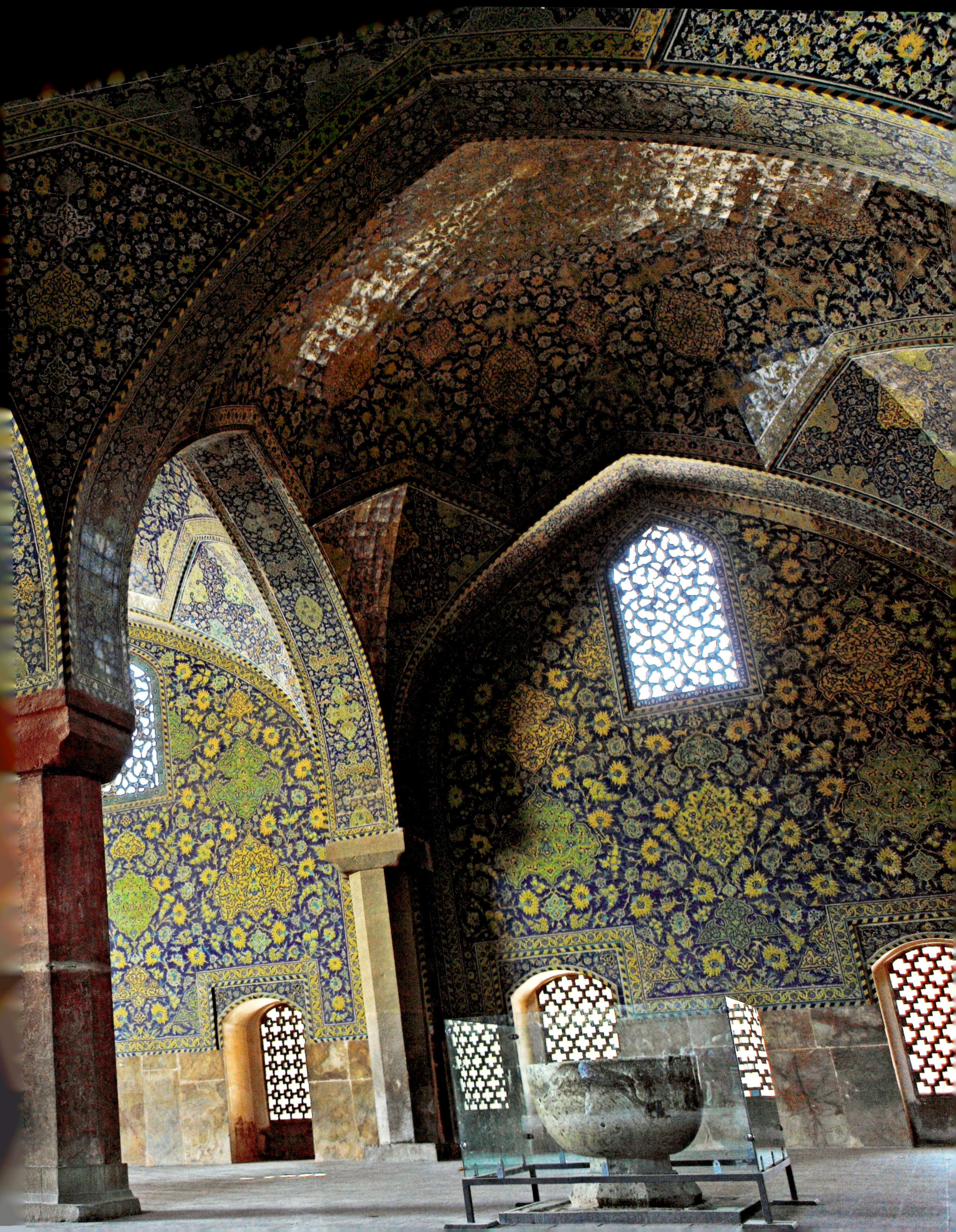

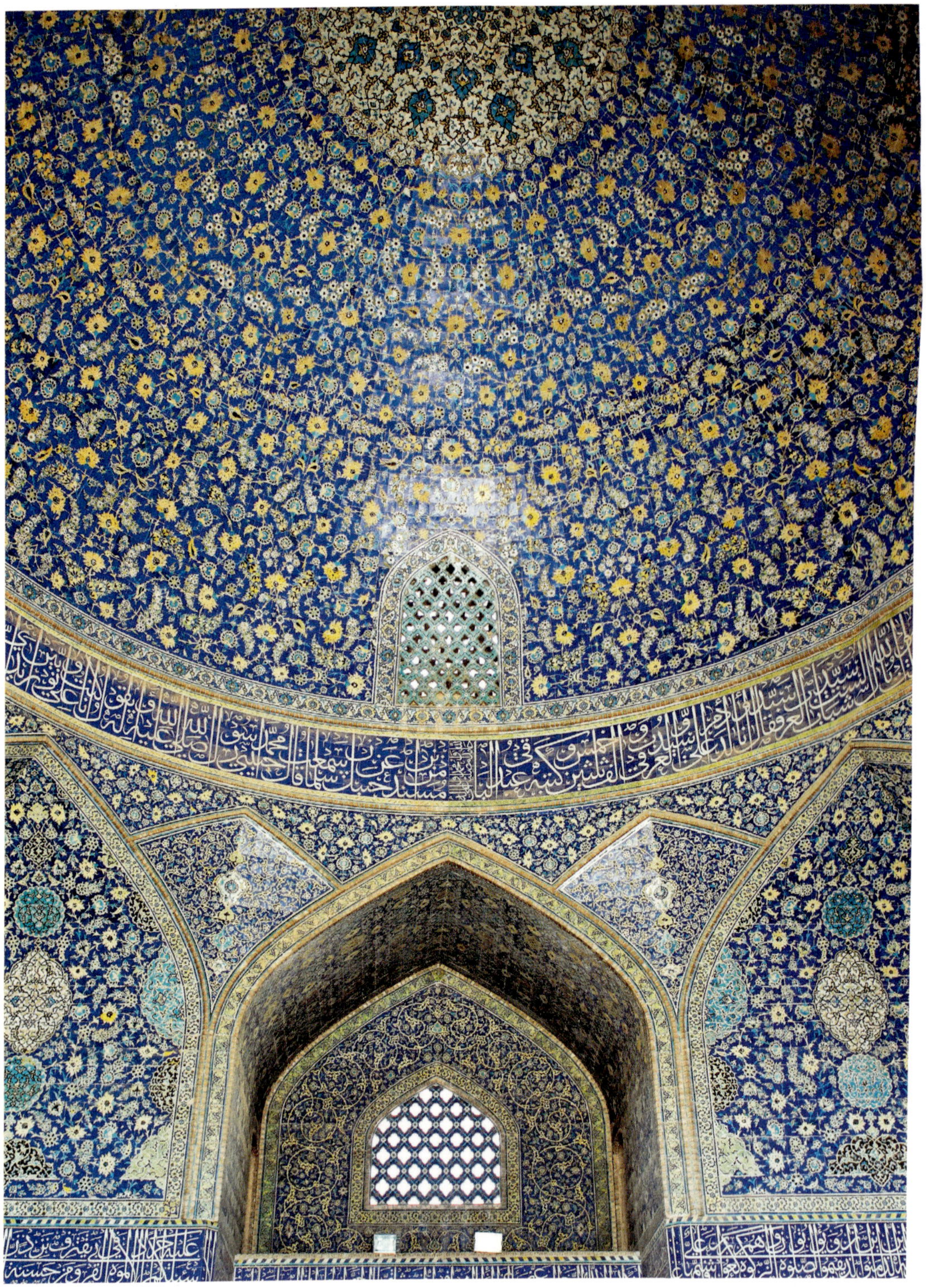

Left: Domed prayer hall.

Opposite top and bottom: Ceiling of the entrance portal. Even the motifs that draw inspiration from nature, such as vines and floral patterns, are produced in a stylized rather than lifelike way.

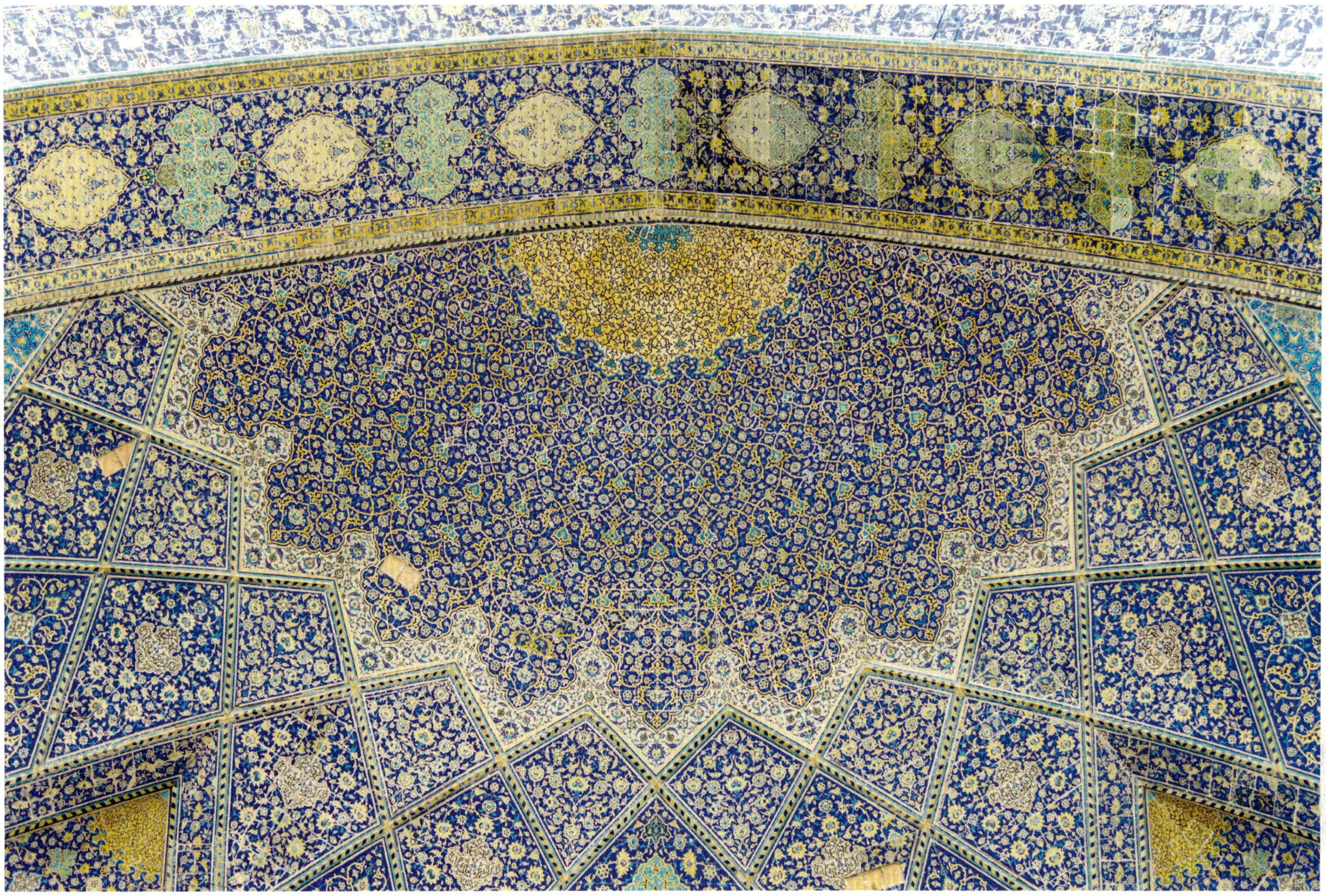

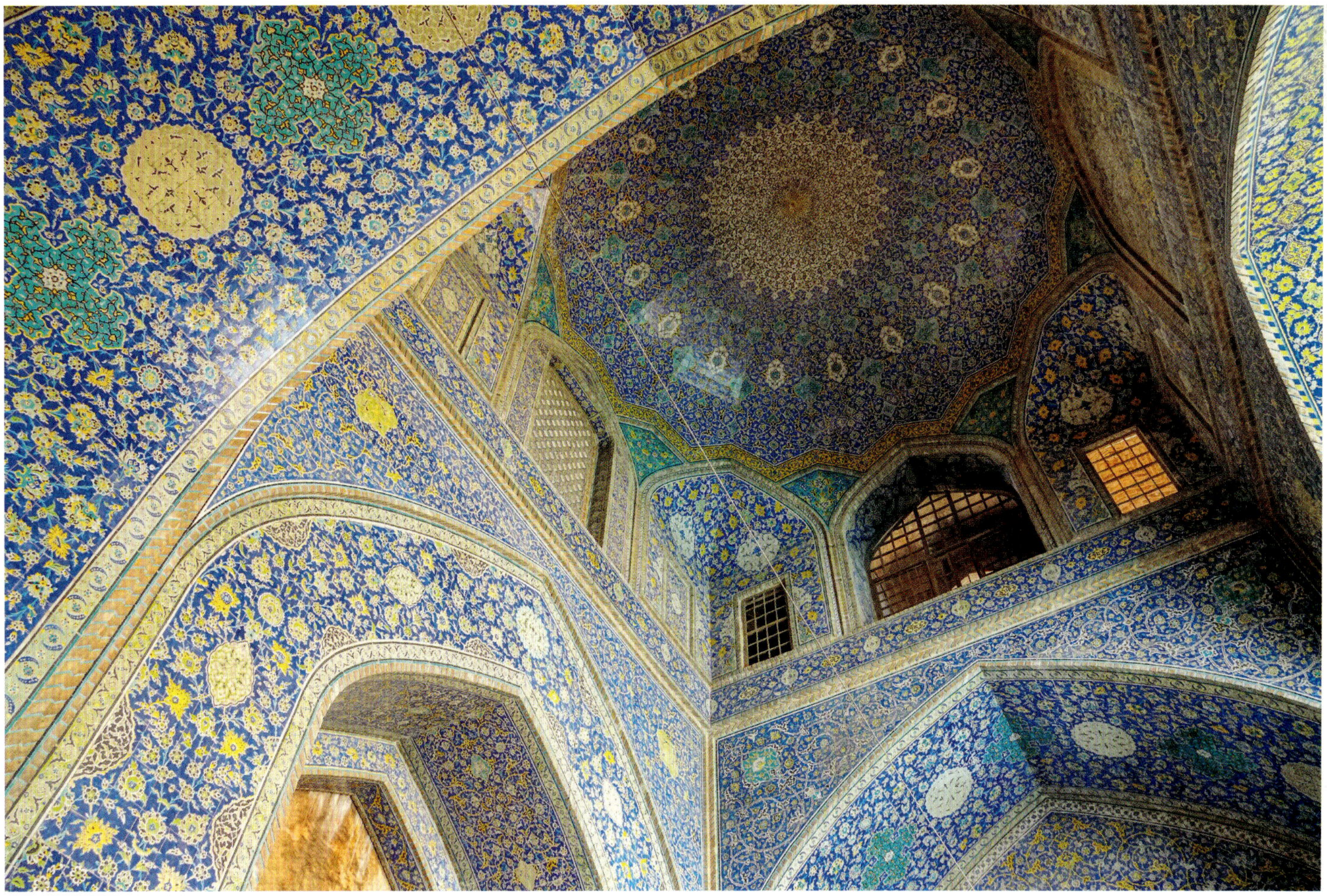

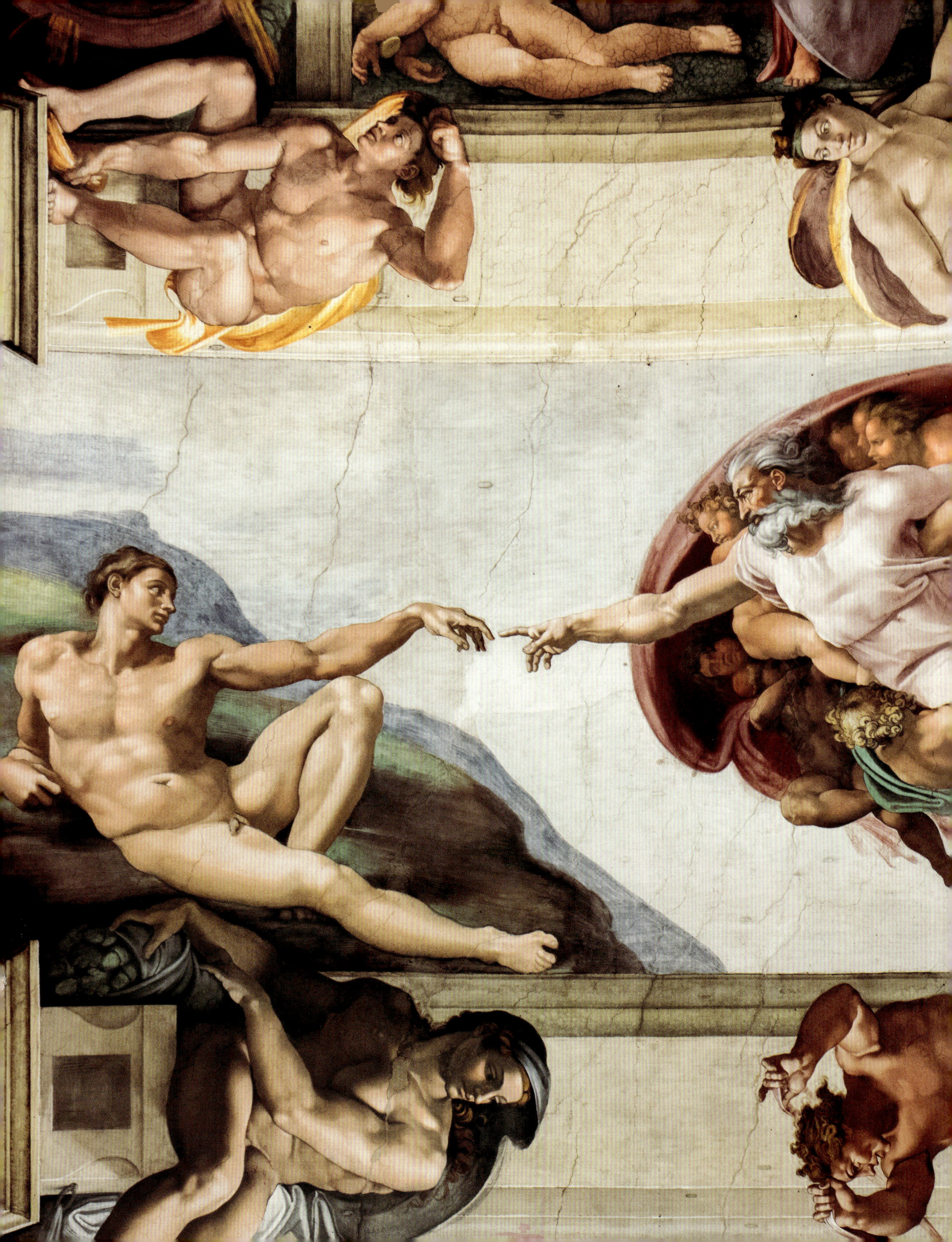

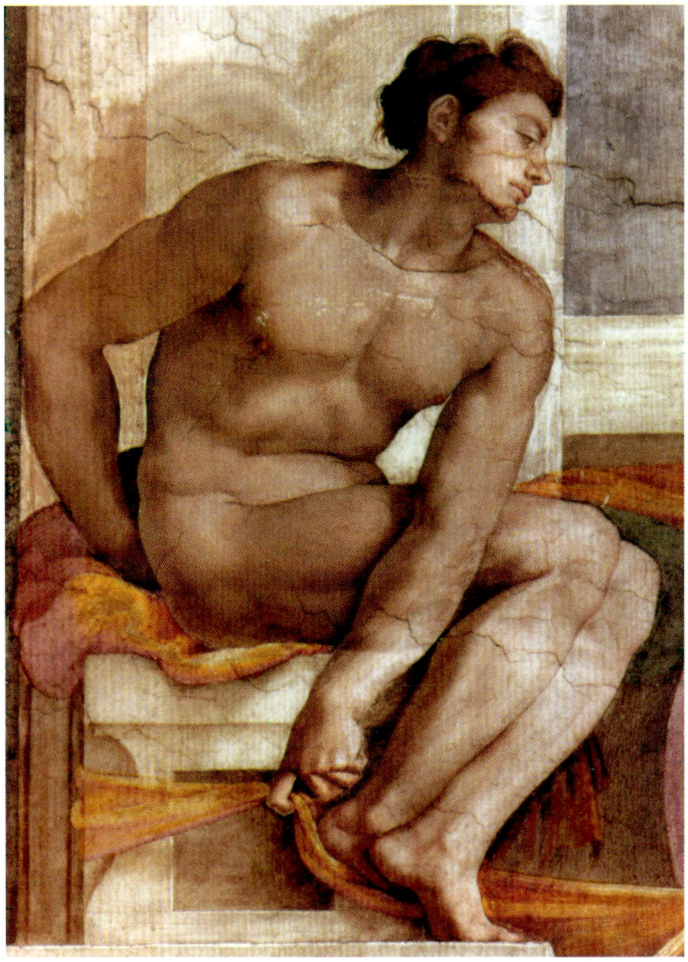

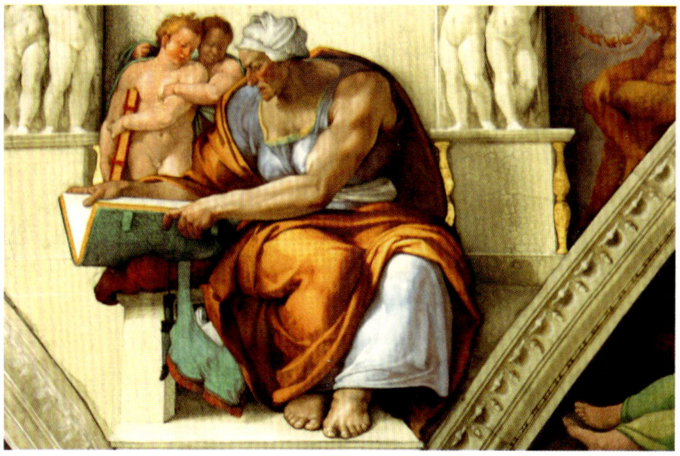

Opposite bottom: The Belvedere Torso fragment of the ancient roman (first century BCE) sculpture of a monumental male nude. The fragment was discovered in Rome at the end of the fifteenth century and became a recurrent source of inspiration for artists such as Michelangelo. Similarities can be seen between the fragment and the body of Adam on the Sistine Chapel ceiling.

Left: One of the male figures on the ceiling known as the *ignudi*. For Michelangelo, these powerful super-human male bodies constituted something of spiritual being acting as alternatives to traditional angels.

Below: The Cumaean Sibyl, one of the prophetesses who predicted the coming of Christ. Associated with the oracle of Apollo at Cumae, a Greek colony near modern-day Naples, the Cumaean Sybil holds special significance for the city of Rome because of this proximity.

Bottom: The temptation of Adam and Eve by the serpent offering them fruit from the Tree of Knowledge on the left, and their subsequent expulsion from paradise on the right.

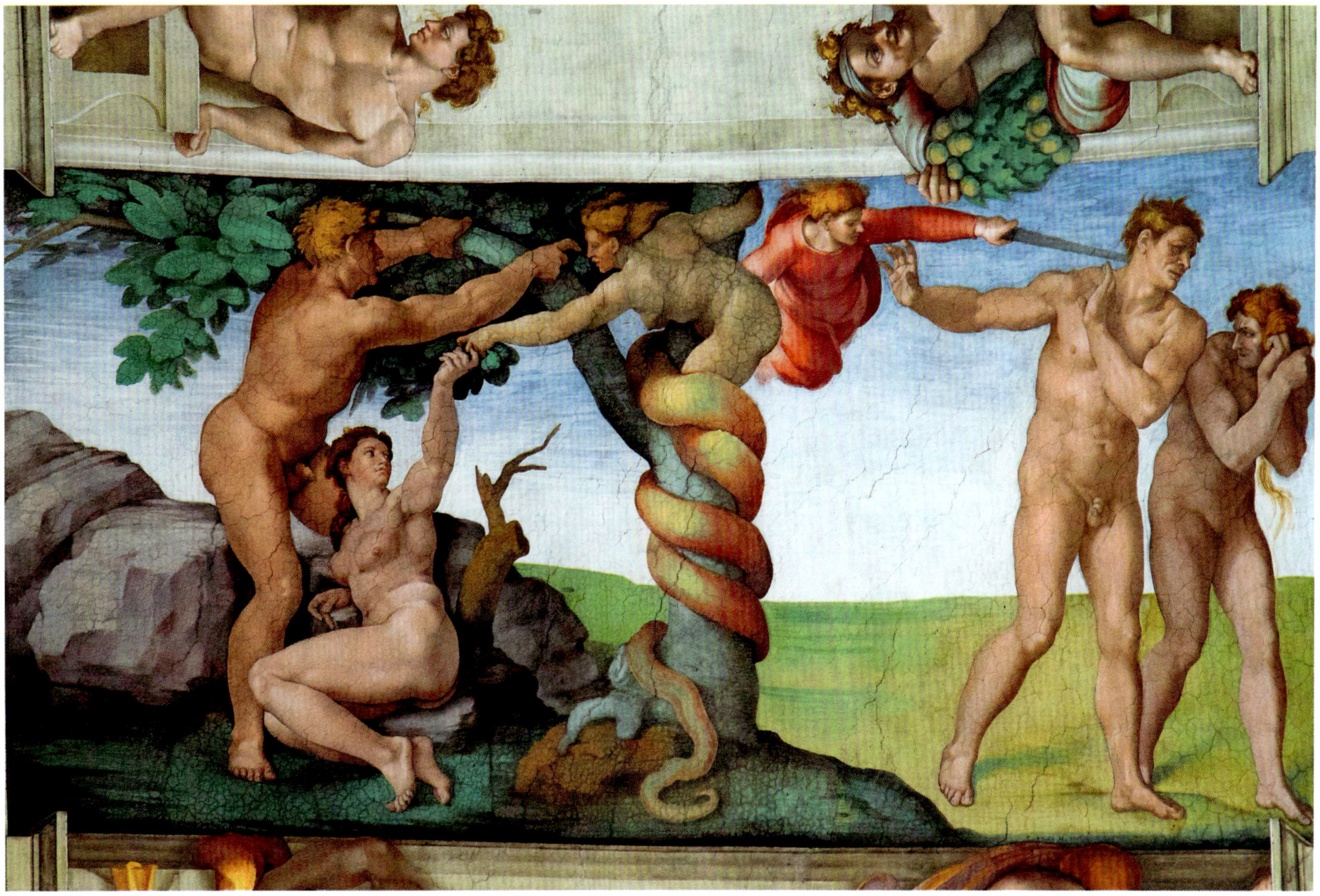

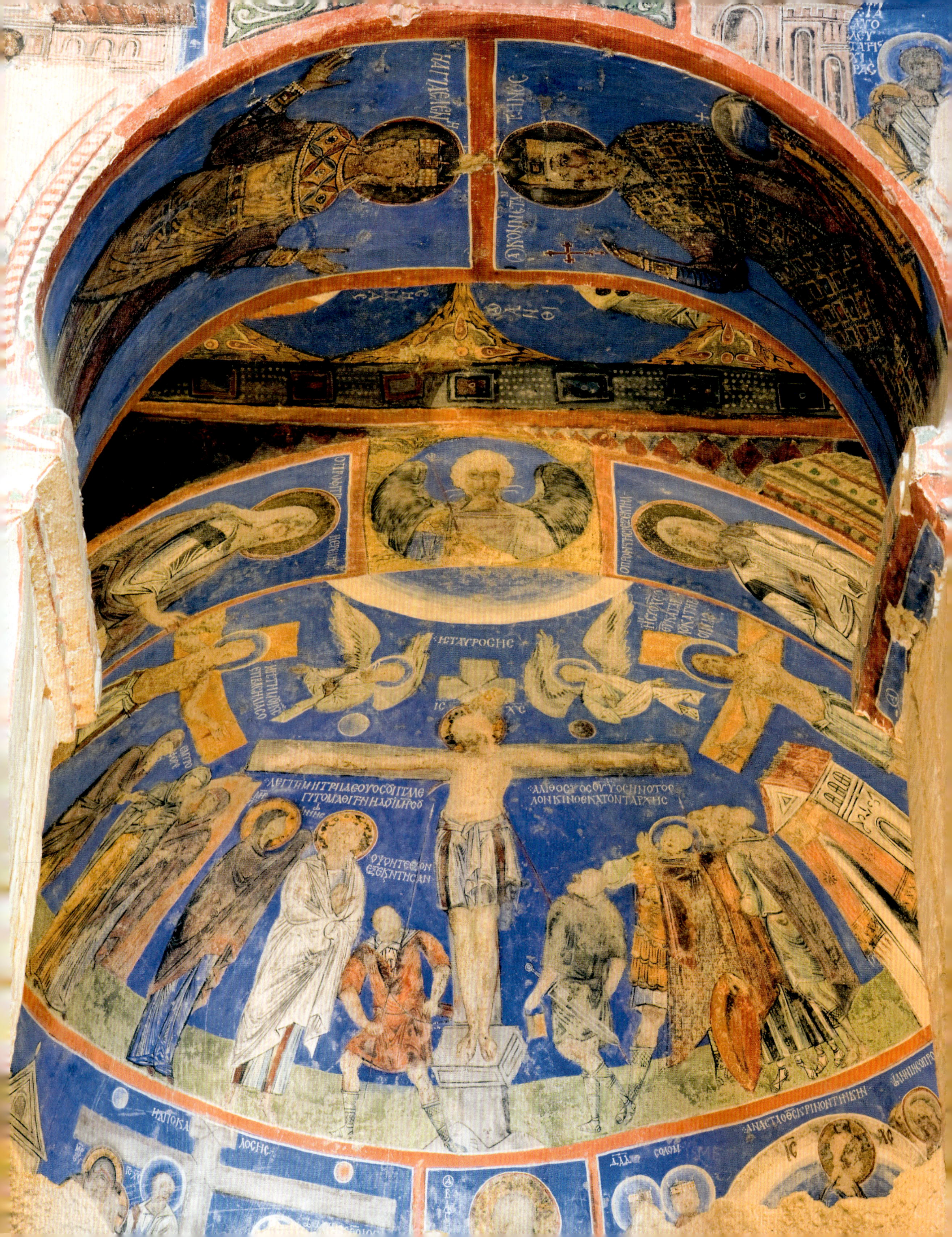

Frescoes

10th Century

Church of the Buckle, Göreme, Turkey

Left: Apse of the side chapel (paracclesion) in the New Church with central scene of the crucifixion.

Overleaf: A view of the Christological cycle in the New Church.

Church of the Buckle, Turkey

Beneath the golden, almost lunar landscape of the Göreme region in Turkey, the frescoes in the Old Church of Tokalı Kilise tell a story of humankind's mediation with nature and with God. Painted predominantly in ultramarine and a blood-like red, they are sheltered beneath great hulks of pitted rock that undulate in spiky patterns, hiding the internal cavities that were once ancient dwellings, sanctuaries and churches with idiosyncratic origins.

The eruption of Mount Erciyes in the Kayseri province of Turkey 2.6 million years ago washed the surrounding area with volcanic lava and ash, forming a 20,000 sq km (7,700 sq mi) crust of soft volcanic rock that partly eroded over time, but was also partly hewn by the inhabitants of the historical region of Cappadocia in central Anatolia, to make churches such as this, which is sometimes known as the Church of the Buckle.

The Old Church is one of four chambers in the Tokalı Kilise complex that, in the Middle Ages, served as the katholikon, or main church, of the Archangel Monastery. The monastery served the remote communities of anchorites – hermits living a withdrawn life of asceticism and spiritual contemplation in the harsh terrain of stone and sky. Cappadocia, ruled by the Christian Byzantine Empire, was one of the earliest regions to embrace early Christianity, and its people are mentioned in the New Testament as some of the first to have heard the gospel of Christ in their own tongue during the mystery of Pentecost following Christ's resurrection.

It is this story of Christ that is committed in pictorial form on the barrel vault of the Old Church in thirty-two frescoed scenes. These appear in three registers on each side of the vault, and span the life of Jesus from his conception to his crucifixion and resurrection. The first register of images starts with the *Annunciation* and ends with the *Murder of Zacchariah*. The cycle continues with depictions of the miracles associated with Christ's life in the middle register. This commences with the *Flight of Elizabeth* and concludes with the *Raising of Lazarus*. The third register depicts Christ's passion, starting with the *Entry into Jerusalem* and ending with Christ's *Descent into Limbo*. In this final scene, Christ is seen grasping the arm of Adam, the first man of the Old Testament, in Hell. This acts as a reminder that the death of Christ was a sacrificial act to atone for the sins of Adam and Eve in the Garden of Eden. Unfortunate Adam appears elsewhere in the vault too, with his deceased skull between the feet of Christ in the image of the *Deposition from the Cross*, as a further pathos-laden reminder of mankind's disobedience.

The narrative sequence of images runs from left to right with an additional two tympana at either end of the vault depicting the episodes of Christ's transfiguration (to the west) and his final ascension as a resurrected body (to the east). There are no vertical borders to distinguish the beginning and ending of an episode. Instead, these are delineated by a change in direction of the figures or the appearance of an architectural prop to conclude the passage of each particular scene.

Today, the vault serves as an entrance to the additional buildings that are known as the New Church, but it was once the single-aisled nave of the Old Church, and was built from the hollows in the volcanic rock in the tenth century. This simple architecture, pure in its essential geometry, recalls the roots of Christianity in the Roman Empire, as the form echoes the triumphal arch, a much-repeated architectural showpiece of the ancient Romans that was usually

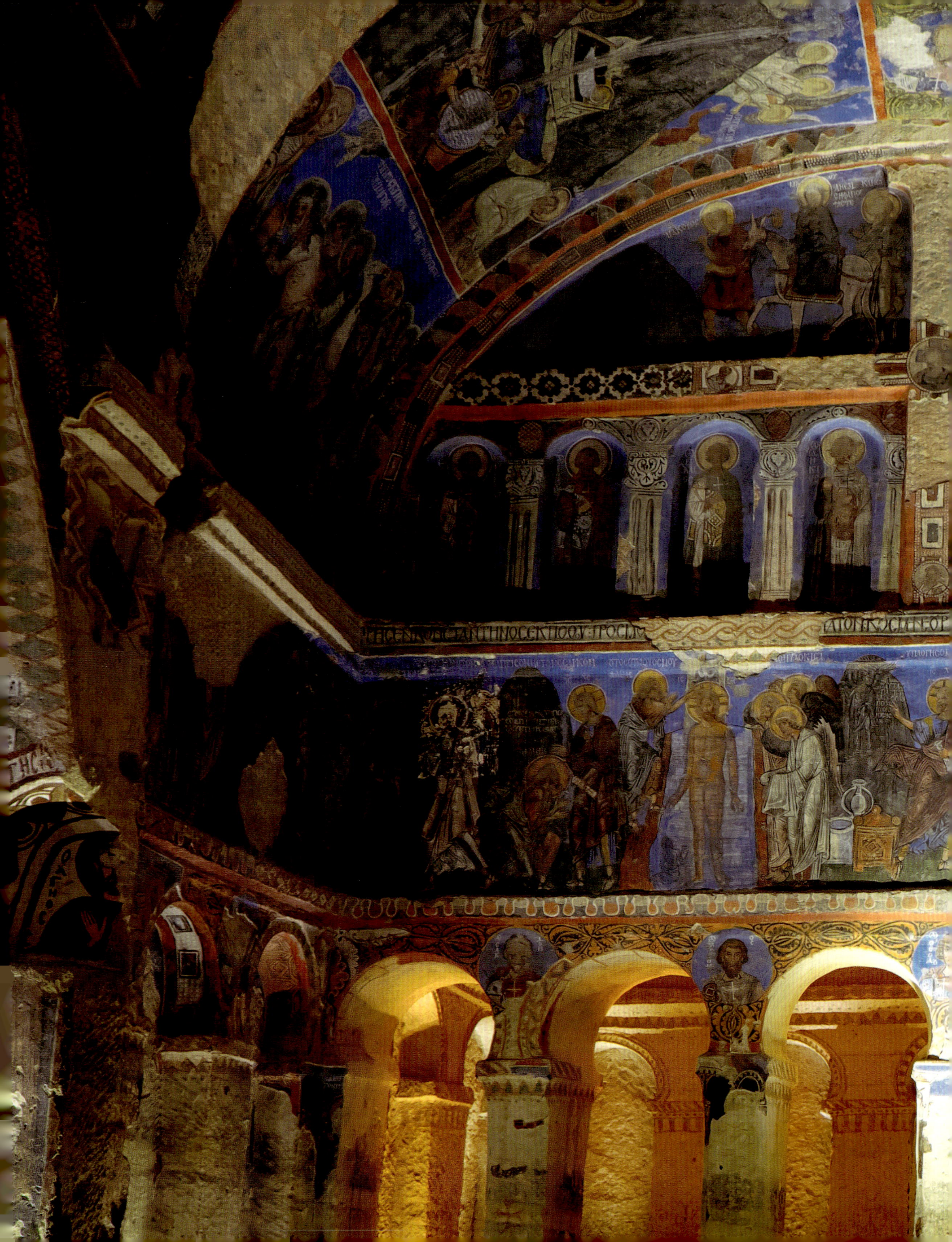

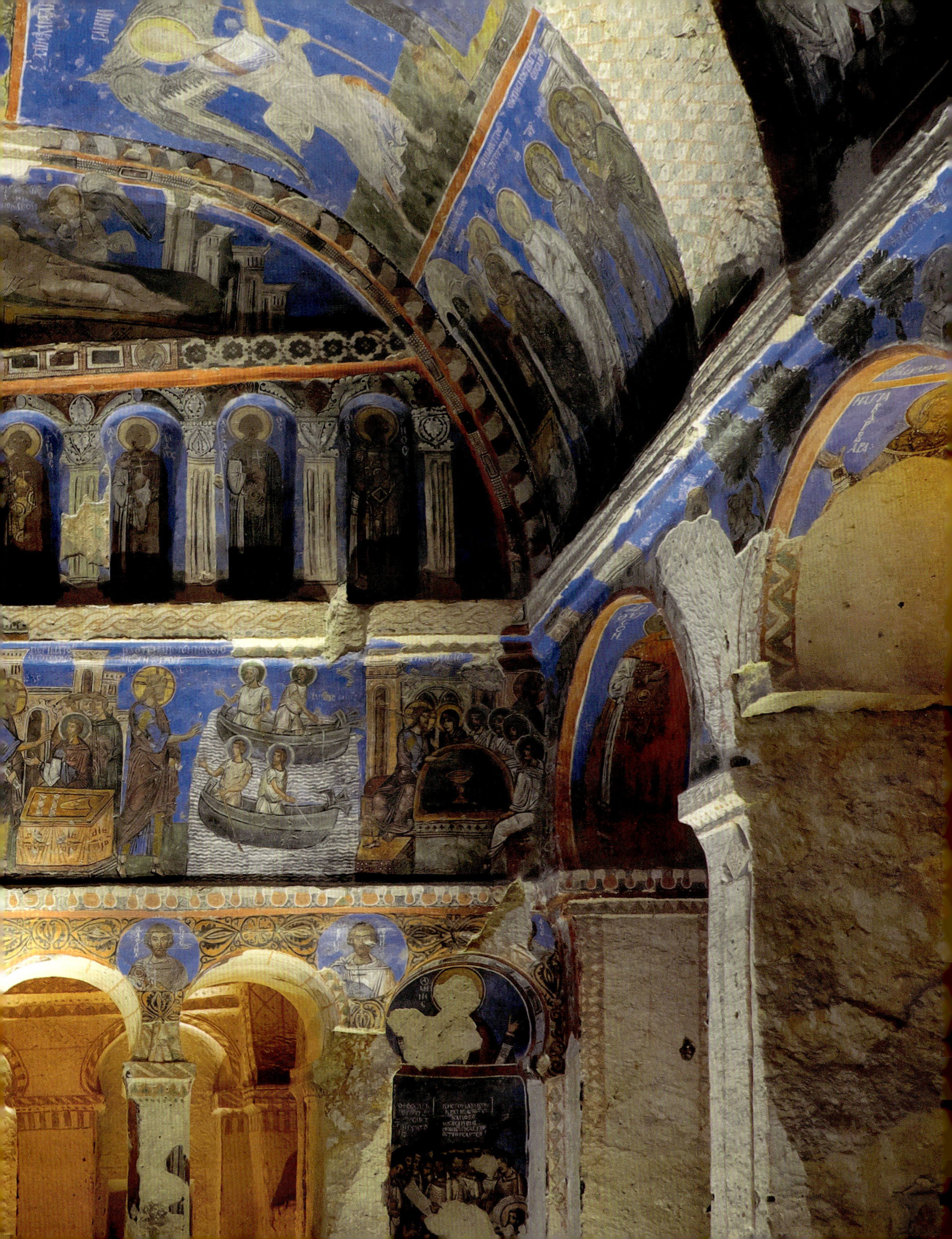

Below: A fresco from the New Church depicting the Virgin and Child, showing the Byzantine painting from outside of Cappadocia.

Bottom: View of the single-aisled basilica of the Old Church.

Opposite: Scenes from the life of Christ on the barrel vault of the Old Church.

decorated with narrative scenes in sculpted relief. In a church such as this, which is homogenous with the landscape that rises above it, and not built on top of it, the barrel vault became the equivalent space to the cupola, the decoration of which provided the visual climax to the experience of looking up inside buildings of a similar period such as the early Christian Neonian Baptistery (see p. 14).

The New Church extends from the barrel vault of the Old Church into a larger additional part of the building, which is also decorated with two separate narrative fresco cycles. One of these is another Christological cycle detailing stories of the life of Christ, from his infancy, to the Miracles and Passion. The other cycle is dedicated to St Basil, who was the principal religious figure of the Cappadocian region. Whereas the artisans who produced the frescoes of the Old Church remain anonymous, an inscription attributes the images in the New Church to the painter Nikephoros and also includes the names of the patrons, known as Constantine and his son, Leon, who were presumably wealthy and influential enough to be known only by their first names. Stylistically the frescoes in the old and new parts of the church are also different – the earlier ninth-century frescoes in the Old Church with their huge umber eyes are referred to as the 'provincial style' in contrast to the eleventh-century frescoes of the New Church , which are known as the 'metropolitan style'. However, these labels are arguably superfluous, pertaining to attempts to categorize the production of spiritual art in terms of progression in picture-making to achieve the illusion of three-dimensional modelling and depth. Better to soak oneself in these mysterious subterranean surfaces, where the simple profound poetry of man, God and stone is laid bare.

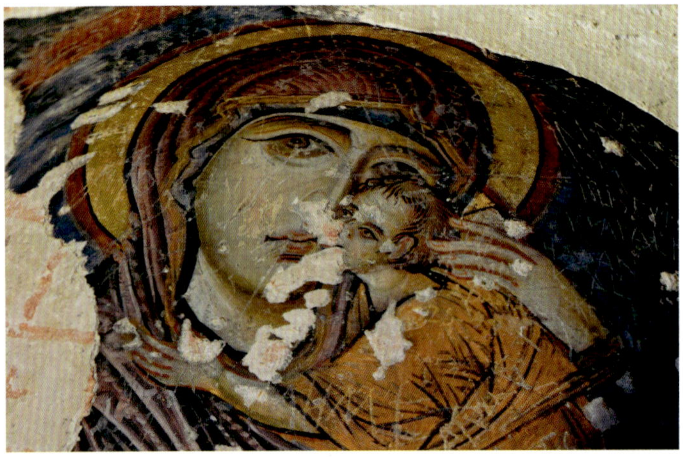

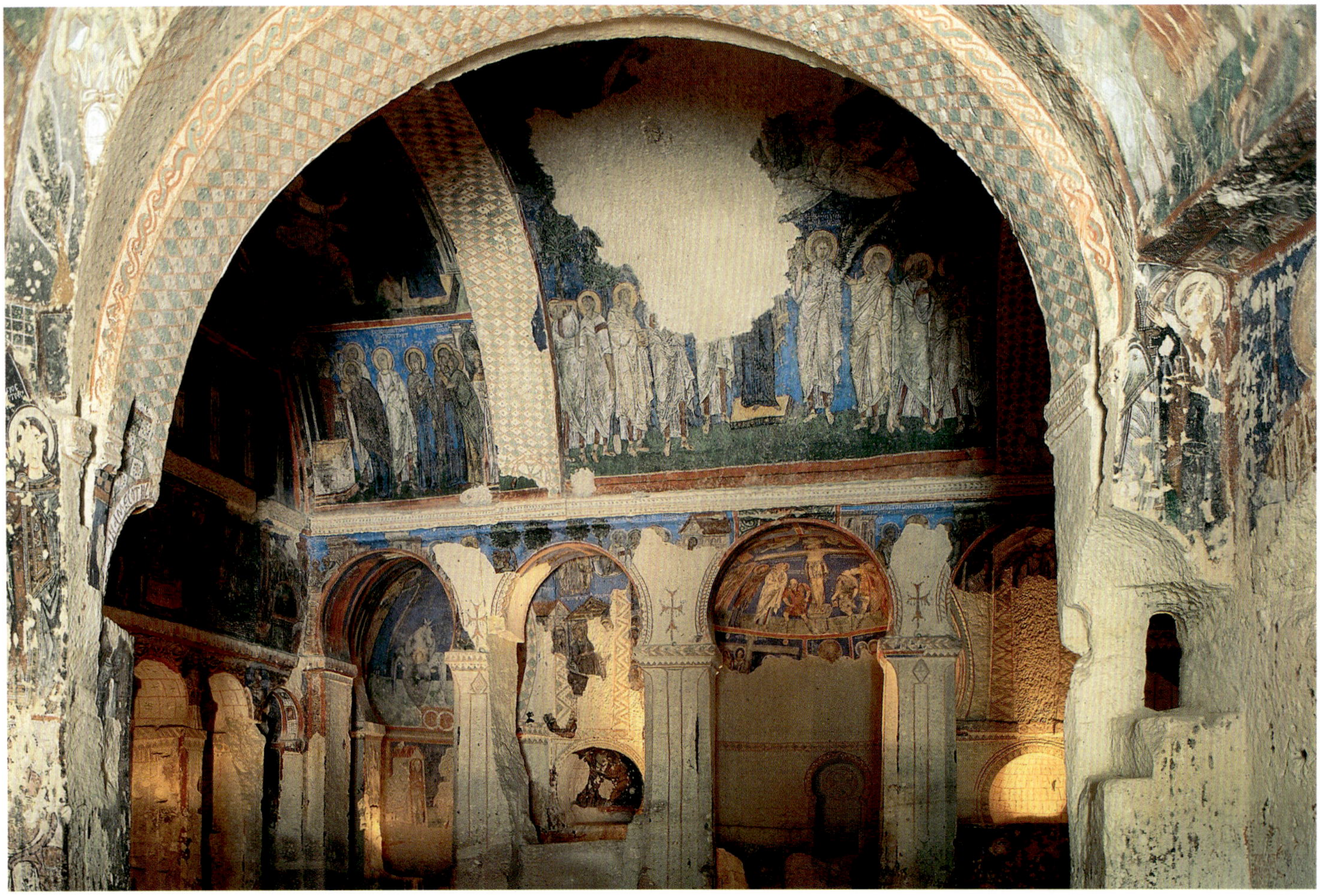

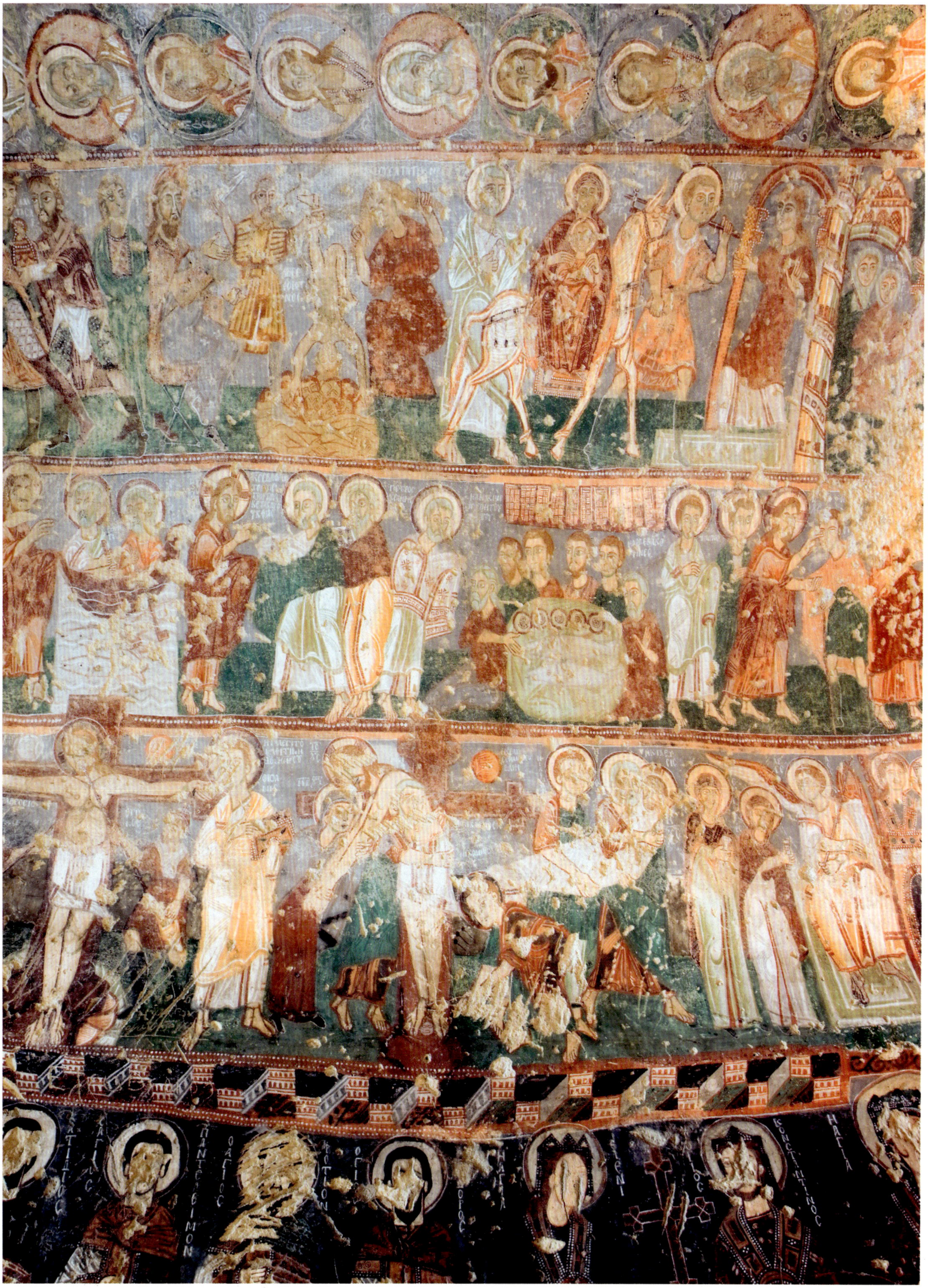

49 Church of the Buckle

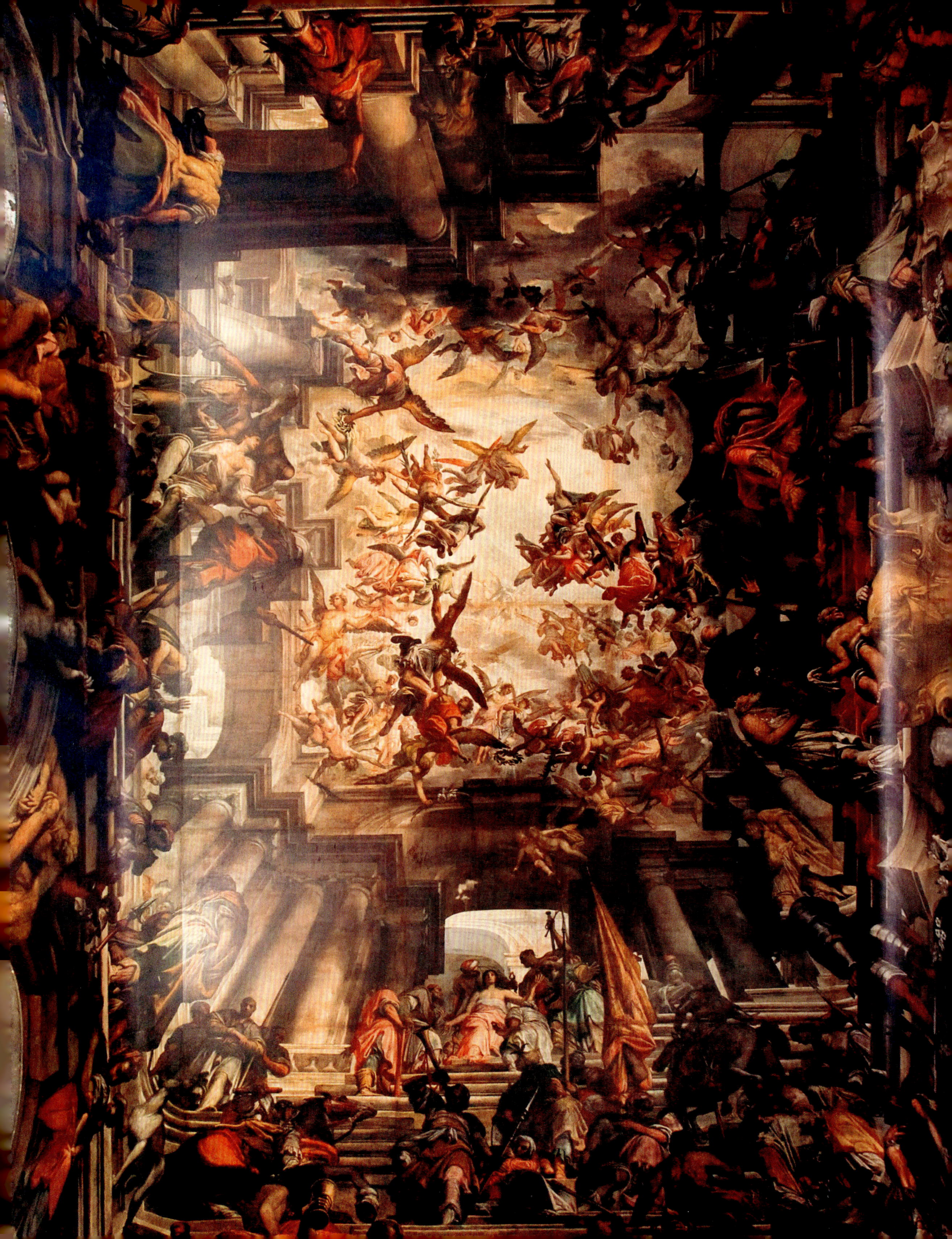

Gian Antonio Fumiani

The Martyrdom and Apotheosis of San Pantalon

1704

San Pantalon, Venice, Italy

Left: Fumiani's illusionistic ceiling at San Pantalon tells the story of the early Christian saint to whom the church is dedicated.

San Pantalon, Italy

Behind the unfinished facade of Chiesa di San Pantaleone Martire (San Pantalon), in the bustling Campo Santa Margherita, Venice, is a church thick with dense damp shadows. These slowly give way to a ceiling that claims to be the world's largest oil painting. Painted by Gian Antonio Fumiani between 1680 and 1704, it is titled *The Martyrdom and Apotheosis of San Pantalon*, and tells the story of the early Christian saint to whom the church is dedicated.

Unfolding over 41 sq m (443 sq ft), the scenes from his martyrology play out over sixty canvases. Son of a wealthy pagan from the ancient Greek territory of Nicomedia (now in Turkey), and educated by a Christian mother, Pantaleone drifted from religion after his mother's death. He studied medicine, subsequently becoming a physician to the Roman emperor Maximian. He was later converted back to the Christian faith by a priest known as Hermolaus , who argued that medicine was nothing compared to salvation and healing offered by Christ. Pantaleone distributed all his wealth to the poor and, through his faith, was able to cure the blind and disabled. Condemned to death for his beliefs, which challenged the orthodoxy of pagan religion in ancient Rome, he was killed in 305 [CE], during the most severe purge of Christians under the Roman emperors Diocletian, Maximian, Galerius and Constantius. The saint's official capacity within the Catholic Church is as the patron saint of physicians and midwives. However, in contemporary Italy, San Pantaleone is known to appear in dreams with fortuitous lottery numbers. The name was an extremely popular choice for the sons of well-to-do Venetian families during the sixteenth century.

The San Pantalon ceiling follows the, by then, established *sotto in su* (from below to above) tradition in Italian ceiling painting, in which the composition is painted with severe foreshortening and the dramatic illusion of elements extending vertiginously upwards while others seem about to topple downwards onto the viewer. As such, it is comparable to the illusionistic compositional format of other Italian ceilings, such as Pietro da Cortona's *Allegory of Divine Providence* at the Palazzo Barberini in Rome (see p. 144), which also depicts an apotheosis (of the Barberini pope). As in da Cortona's ceiling, Gian Antonio Fumiani employs the *quadratura* technique to create the illusion that the vault is open to the sky. Fumiani's ceiling delivers a far less triumphalist tale, however. Through a dusk-like haze, winged angels swarm like chaotic bats in and out of a portico of severe classical architecture around which the tumult takes place. The crepuscular tangle of figures in motion comes into focus around the central light that silhouettes the figure of the saint as he is welcomed into heaven, accompanied by attributes such as the martyr's palm, while organs bellow and trumpets squeal.

To the right of centre (under a tent), Emperor Diocletian commands and observes the execution of San Pantaleone, while in front of this, the executioners set about the grisly work, but to no avail. As was customary in the early martyrologies of Christian saints, their bodies miraculously repelled many of the violent assaults inflicted upon them. In this case, baths of molten lead turned cold, torches for burning flesh were extinguished and wild beasts were tamed before San Pantaleone gave in. Only when the martyr desired his own death was he successfully beheaded to find milk rather than blood flowing from his severed body.

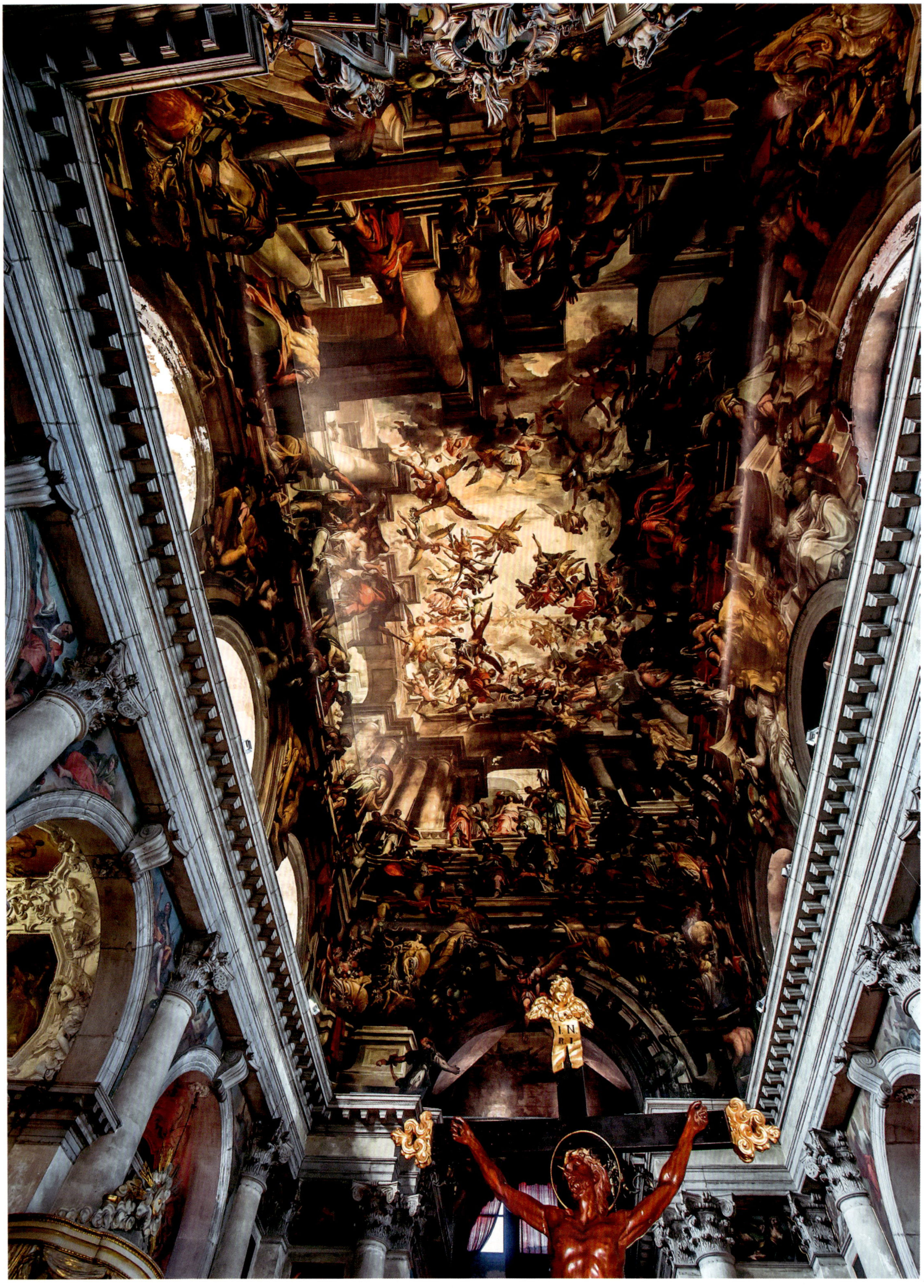

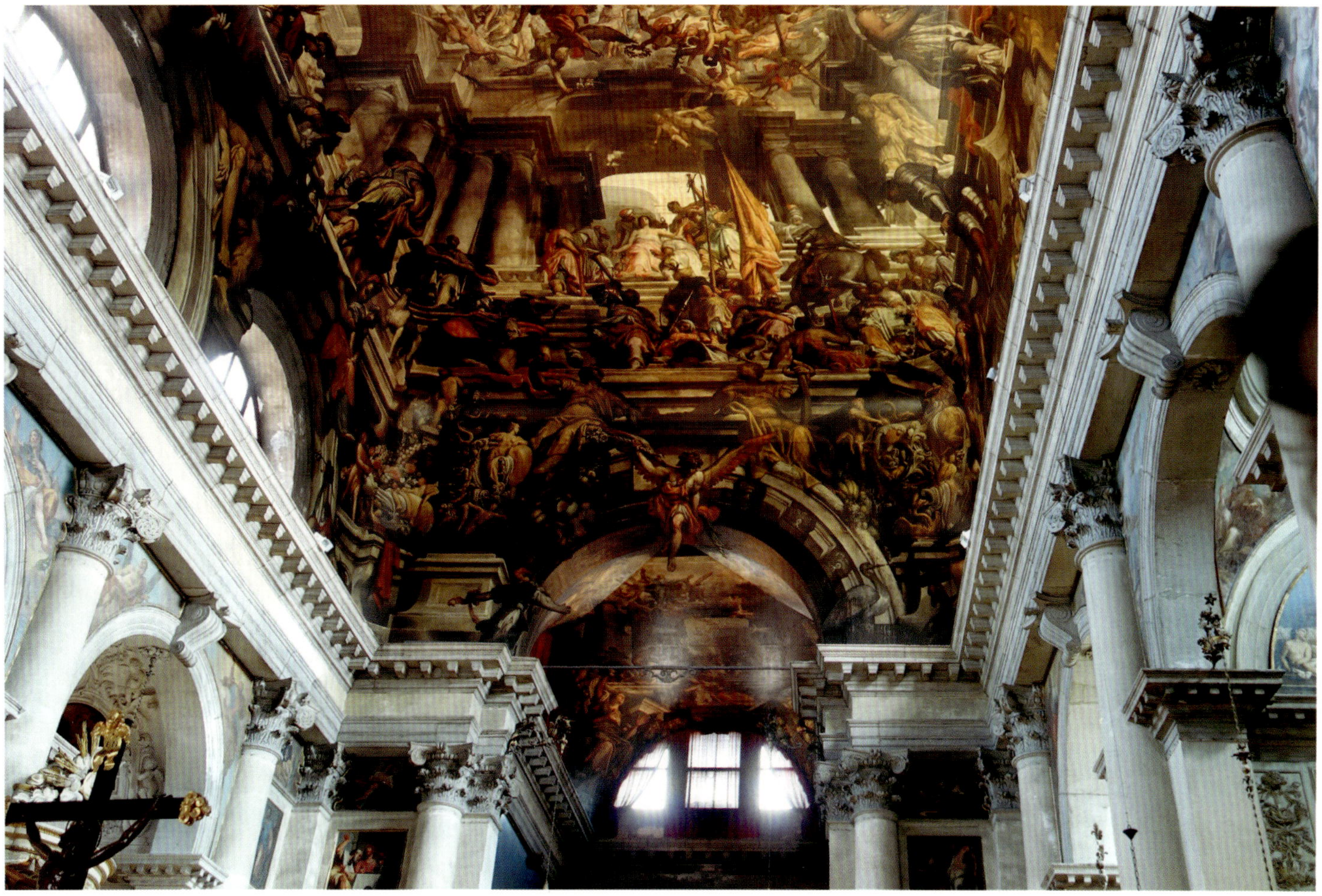

Opposite and above: Claimed to be the world's largest oil painting, Fumiani's work unfolds over 41 sq m (443 sq ft).

Native to the watery city of Venice, Fumiani had trained in Bologna and had worked on theatrical sets for the ducal theatre in Piacenza in the 1660s. This proved useful for the special effects required for religious painting in the service of the Catholic Church, to help produce works that would stimulate the senses and emotions of the viewer, engaging them and instructing them in their devotion. Fumiani is buried in the church, which by some accounts became his final resting place more prematurely than perhaps anticipated, as some suggest that he fell from a scaffold while finishing the work, although this fact is contested.

Fumiani's vast life's work hasn't always suited all tastes. The nineteenth-century artist and critic John Ruskin found it something of an aberration with 'the rags and ruins of Venetian skill, honour and worship exploded all together sky high. Miracles of frantic mistake, of flaunting and thunderous hypocrisy – universal lie, shouted through speaking-trumpets . . . [It is] the most curious example in Europe of the vulgar dramatic effects of painting.'

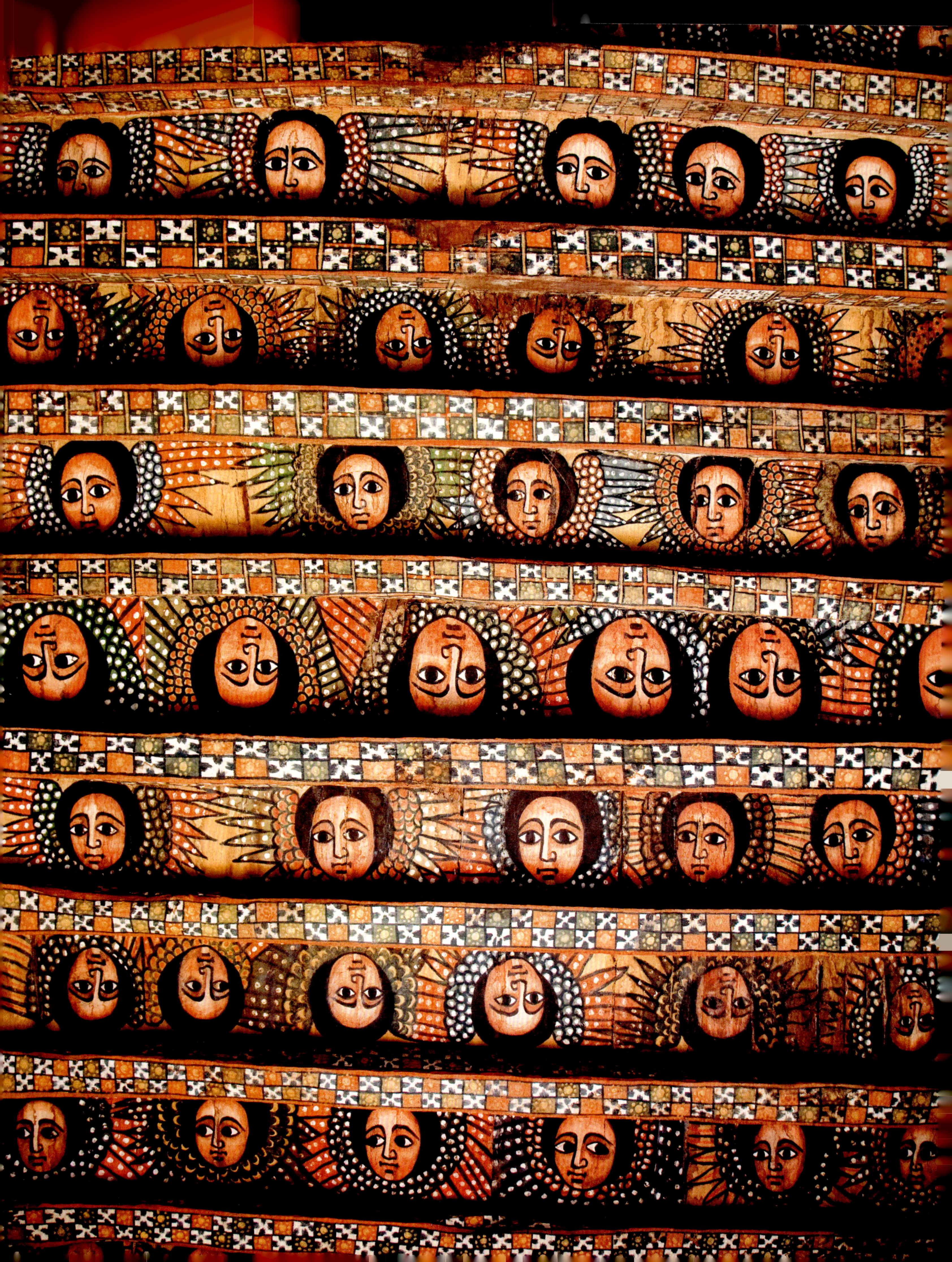

Left: On the ceiling of Debre Berhan Selassie, the heads of 135 angels gaze down on visitors.

Debre Berhan Selassie Church, Ethiopia

A patchwork of red, blue and gold clings to every available surface on the walls and ceiling inside the Debre Berhan Selassie Church in Gondar. Within this sprawling composition, biblical stories are vividly narrated with an abundance of figures, from men with white beards to saints on horseback and even a thorny-clawed black devil with huge horns squatting in a nest of flames. The disembodied heads of 135 angels gaze down from the flat-beamed roof like custodians waiting in a court of heaven, each with its own individual expression. It is beneath their benign gazes that the biblical stories are played out.

Painted in the hieratic style of early Christian imagery that originated in Byzantium, the importance of religious figures in this work is signified by their size. This explains the dominant position of three identical men with white beards and white hair who sit above Christ in a hexagonal frame. Both position and size hold clues to their symbolic value: they represent the Holy Trinity of God the Father, God the Son and God the Holy Spirit. Around the outermost corners of the frame that holds them are symbols representing the four gospel writers (the evangelists). A lion for St Mark, an eagle for St John, a bull for St Luke and an angel for St Matthew. And there is another figure, huge in comparison, who strides across the left-hand wall in various scenes. This is the warrior knight St George, the famous dragon slayer of Christianity who represents the triumph of Christian valiance and goodness over heresy and evil. St George, despite his origins in third-century Cappadocia (he died in 303), was widely venerated across Ethiopia and features in Christian art and icons of the region almost as regularly as the Virgin Mary. Despite his non-Western origins, he has been whitewashed for the most part in art history and even adopted as the patron saint of England.

The main compositional focus of the room is a huge crucifixion that resembles early Florentine Renaissance paintings of the subject such as Cimabue's *Crucifixion* at Santa Croce (c. 1265). In fact, the frescoes here seem to belong to a much earlier point in time than the eighteenth century, when they were painted. The flatness of the scenes, without any perspectival recession into space, the stylized faces and the striated clothing resemble the early icons of the Byzantine Church. This pictorial language of Christianity arrived in Ethiopia as a result of the country's ties with monastic leaders beyond its borders, in turn leading to the employment of European and Middle Eastern artisans to decorate the region's churches. This explains the absence of indigenous black complexions on the walls of the church. This adoption of artistic styles from outside of Africa was enhanced by extensive international trade relationships; Ethiopia was an interface between Europe and Africa between the thirteenth and seventeenth centuries, when European merchants sought alternatives to Islamic-controlled trade routes.

The church itself dates to the seventeenth century, when the Gondar region of Ethiopia became the territory's new capital and home of kings, as decreed by King Fasilides in 1632. (Ethiopia's church has a much longer history, however, as the second nation in the world to adopt Christianity as its state religion, after Armenia.) An original place of worship was built by Iyasu II in the late seventeenth century and took its name Debre Berhan, meaning 'mountain of light', from his nickname Berghan

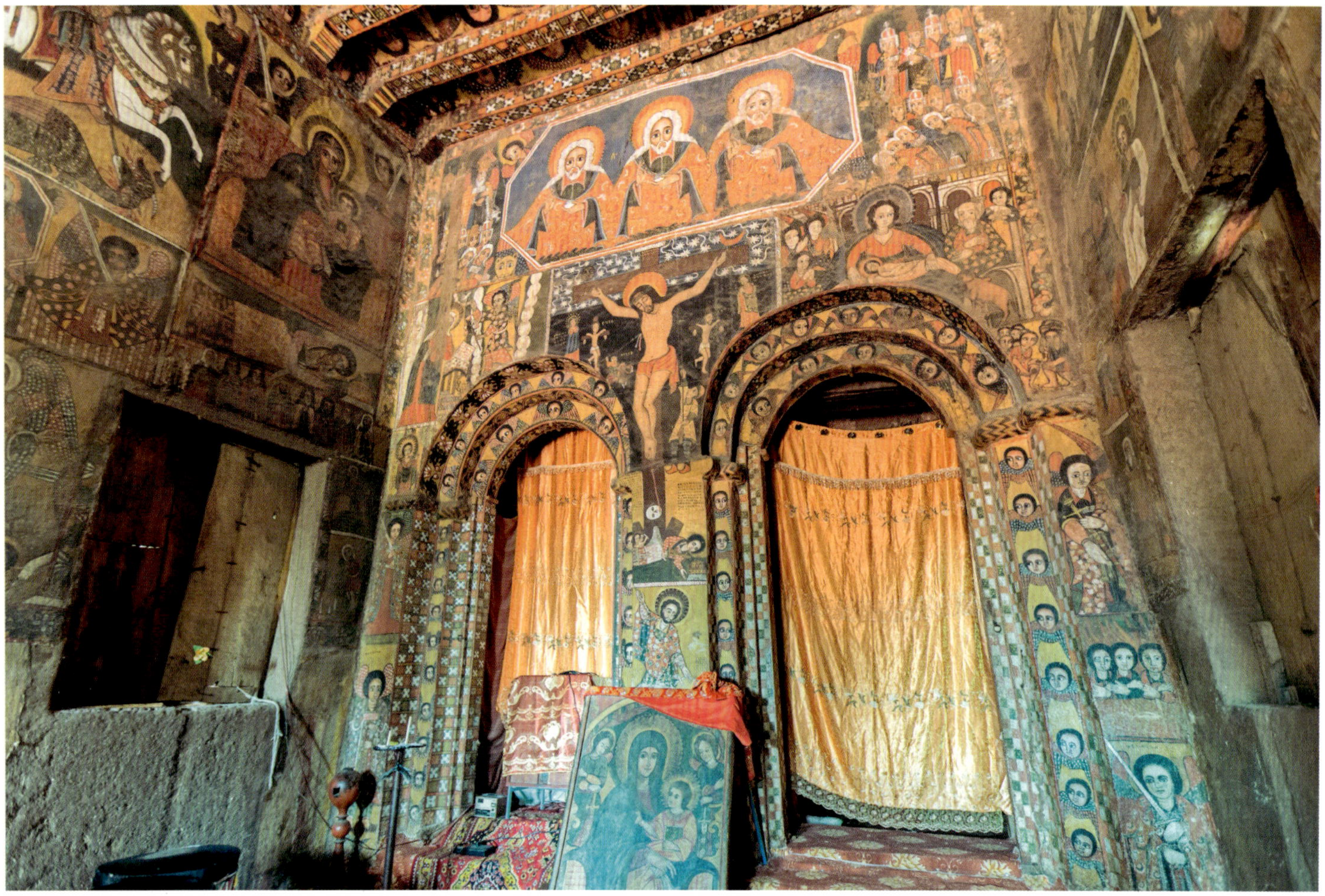

Above and opposite top: The central image of the crucifixion, above which is an image of three bearded men symbolizing the Holy Trinity of God the Father, Son and Holy Spirit.

Below and opposite bottom: The hieratically proportioned figures of St George on a white horse and the Virgin Mary and Jesus on the left wall.

Seged (to whom the light bows). However, light was also to be its downfall – quite literally – when the church was struck by lightning and destroyed. The current structure dates to the eighteenth century, which is when the frescoes on the interior were completed. It has survived against the odds – perhaps the angels on the ceiling have gifted some protection, the power of their collective gaze too overwhelming for potential marauders. In fact, one of their number is said to have protected the church from destruction in the nineteenth century; when the Mahdist dervishes of the Sudan sacked the city of Gondar in 1888, they burned down every church in the city except Debre Berhan Selassie. According to local legend, a swarm of bees descended on the compound, repelling the troops, while the archangel Michael himself stood before the large wooden gates armed with a flaming sword.

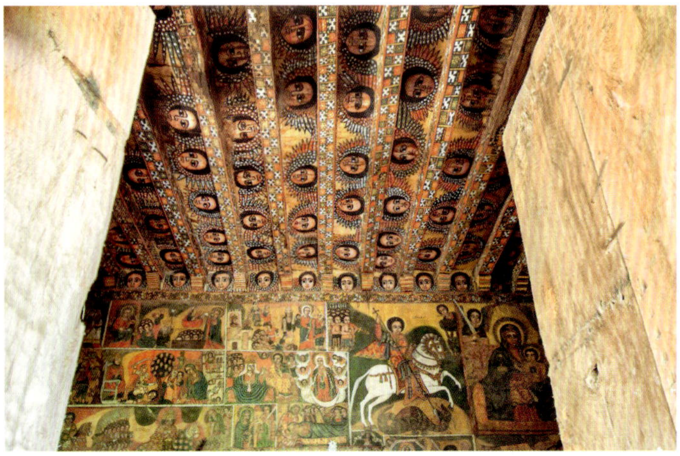

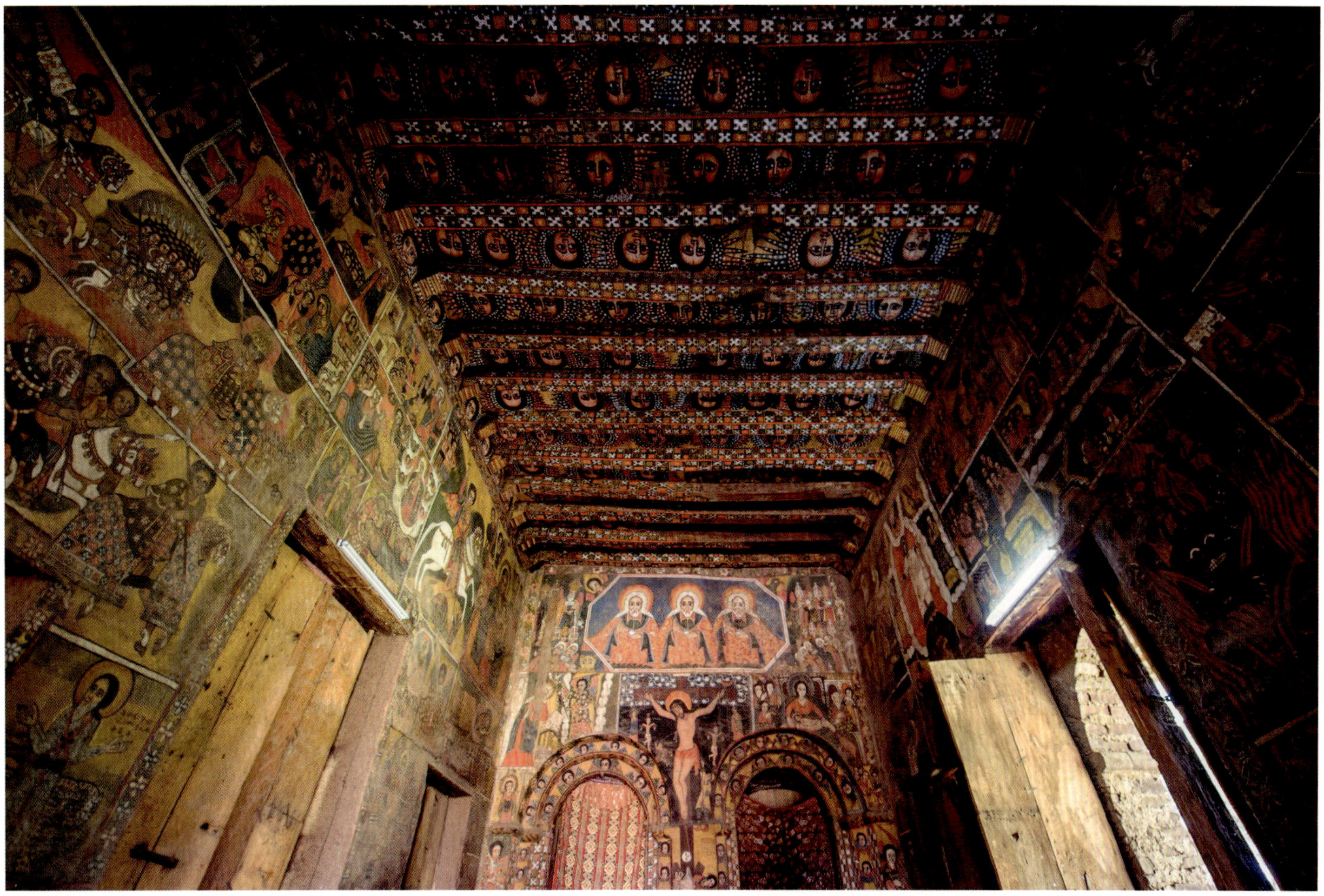

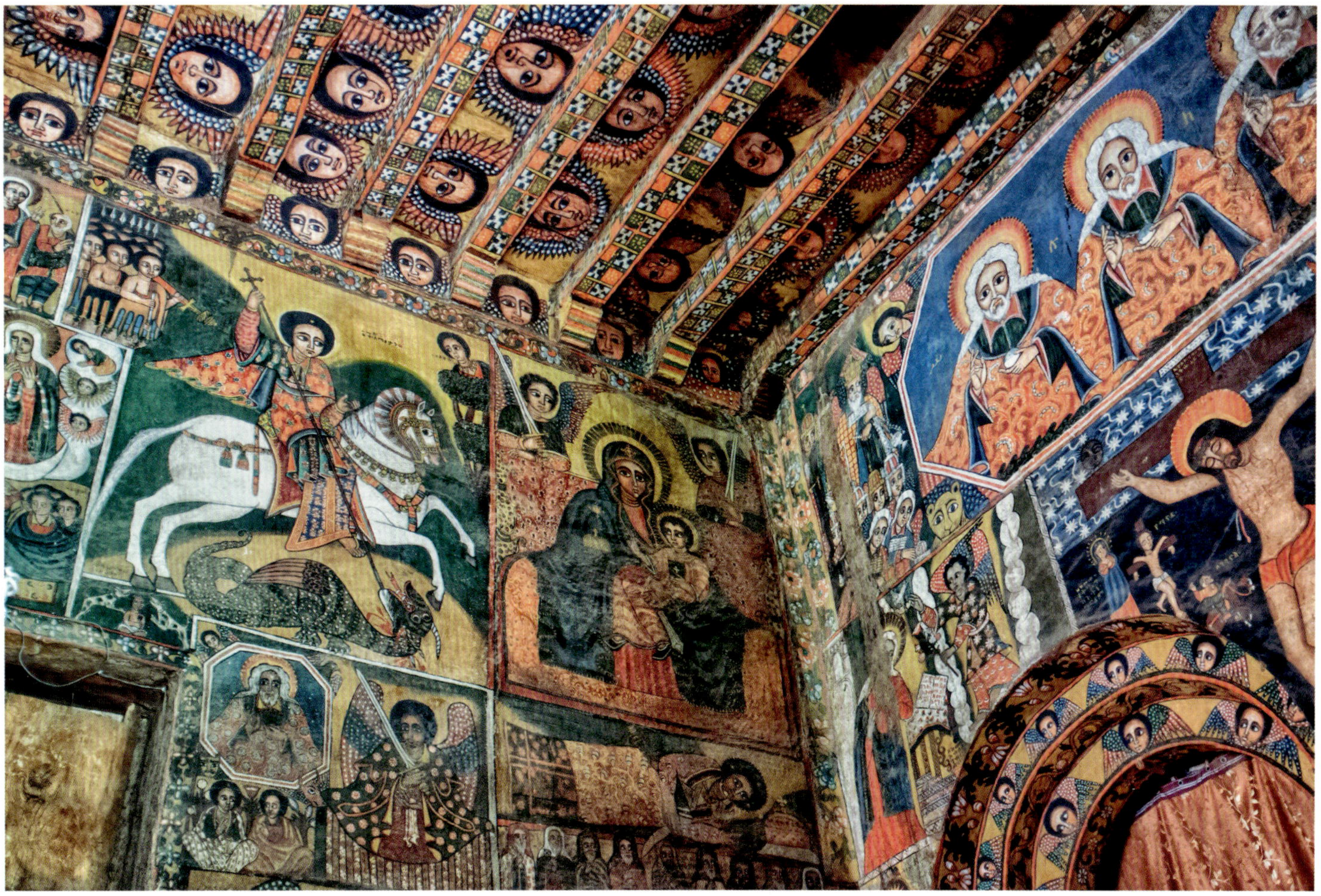

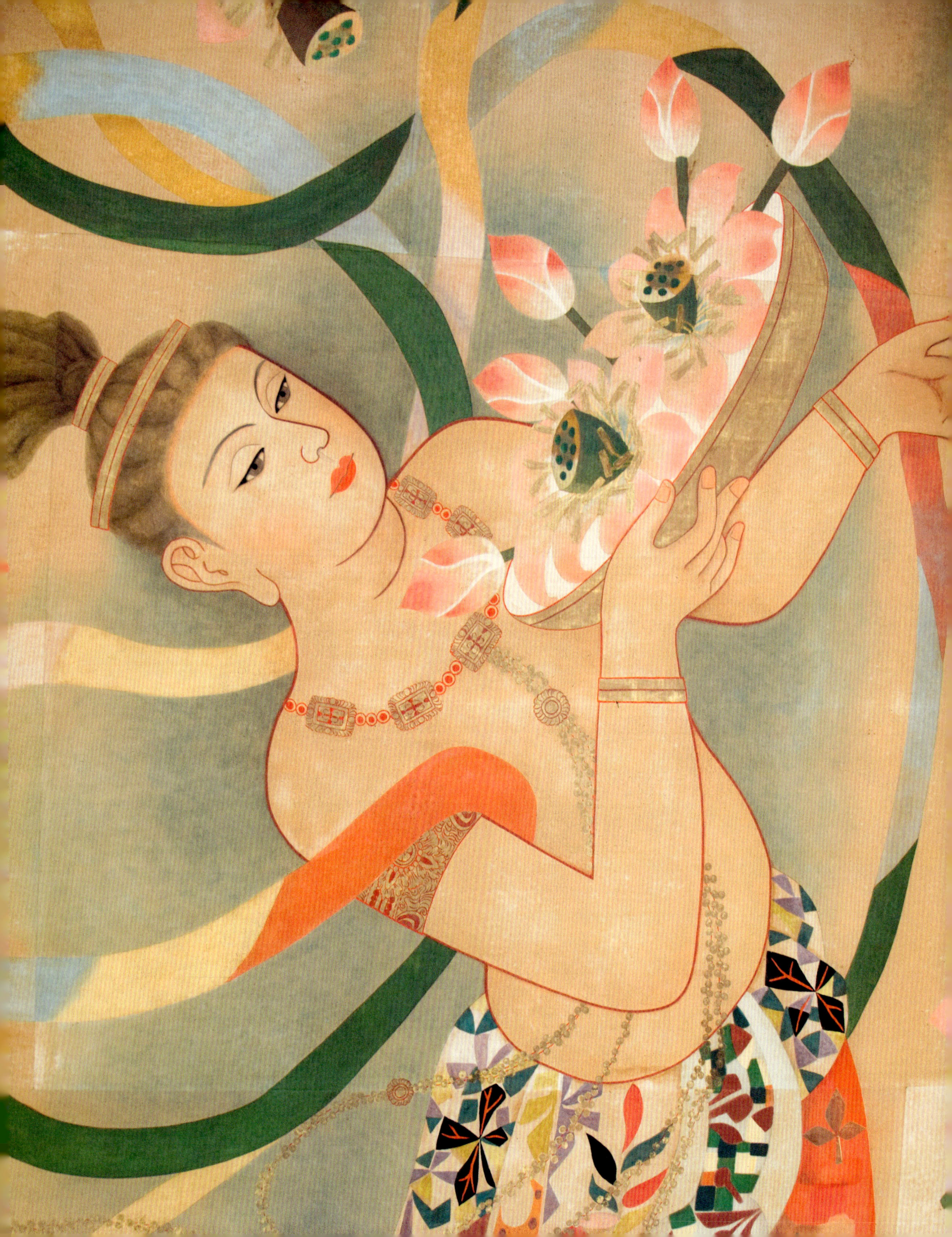

Inshō Dōmoto, Ryūshi Kawabata

Sensō-ji Temple

1957

Tokyo, Japan

Left: One of the two angel-like figures, scattering her lotus blossoms over the temple.

Overleaf: Although originating in the fifth century [BCE], the current invocation dates back to the 1950s.

Sensō-ji Temple, Japan

Two giant maidens bedecked in a web of swirling multicoloured ribbons hover in mid-flight, scattering lotus blossoms that seem to catch on an overhead breeze. The lower parts of their bodies are wrapped in gauzy crimson scarfs that unfurl behind them, while delicate jewellery adorns their necks and wrists. These figures are celestial beings from Japanese Buddhism known as *tennyo*, angel-like figures devoted to giving praise to the gods, who are often depicted dancing or sweetly thrumming on musical instruments. From their vantage point here, in the outer chamber to the *hondō* (main hall) of the Sensō-ji temple in Asakusa, Tokyo, they watch over and bless the heads of those on the threshold of the hall, a space that also serves, perhaps unexpectedly, as a shopping arcade, and accommodates the thirty million people who visit each year, making this the world's most visited religious site.

Japanese Buddhism adopted these angelic attendants from India's earlier Vedic traditions in Hindu mythology, when the religion became diffuse across China, Japan and Southeast Asia in the sixth century. Although the *tennyo* is an ancient spiritual being with roots in Indian Buddhism of the fifth century [BCE], the visual invocations here date from 1957 and were created by the Japanese *nihonga* artist Inshō Dōmoto, whose prolific output comprises around six hundred interior screens and ceilings for Buddhist temples and shrines.

The origins of the Sensō-ji temple date to the year 628 when, according to the foundational legend, two fishermen discovered a statue of the goddess of mercy and compassion known as Kannon in the Sumida River. Kannon is a Japanese adoption of the Taoist goddess Guanyin and the Indian deity Avalokiteshvara. She is a *bodhisattva*, a being that postpones their own eternal enlightenment in order to provide assistance to those on Earth. The theme of recurrence and reincarnation continues, for no matter how many times the fishermen discarded the statue, it kept returning to them, until they brought it to the village chief of Asakusa, who created a shrine for it in his own home – the first invocation of the Sensō-ji temple. In the tenth century, Taira no Kinmasa expanded the temple into a seven-structure complex, in order to give thanks for his becoming lord of the ancient Musashi district. Destroyed by an earthquake in 1041, the temple was rebuilt only to be razed to the ground by fire in 1079; it was not rebuilt again until a century later. Sensō-ji's penultimate refurbishment, which began in 1649 and lasted three centuries, was destroyed during an air raid by Allied forces in 1945.

This current reconstruction commenced in the postwar period of the 1950s, which is when Inshō Dōmoto's graceful *tennyo* were introduced. They are accompanied by a central image of a dragon, created by fellow *nihonga* pioneer Ryūshi Kawabata, an enthusiastic voice who advocated widely for the public benefits of art. After a period spent studying the Western trajectory of art in the United States, Kawabata returned to the heritage of Japanese imagery, choosing to invoke traditional iconography from Japanese folklore and religion. This is encapsulated in the figure of the dragon, which was a traditional symbol of enlightenment in Japanese Buddhism and believed to be the ancestral parent of Japanese emperors, as well as the focus of worship as a water deity associated with rainfall.

But beyond their iconographical function in Japanese religion

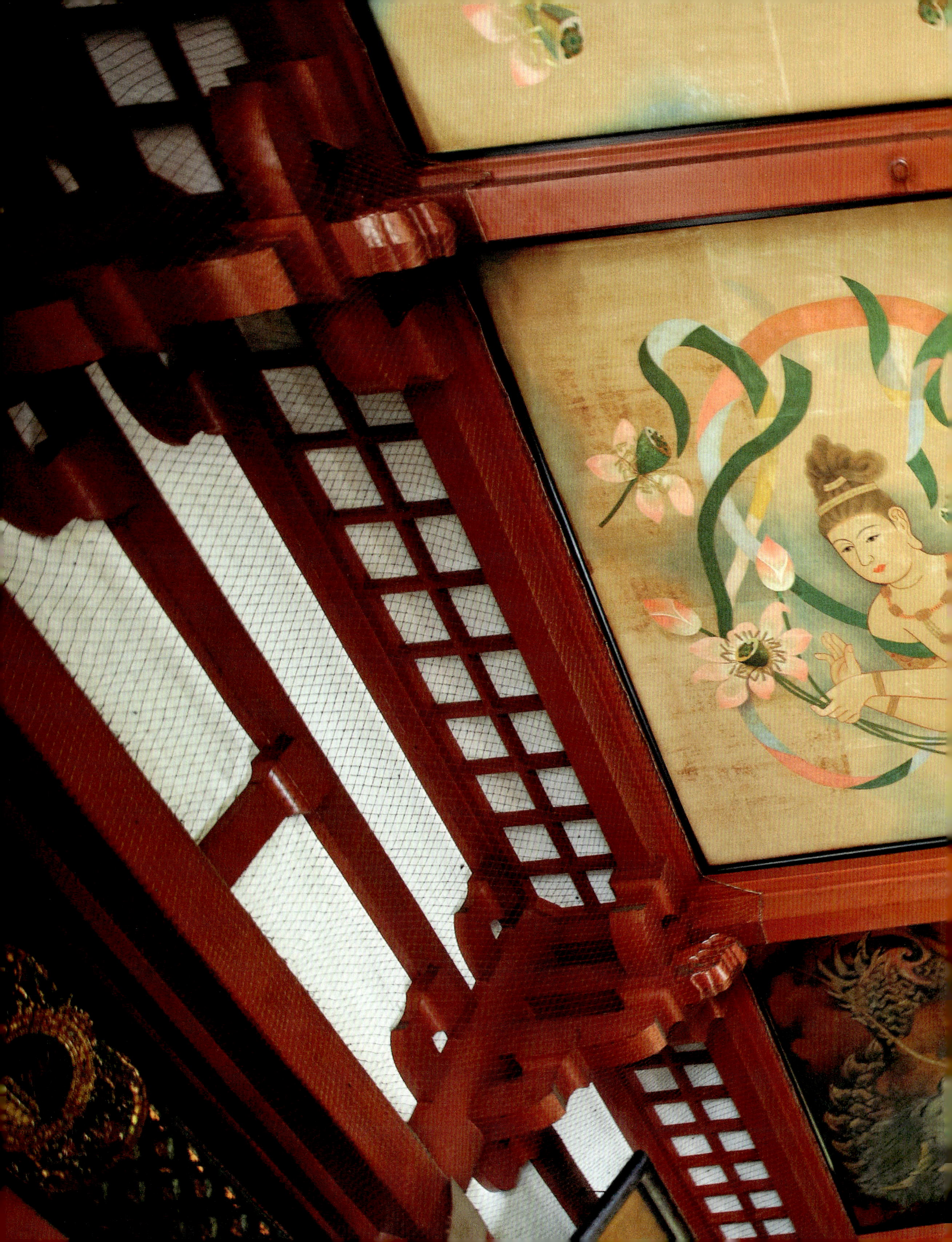

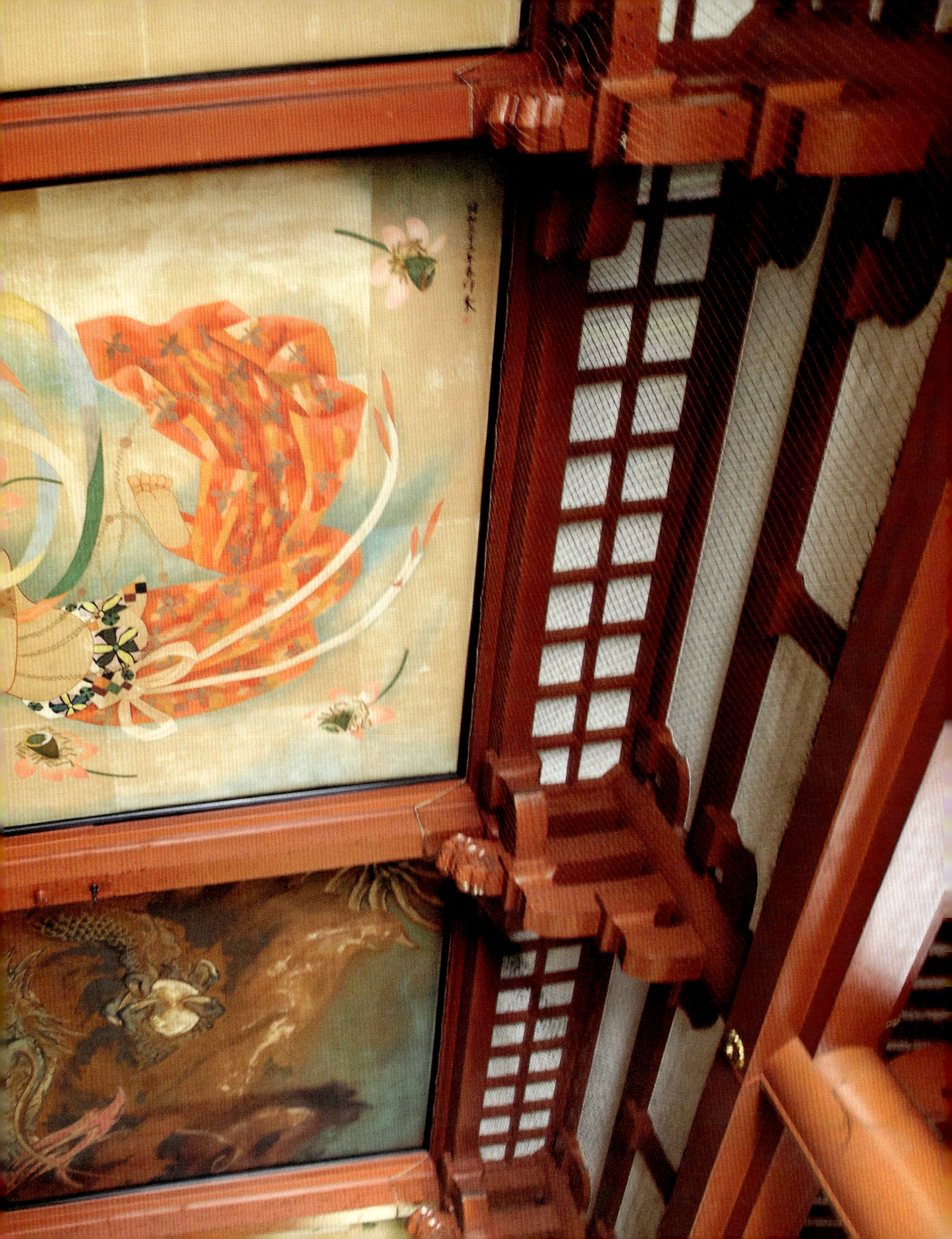

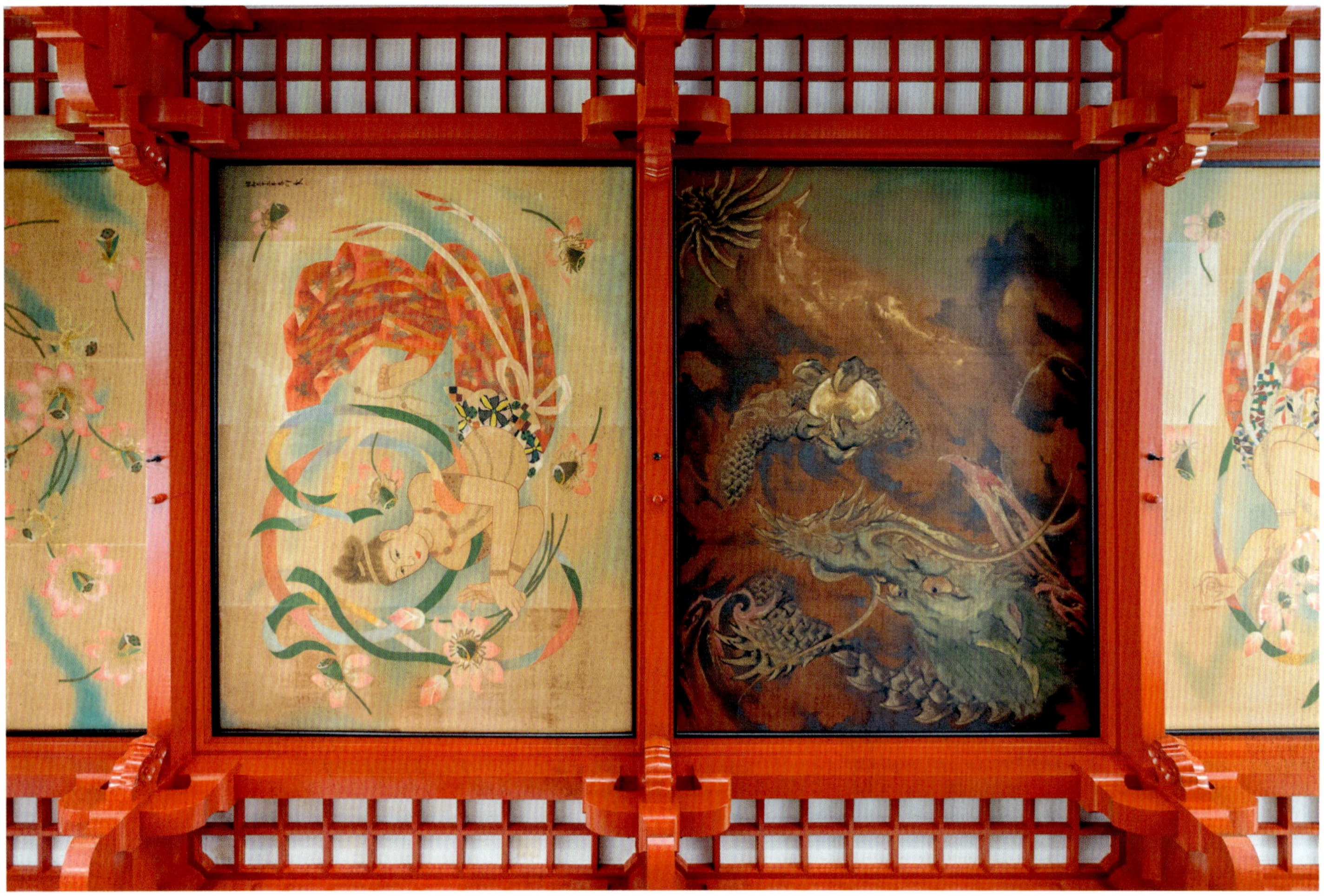

Above and opposite top: The figures of the *tennyo* and dragon take centre stage.

and mythology, these images also tell a story of the culture clash between Eastern and Western art traditions. One of the primary distinctions between the visual arts of the East and West revolves around the use of perspective and the creation of three-dimensional depth in drawing and painting. While there is a perceived 'flatness' with blocks of empty space in traditional Japanese images, Western European art of the early modern period is characterized by a depth of field and three-dimensional modelling, achieved through the manipulation of light and shadow.

The possibility of any dialogue between the differing approaches was tightly controlled, as the consumption of images from Europe and the West was curtailed in Japan during the country's Edo period (1603–1868), when foreign influence of any kind was actively restricted. In this way, Japan cultivated a prosperity borne out of seclusion, which came to an abrupt end with the arrival of four US battleships in Edo Bay in 1853. Eventually the ruling order gave way to the Meji period (1868–1912), which opened the floodgates to oceans of foreign images and an engagement with the 'exotic' world outside of Japan.

However, with the Japanese enthusiasm for these Western artistic styles there came a backlash, in which the *nihonga* style emerged as a revival of ancient Japanese themes and artistic techniques, but with a broadening of subject matter and diversification of style. Painted on Japanese washi paper with pigment derived from crushed minerals, shells, coral and semi-precious stones, the dragon and *tennyo* at Sensō-ji embrace the delicacy and ancient folkloric and religious motifs of Japanese artistic tradition in the face of twentieth-century globalization and commerce with the West.

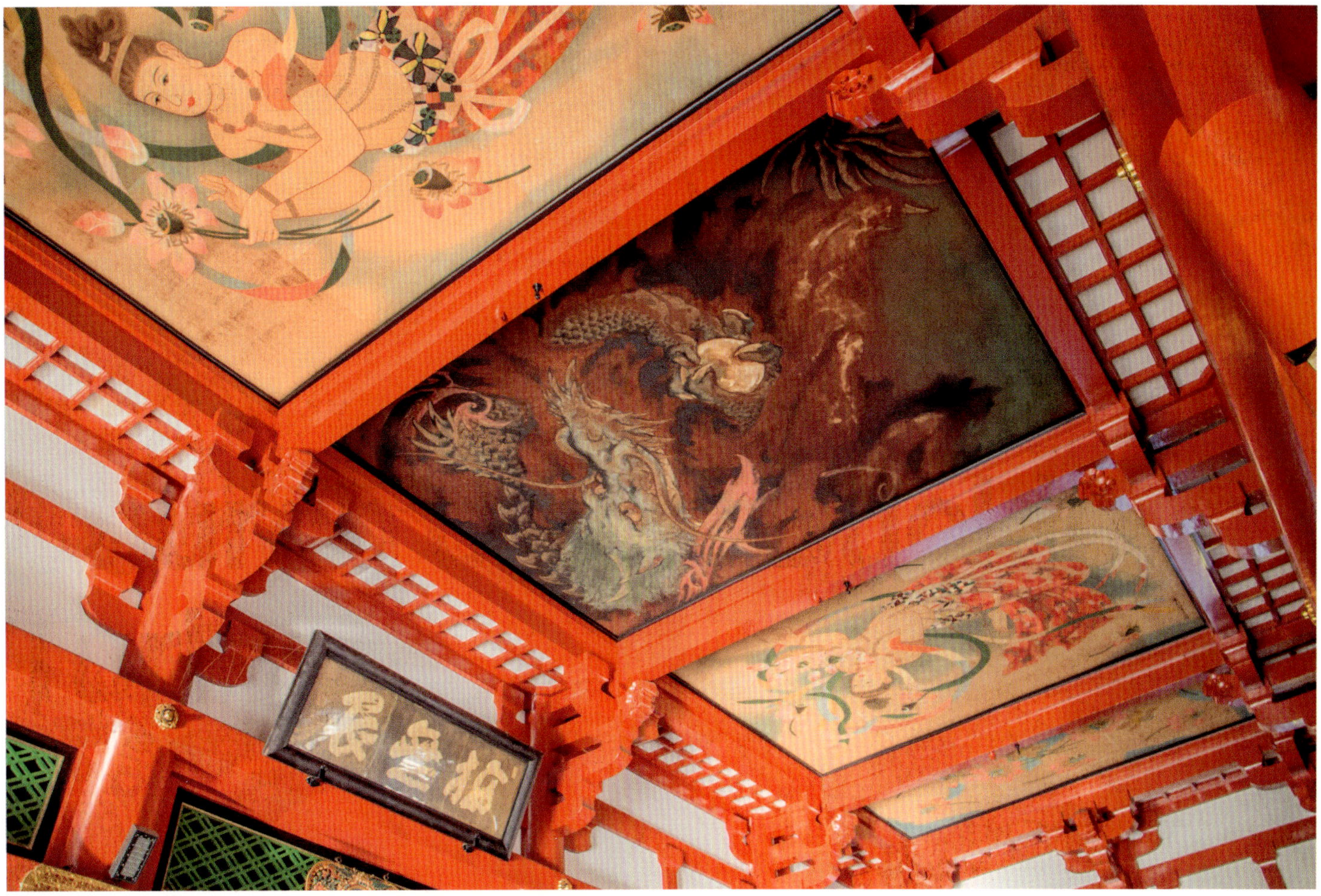

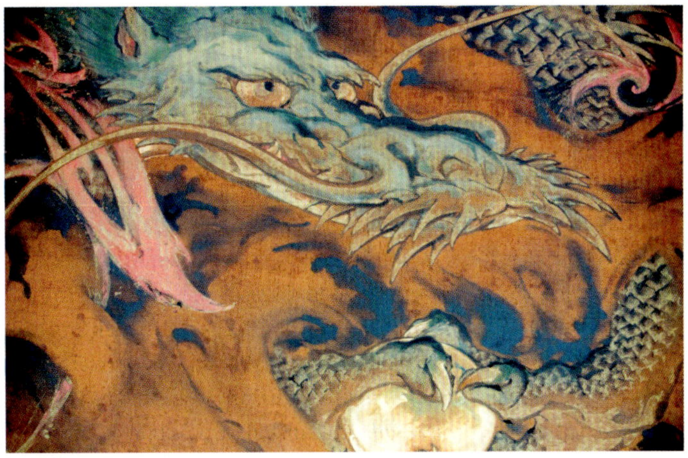

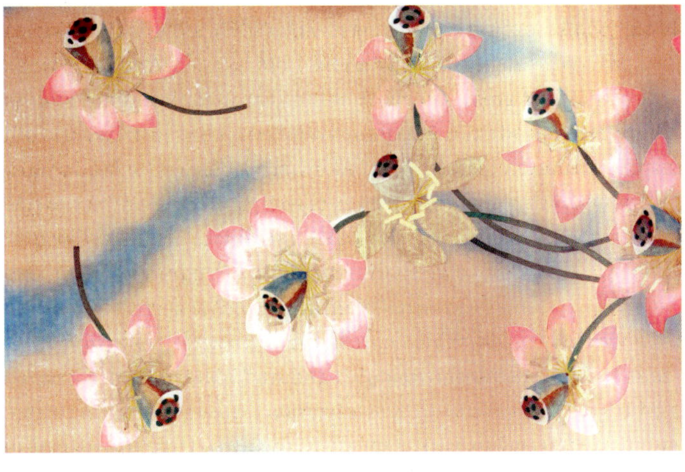

Centre: The figure of the dragon encapsulates traditional Japanese folklore iconography.

Bottom: Detail of the painted lotus flowers that make up parts of the ceiling.

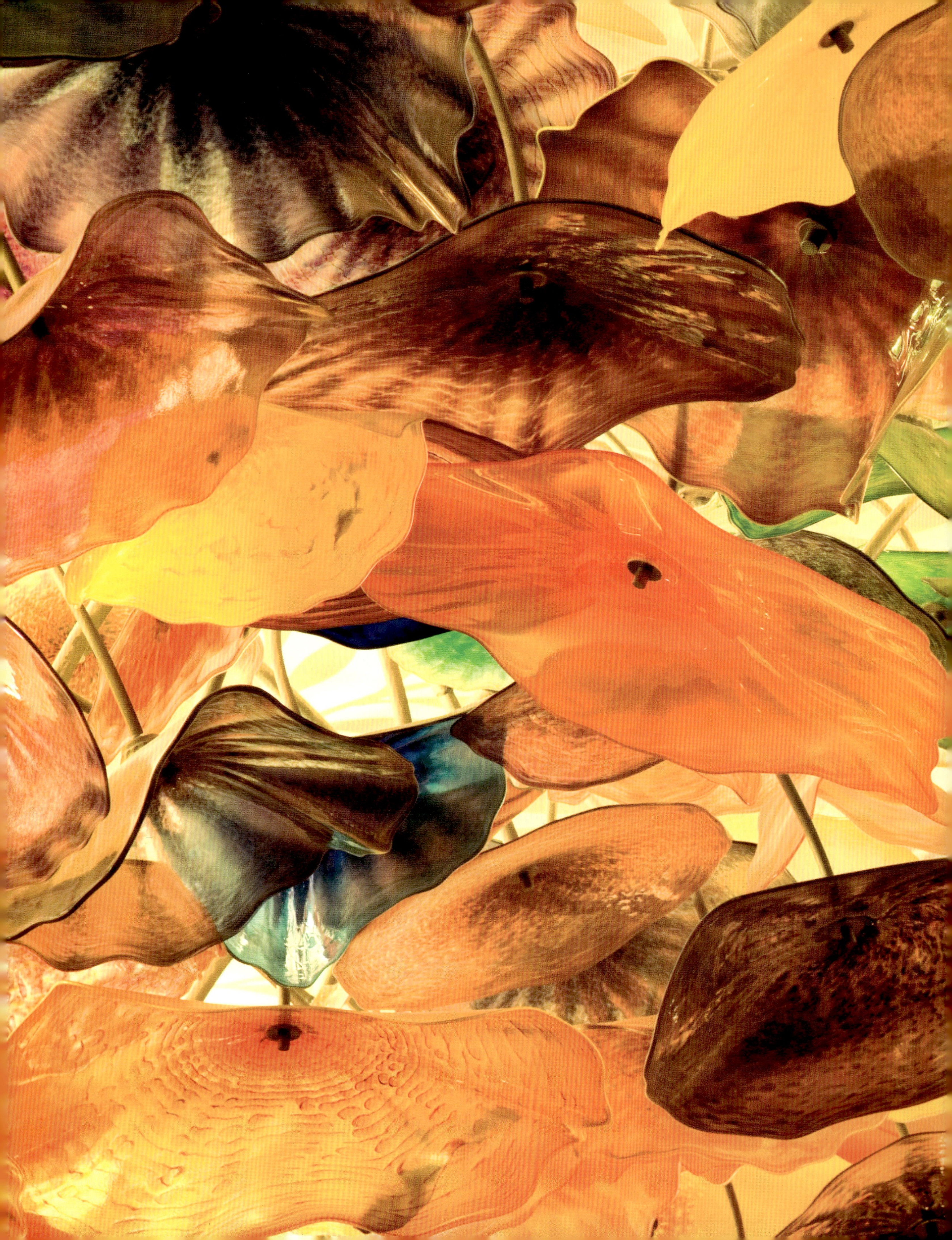

2

Culture

A well-placed ceiling can achieve many things, from entertaining the wandering minds of a distracted audience at the Paris Opera House to flattering the patrons in Vienna's Burgtheater, or from enlivening the monotony of the daily commute across Stockholm's city metro network to nourishing intellectual contemplation within the library at Strahov Monastery. It can, perhaps, even keep clients in the casino, mechanically parting with their cash, as Dale Chihuly's *Fiori di Como* in the Bellagio Resort and Casino would seem to aspire to, with its upside-down seabed of glass flowers.

And while it is no surprise that world-class art galleries and museums (the so-called temples of culture) have fantastically decorative ceilings, these often receive little attention from the flow of visitors keen to tick off the highlights that appear on the walls and in cabinets of display. And yet, looking up means enjoying the ceilings of the East Wing at Uffizi Gallery, Florence, which contextualize the intellectual and cultural aspirations of the early collection. Looking up means drowning in the impossible azure infinity of Cy Twombly's *The Ceiling* in Salle des Bronzes, at the Louvre Museum, Paris.

The ceilings of the cultural locations discussed in the pages that follow are diverse and varied. They often express political and spiritual themes that overlap with other chapters in the book. For example, the ceiling of the staircase at the Teatro Nacional in San José celebrates an allegory of the export trade in coffee and bananas that brought the riches of modernity (including the arrival of electricity) to Costa Rica, so making a marriage between the economic market and the financing of the arts. In another more supernatural vein, the Toluca Botanical Gardens in Mexico City are centred around the cosmic oneness of humankind and the stars, while the surrealist apotheosis of Salvador Dalí and his wife in the *Palace of the Wind* ceiling shares much with the self-aggrandizing mythologies seen to flagrant effect in the ceilings of powerful palaces.

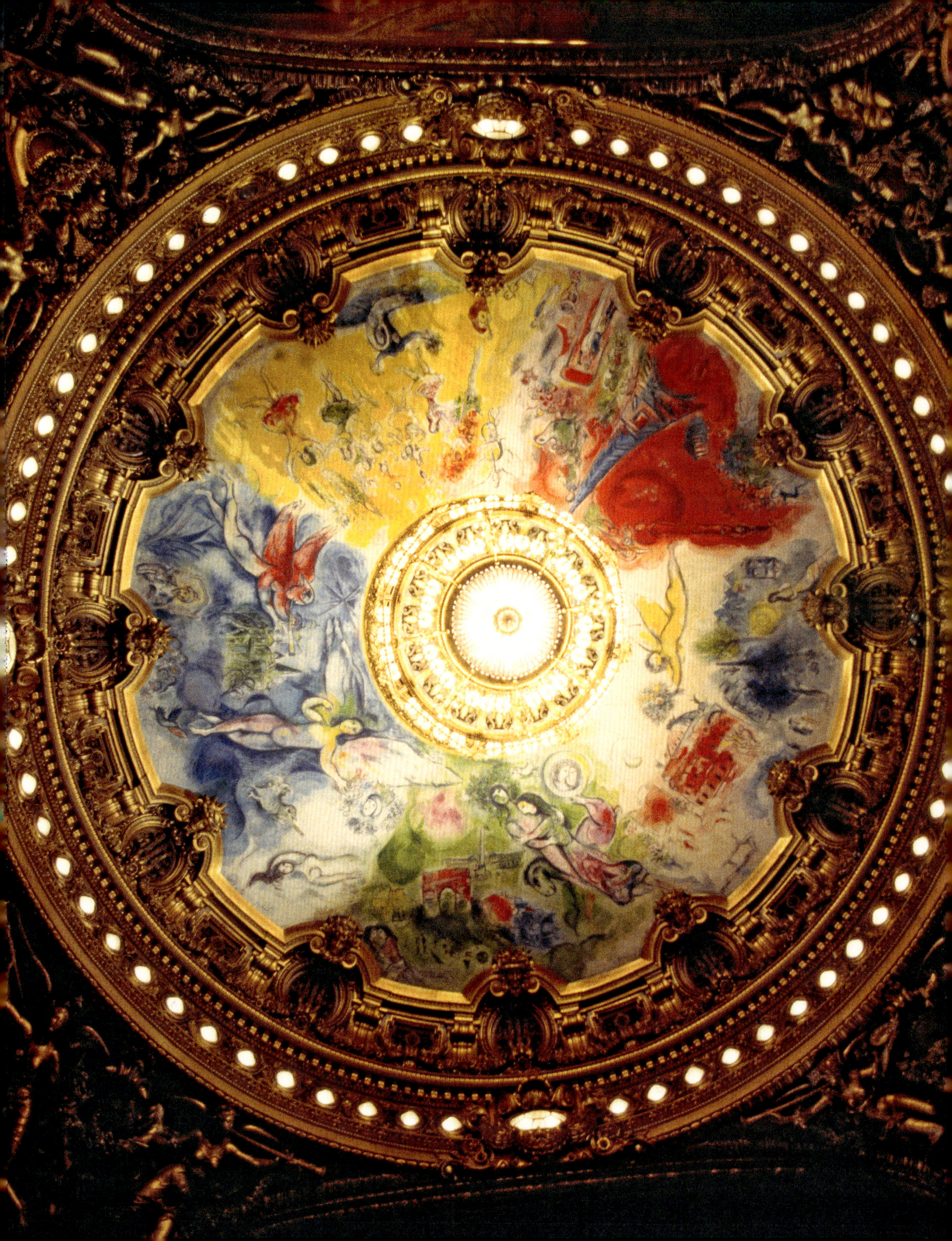

Marc Chagall

Ceiling for the Paris Opera

1964

Palais Garnier, Paris, France

Left and overleaf: Marc Chagall's rich colours, made up of five symbolic 'petals'.

Palais Garnier, France

One evening in 1962, the French arts and culture minister André Malraux spent a disappointing night at the Palais Garnier, the gilded temple to the arts that first opened its doors as the home of the city's ballet and opera in 1875. The focus of Malraux's frustration was the dome's interior, painted by Jules Eugène Lenepveu from 1869–1871, and its seminude figures in languorous drapery surrounded by winged deities in a pastel sky. To him, the work represented *l'art pompier*, an art too much concerned with conservative and bourgeois tradition and taste, and no longer relevant to the Paris of the 1960s.

The decision to repaint the ceiling is poorly documented, but seems to have been decided through a series of conversations and tacit approvals that concluded in asking Russian artist Marc Chagall to take on the job. A shrill exchange between the reactionary press and Malraux ensued. Attacks were personally directed towards Chagall as a foreign, Jewish, avant-garde artist, but to all public protestations, the Ministry of Culture bluntly replied, 'the ceiling will be repainted by Chagall or we shall close down the Opéra'.

Malraux and Chagall had been close friends since 1924, when they met at Chagall's first exhibition in Paris. The artist was a natural choice, based on his experience working in the theatre and especially with dance. In 1911 he had assisted his teacher Léon Bakst in producing set designs for Diaghilev's Ballet Russes, and was exposed to the guiding principles of theatre in the early twentieth century as an experimental convergence of music, art and dance. Chagall went on to design stage sets and costumes for the Moscow State Jewish Theatre and the director Alexis Granowsky as well as the New York City Ballet's version of *The Firebird* and modernist ballet *Aleko* by Léonide Massine.

The work began on 240 sq m (2,600 sq ft) of canvas and was carried out at the Gobelins tapestry factory. The artist reportedly worked without eating or drinking, listening to Mozart all day. Such was his vigour, that he could apparently destroy a brush within fifteen minutes of painting. Chagall's art was underpinned by the relationship between colour and freedom, which was synonymous with the French national identity bound up in the tricolore flag. For him colour and light were the most potent expressive channels and the work at Palais Garnier sings with all the chromatic vibrancy of Provence in summer.

The circular design of the ceiling takes shape in a flower representing France, made up of five petals of different colours. Chagall developed an ideology to accompany the work: each 'petal' refers to two composers in the Paris Opéra's repertoire and also references the city of Paris with images of architectural landmarks.

The white petal honours the composers Rameau and Debussy and commemorates the creation of the work. A portrait of Chagall's patron Malraux looking from the window doubles as an episode from Debussy's ballet *Pelléas and Mélisande*. This also marks one of Chagall's self-conscious references to the art of the past, in particular, the tradition of Renaissance painting, in which portraits of patrons often featured. A voluptuous nude leads on to the green petal, which is devoted to Wagner and his tragic lovers Tristan and Isolde, and Berlioz's choral symphony of *Roméo et Juliette*. This work had a certain political resonance intended

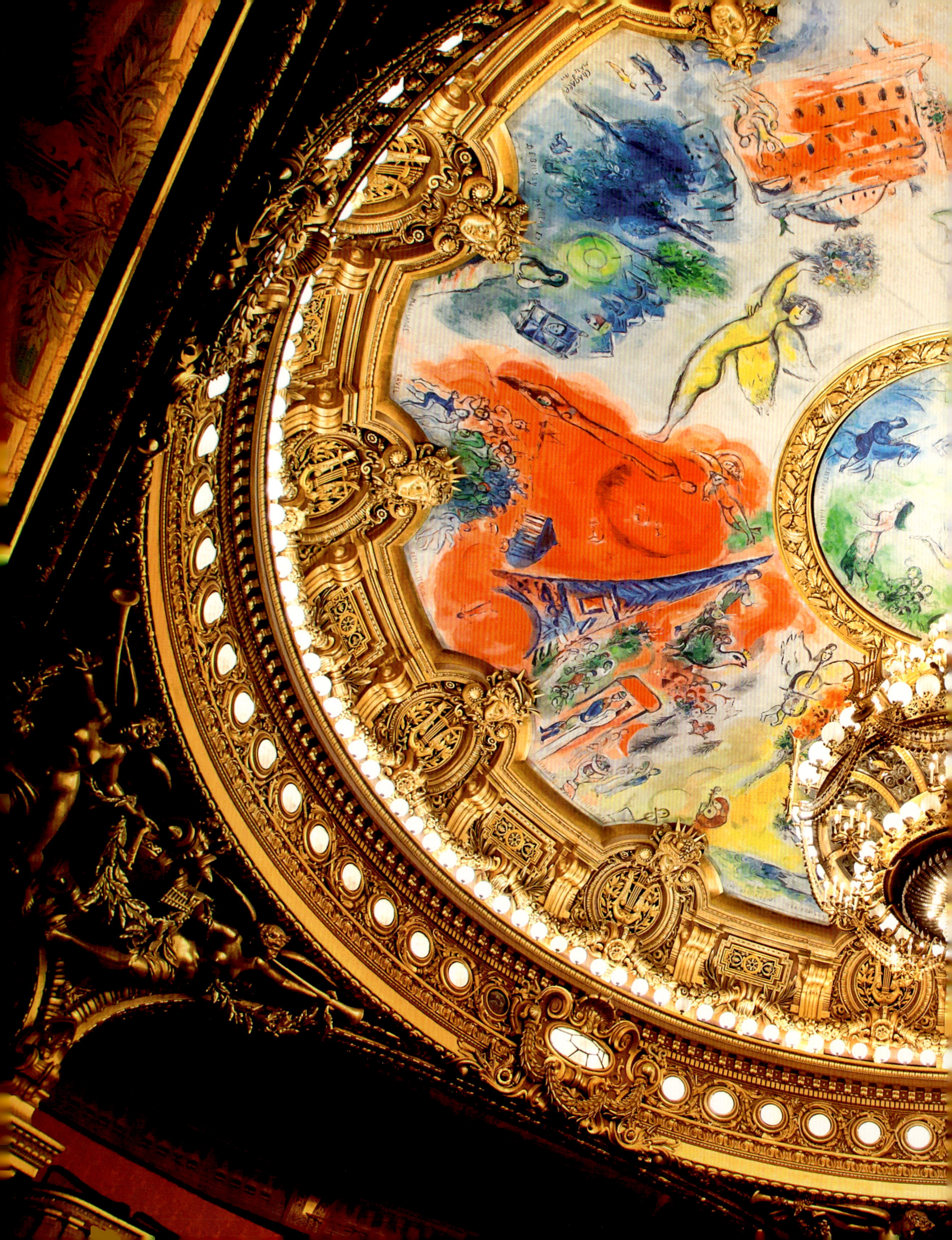

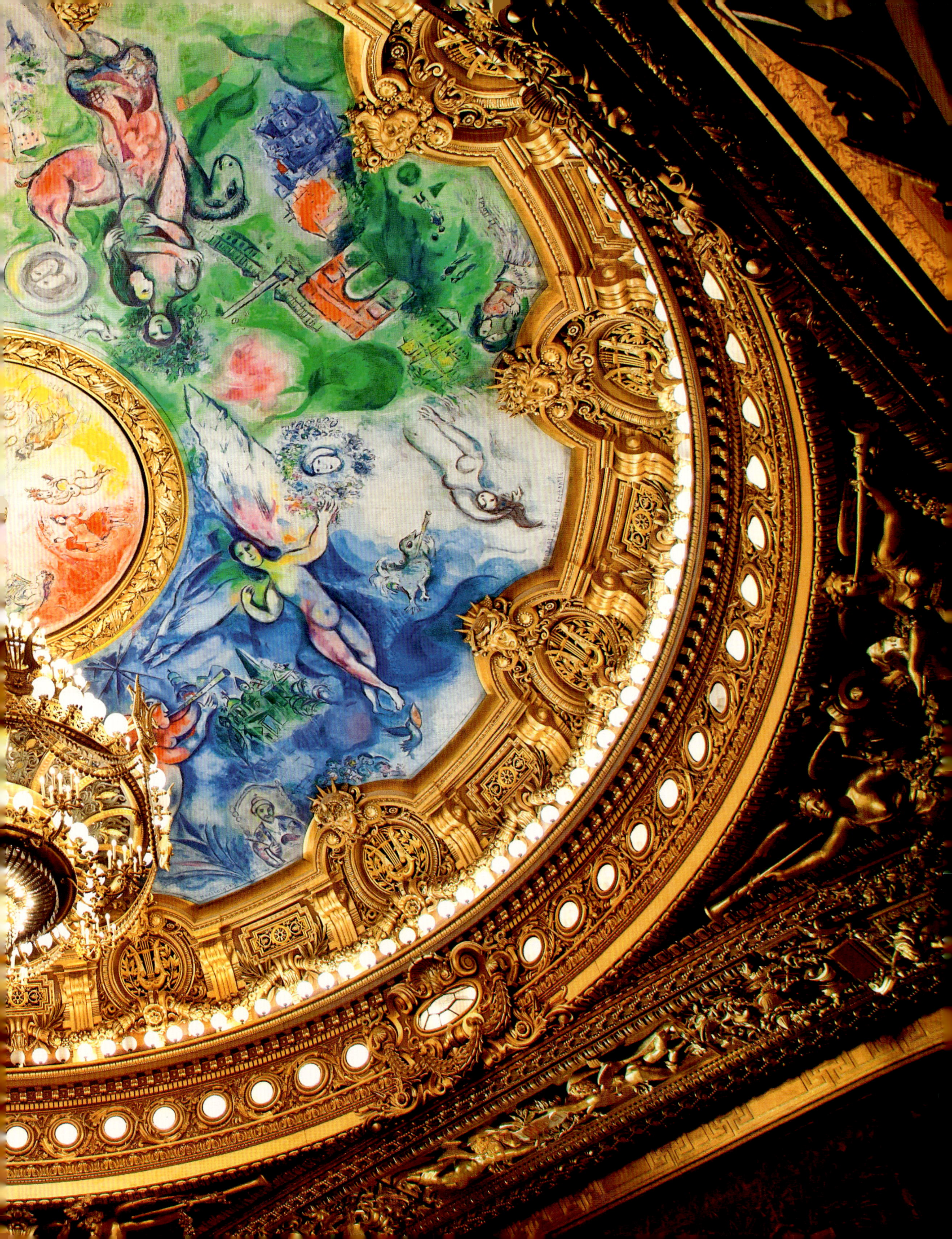

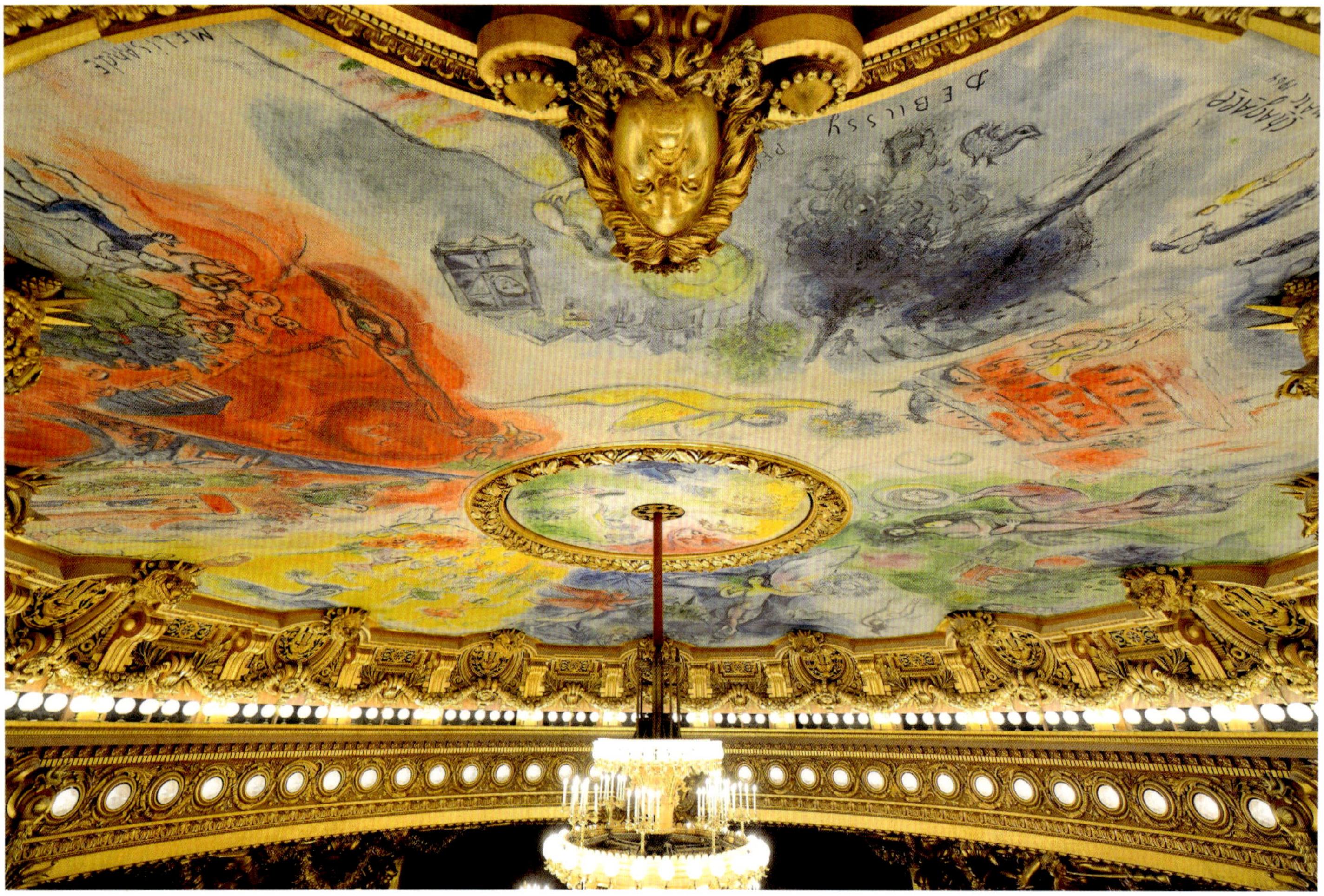

to reflect reconciliation between France and Germany in the decades after the Second World War. Chagall includes the Parisian landmarks of the Arc de Triomphe and the Place de la Concorde, further symbols of celebration and peace.

The red petal unites France with Russia and honours the creative innovation of the Ballet Russes with depictions of Stravinsky's *The Firebird* and Ravel's ballet *Daphnis et Chloé*, the work chosen for the inauguration of the ceiling. A mystical figure – half man, half bird – features a self-portrait of the artist, securing his place among those immortalized here. A colossal Eiffel Tower, the symbol of the spirit of Paris itself, separates the depiction.

The red heat of *The Firebird* softens into the joyous yellow of the next petal, where Chagall's colour symbolism takes an unexpected turn. He associates yellow with madness and frenzy, represented here in the figure of Giselle from the eponymous ballet by Alphonse Adam, a heroine who goes insane as a result of a broken heart. A giant swan-woman arching her back represents Tchaikovsky's grand ballet *Swan Lake*, which explores the interlocking themes of love and sadness, the animal and human, shadow and light.

For the last petal, which is blue, Chagall draws on his own heritage and musical tastes. He pays homage to the father of Russian music, Modest Mussorgsky, with an episode from his opera *Boris Godunov*. A nude angel with the monumental simplicity of a Cycladic figure holds a garland with a portrait of Mozart. This is where Chagall expresses an alternative divine to the mythological figures concealed beneath his work on Lenepveu's hidden canvas. For Chagall, Mozart was a god, and his opera *The Magic Flute* was the height of spiritualism.

Above: Chagall's ceiling is a departure from the Palais Garnier's architecture.

Opposite top: Detail of the green 'petal' includes two pairs of lovers on either side of the Arc de Triomphe. These are Romeo and Juliet flying away on an inverted horse and Tristan and Isolde laying in the green waters close to the gilded external edge of the dome. Also visible is the huge angel holding a portrait of Mozart on the blue petal.

Opposite bottom left: *La Danse*, by Jean-Baptiste Carpeaux, one of four sculpture groups in Echaillon marble on the outside of the Palais Garnier.

Opposite bottom right: The striking red petal unites France and Russia, whilst the yellow petal is associated with madness and frenzy.

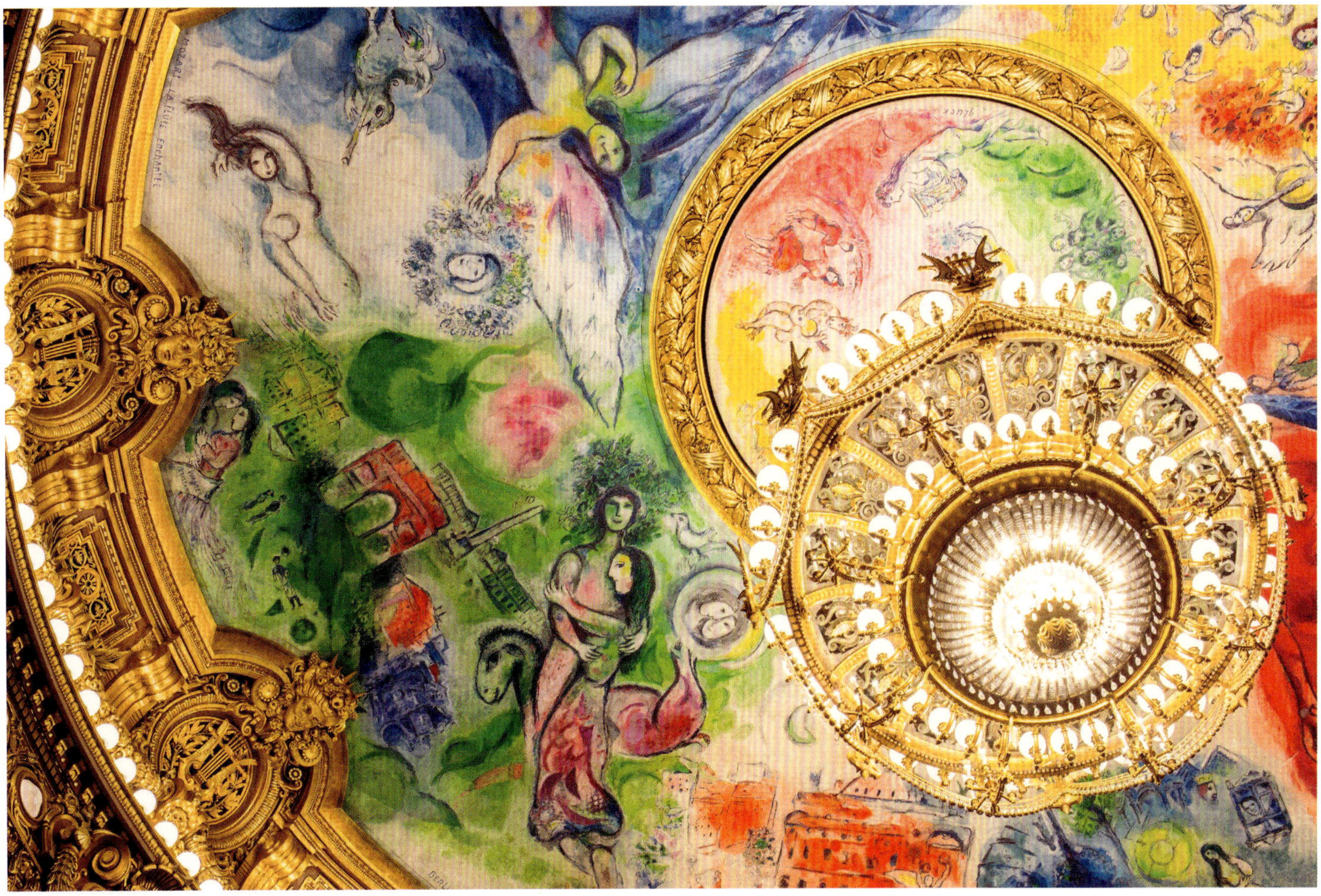

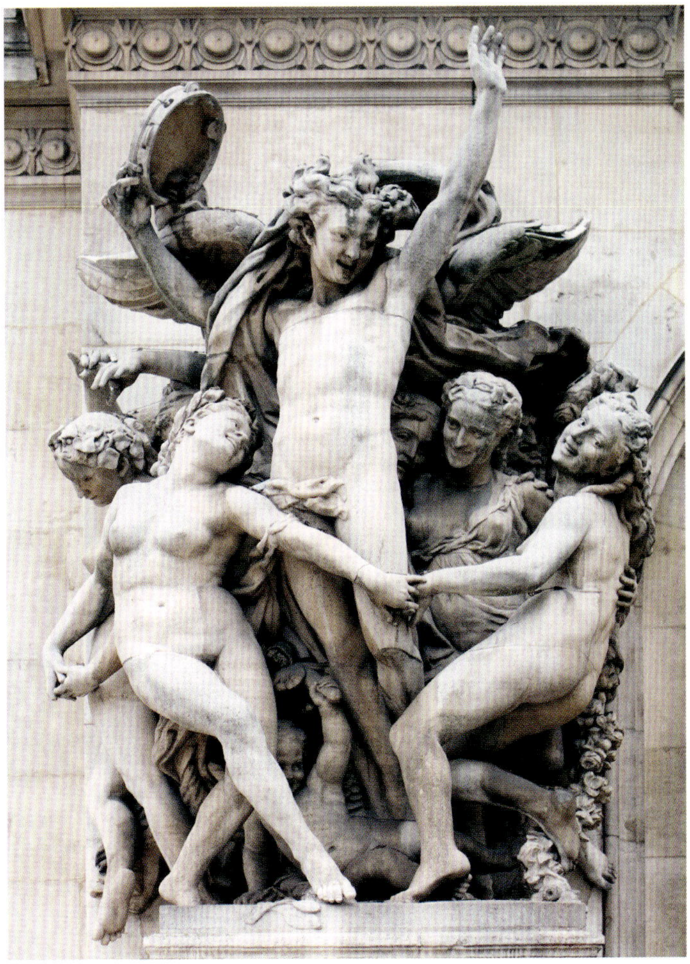

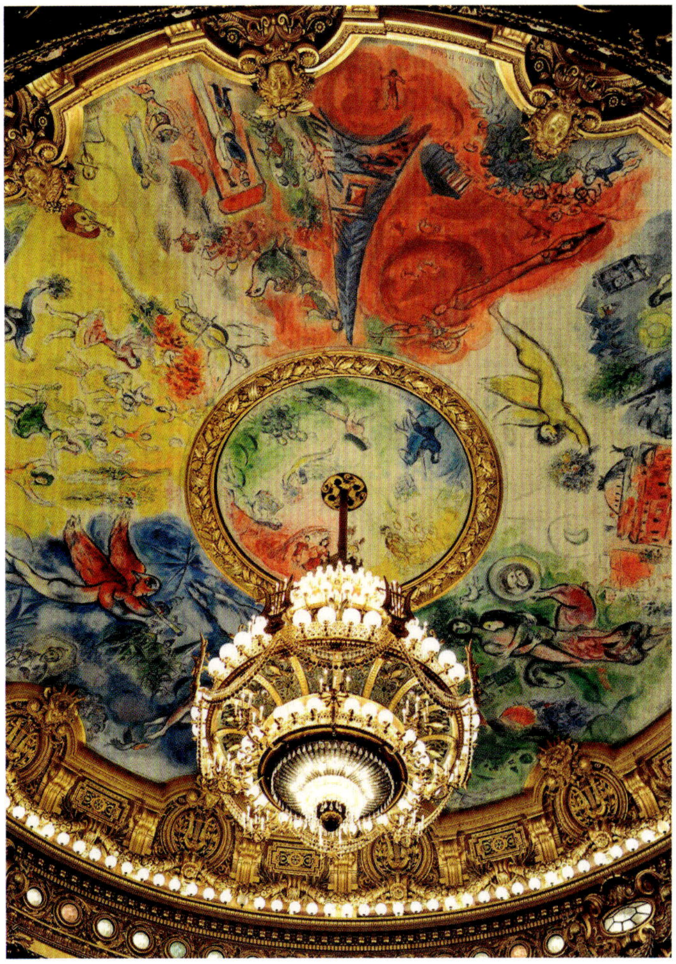

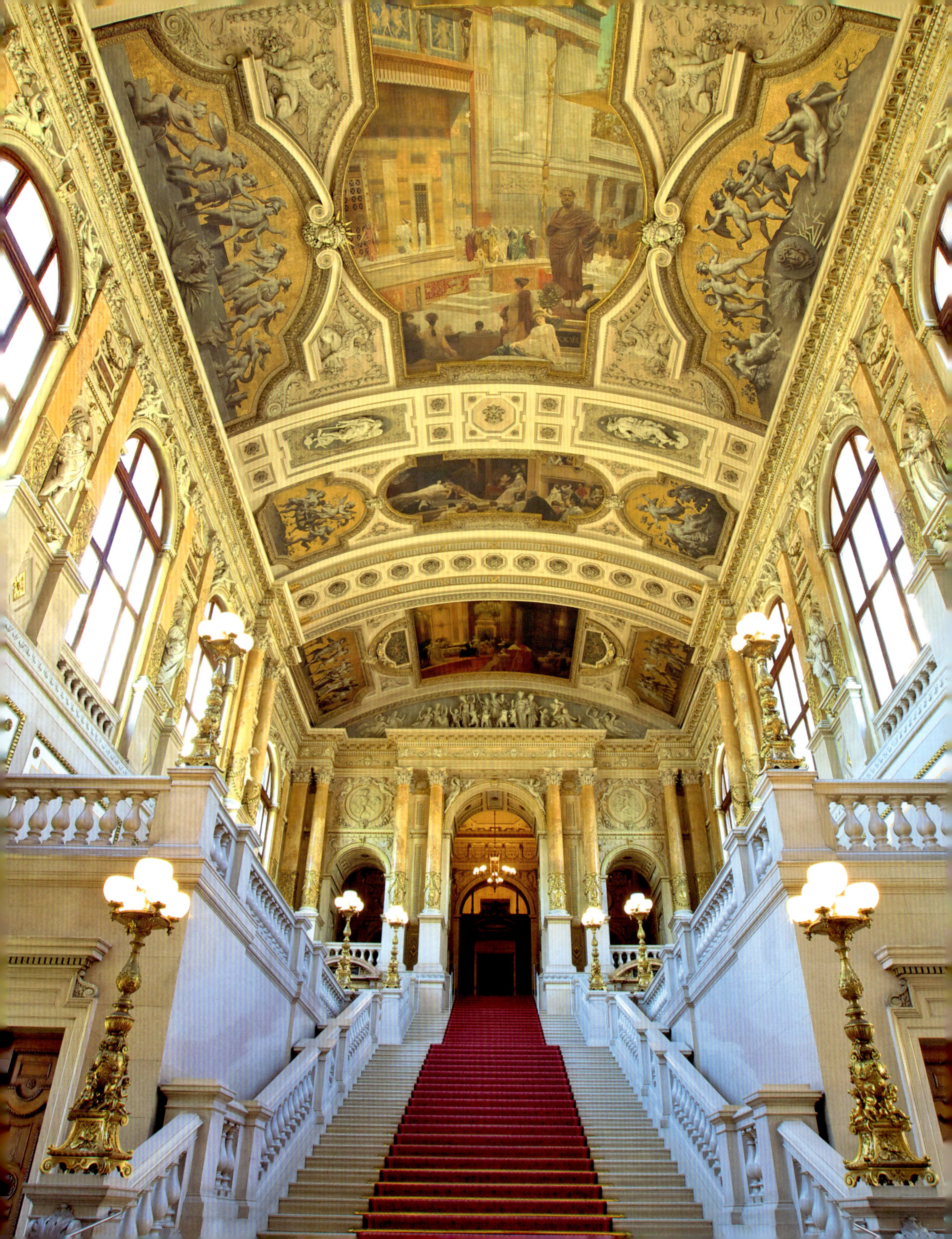

Gustav Klimt

Painted murals

1887

Burgtheater, Vienna, Austria

Left: Klimt's painted murals loom over the grand staircase at Vienna's Burgtheater.

Overleaf: *The Cart of Thespis*, 1886–87. According to ancient Greek sources including Aristotle, Thespis is thought to have been the first ever person to appear on stage as an actor in the guise of a character. He is also credited with pioneering the concept of the touring theatre, as he travelled with his cart of props, costumes and masks. The term 'thespian' is inspired by him.

Burgtheater, Austria

The Burgtheater sits in the imperial heartland of Vienna's boulevard of palaces and monuments known as the Ringstrasse. Originally commissioned in the 1740s by the Hapsburg empress Maria Theresa of Austria, who wished for the convenience of a theatre in close proximity to her palace, the building underwent renovation in the 1870s, eventually reopening its doors to the great and the good of *fin de siècle* Europe in 1888.

A trio of fresh-faced young artists known as Künstler-Compagnie were given the prestigious commission of decorating the two magnificent interior staircases. The men were Gustav Klimt, his younger brother Ernst, and their associate Franz Matsch, who had banded together in 1883. The Burgtheater staircase was their first-ever group commission and proved to be so successful, that it led to the award of a Golden Cross of Merit in 1888 from Emperor Franz Joseph I. Executed in the prevailing academic style of history painting, as officially sanctioned by the Viennese Academy of Arts, the success of the Burgtheater paintings marked the coronation of the newcomers as the new darlings of the cultural establishment.

Within time, the pivotal figure of the group, Gustav Klimt, tired of the stifling grand manner of history painting that flattered bourgeois and aristocratic taste. In 1897, he became a founder member and the first president of the Viennese Secession movement of artists, who broke away from the cultural conservatism of the period to embrace a new freedom of expression in the arts. Klimt would later provoke the establishment with the sensuality and decadent eroticism of his later work, for which he is best known, creating such controversy that his writhing female nudes for the ceiling of the University of Vienna (destroyed in the Second World War) sparked a parliamentary debate. But at the Burgtheater, the prescriptive style and carefully crafted subject matter for the work was set by Adolf von Wilbrandt, the theatre director and author.

The ten paintings collectively depict the evolution of theatre and portray three classical playwrights amid the themes of music, dance, medieval mystery plays and actors and audiences. On the staircase to the right, three of the five images are by Gustav Klimt. These are the *Altar of Dionysus*, *The Cart of Thespis* and *Shakespeare's Globe Theatre*. The first is in reference to the cult of the Greek god, who presided over comic and tragic theatre in ancient Greece (as well as ecstasy and wine). Here, two of his female followers known as maenads lay supine at an altar, one holding a votive statuette of Pallas Athena in offering to the god, while the other lounges languidly on leopard skin, betraying a hint of the luxurious sensuality and attention to texture that would characterize Klimt's later work.

In *Shakespeare's Globe Theatre*, the tragic climax of *Romeo and Juliet* plays out to an audience dressed in the historical period detail of Elizabethan England, including a figure of the Faerie Queene herself. And in the box, in front of the stage to the far right, a handsome young man in a ruff is the only self-portrait of the artist himself, with his brother Ernst behind him and Franz Matsch bedecked in a black velvet cape at his side. Joining them, in various guises across the ceiling paintings, are the Flöge sisters and their bohemian circle of friends. Ernst Klimt married the eldest Flöge sister, Helene, in 1891, while Emilie Flöge became the life companion of Gustav Klimt and inherited half of the artist's estate on his death in 1918.

As with *Thespis's Cart*, which depicts the ancient tragic actor who toured Attica with a cart that doubled as a stage, the historical

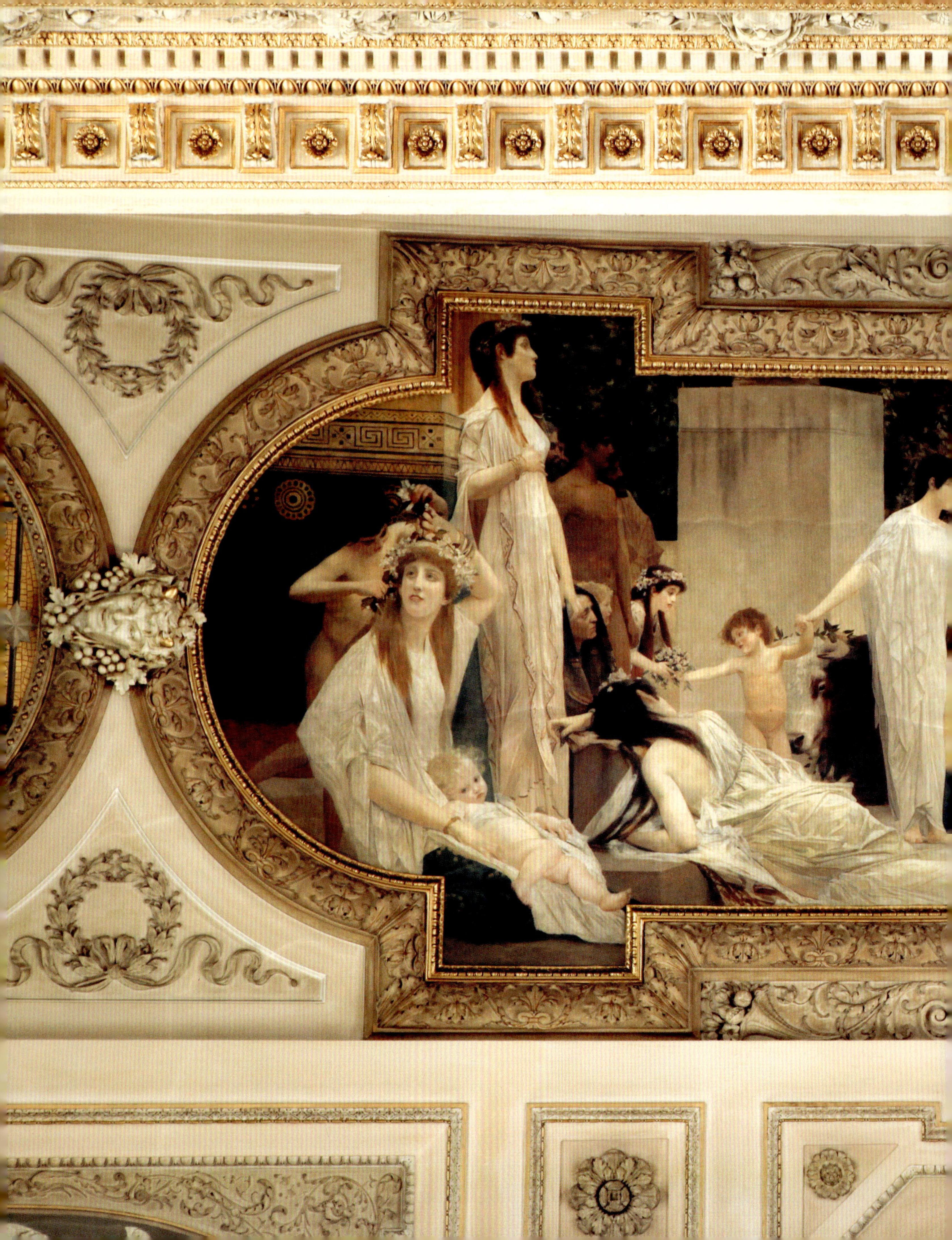

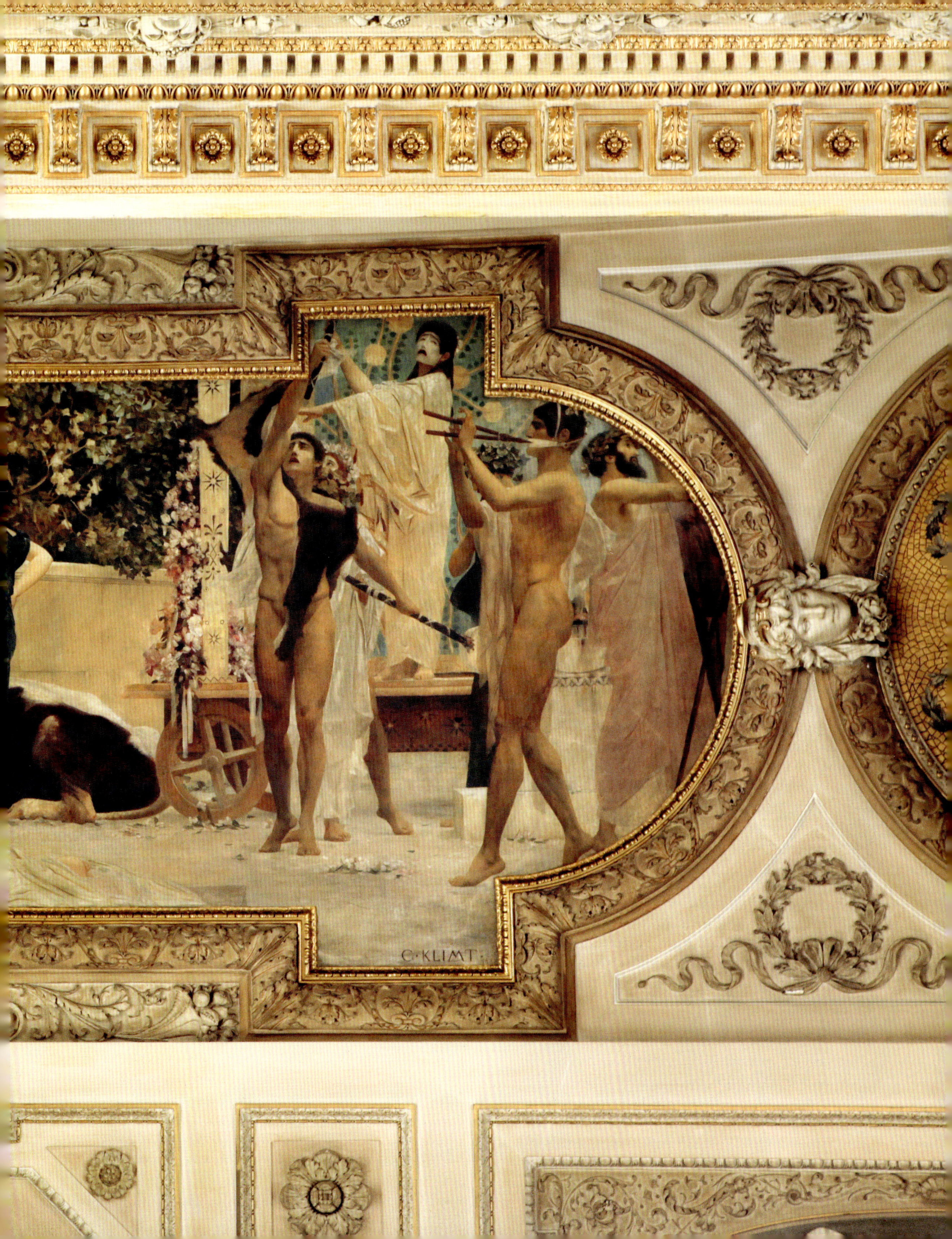
G·KLIMT

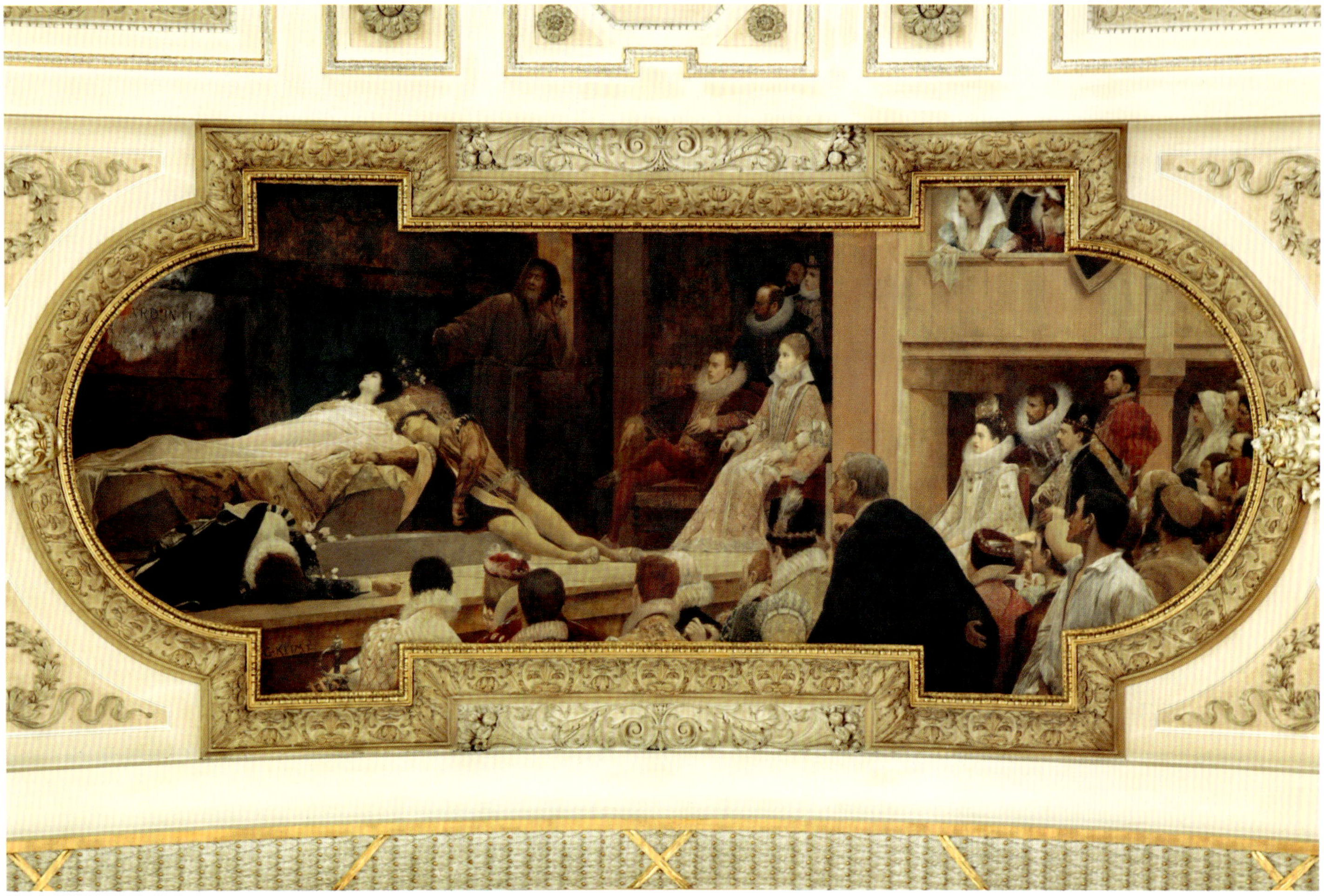

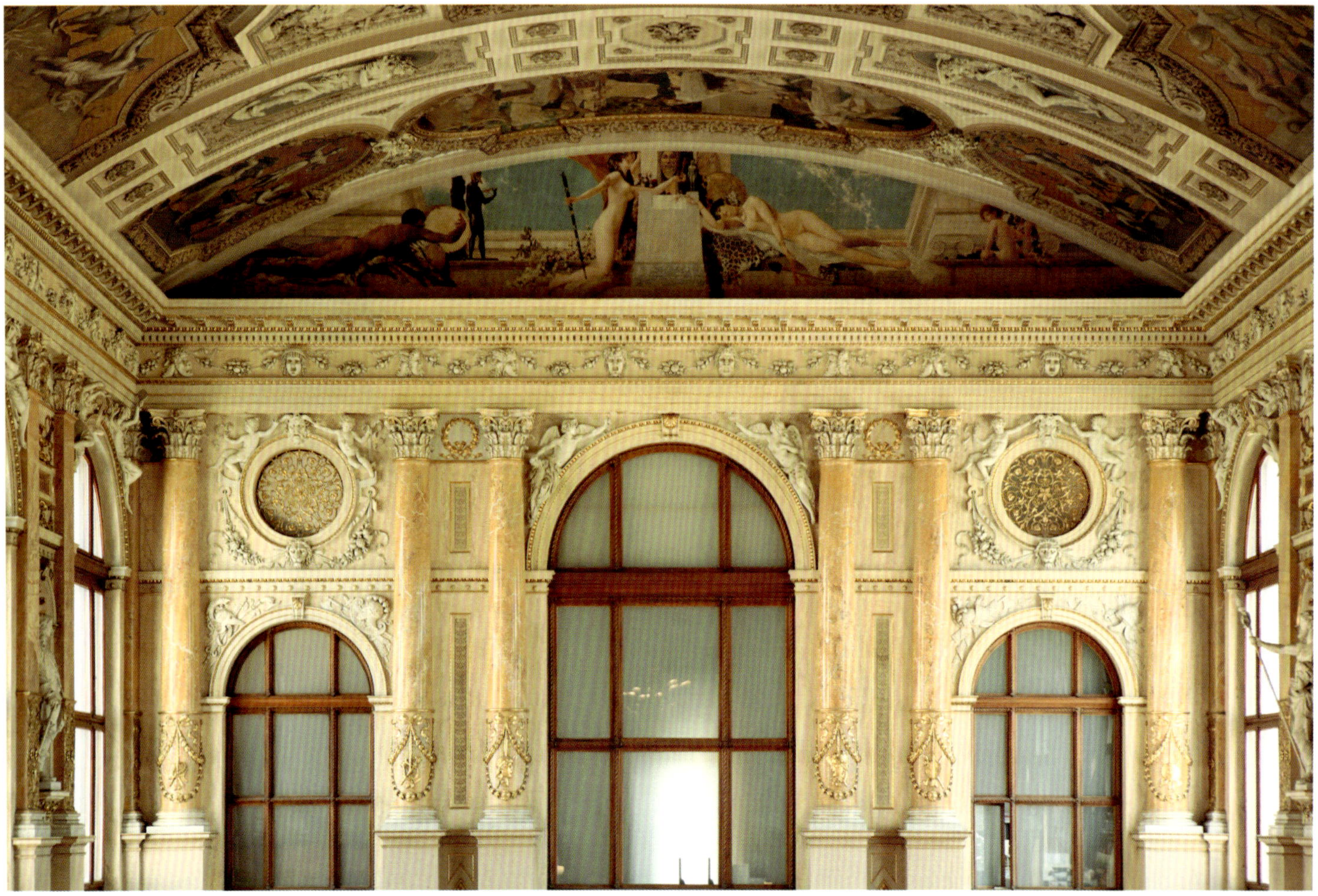

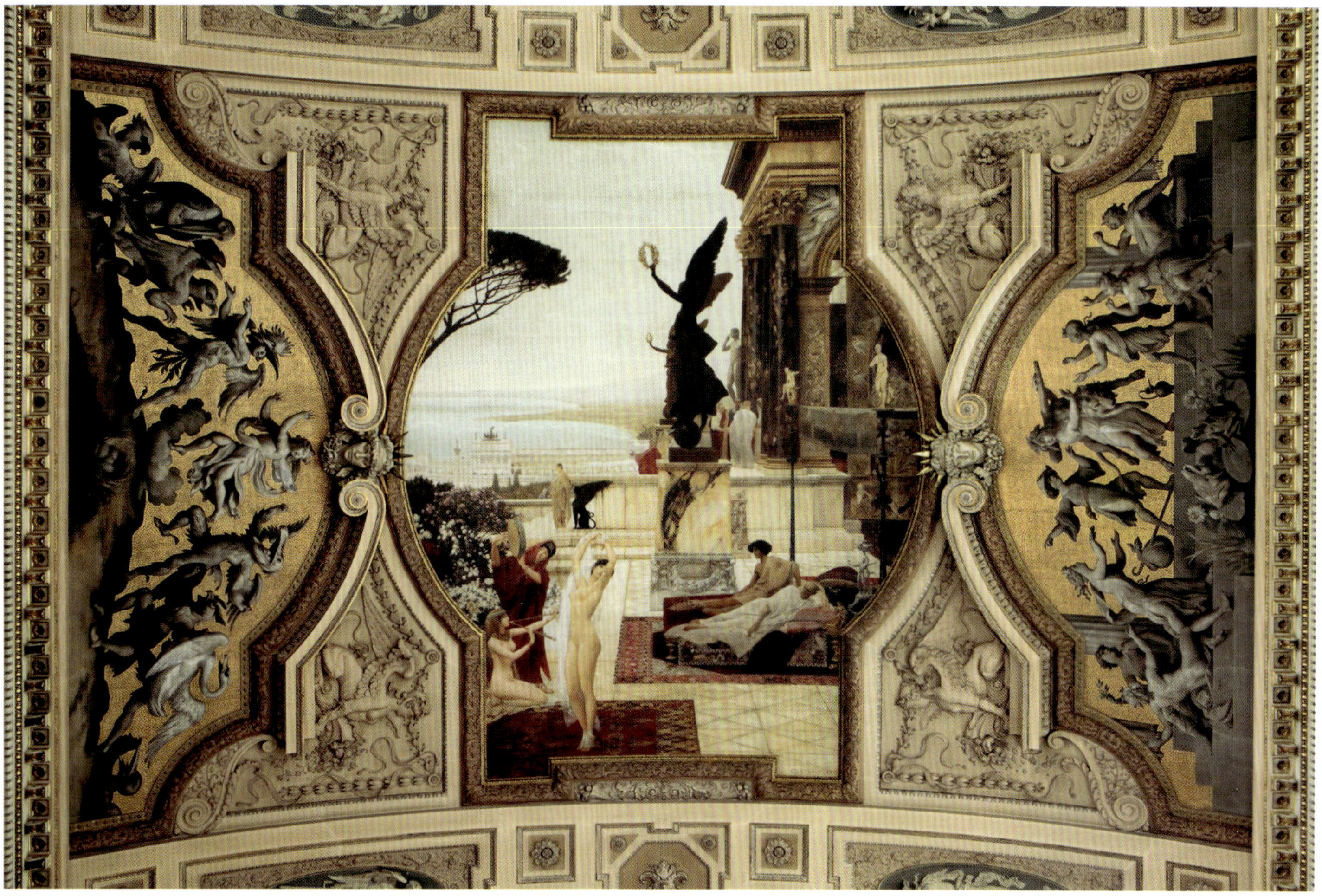

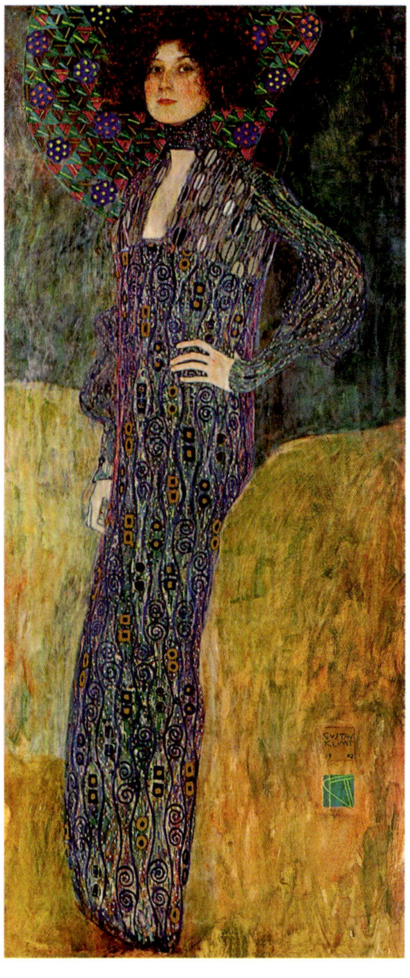

audiences (with classical robes and hairstyles in this example) take up much of the image space. For, although the staircase decoration was inspired by the history of theatre and its most illustrious dramatists, the majority of the painted scenes also feature the historical audiences who make up the essence of the theatrical experience. After all, these staircases facilitated the flow of the dazzling throng of self-regarding spectators who attended the Burgtheater as much to be seen in society as to be enriched by the dramatic productions. Looking up from their interval refreshments, they could see themselves depicted in the vaults of the building, as much a part of the contemporary spectacle of the theatre as the players themselves.

Opposite top: *Shakespeare's Globe Theatre* (1886–87), featuring portraits of the three artists of the Künstler-Compagnie. Gustav Klimt sits in the theatre box wearing a ruff, and his brother Ernst Klimt sits behind him, while Franz Matsch sits next to the brothers in a black velvet cape.

Opposite bottom: *Altar of Dionysus* (1886–87).

Above: Central painted panel shows Gustav Klimt's *Theatre at Taormina* (1886–87). The ancient theatre at Taormina in Sicily dates to the early seventh century BCE.

Left: *Portrait of Emilie Flöge* (1902) by Gustav Klimt.

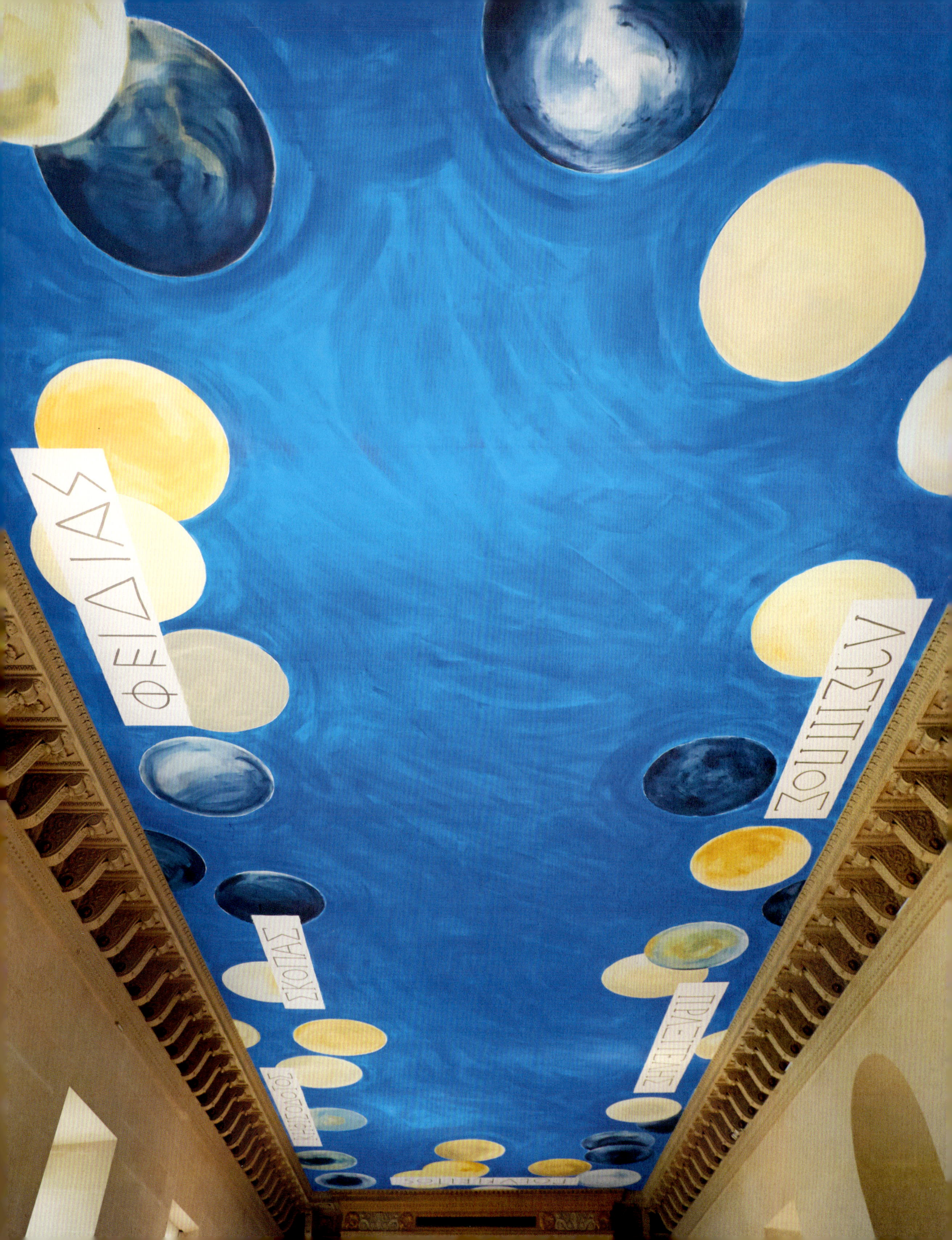
ΦΕΙΔΙΑΣ
ΛΥΣΙΠΠΟΣ
ΣΚΟΠΑΣ

Cy Twombly

The Ceiling

2010

Salle des Bronzes, Louvre Museum,

Paris, France

Left: View of Cy Twombly's *The Ceiling* in Salle des Bronzes, Louvre Museum.

Louvre Museum, France

Cy Twombly's ceiling of the Salles des Bronzes fills the overhead vault with a field of azure that is, perhaps, more blue than is comfortable. It emerges somewhat unexpectedly as you pass through the Musée du Louvre (Louvre Museum), as a vigorous chord of modernism echoing in the oldest part of the building. On this blue ceiling, overlapping discs of gold, silver and petroleum grey eclipse one another like celestial bodies in orbit. Some extend beyond the confining borders of the sturdy gilded cornice to suggest an infinite vastness that reaches beyond the almost 400 sq m (4,300 sq ft) of painted expanse. White insets hover like geometric clouds, engraved with the names of Hellenic sculptors from the fourth century [BCE]: Cephisodotus, Lysippus, Myron, Phidias, Polyclitus, Praxiteles and Scopas. These artists of antiquity took rocks and transformed them into images of gods, and of mankind, and used them to decorate temples, homes and cities.

The vitrines and cabinets beneath this glorious canopy house the Musée du Louvre's collection of around one thousand objects in bronze and other precious metals, ranging from signet rings and helmets to crowns of laurel rendered in gold. These are things made from the stuff of the earth, metal ore that was mined and polished and burnished to make it glisten in the light from the sun and stars. As objects, these works tell a story of how human hands mined the ground to produce the enduring emblems of civilizations – our trophies, jewellery and tools, the commemorations of who we are. But then, above all of this, there is the sky, Earth's ceaseless vault, the abyss that we can never occupy.

Known only as *The Ceiling*, any interpretation of Twombly's painting is left deliberately open-ended, not least because the artist was famously tacit about his work. We could argue that *The Ceiling* of the Salles des Bronzes speaks of human experience, suspended as we are between the ground we have mined and exploited and the sky that we yearn for and onto which we project all of our dreams and spirituality.

Twombly was born in Lexington, Virginia, USA, in 1928, but spent most of his life in and around Rome, deeply and emotionally invested in the art and myths of the antique Mediterranean past. This may seem incongruous with his signature style of image-making, with its abstract shapes and the trademark trailing scrawled text that was often erased and overwritten and for which he became known. But despite his experiments in modernism, Twombly's works often bear the names of mythological deities and narratives and, because of this, the philosopher Jean Luc Nancy said: 'Twombly paints "gods but without faces"'. With this in mind, we can perhaps read his ceiling in a similar vein, as a chromatic expression of something deeply spiritual, yet agnostically so, that exists outside of time and tradition.

Having said this, the work is not without art-historical precedent. Twombly himself admits taking inspiration from the ceilings of medieval Italian churches, in particular Giotto di Bondone's painting in the Scrovegni Chapel in Padua from 1305. Here, the intense blue backdrop on the walls and the vaulted ceiling offers another example of the way in which colour communicates loquaciously where words, and even pictures, fall short. In Giotto's time the semiprecious rock known as lapis

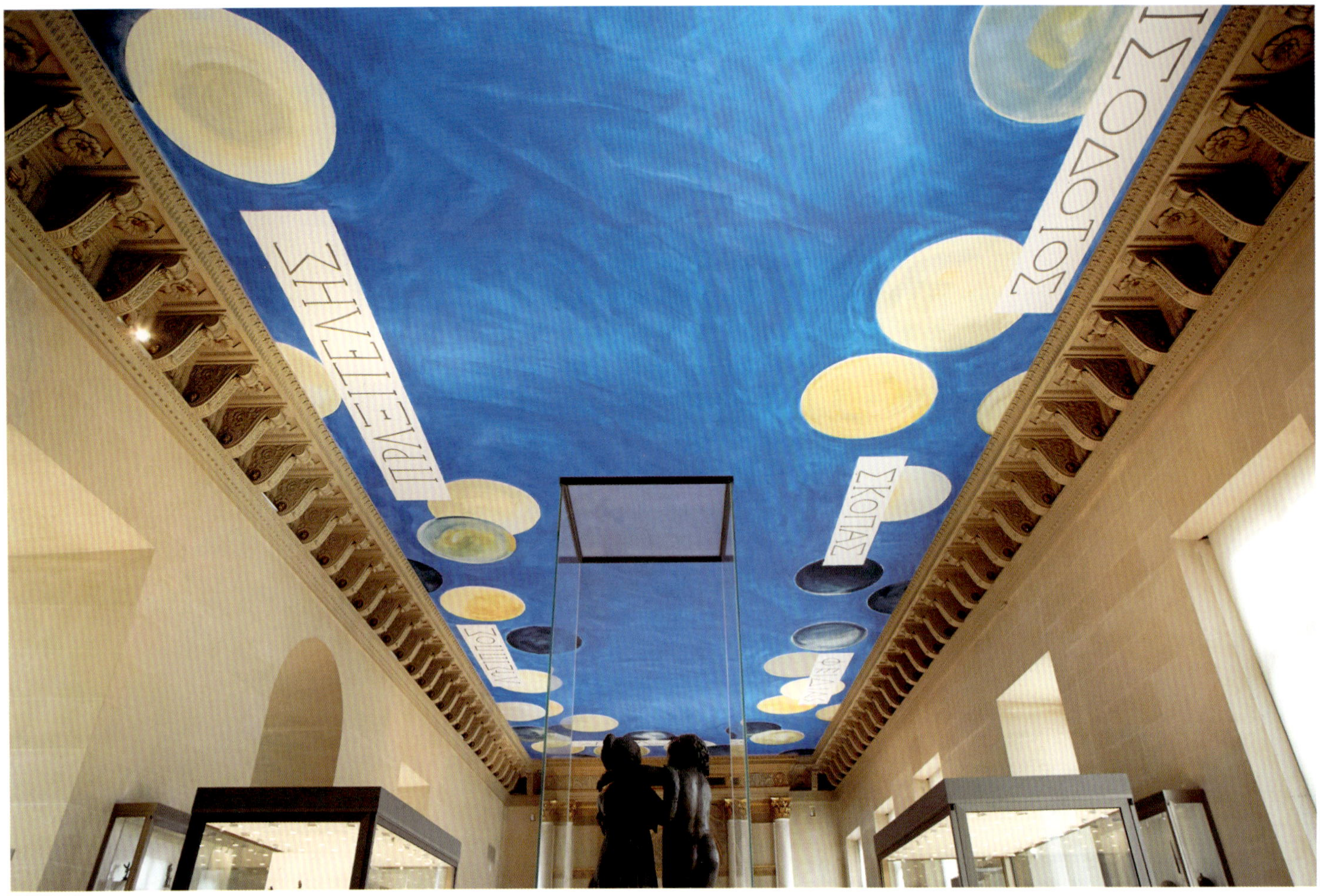
ΠΡΑΞΙΤΕΛΗΣ
ΣΚΟΠΑΣ

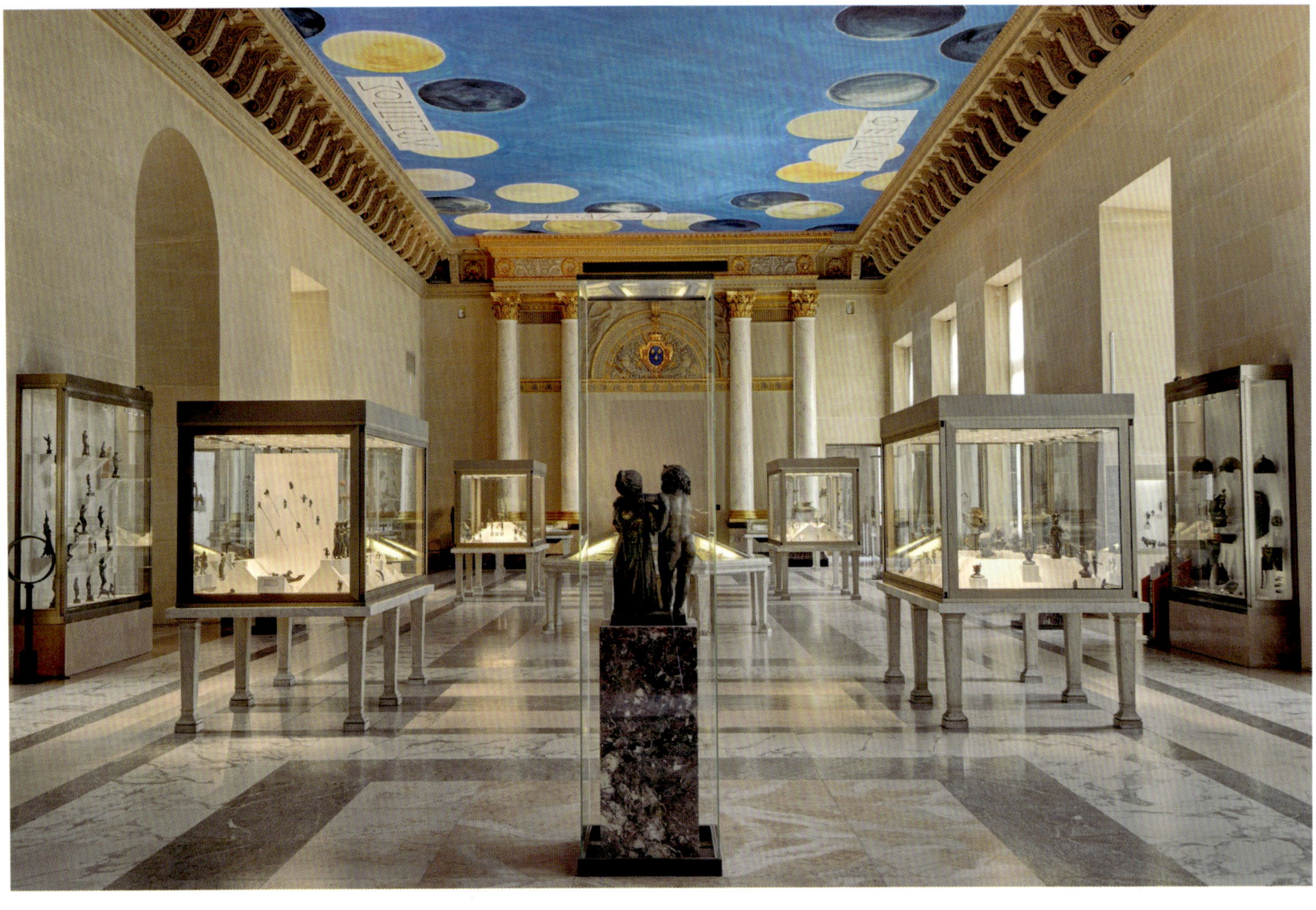

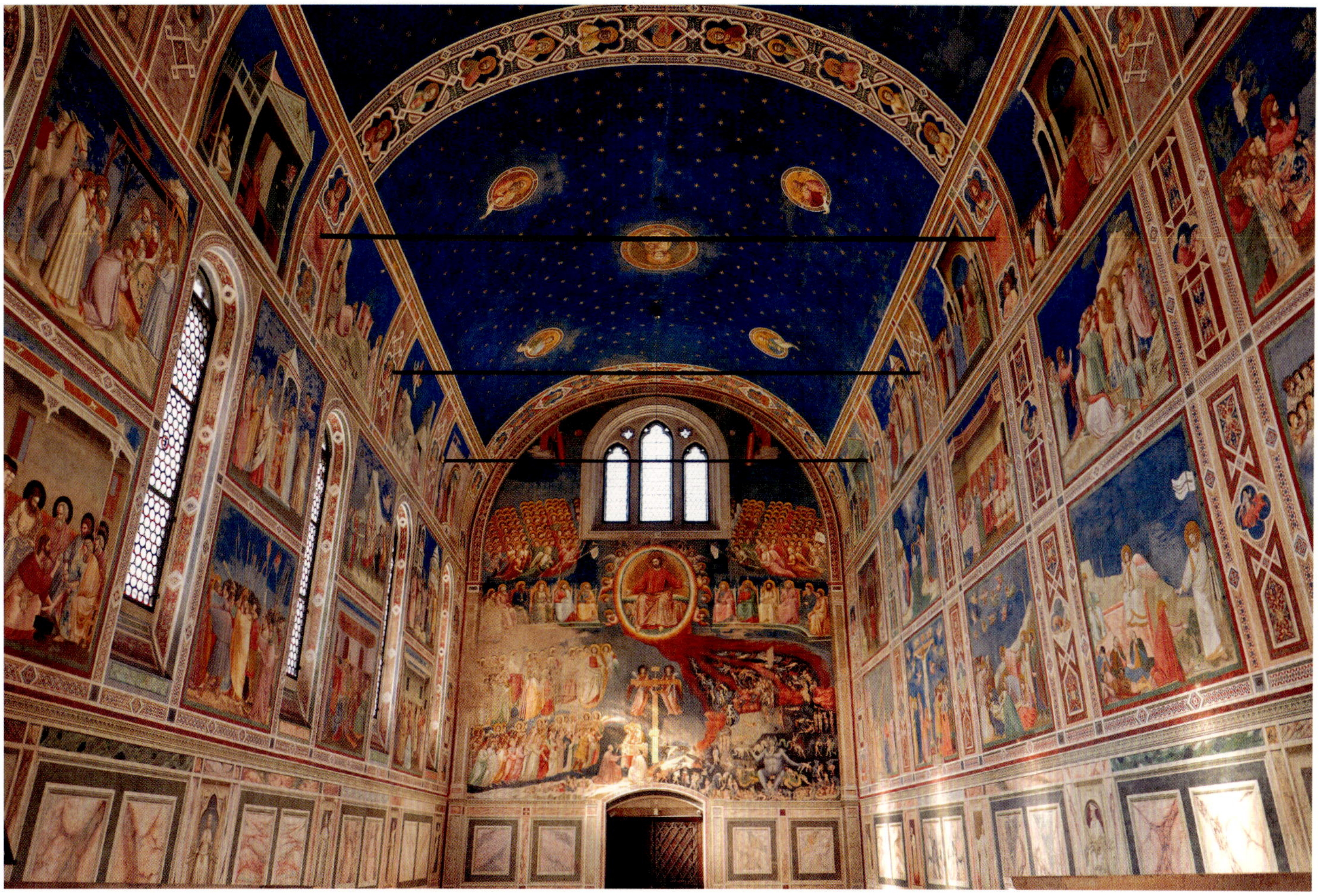

lazuli was being imported into Europe to make the pigment 'ultramarine'. By the fifteenth century, large painted areas of blue in works of art were a mark of conspicuous consumption, reflecting the wealth of the patron to dazzling effect. So there is potentially a double edge here: while the blue ceiling floats above us as a peaceful promise of immortality, it also draws on the history of the building as a royal palace in an era of absolutist wealth and privilege, in particular during the reign of King Louis XIV who resided in the palace between 1654 and 1678.

During the first decade of the twenty-first century, Twombly was one of three contemporary artists (along with François Morellet and Anselm Kiefer) invited to add a permanent fixture to the Musée du Louvre as part of a long commitment to set up ways in which the historical and contemporary can converse with one another.

Opposite top and bottom: Twombly's *The Ceiling* injects a sea of colour into Salle des Bronzes, Louvre Museum.

Above: An avid admirer of Italian Renaissance art, Cy Twombly acknowledged the blue frescoes of Giotto di Bondone's Scrovegni Chapel (1305) in Padua next to the Monastero degli Eremitani, as a source of his inspiration.

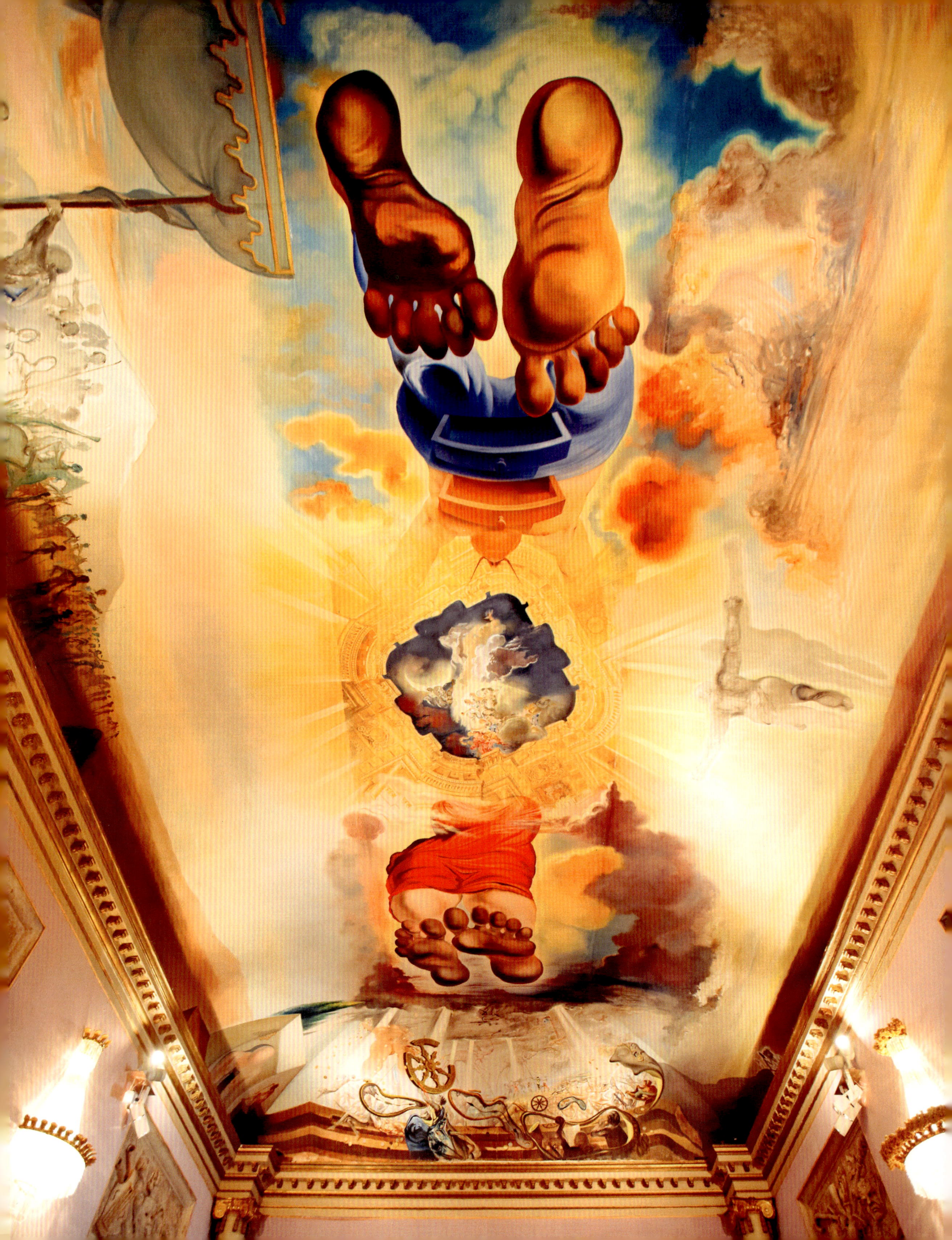

Salvador Dalí

Palace of the Wind ceiling

1972

Dalí Theatre-Museum, Figueres, Catalonia

Left and overleaf: The viewer is right at the heart of Dalí's *Palace of the Wind* ceiling, looking up at gigantic feet and into the opened vault in the centre.

Dalí Theatre-Museum, Catalonia

It is a most unusual view. The soles of two pairs of enormous feet bear down from above. Showers of coins cascade out of bodies and over melting clocks, while elephants with insect legs parade across the landscape. A fictitious vault in the centre opens to a dark night sky behind the sun, where details as separate as the invention of submarines to a hovering crucified figure of Christ appear.

We are at the heart of the artist Salvador Dalí's surrealist imagination, the prolific Catalan provocateur whose work embraced myth, literature and the suppressed desires and fantasies of the mind. We are also in the artist's ancestral heartland, the Dalí Theatre-Museum, a converted municipal theatre in Figueres in the Empordà region of Catalonia, a place of maddening winds, evocative mountains and dazzling sea. The development and contents of the museum were a gift from Dalí to his home town and a eulogy to Empordà – a landscape with its own artistic and literary mythology that occupied a central thematic space in Dalí's work. The Figueres former theatre even played host to Dalí's first-ever exhibition in 1919.

The *Palace of the Wind* ceiling was painted on five huge canvases at Dalí's studio in Port Lligat. The painting's name comes from the poem *L'Empordà* by the Catalan poet Joan Maragall, a work that explores the mythological origins of the region as borne from the love between a shepherd and a siren. The shepherd loves the mountains and sings of their incomparable beauty during the day, while, by night, the siren eulogizes the watery paradise of the sea under the light of the moon. Sea and mountain come together to give birth to the plains of Empordà, across which the distinctive 'tramuntana' wind blows, turning the territory into a 'palace of the wind'. This wind, energized by its passage through the mountains, features regularly in Spanish storytelling as an inclement and inscrutable natural force seeding the germs of madness, but also as a light that cleans the eyes and calms the breath. The two extremely foreshortened central figures on the ceiling image (one with a characteristic upturned moustache as seen from below) are Salvador Dalí and his beloved wife Gala. She was a recurrent muse, often appearing in sanctified roles such as the Virgin Mary, and was said to have adopted Dalí (who was a decade her junior) as newborn baby, lover, son and protégé, often signing his canvases to acknowledge her influence as something of a divine muse. Even Dalí admitted with regard to his wife: 'It is mostly with your blood that I paint my pictures.'

In the *Palace of the Wind* ceiling, husband and wife ascend towards the night sky and the subconscious mind, access to which drove the surrealist movement's quest for enlightenment through art and literature. True to Dalí's surrealist style, there is no conventional narrative logic to the scenes that play out here, more a slipping and montaging of disassociated forms and symbols as if in a dream sequence. One of the mantras adopted by the artists and writers who identified with the surrealist movement, was the concept of a 'chance encounter of a sewing machine and an umbrella on a dissecting table', a line taken from the poetry of the Comte de Lautréamont, whose work was cited often as an example of the beauty and latent menace of seemingly dislocated objects that could only come together in the realms of the marvellous and of dreams.

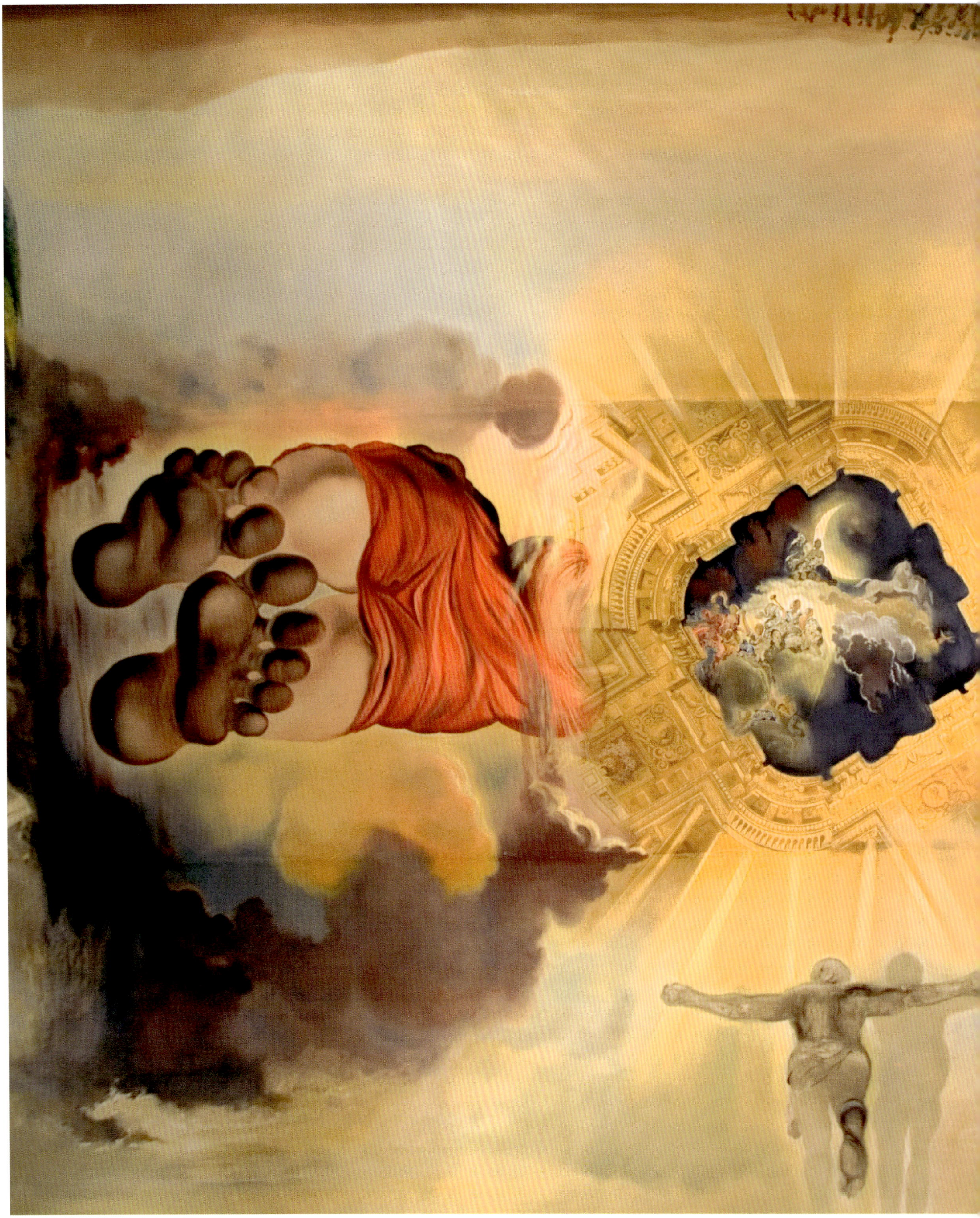

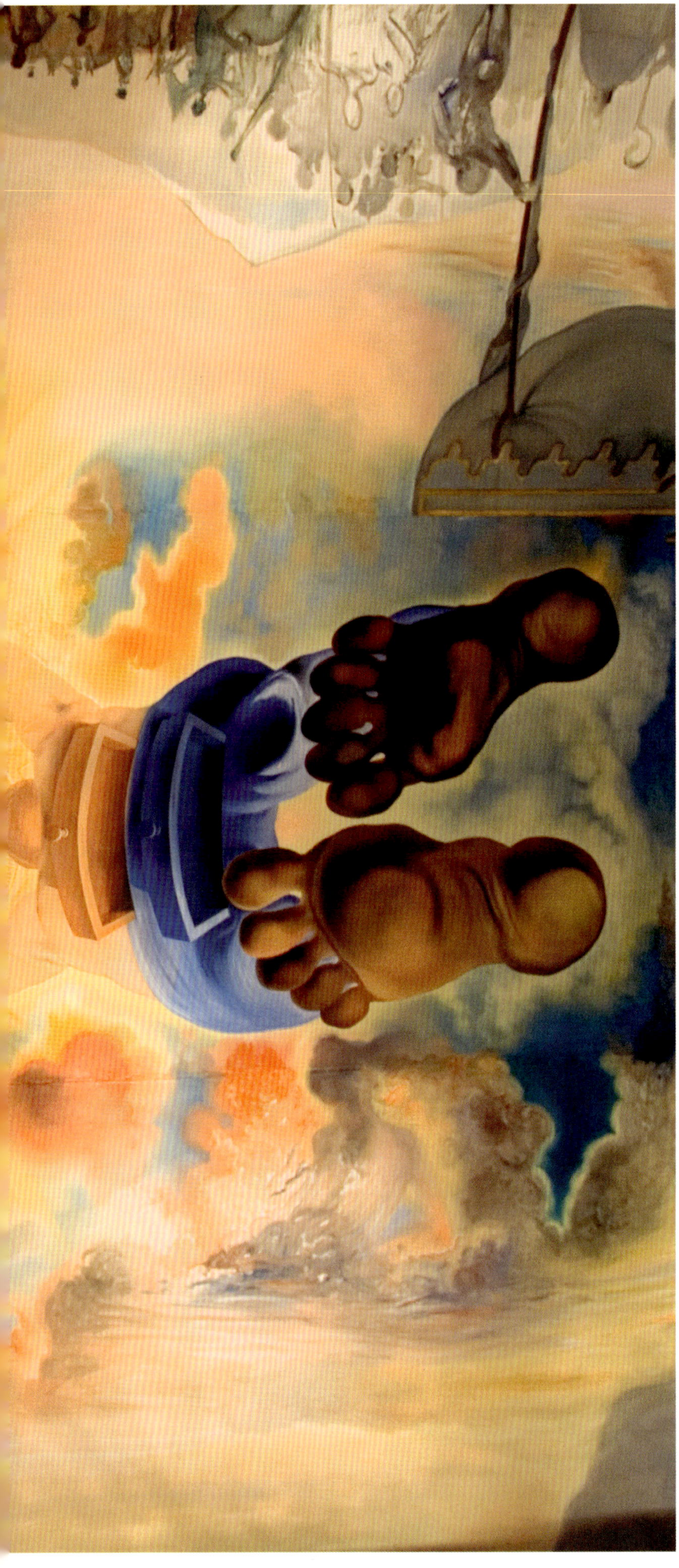

The depiction of Dalí and Gala also represents the coupling of the siren and shepherd in Maragall's poem, which makes the image not just an apotheosis of Dalí and Gala, but an apotheosis of Empordà as well, conferring immortal status to the environment that permeated Dalí's art and the wider canons of Spanish art and literature so profusely. However, some sources have provided the alternative title *Gala and Dalí Generously and Jesuitically Throwing Out all The Gold I Earned Over the Heads of My Fellow Citizens*. In simple terms, this title underlines Dalí's gift of his work and the museum to his ancestral home, but there are other metaphorical associations, too. Underneath the central figure of Gala is a nude woman with an open door on her hip from which gold coins issue forth (including one real coin according to Dalí). This element is an echo of the classical myth of Danae, the woman who was impregnated by Zeus (king of the Greek mythological gods) who had shape-shifted into a shower of gold, resulting in the birth of the hero Perseus who later slayed the Gorgon snake-haired queen Medusa.

Dalí and Gala appear again along the lower register of the image, gazing at a distant ship of destiny as it embarks across the waves. This reflects the artist's admiration of art history, as it is a reference to the well-known painting *Voyage to Cythera* by French eighteenth-century artist Jean-Antoine Watteau, and which was a compulsive source of inspiration for Dalí. Cythera was the mythological birthplace of Venus (goddess of love and beauty) and another landscape infused with sexual desire and the imagination, in many ways much like Dalí's beloved Empordà.

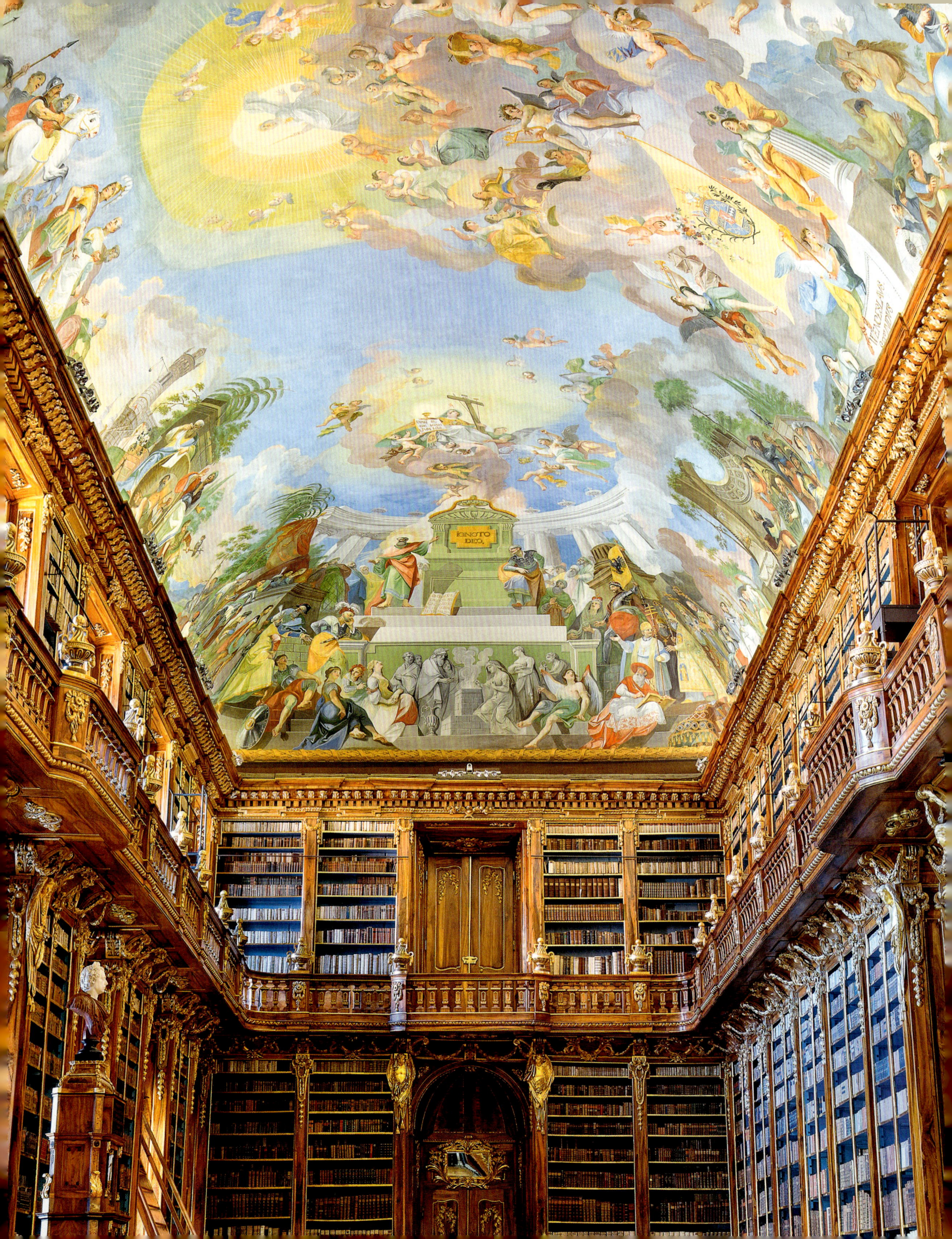
IGNOTO DEO.

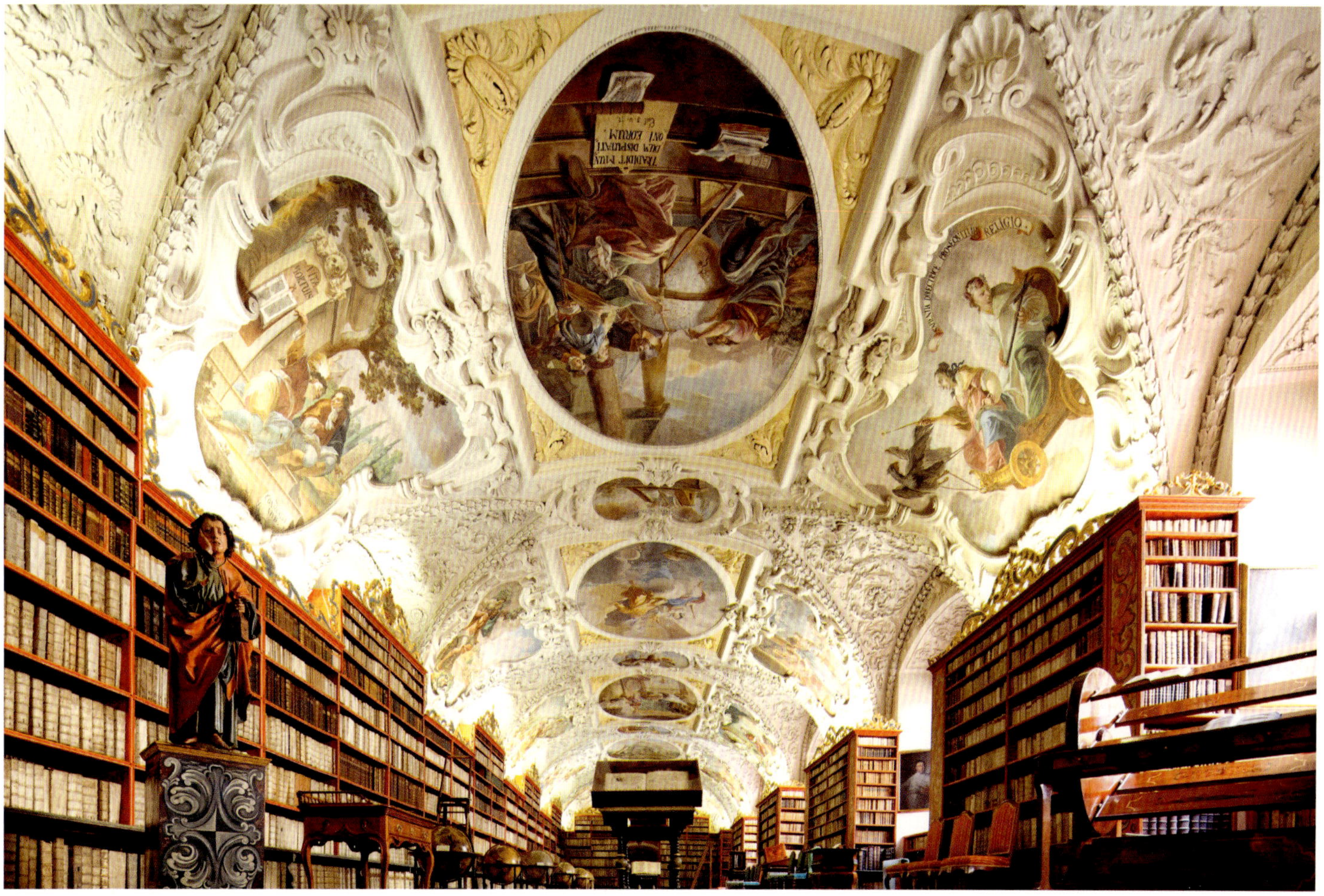

On the right-hand side of the ceiling, is the development of Greek civilization and philosophy, featuring Alexander the Great in the presence of his teacher Aristotle through to the philosophers Socrates, Diogenes and Democritos. On the other side of the ceiling is the evolution of science, depicted through figures such as Aesculapius and Pythagoras, whose endeavours in the fields of medicine and mathematics constituted the premodern study of natural philosophy.

Members of another group are cast as the defeated reprobates of Enlightenment knowledge, the misbelievers who rejected Christianity as the model for understanding in favour of new systematic and secular models of learning as were communicated in texts such as Denis Diderot's *Encyclopédie*. These outcasts were held as partly responsible for the recent trauma of the French Revolution, which saw the suppression of the Church and organized religion. However, tolerance proves to be the chief god in this library, as (again somewhat paradoxically) the *Encyclopédie* is stored among the first volumes in the Philosophical Hall.

Alongside Diderot and his like – intellectual incendiaries who argued for alternatives to church and crown – there was another, far larger group of outcasts who were denied access to the monastery's library and the nourishing visions of the ceiling painting in each of its halls: no women were allowed over the threshold until the start of the nineteenth century. Ever at the forefront of new trends and fashions in Europe at the time was Lady Emma Hamilton, wife of British statesman and antiquarian Sir William Hamilton, was one of the first to enter into this hallowed space of learning, knowledge and collecting.

Opposite and above: The overriding dictat of the imagery contained in the stuccos that make up the ceiling in the Theological Hall is the belief that true wisdom was gained through humility and piety, as opposed to a rationalist understanding of the world.

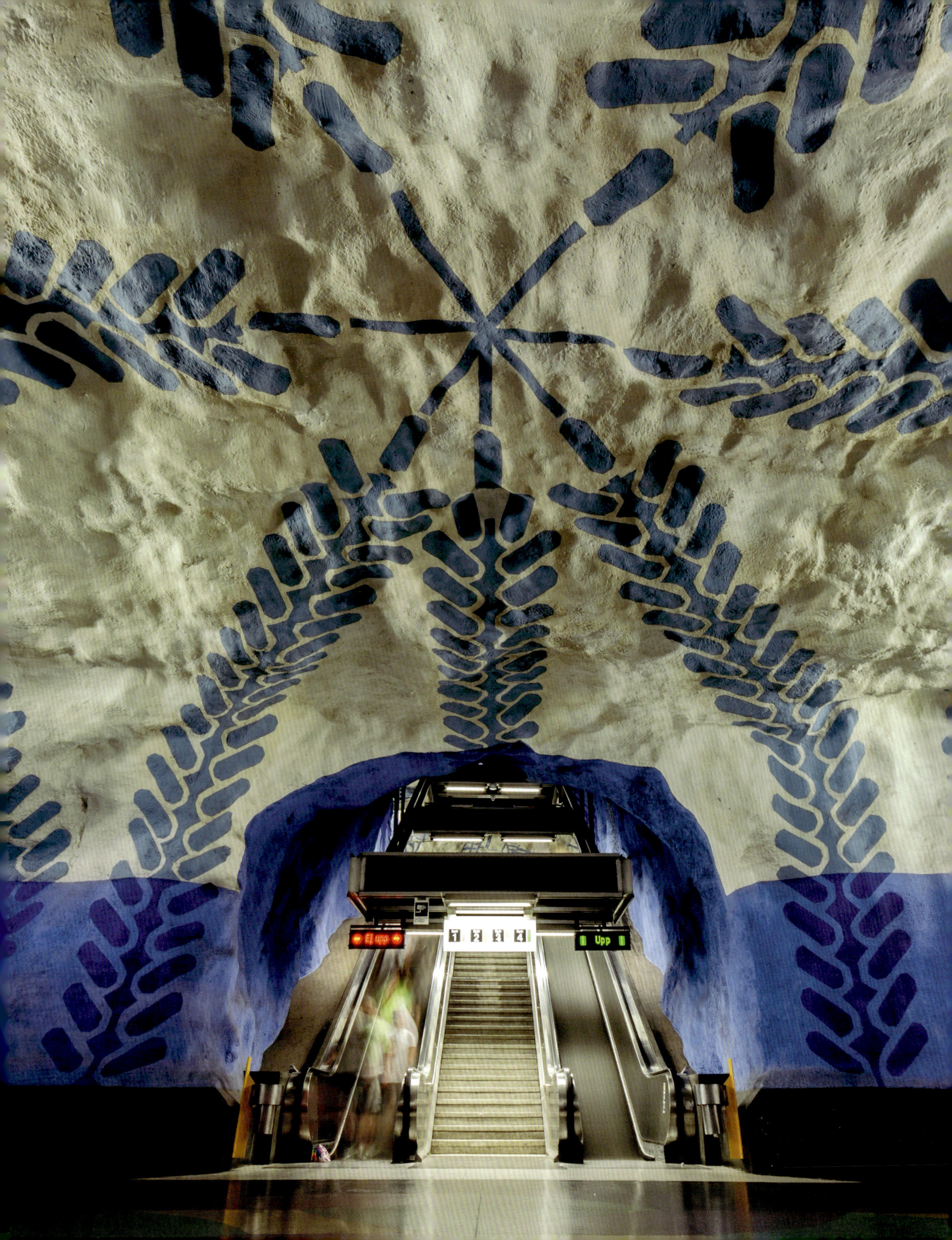
Ej upp
1 2 3 4
Upp

Various artists

Metro stations

1950s–70s

Metro stations, Stockholm, Sweden

Left: T-Centralen station.

Metro Stations, Sweden

Sometimes, looking up involves going underground first. This is the case when it comes to the subterranean channels of the Stockholm city metro system, the unusual home for a display of art that snakes through the underground thoroughfares of the Swedish capital. The project, which dates back to the 1950s, was motivated by the realization that the train stations – often dreary, functional spaces – could serve a cultural purpose, with artists crafting a more engaging experience for city-dwellers as they commuted across the city. So, replacing cavernous exposed rock and bleaching strip lighting, a series of murals and objects provide the one hundred or so stations in the network with a different aesthetic experience.

The earliest station to receive such treatment – and the birthplace of subway art in the 1950s – is T-Centralen, where an abstract design of tiles graces the platform walls. However, the most significant phase of decoration took place in the 1970s, when artist Per Olov Ultvedt produced soothing, blue murals with floral motifs that recall both the late work of Henri Matisse and the colours of white-washed Greek islands, bringing a blast of southern European brightness into the clinging darkness of the Scandinavian winter. In a similar vein, a giant rainbow set against a limpid blue sky arcs overhead at Stadion station. The station serves the nearby Stockholm Olympic Stadium, constructed for the 1912 Stockholm Olympics. The five colours of the rainbow here refer to the five interlocking Olympic rings, however the motif also has an unwittingly symbolic resonance for LGBT festivalgoers to the annual Pride celebration that takes place at nearby Östermalms IP.

Not all of the stations are so perky and illuminated. Tekniska Högskolan, on the red line, serves the Kungliga Tekniska Högskolan (Royal Institute of Technology), which first opened its doors to science students in 1827, and has had a station stop since 1973. Here, artist Lennart Mörk is responsible for crepuscular and atmospheric interior decorations that draw on the mysterious power and forces of the laws of physics and other sciences, with a violently marbled mural on the ceiling, paired with five regular polyhedra located on the platform, each one representing one of Plato's five elements: fire, water, air, earth and ether. Elsewhere, at Kungsträdgården, on the blue line, the feeling is one of being submerged in a vast, mossy, archaeological ruin, complete with relics from the location's former identity as the site of the majestic Makalös Palace. The red, white and green colour scheme of the station mirrors that of the French garden that accompanied the bygone palace, while the name 'Kungsträdgården', meaning King's Garden, refers to the area's royal history. One of the internal vaults of this underground warren is decorated with a patchwork of tessellated images depicting what looks to combine fossils, knotted rope, flowers and chequerboard designs in a veritable museum of the imagination. These give the feeling of being in a premodern cabinet of curiosities, where objects from the man-made world were displayed alongside gems, shells and stones as well as different flora and fauna. This station could be described as an example of life imitating art, as its ceiling and walls happen to be home to an idiosyncratic ecosystem. The station is the only place in northern Europe where the cave-dwelling Lessertia dentichelis spider can be found. There is also evidence of a previously unknown fungus on the station walls, discovered by scientists in 2016.

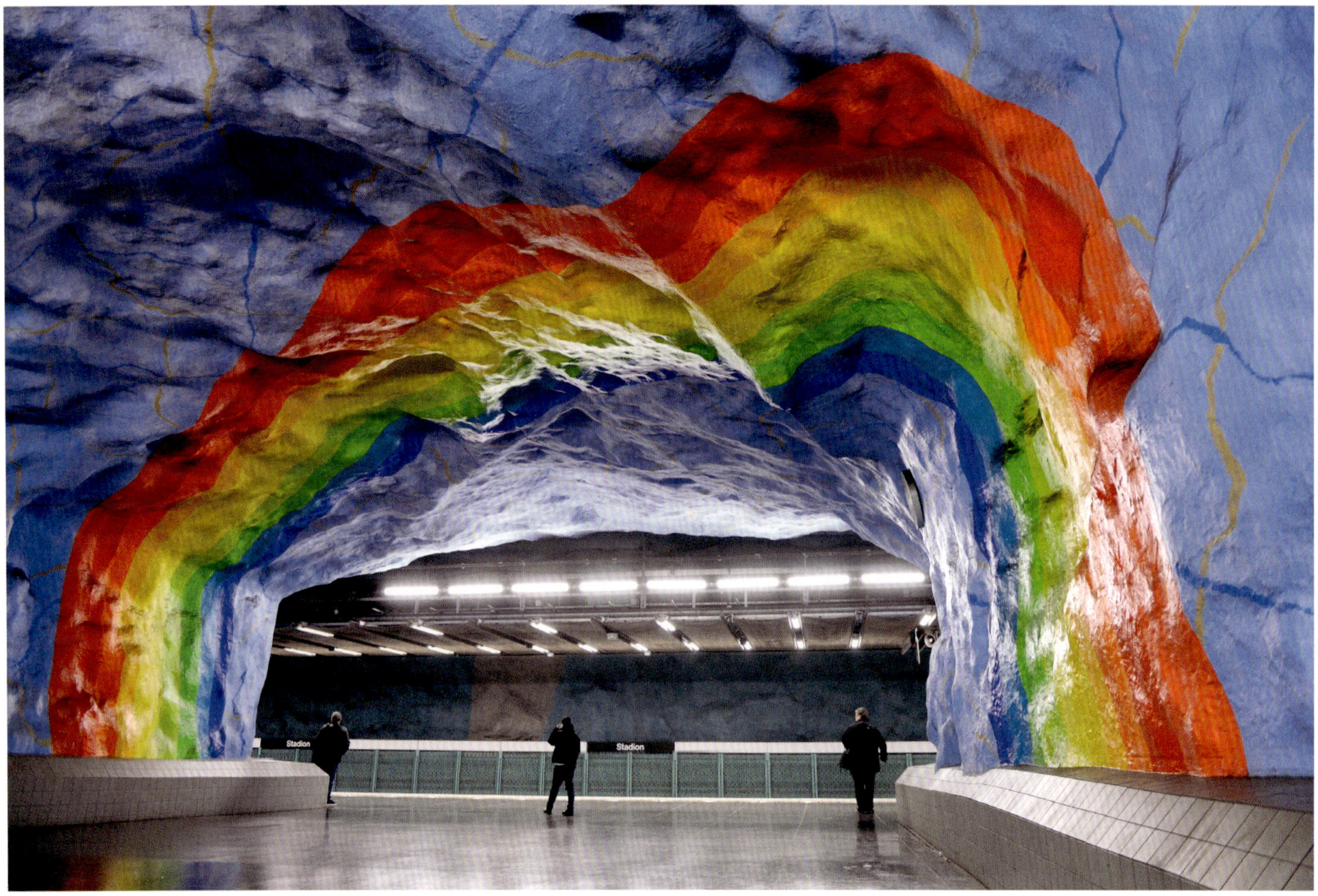
Stadion
Stadion

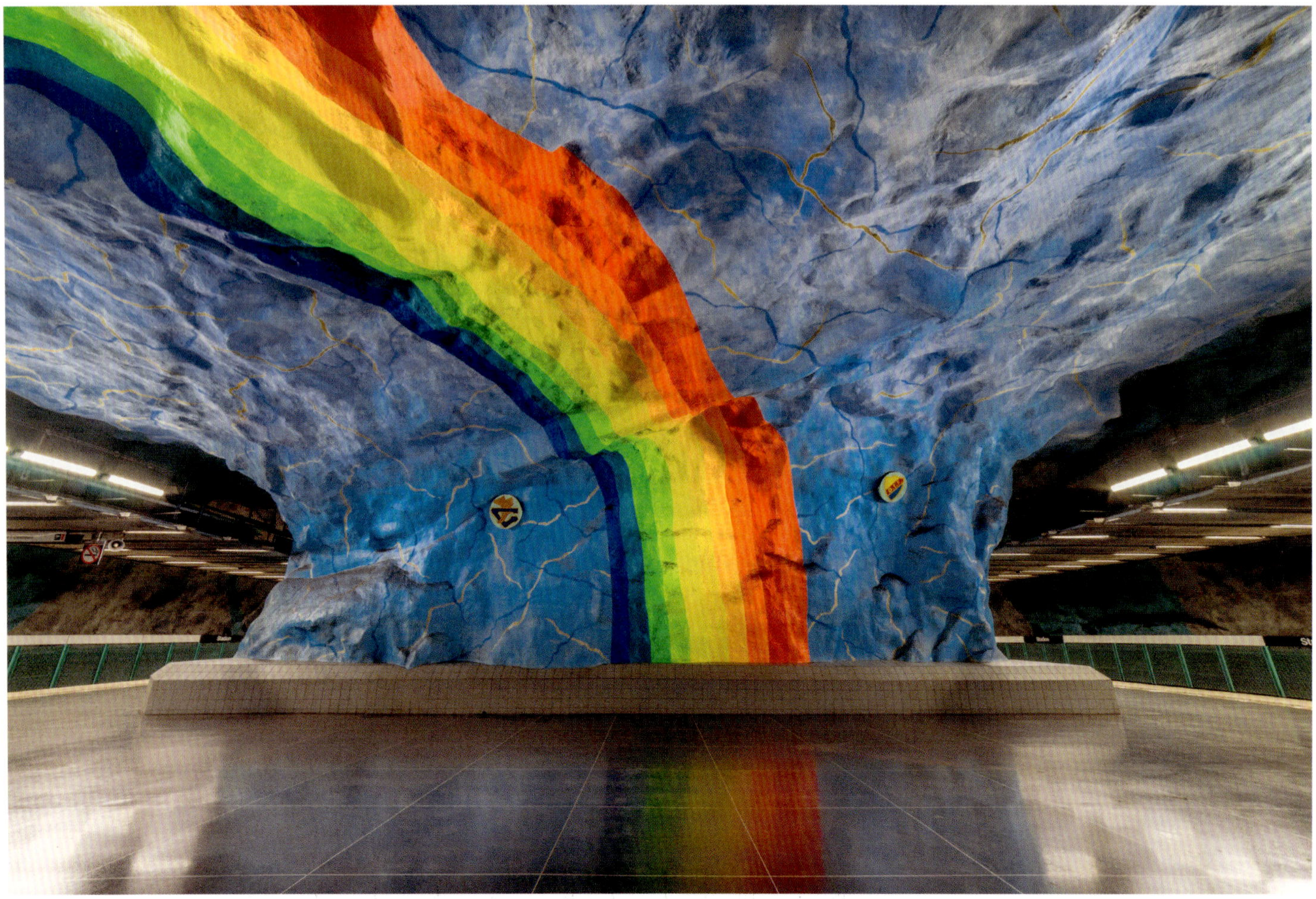

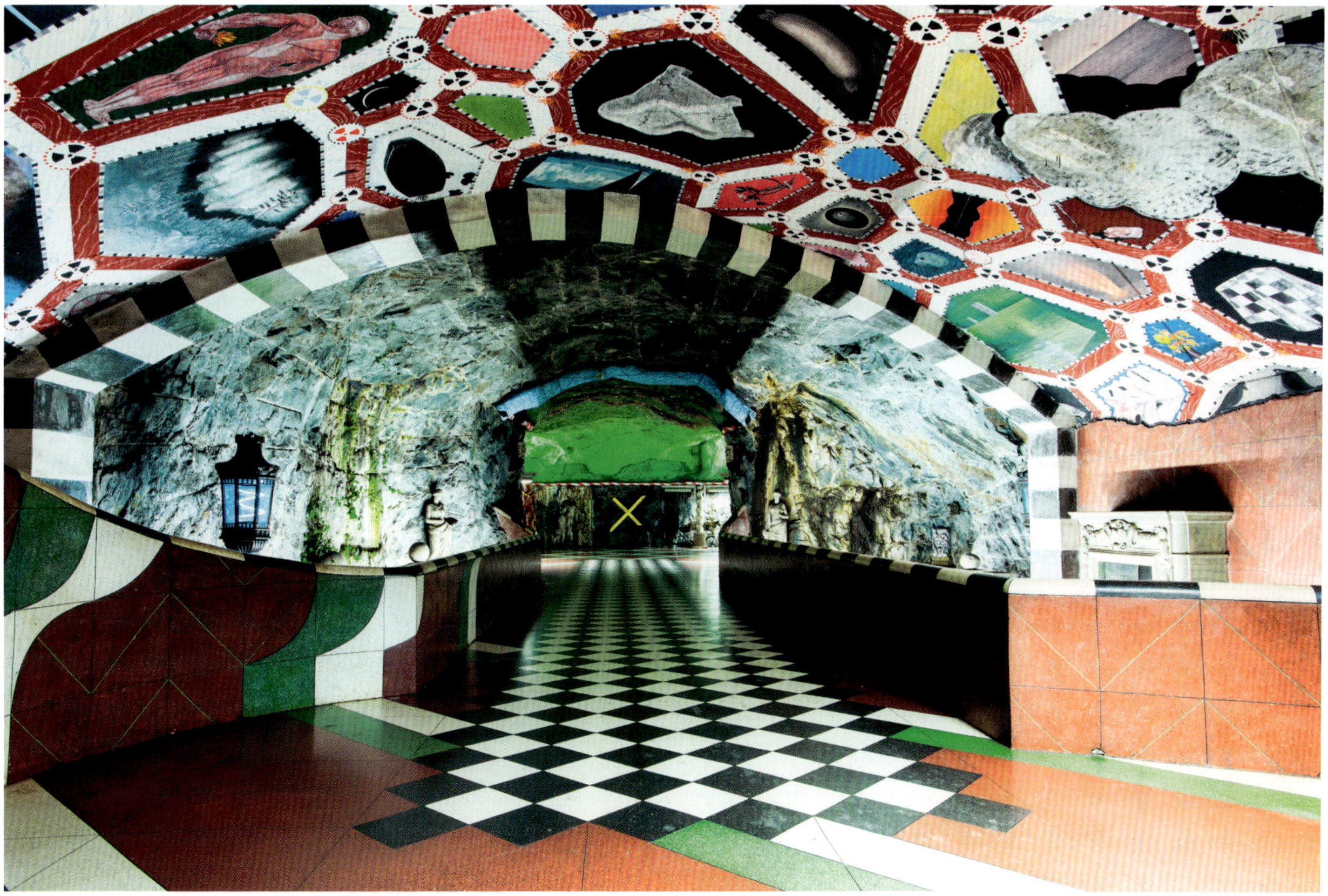

Left: The vibrant rainbows sprawl across the ceiling and walls of the Stadion station.

Above and bottom: The red, white and green colour scheme of Kungsträdgården station engulfs cavernous spaces of the station.

Centre: The entrance to Kungsträdgården station was intended to be in the park but, due to the Elm Conflict in 1971, these plans had to be changed.

Overleaf: Tekniska Högskolan station, which includes five regular polyhedra located on the platform, each one representing one of Plato's five elements: fire, water, air, earth and ether.

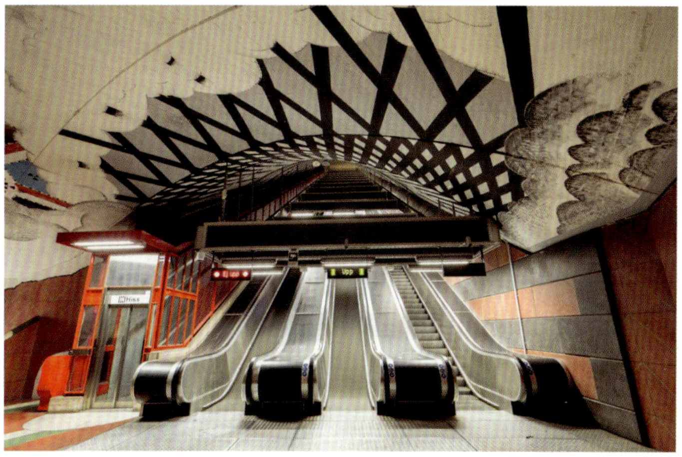

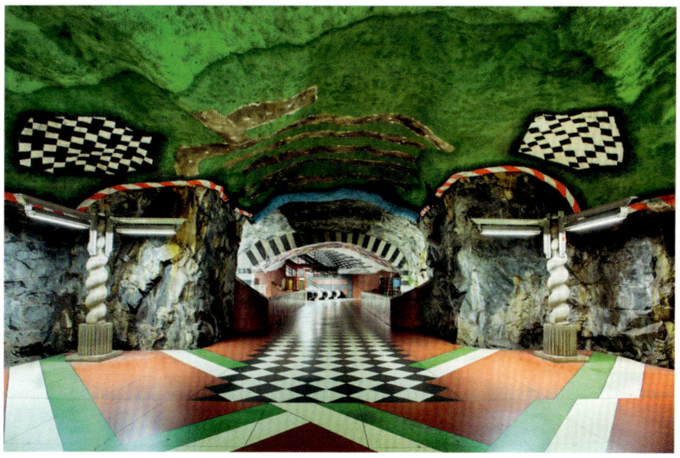

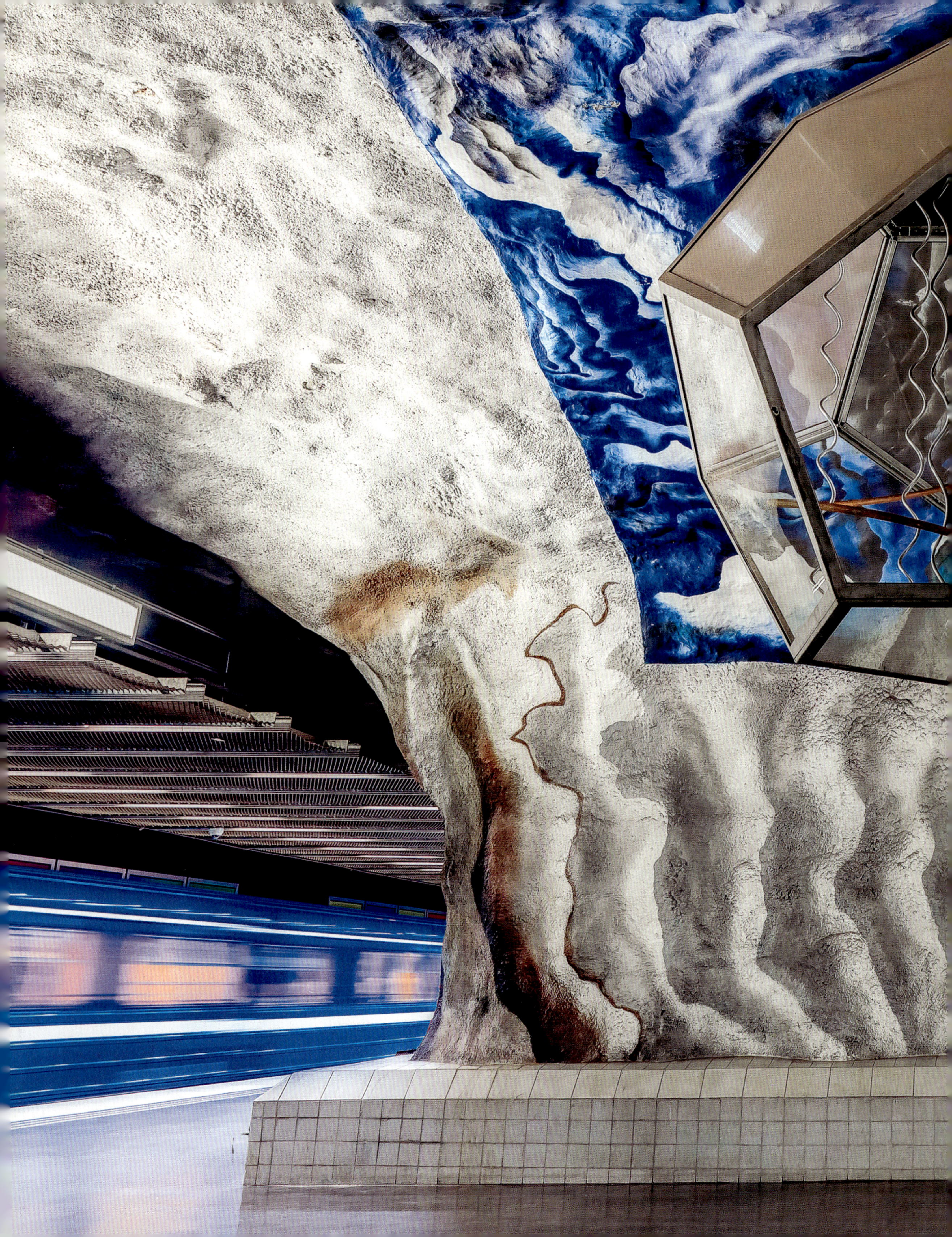

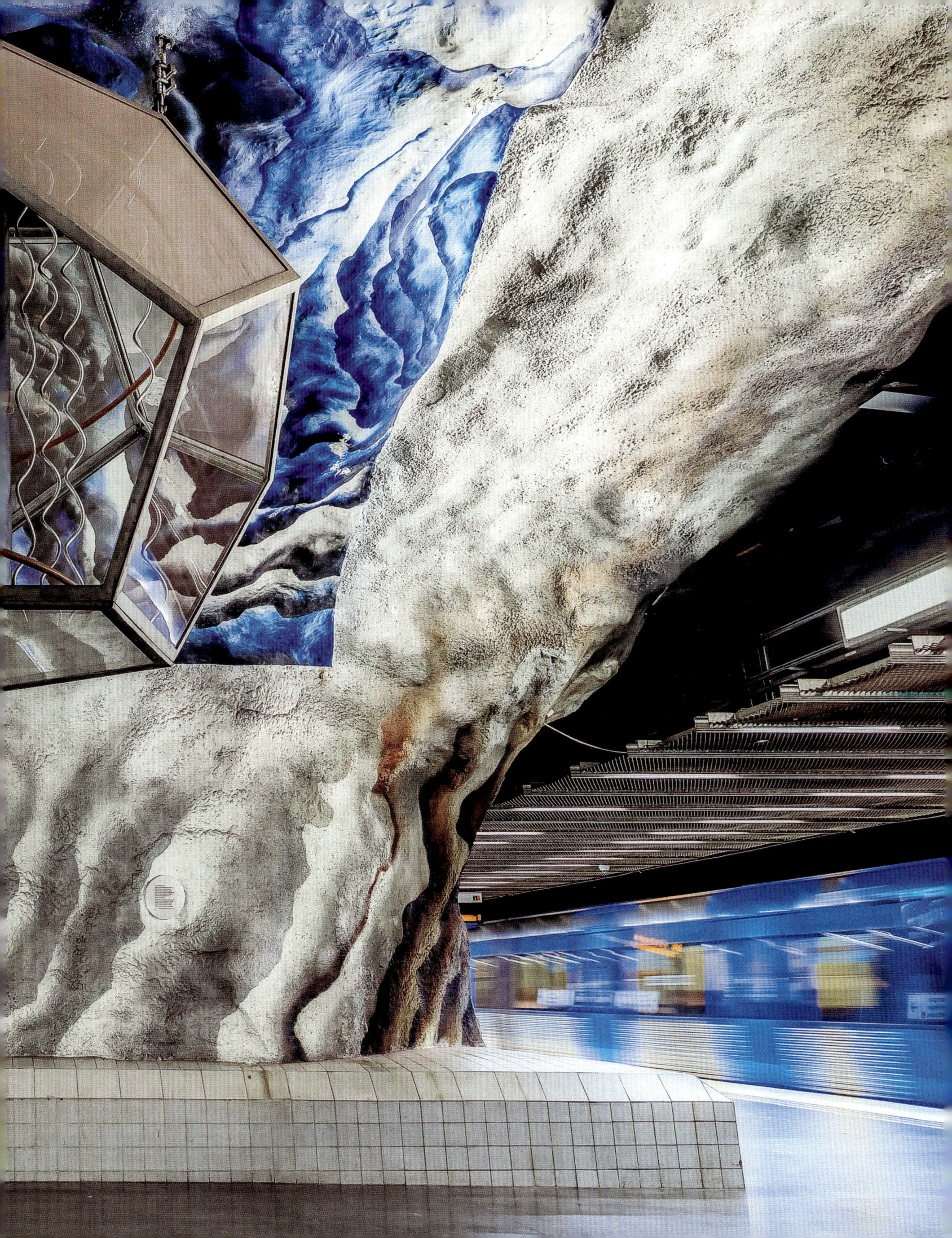

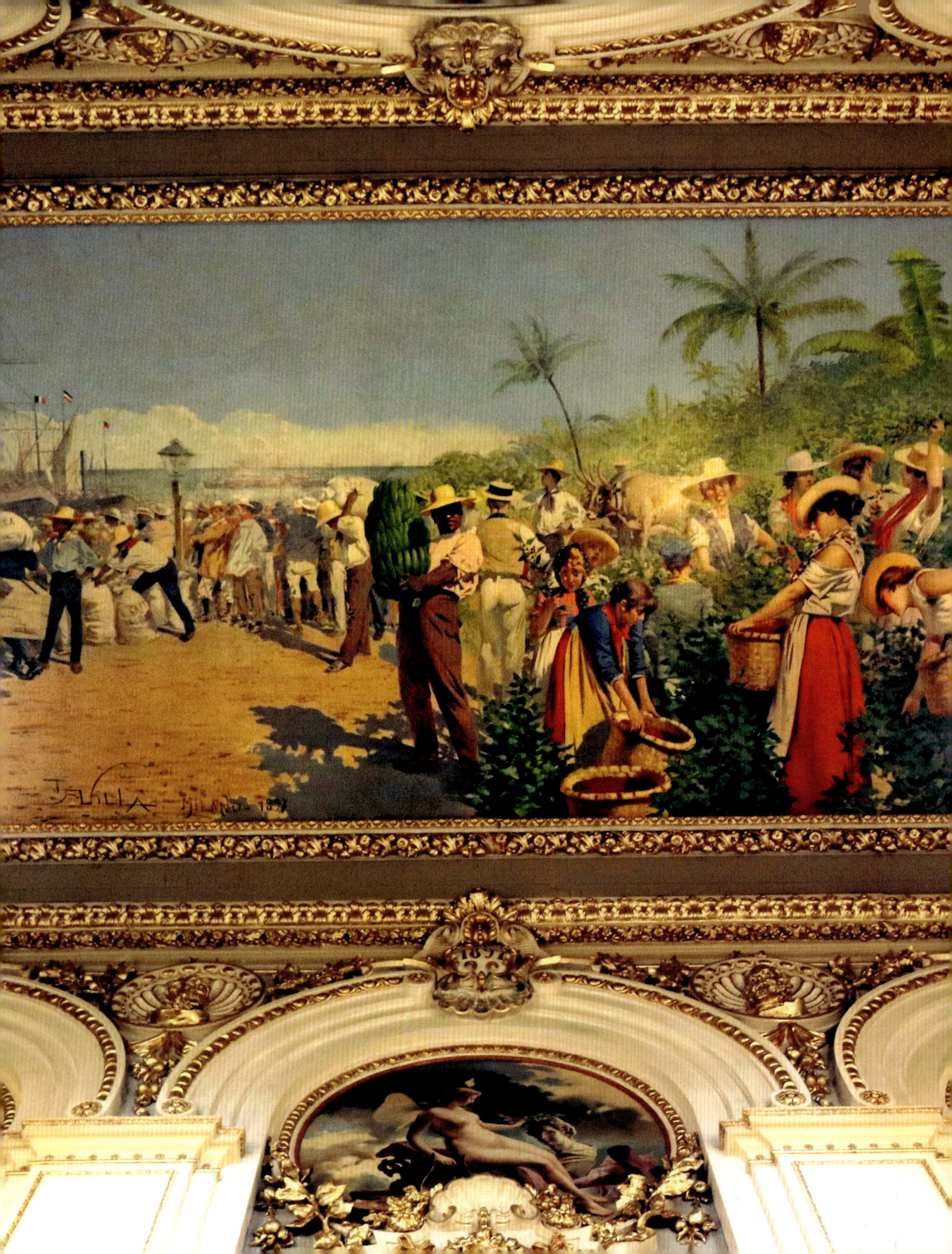
J VILLA
MILANO

Aleardo Villa

Allegory of Coffee and Bananas

1897

National Theatre, San José, Costa Rica

Left: Detail of Aleardo Villa's *Allegory of Coffee and Bananas*.

Overleaf: A view of the *Allegory of Coffee and Bananas* from the hall of the National Theatre.

National Theatre, Costa Rica

Art historians revel in unpacking allegorical significance in an image, unveiling the stories or messages that lurk like precious pearls within a picture's immediate and literal reading, to be glimpsed only by the worthily informed. A number of allegories appear frequently – for example, the passage of time; victory; peaceful governance; and resurrection. Sometimes allegories seek to persuade the viewer of a certain superiority of an attribute or an abstract ideal, such as pitting an allegory of painting against one of poetry, or an allegory of sight against one of touch. Allegories do not always have to be glorious, they can be tragic or express vice, ill-judgment and mortality.

But the *Allegory of Coffee and Bananas* on the ceiling of the staircase at the National Theatre of Costa Rica does something that bucks the trend: it functions as an allegory of transformation and capitalist prosperity through the export of commodities in the New World. As such, it replaces the familiar images of gods and governments and mythology, immortalizing instead the power of the market and trade in providing an idealized dream of stability and prosperity.

Painted for the grand opening of the theatre in 1897, the rectangular mural depicts a happy throng of workers busily engaged in the supply of bananas and coffee for a hungry international market in a country transformed by its export. The coffee plant was originally introduced to Costa Rica from Ethiopia in the 1770s. By the nineteenth century, coffee had surpassed cacao, sugar and tobacco as the country's main export, fuelling the aspirations and energies of an international appetite for caffeine, and transforming the humble agricultural economy and the country's identity on the world stage.

Costa Rican coffee was so in demand at the time, that export taxation by the country's government generated enough income for a number of enterprises, from funding the travel of young academics to Europe, to the development of a railway linking the country to the Atlantic Coast in the 1890s. The coffee trade not only financed the infrastructure and intellectual development of Costa Rica, it also provided the necessary income to build the National Theatre as a lavish projection of the nation's ability to invest in the arts.

On the left of the ceiling mural, men haul gleaming sacks of coffee beans at the waterfront of a sandy beach where, behind them in the background, a story of development and obsolescence plays out among the vertical masts of the sailing ships of the Old World standing, as they do, alongside the steamship funnels of the New World, that will replace them. The thrill of the technologically new can also be found in the erroneous detail of a lamppost, sprouting mystically out of the sandy ground. This is a reference to the arrival of electricity in San José, which was one of the earliest cities in the world to adopt it.

Before becoming easily available across the globe, the exotic banana also arrived in Costa Rica from foreign climes, bringing with it wealth and good fortune. Originating in India and Southeast Asia, banana plants were introduced to Costa Rica and mass-cultivated from 1834, becoming increasingly widespread as a commodity and reaching well into the millions by the close of the nineteenth century. A bevvy of coquettish workers on the right of this ceiling mural are seen harvesting the fruits, but another erroneous detail can be spotted in the dark figure who stands at the centre of the image – he's holding the bananas upside down. This mistake can be

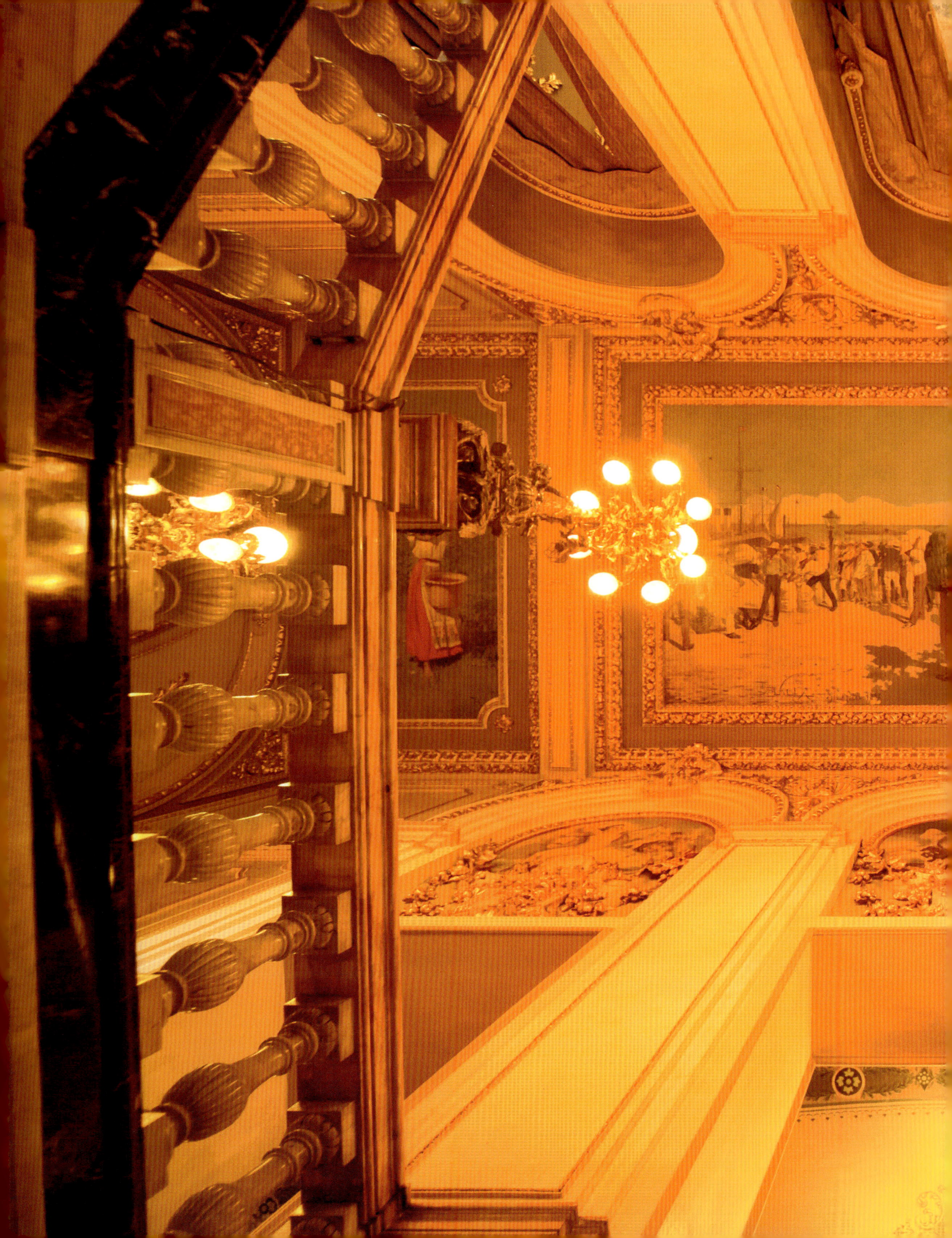

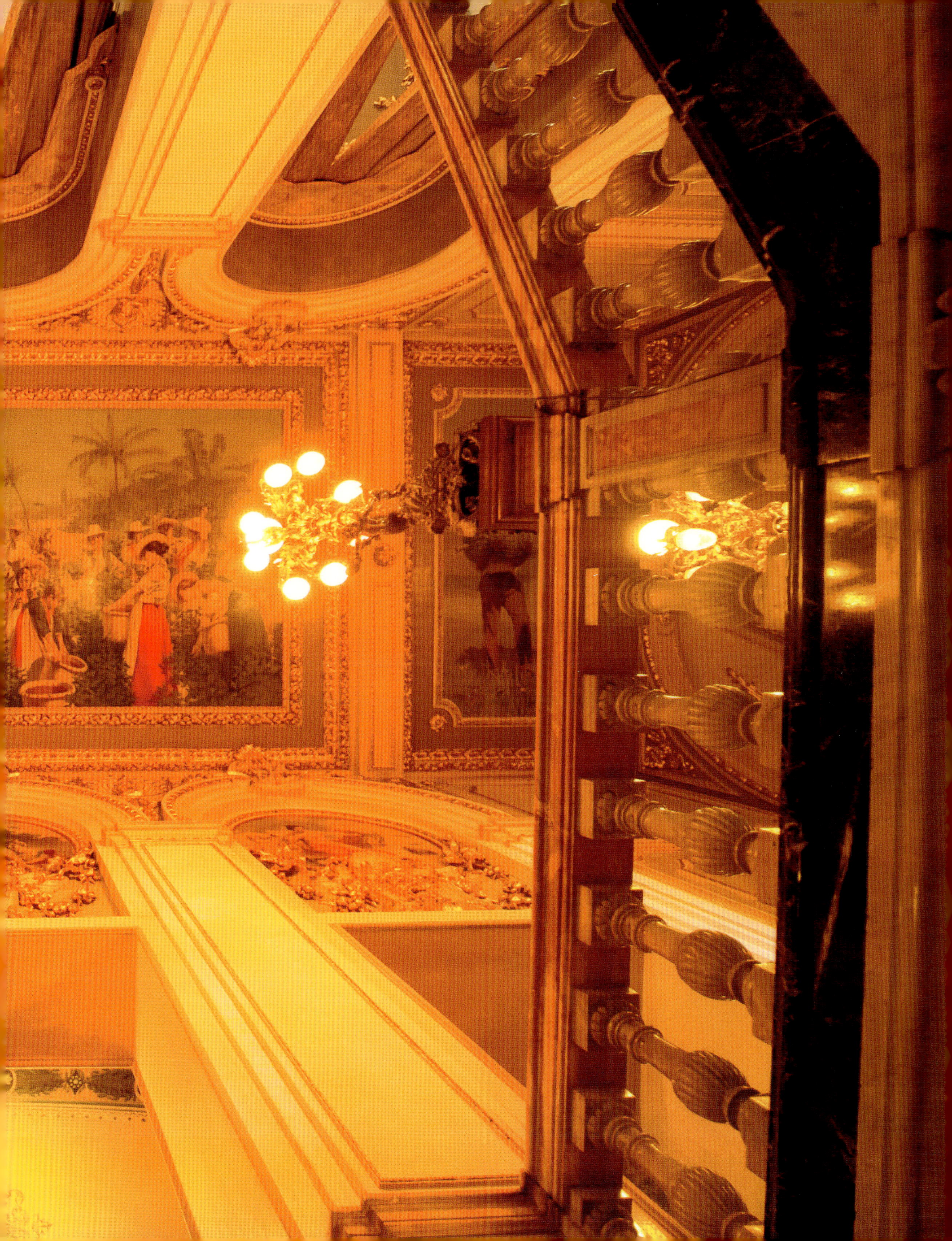

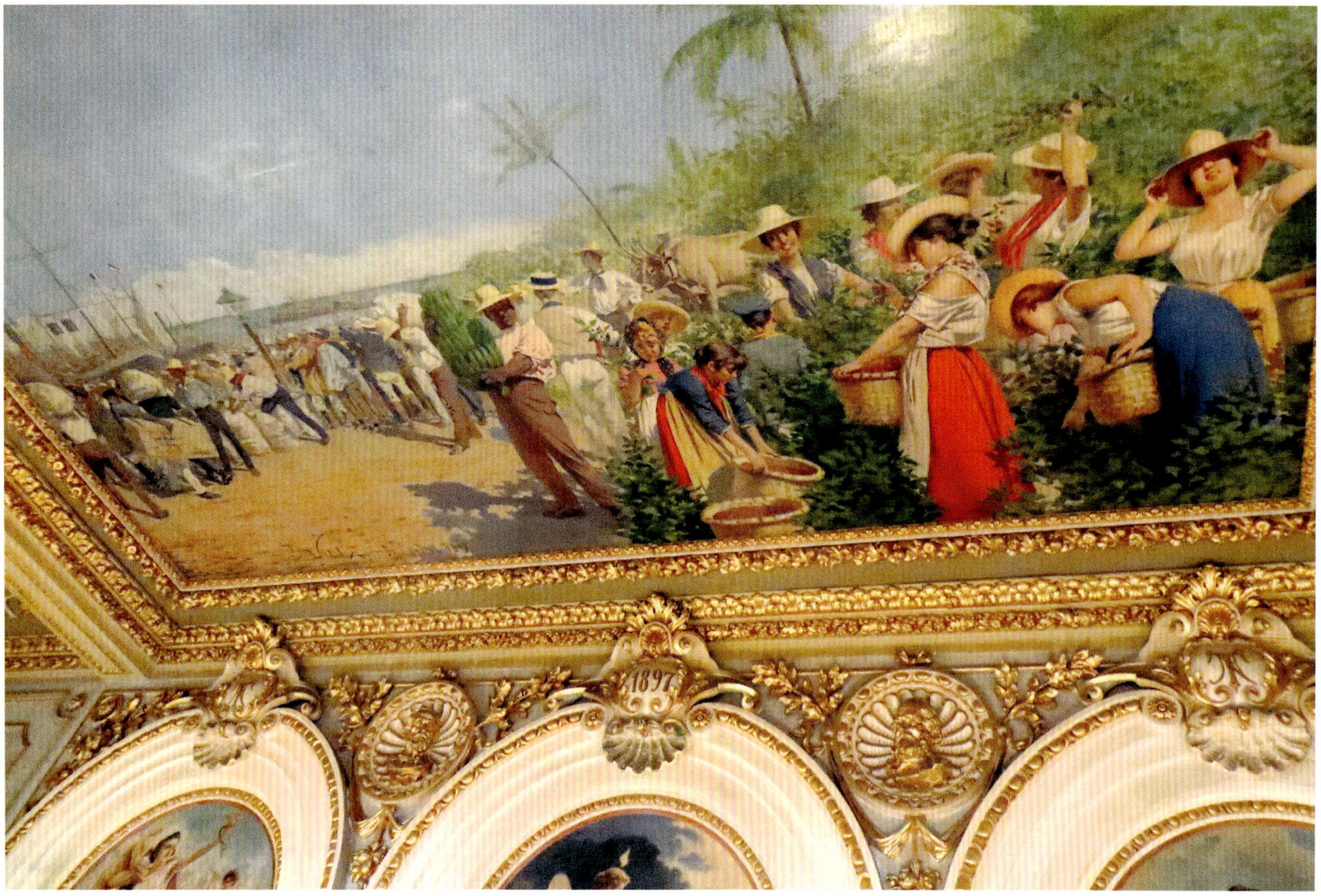

Above: The mural depicts cheery and playful workers gathering bananas and coffee beans that were the main exported commodity in late nineteenth-century Costa Rica.

Below: The *Allegory of Coffee and Bananas* also featured on the 5 colones banknote, which is no longer in circulation.

Opposite: Aleardo Villa's career was characterized by Belle Époque poster designs advertising consumer commodities such as cigarettes.

attributed to the fact that the painter of the work – Italian artist Aleardo Villa – had never set foot in Central America.

Villa, a graphic artist from Campania, had trained at the Milan Brera Academy. He might not have seemed the most obvious choice for immortalizing the transformative cultural impact of Costa Rican trade – that is, were he not already known as an artist devoted to branding the commodities of the belle époque era in Europe with his posters, often adorned with scantily clad beauties selling everything from gasoline to cigarettes and chocolate. Smiling in their conical brassieres as they harvest coffee, coyly pulling at their hats, the banana harvesters bear certain resemblances to their European pin-up poster cousins.

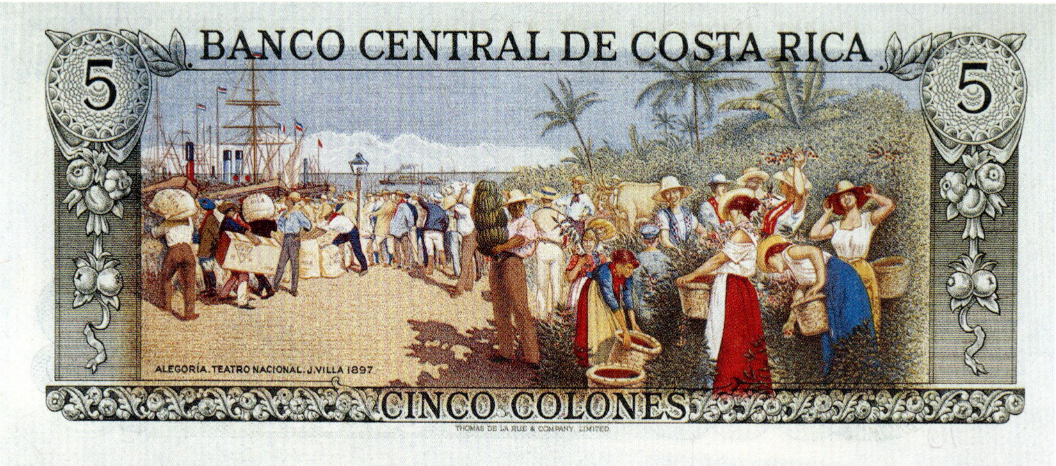

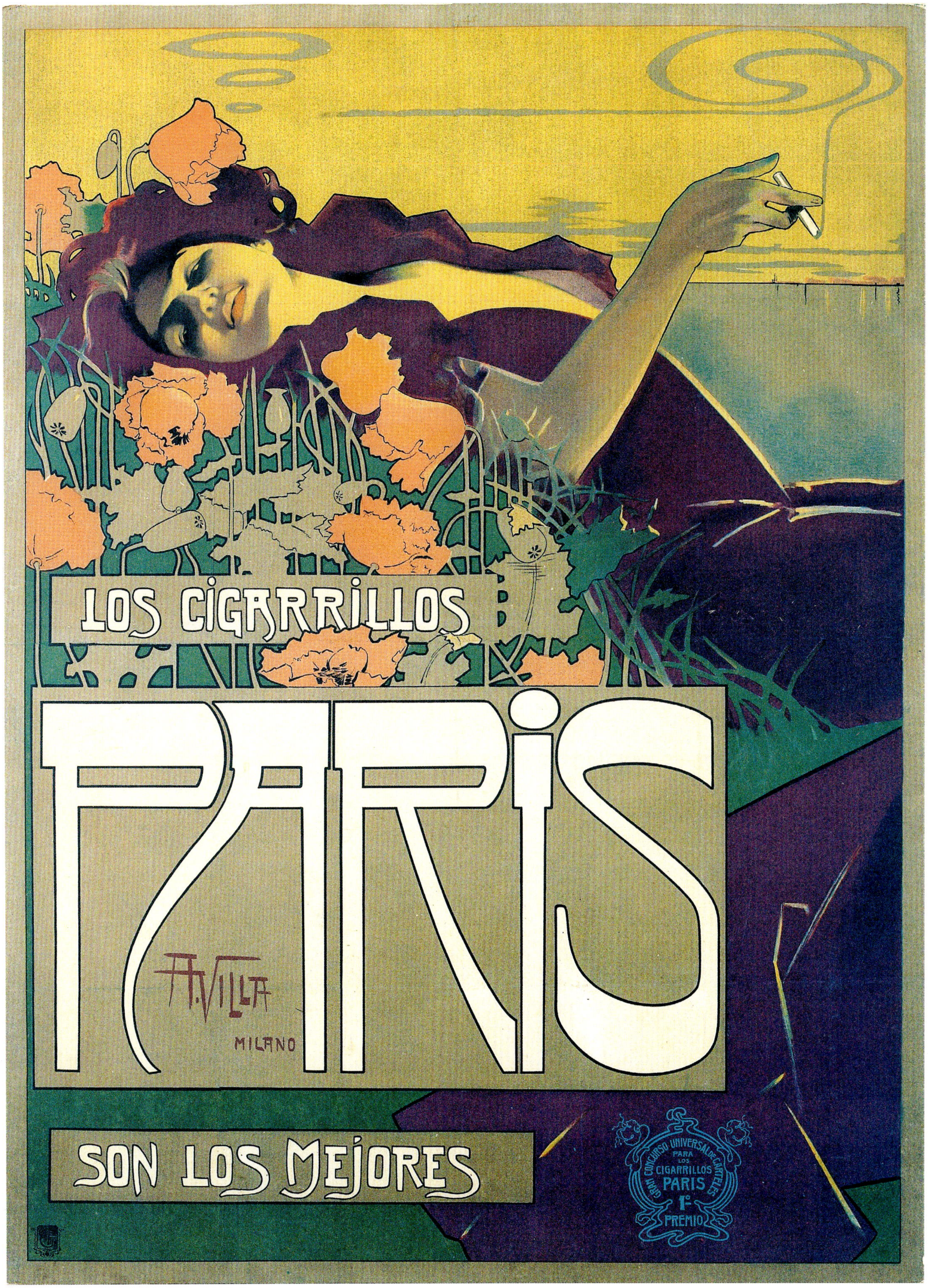
LOS CIGARRILLOS
PARIS
A.VILLA
MILANO
SON LOS MEJORES
CIGARRILLOS
PARIS
PREMIO

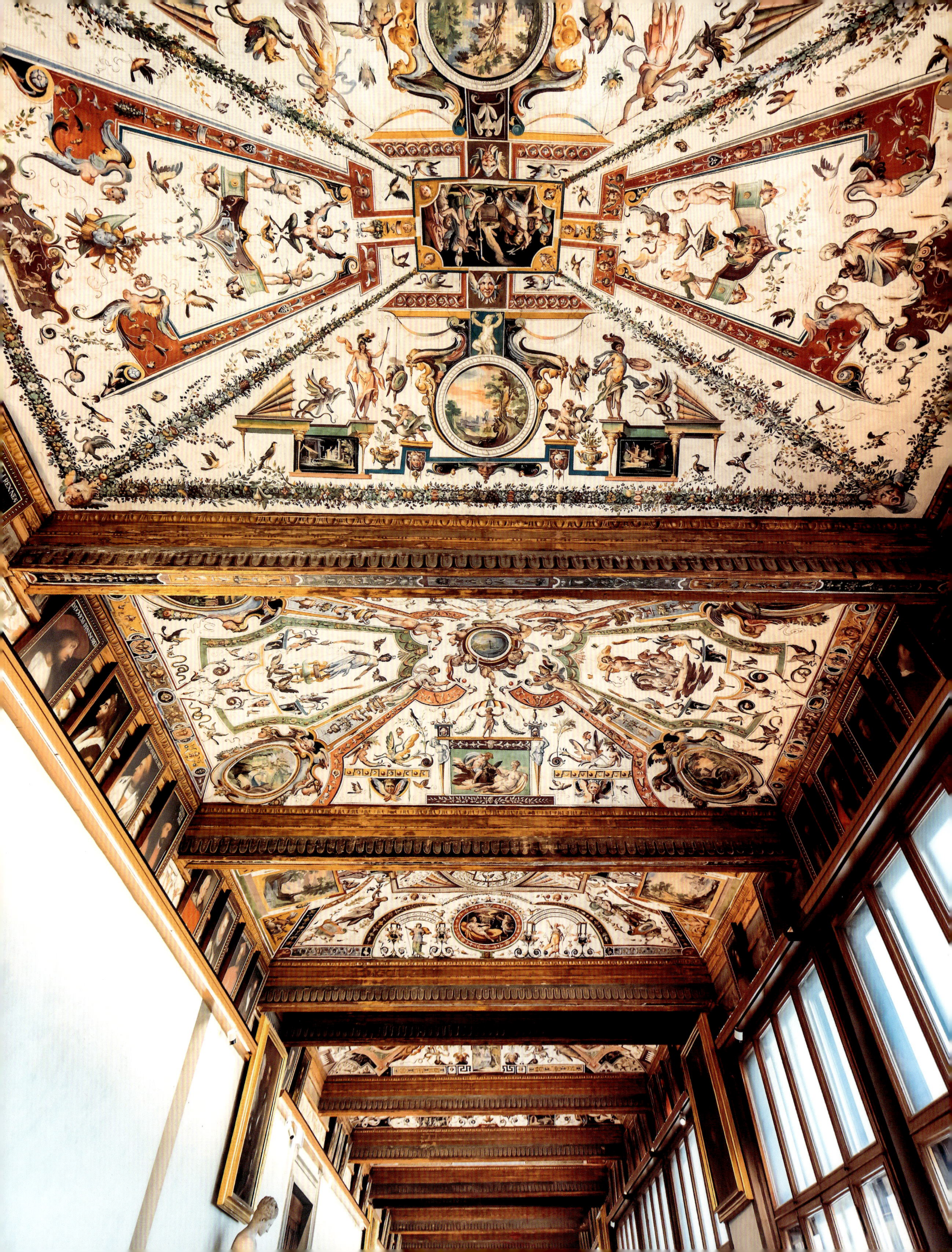

Antonio Tempesta and Alessandro Allori

Various murals

1580–81

East Wing, Uffizi Gallery, Florence, Italy

Left: The interior of the famous Uffizi Gallery in Florence, Italy.

Overleaf: Ceiling frescoes in the East Wing of the Uffizi Gallery.

Uffizi Gallery, Italy

Europe's oldest art gallery, the Uffizi Gallery houses one of the most significant collections of Western art in the world. No wonder, then, that it attracts a relentless flow of visitors year-round. Among the works people make a beeline for is Sandro Botticelli's Birth of Venus borne on the waves. When joining the procession that traipses from one gallery to the next, however, how many of the art pilgrims stop to look up at the ceilings of the museum's East Wing? For it is here, in the forty-six ceilings of the vast corridor and adjacent rooms, that one gains an insight into the political and intellectual context of the Uffizi as a space that, at its inception, communicated the authority of the Grand Dukes of Tuscany through its display of culture and collecting.

The Uffizi (an Italian word meaning 'offices') started life in 1560 as an administrative complex housing the legal and other offices of the city of Florence. It was commissioned by Cosimo I de Medici, the first grand duke of Tuscany. The thirteen offices of the magistrates in charge of overseeing Florentine production and trade were accommodated on the ground floor of the building, while the first floor housed the administrative offices and workshops of the grand duchy, dedicated to the manufacture of precious objects. After the accession of Francesco I, the building also accommodated the first incarnation of the duchy's art collection on the second floor. The eastern corridor housed a series of ancient statues and busts and connected to a number of rooms – such as the famous Tribuna – in which the most highly prized pieces of the collection were stored. It was during this nascent period of the early collection that the ceilings of the East Wing were painted in fresco, first by Antonio Tempesta, and subsequently by Florentine painter Alessandro Allori and his team between 1580–81.

The imagery on the ceilings varies wildly and excitingly, from sylvan landscapes to an arbored dome teeming with various species of birds, to the more bizarre details of sphinxes with dried up teats and leering gargoyles. Despite this cacophony of the natural and the bizarre, a unifying strand here is the recurring 'grotesque' style of geometrically patterned fields alternating with white surfaces and fantastical motifs that include hybrid figures known in the sixteenth century as 'chimaeras'. The grotesque style took root in Rome in the 1480s, following the discovery of similar decorative work in the subterranean ruins of the Domus Aurea. Sufficiently buried beneath the rubble of time, the rooms decorated in this fashion resembled caves (in Italian *grotte*), hence the name of the style (see also Palazzo Chiericati, p. 162).

Taken individually, any interpretation of the images proves elusive, made up as there are of a variety of logic-defying arrangements and secretive symbols. Yet despite what seems rather arcane iconography (at least to the contemporary viewer), as a whole the ceilings give insights into the original display of objects in the collection. As such, they also suggest a synchronicity between the fine arts and the philosophical and scientific knowledge of sixteenth-century Florence. For example, in Room 17, putti skim and skirmish across the ceiling holding scientific objects such as scales and astrolabes, while pictorial vignettes depict practical efforts in pulling ashore a ship run aground. While it is impossible to know the

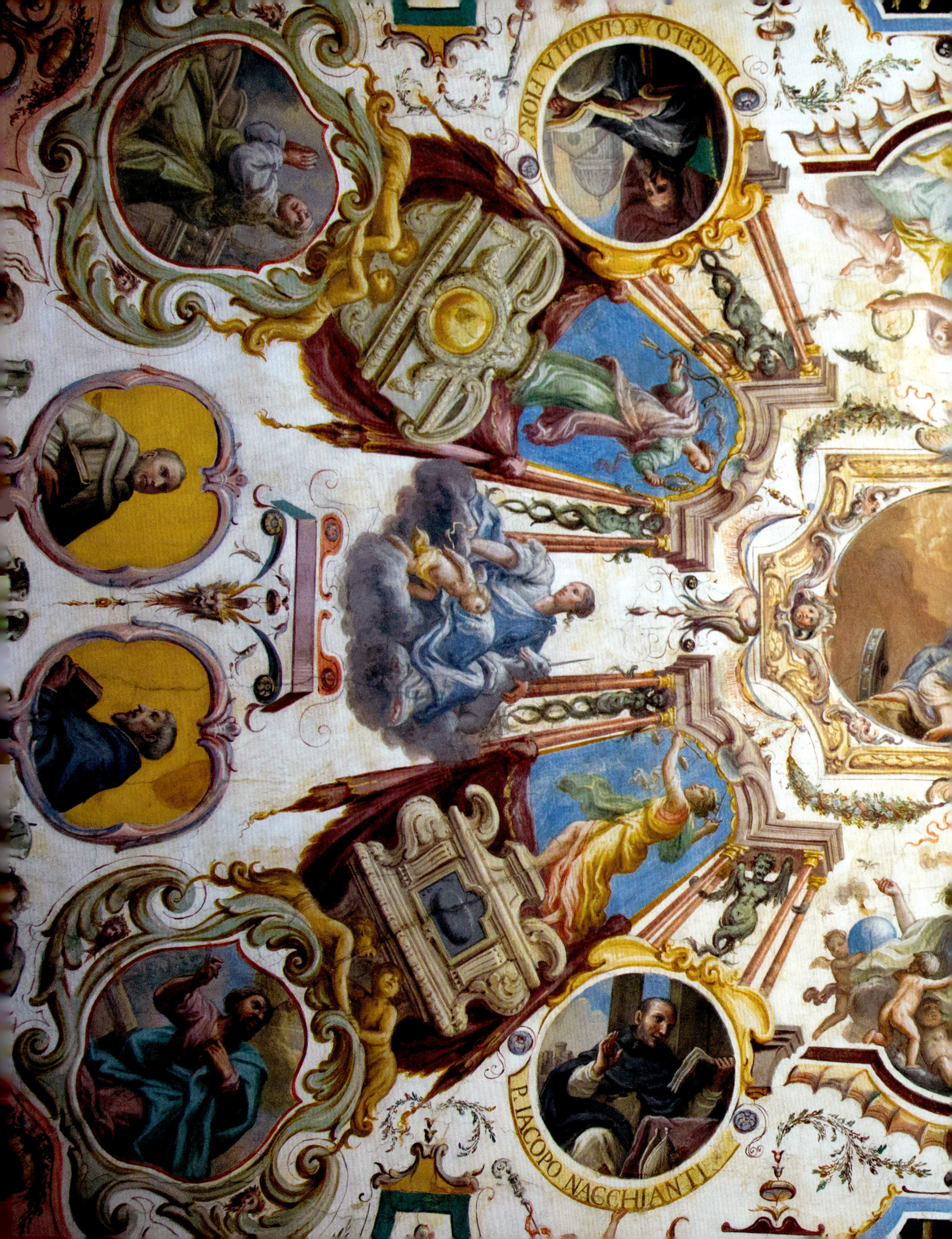
ANGELO ACCIAIOLI A. FIOR.
P. IACOPO NACCHIANTI

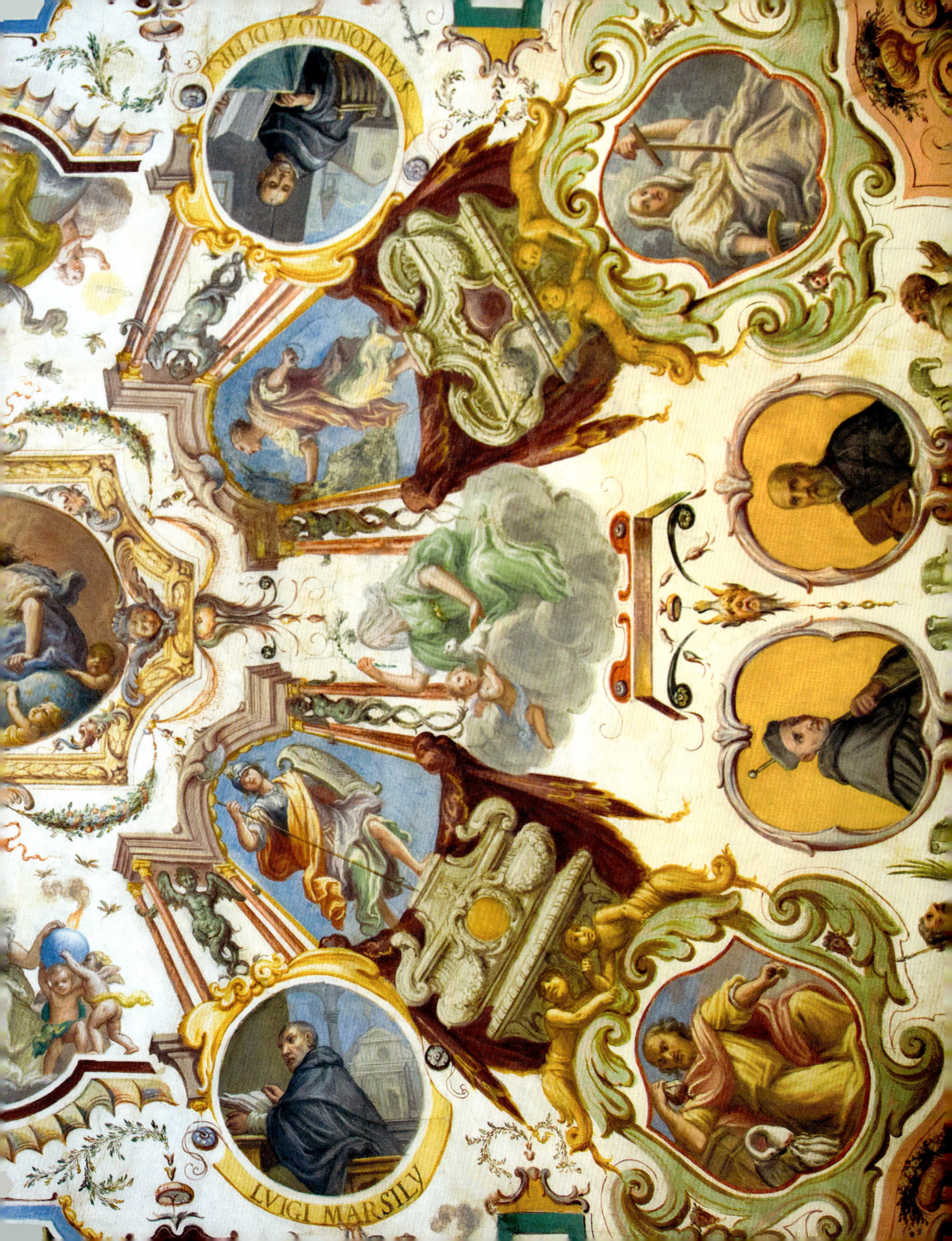
S. ANTONINO A. DI FIR
LVIGI MARSILY

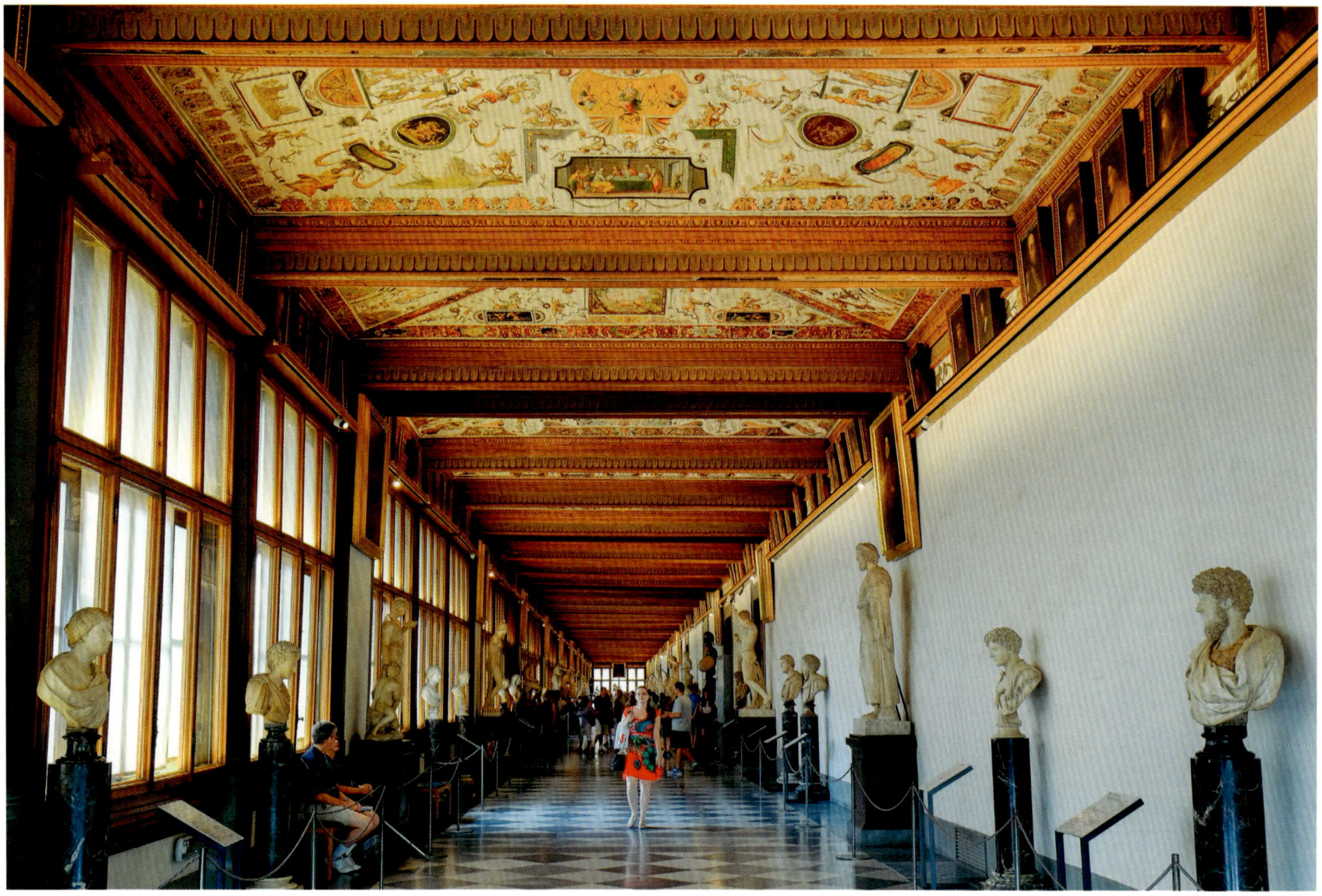

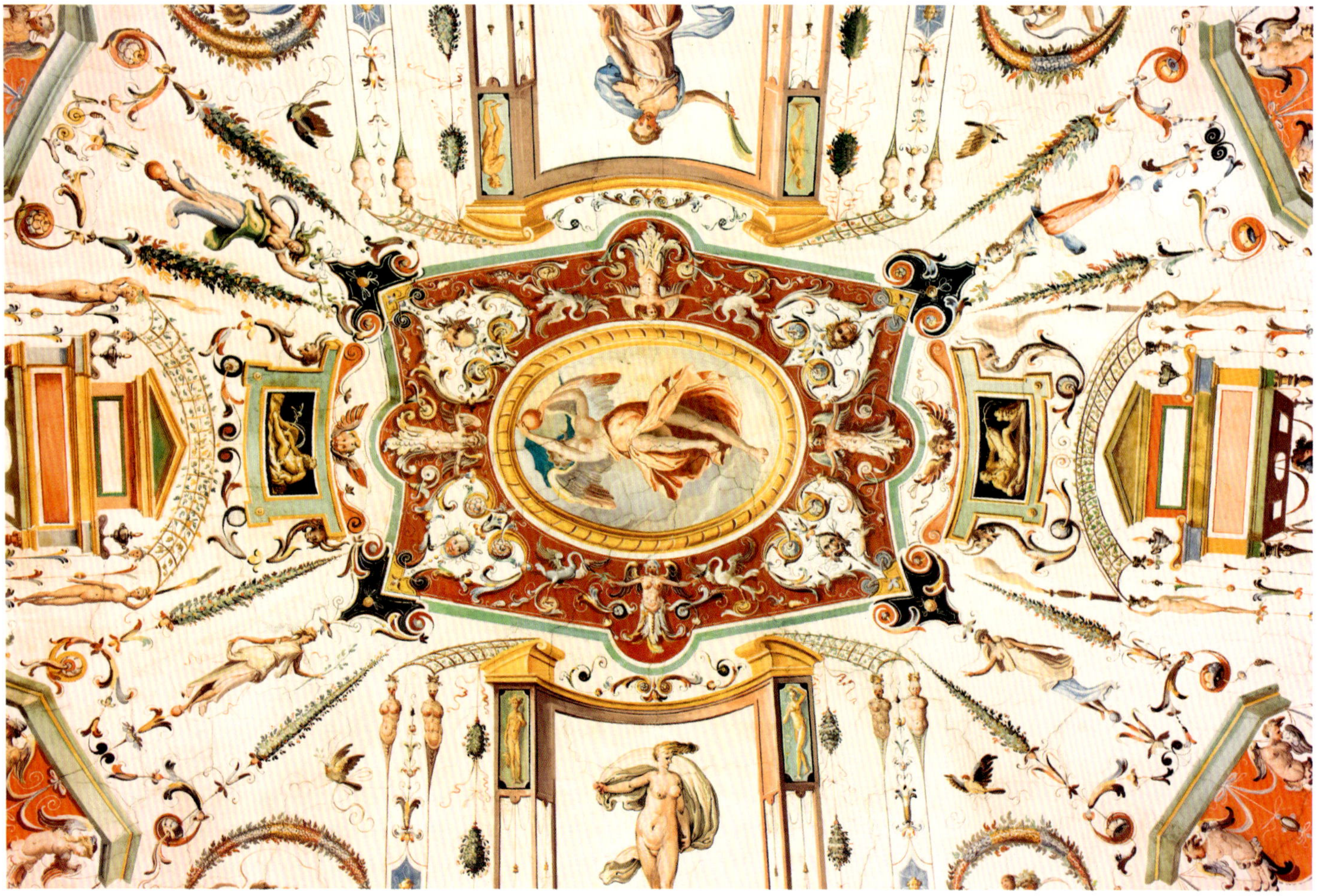

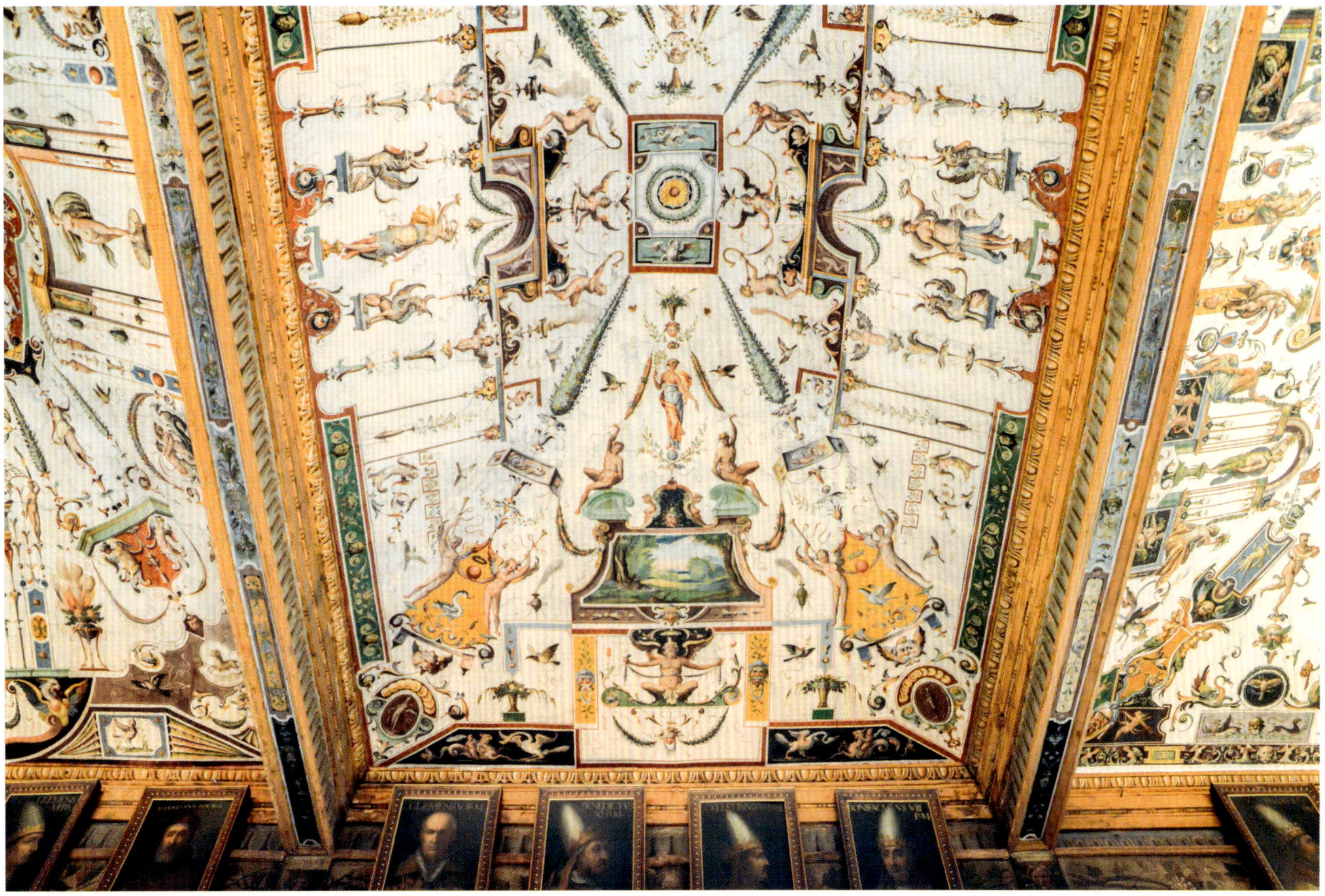

original arrangements of this room, it is likely and logical that it contained scientific objects of the sort that corresponded with Francesco's interests as a devoted natural philosopher and alchemist. Likewise the ceilings of Room 23 contain more putti, this time nestling among mounds of armour, while large vases showcase other objects made of metal, perhaps inspired by the grand duke's interest in metallurgy, as well as a space for displaying his collection of antique and modern weaponry (itself an indication of his power and not without the subtle threat of intimidation).

However, not all ceilings correspond to the presumed original contents on display. Room 20's ceiling, for example, contains a portrait of the city of Florence, with cityscapes of surrounding piazzas, while Room 19 showcases the heraldry of the illustrious Medici dynasty, featuring symbols such as Cosimo's turtle and Francesco's fox insignia. Also pictured here are historical feats of military prowess, such as Alexander the Great's famous crossing of the Hydaspes River.

Collectively, the ceilings of the East Wing depict a stream of the possibilities of natural and human creativity, endeavour and transformation, and these images supported the function of the Uffizi building as symbolic of Medici wealth, taste, influence and intellectual interests as presented to its original audience of dignitaries, scholars, scientists, and those rulers who were Francesco I's peers.

Opposite top: The corridor of the East Wing of the Uffizi Gallery.

Above and opposite bottom: Details of the ceiling in the Uffizi Gallery's East Wing, flanked by a collection of portraits of illustrious figures.

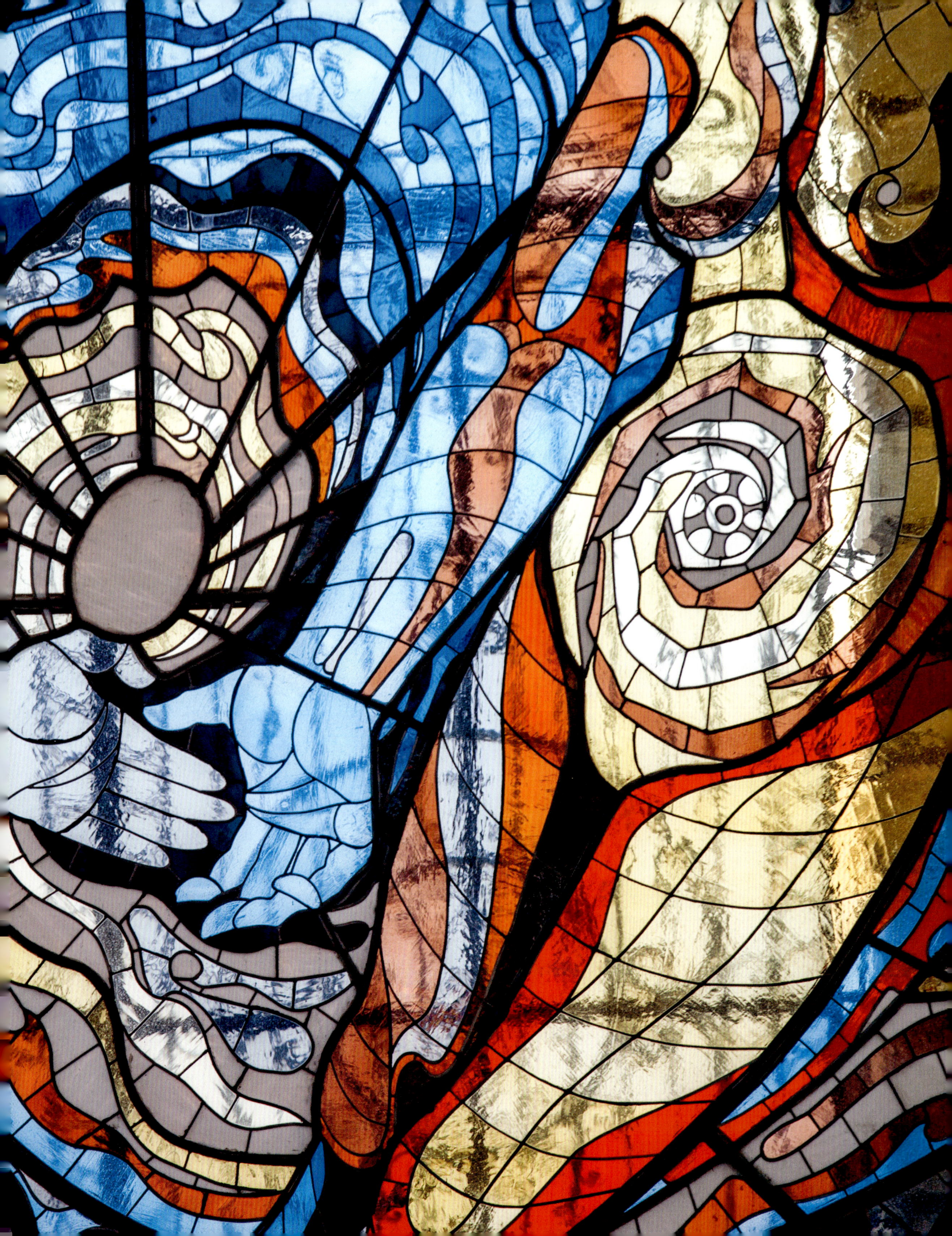

Leopold Flores

Cosmovitral

1978–80

Toluca Botanical Gardens,

Mexico City, Mexico

Left: The concentric circles on the stained glass in the Toluca Botanical Gardens reach their centre in the navel of the female – the symbolic centre of human creation.

Overleaf: The coloured light from the stained-glass windows drapes over the botanical garden.

Toluca Botanical Gardens, Mexico

At the centre of the ceiling, the figures of a man and a woman lit from within with amber and golden hues extend their arms in an embrace. Star belts and astrological matter surround them in energetic circles, creating a rhythm that is echoed across the ceiling's composition and down the walls. Beneath these figures more than five hundred species of plant absorb the shafts of coloured light that permeate through the vast canopy of coloured glass, while fountains trickle and burble. We are encased in the chromatic wonderland of the *Cosmovitral*, a meditation of humankind's philosophical relationship with the universe as conceived in the spiritual, utopian vision of the Mexican artist Leopold Flores. The *Cosmovitral* draws on the senses as an all-encompassing experience, exploring the cosmic theme of creation amid the forces of darkness and light and elemental nature, where images of flying birds transform into humans and we look into the enigmatic eye of the Milky Way.

The iron-framed building that now houses the *Cosmovitral* was initially conceived of in 1910, as an indoor marketplace celebrating Mexican national independence with the sale of handmade folk products. Exhibiting turn-of-the-century beaux-arts and art-nouveau styling, it was intentionally situated next to government offices in Mexico City to encourage a dialogue between art and politics. Once the market became defunct, in 1972, the space was transformed into a botanical garden enshrined in 1,500 sq m (16,000 sq ft) of coloured glass, so becoming a space of spiritual contemplation rather than commerce.

The strong spirituality running through the *Cosmovitral* is one that centres on the place of the human within the cosmos and elemental nature, as opposed to celebrating orthodox devotion to a godlike figure. However, despite this, the manipulation of light through the use of coloured glass draws inevitable parallels with medieval Christian church building, when coloured light radiating through stained-glass windows became symbolic of divine supernatural forces. Here, in the botanical gardens, coloured light becomes a metaphor of the spirit, and its ability to pass through matter (glass) reflects the transcendental nature of the spirit as something that moves beyond the body. This is further expressed in even more grandiose metaphor, in the repeated reference to light-emitting matter in the cosmos through the depictions of constellations that dominate the ceiling imagery.

On the north side of the ceiling, the evocative period of generation and new birth, the spring equinox, is depicted in the Andromeda constellation and the stars of Orion's belt, which gleam like black diamonds on celestial blue. The mythology of Orion is born from Greco-Roman mythology in which Orion was the lover of the moon goddess Diana who immortalized him in the night sky with the brightest stars in the firmament. Around Orion, three circular nebulae explode in indigo, purple and violet as they converge on a central glass mantel that hangs from the ceiling. As a counterpoint on the eastern part of the ceiling, the autumn equinox is depicted in the Sagittarius constellation, the part of the sky ruled by Jupiter, king of the gods and associated with the fire of creative forces that is portrayed here using amber, yellow and red glass. It is amid these astrological poles that the figures of the man and woman take centre stage.

A seething swarm of concentric circles creates a vertiginous

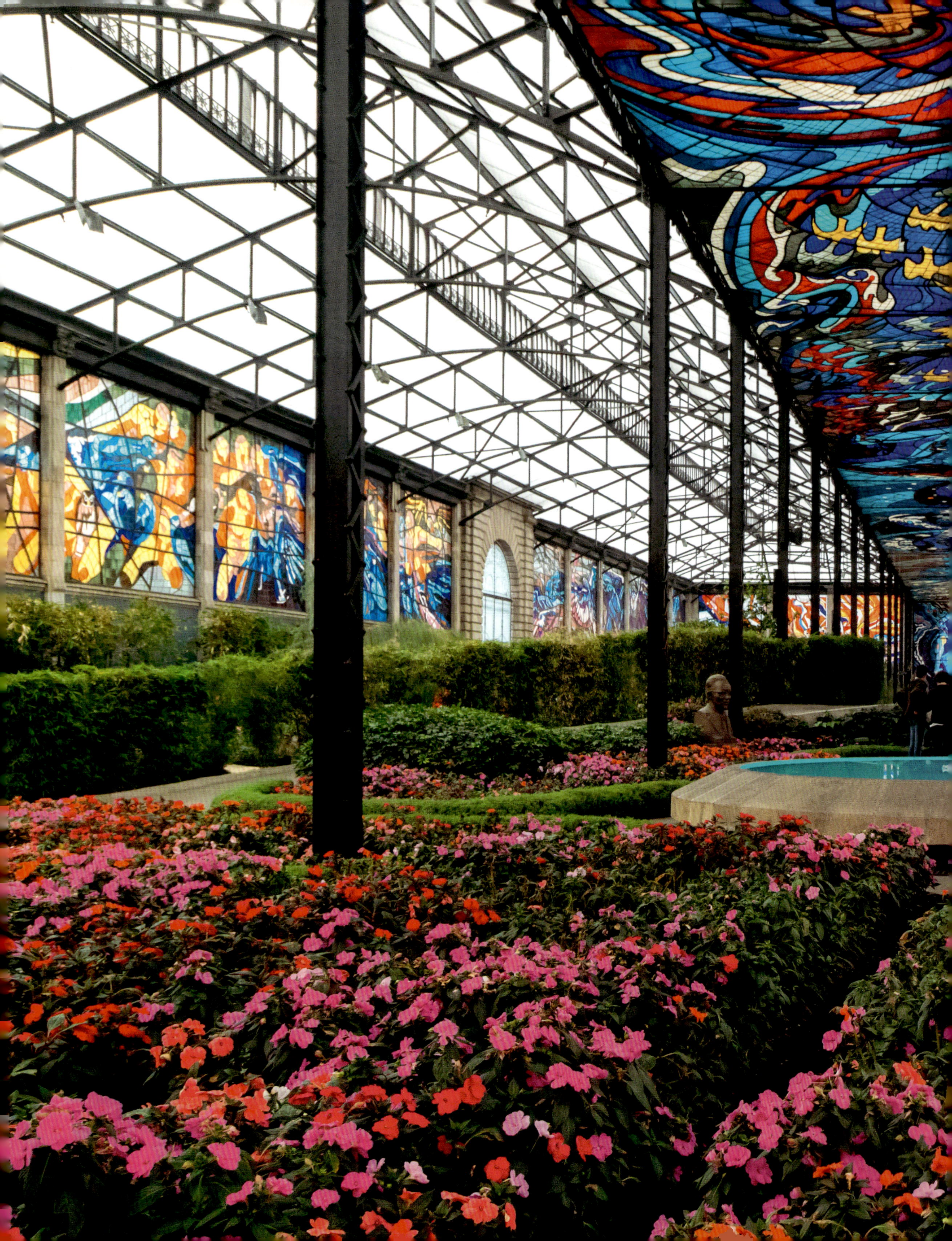

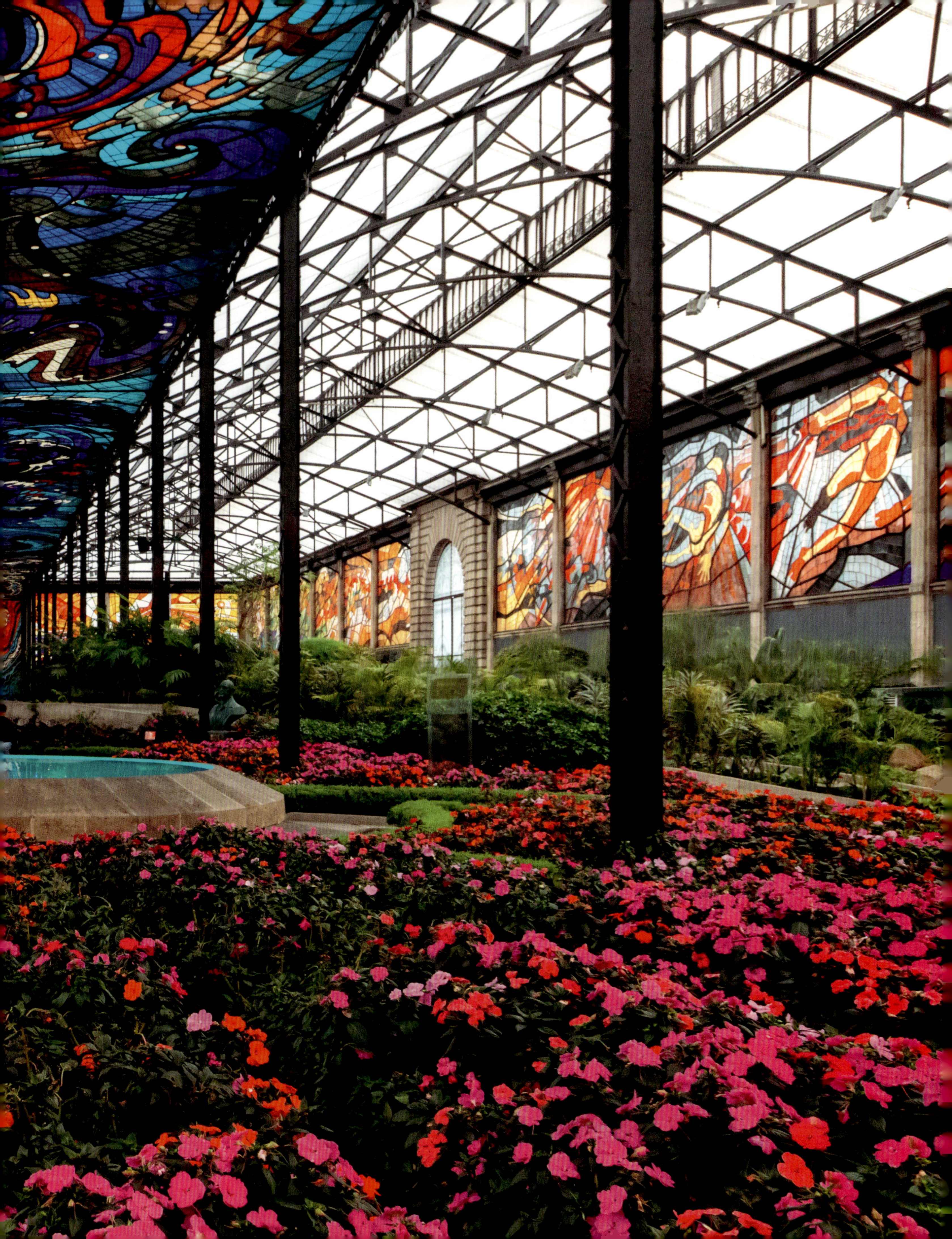

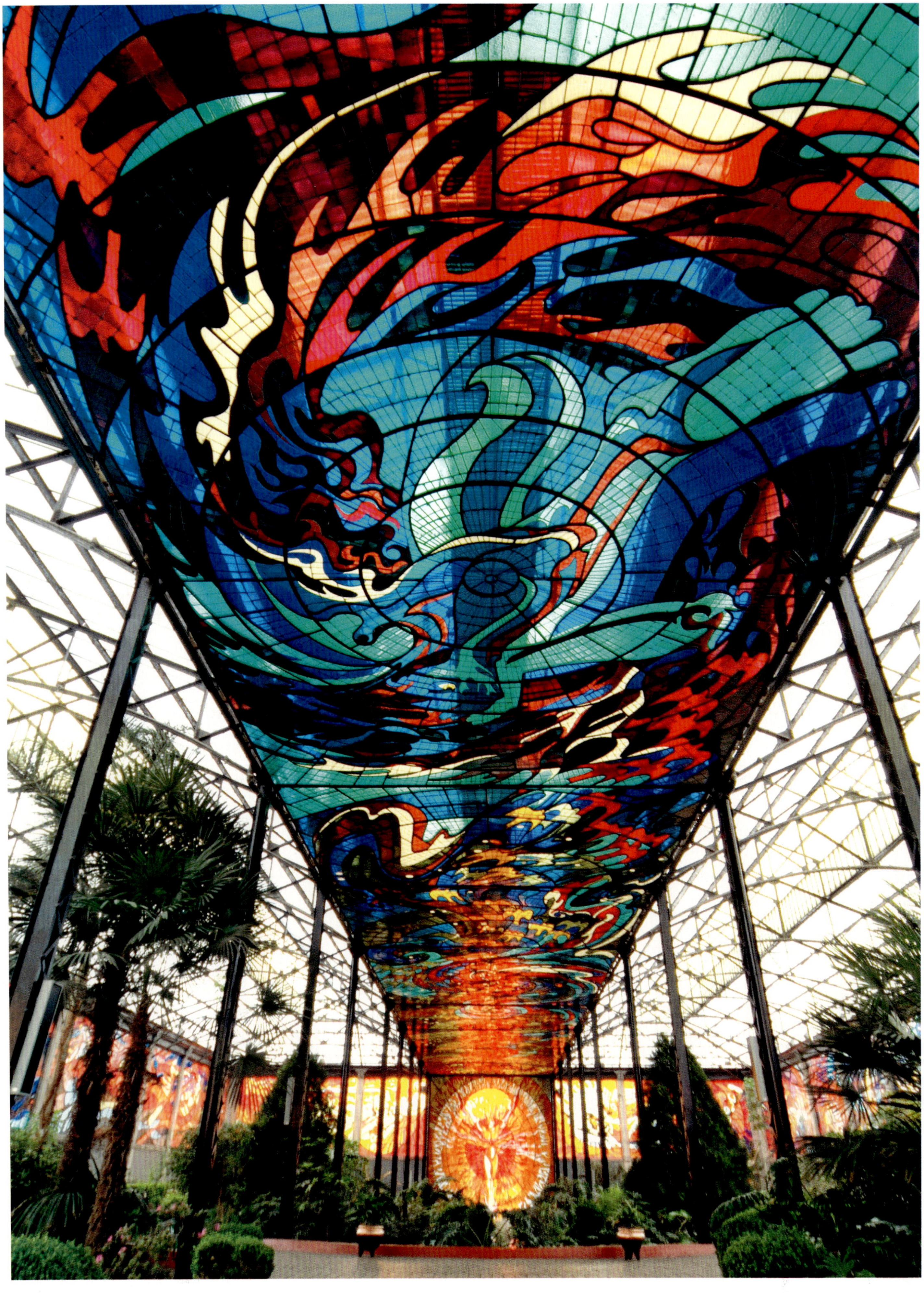

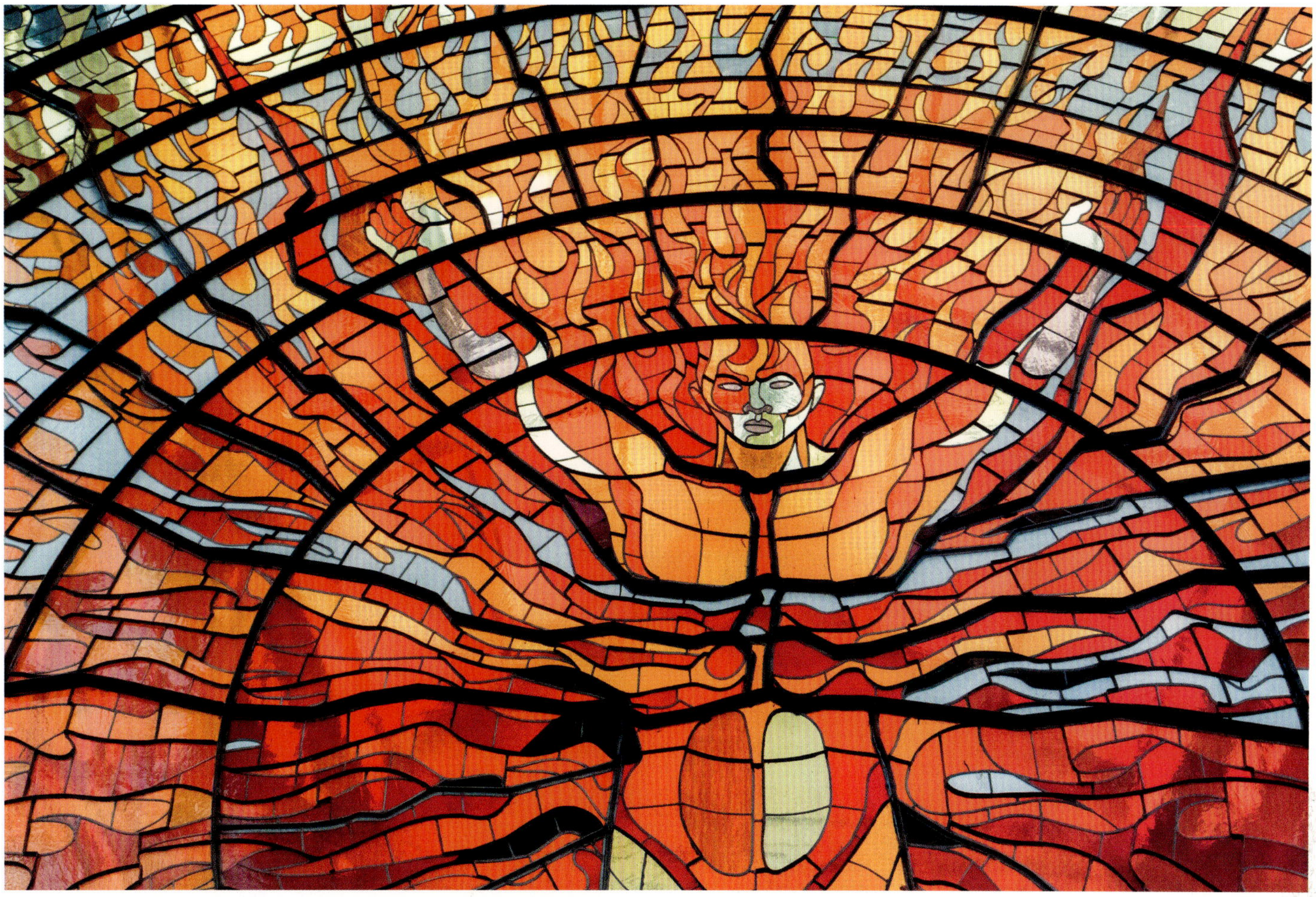

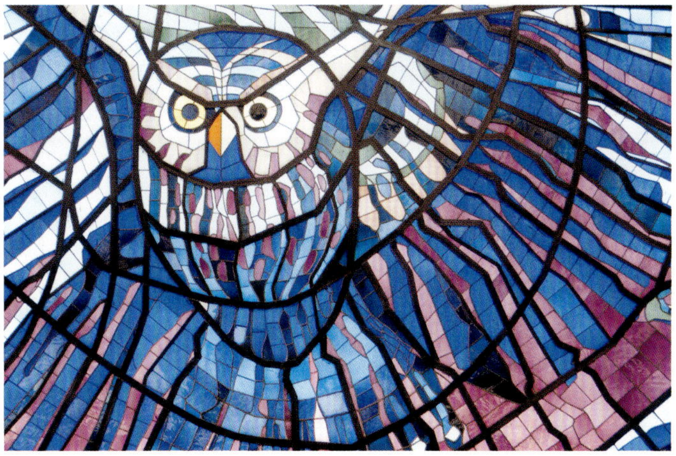

pattern around each constellation, and these reach a symbolic crescendo in the navel of the female figure, who is in other words the cosmic centre of human creation. The genesis of man, it seems, is the same as the genesis of stars – we are, it has been said before, all stardust.

The *Cosmovitral* reminds us that we are all children of the biggest star – the sun. On the eastern wall, a huge figure of a sun man (*hombre sol*) reaches towards the Sagittarius constellation, arms in the sky, feet on the ground and belly all aflame with passion. Each March, during the spring equinox, the sun aligns perfectly with this figure to flood the internal space of the garden in a rainbow bath of light for a full twenty minutes. He, too, is looking up to embrace the evanescent light from which we came and to which we will return.

Top: The blazing figure of the sun man provides a striking focal point in the garden.

Opposite: The *Cosmovitral* in the Toluca Botanical Gardens is the largest stained-glass artwork in the world.

Above: A blue-hued owl casts its beady eye over the garden.

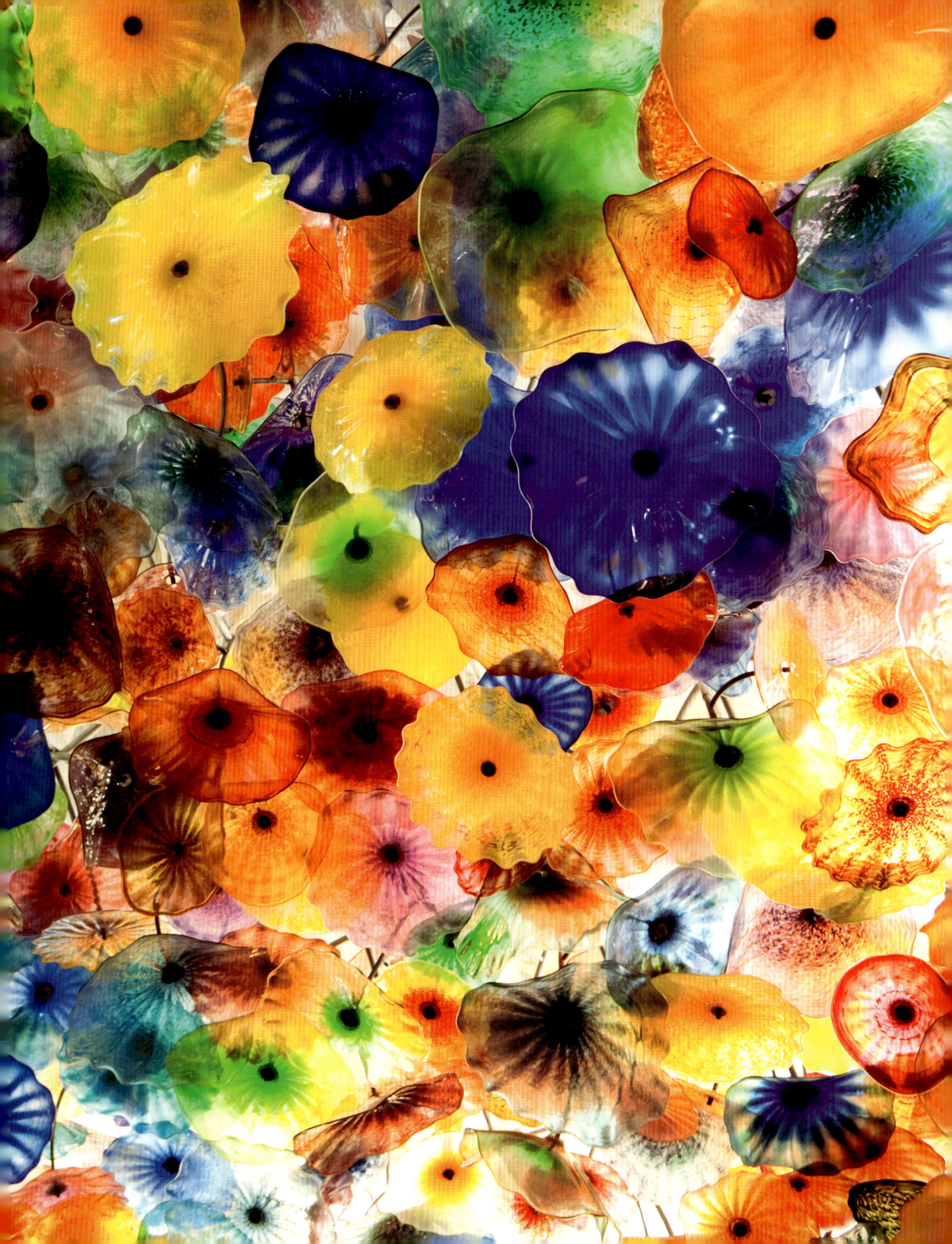

Dale Chihuly

Fiori di Como

1998

Bellagio Hotel and Casino, Las Vegas, Nevada, USA

Left: Detail of the glass flora that make up Dale Chihuly's *Fiori di Como*.

Overleaf: The vibrant and luminous glass, itself synonymous with wealth and luxury, provides a fitting centre-piece to the Bellagio Hotel and Casino.

Bellagio Hotel and Casino, USA

The Mojave Desert is North America's driest. Flanked by the basin of hard-boiled and raw land known as Death Valley, it is a place of extreme and inhospitable nature. Occasionally, and only after the right amount of rainfall, a carpet of desert flowers miraculously pushes through the sand and stone in an unexpected contrast to the otherwise barren environment. The frequency is unpredictable and never mediocre. It is a case of all or nothing, a story of extremes. But here, in the Mojave Desert, everything is extreme, from the harshness of the natural environment to the man-made city of Las Vegas, which has also broken through that severe landscape. For Las Vegas is an empire of spectacle, money, desire and artifice – a place where the natural world is tamed by wealth and the pursuit of luxury. Here, volcanoes erupt on the hour, fountains dance with precious water, rainforests of flora and fauna grow in air-conditioned atriums and gargantuan sharks are contained in tanks. And when nature refuses to blossom in the desert, the lobby of the Bellagio resort and casino is always in full and opulent bloom, with more than two thousand glass flowers suspended from the ceiling like a carpet of intensely coloured anemones.

The behemoth Bellagio complex takes its name from the eponymous Italian town in the Lake Como region, whose unique microclimate supports an abundance of luscious flora. It is from this that artist Dale Chihuly took inspiration when producing his *Fiori di Como* installation. Chihuly was first introduced to glass-blowing in 1965 and, in 1969, he became the first American to study at the prestigious Murano glassworks in Venice, Italy. Murano was the first major glass-making centre in Europe, crafting glassware that is synonymous with wealth, luxury and conspicuous consumption since its origins in the thirteenth century.

By 1980, Chihuly had started to produce large, decorative glass objects along the lines of those in the Bellagio resort, which he coloured using metal oxides and hand-blew into softly fluted shapes or spun using centrifugal forces. At the Bellagio, a frame made using five tonnes of steel holds the fragile blooms in delicate suspension. The installation was commissioned by contemporary art collector Steve Wynn, then owner and developer of the Bellagio resort, who wanted a spectacular showpiece of contemporary art to rival the aquarium at the Mirage, the neighbouring resort (also formerly owned by Wynn). Chihuly's work reportedly cost $10 million.

Fiori di Como allegedly started life as something resembling a 'chandelier', but the story goes that every time Wynn visited Chihuly's work in progress, he requested that more of the ceiling be covered. The result is a fabric of inky efflorescence that bleeds across the line of vision to disorientating effect, creating an opulence and density that is at odds with the emptiness of the desert beyond the walls. Like many in this book, this ceiling intends to overwhelm, helping the viewer to stay lost in a repetitive hallucination of colour and to forget, momentarily, about rational time and space, instead staying at the gambling tables and slot machines.

Chihuly's wildly expensive commission was not the first, or only, time that filthy lucre has made a bedfellow of modern and contemporary art. The Bellagio has played host to exhibitions of

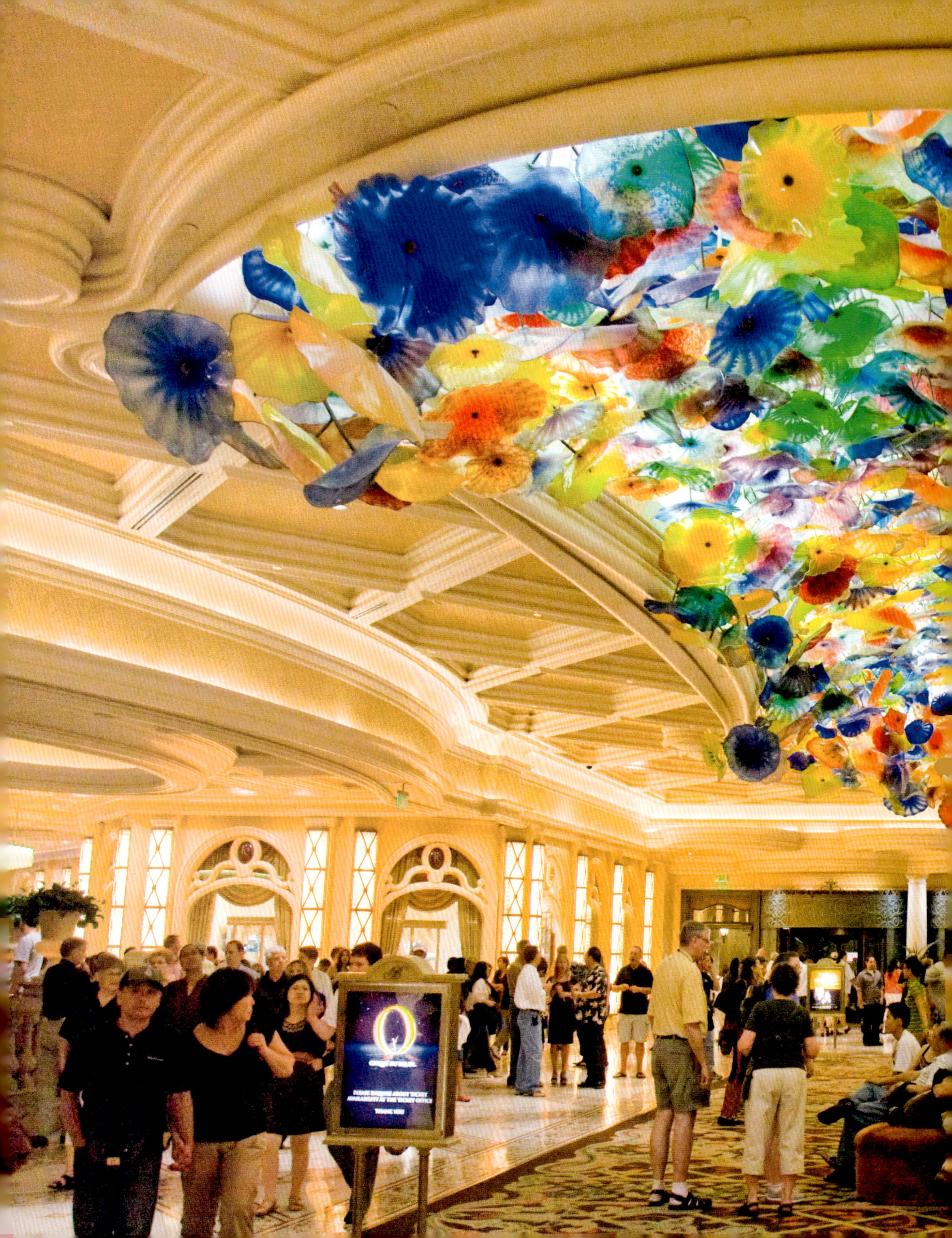
O

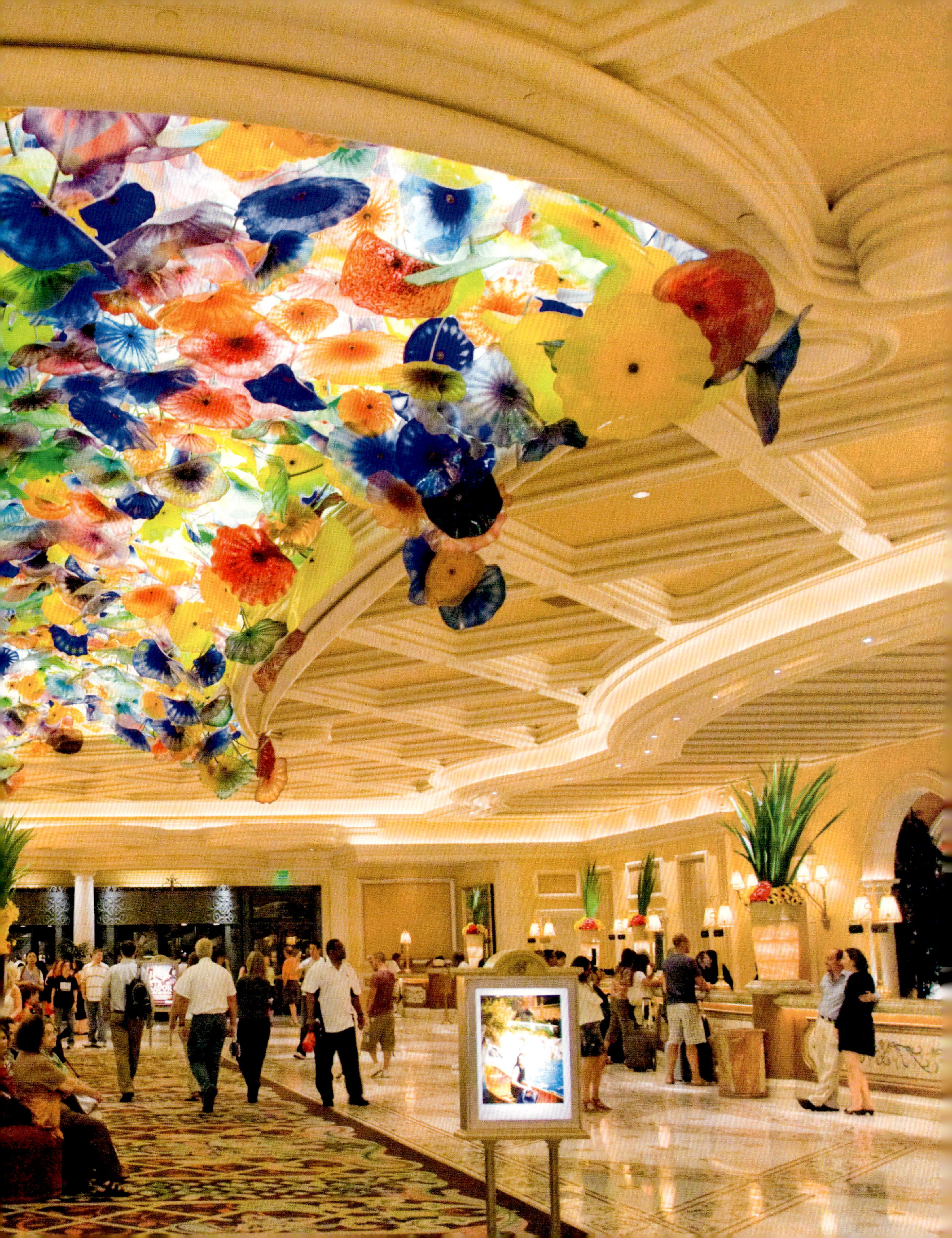

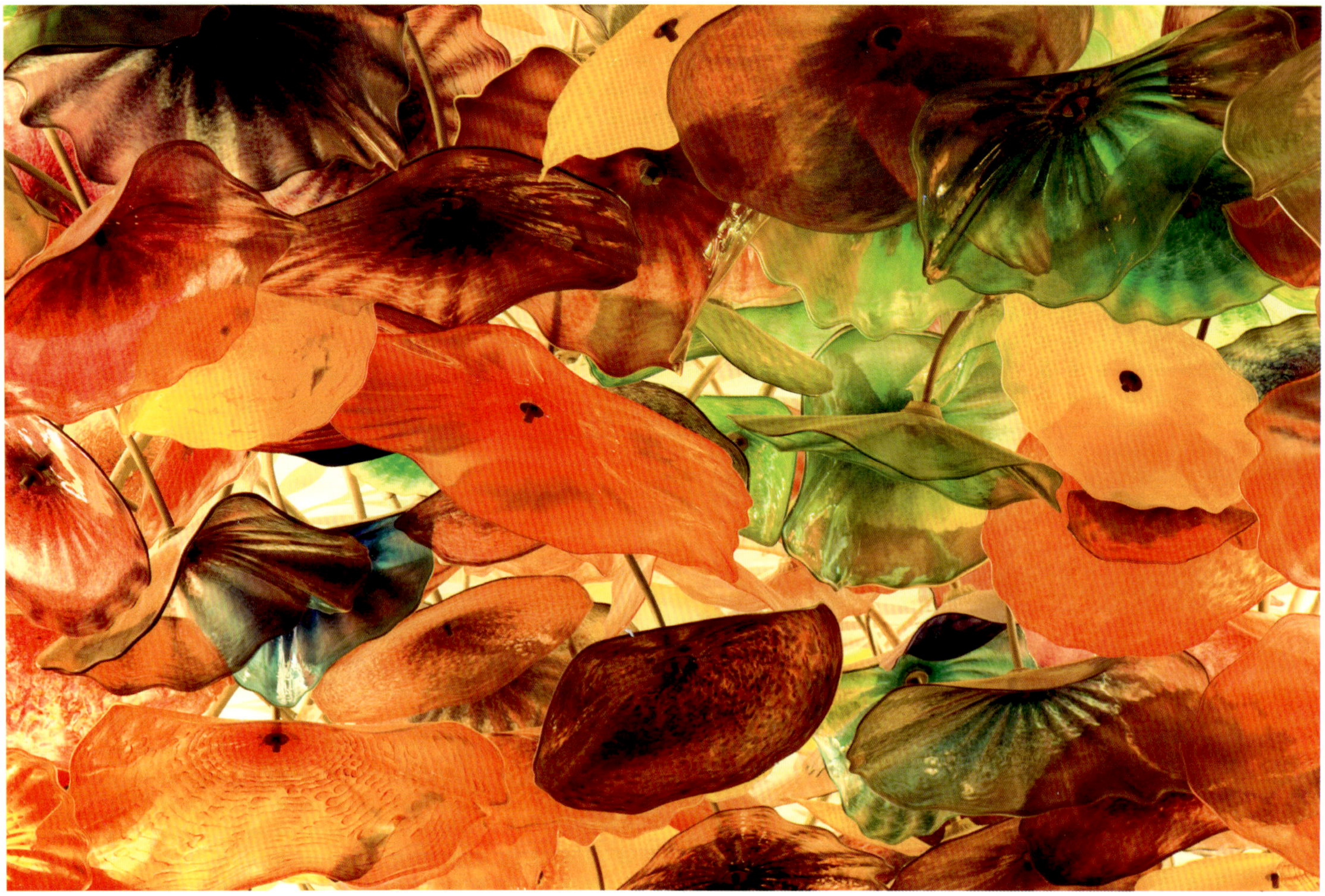

Above and opposite: Chihuly's bold flowers are in stark contrast to the barren wasteland of the desert that lies behind the hotel's walls.

Below: The flowers in Chihuly's artwork are based on those that surround Italy's Lake Como.

art from Picasso to Warhol, whereas the recent renovation of the Palms Hotel and Casino in Las Vegas has seen collaborations with blue-chip contemporary artists such as Damien Hirst, whose artfully butchered tiger shark hangs behind the bar, laughing in the face of death and decay for those who can afford to stay here. And that is what the Las Vegas love of spectacle and gambling does. It repels death in a vortex of non-stop entertainment and leisure that promises infinite resources and the seduction that nothing will end nor wither – not money, not life, not even flowers.

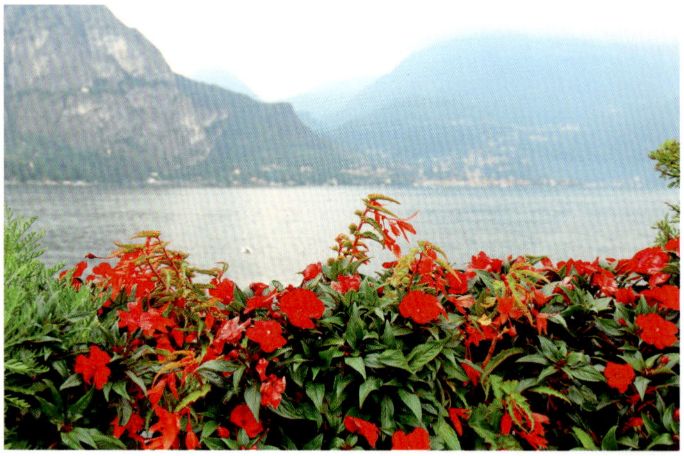

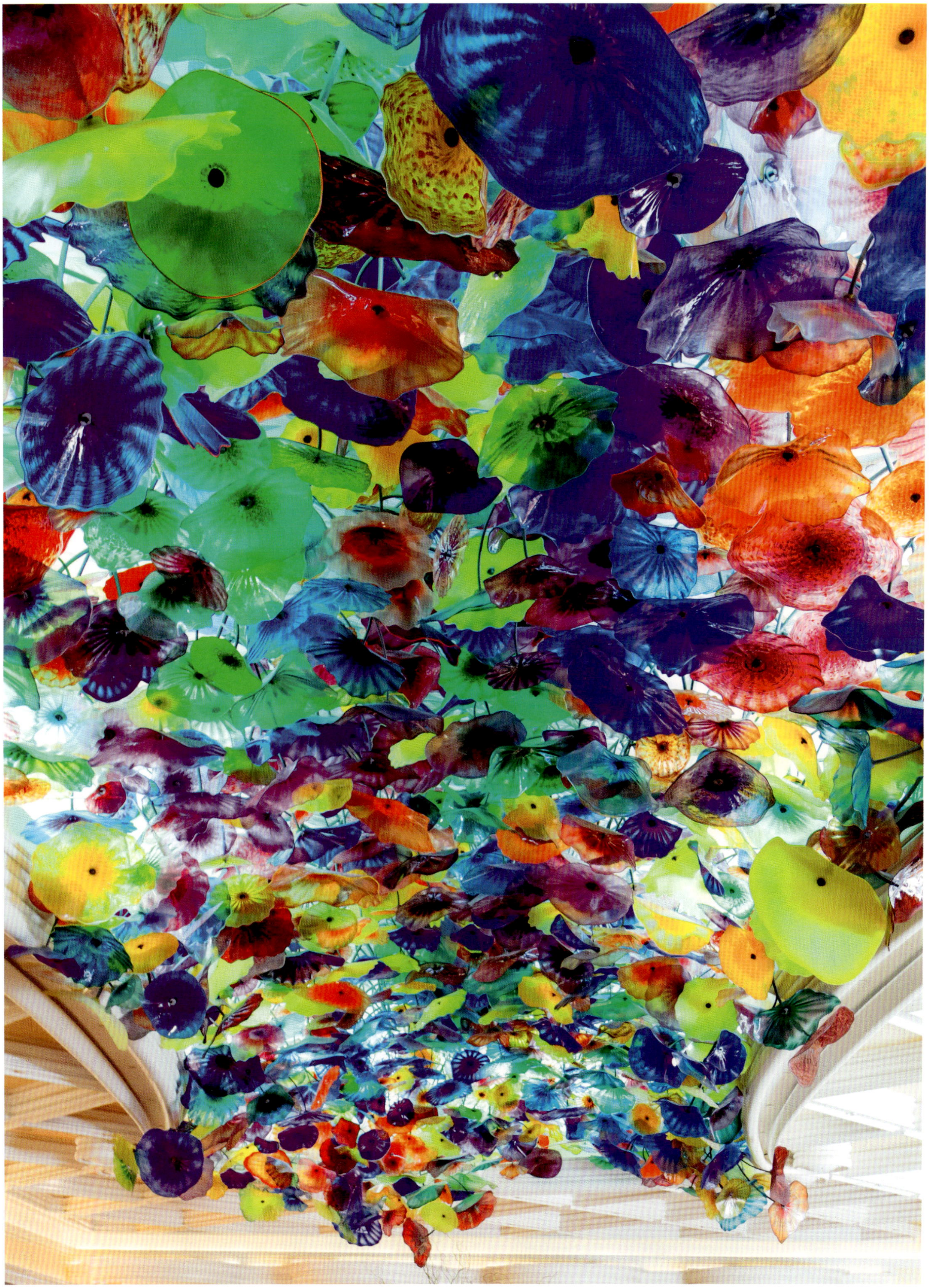

121 Bellagio Hotel and Casino

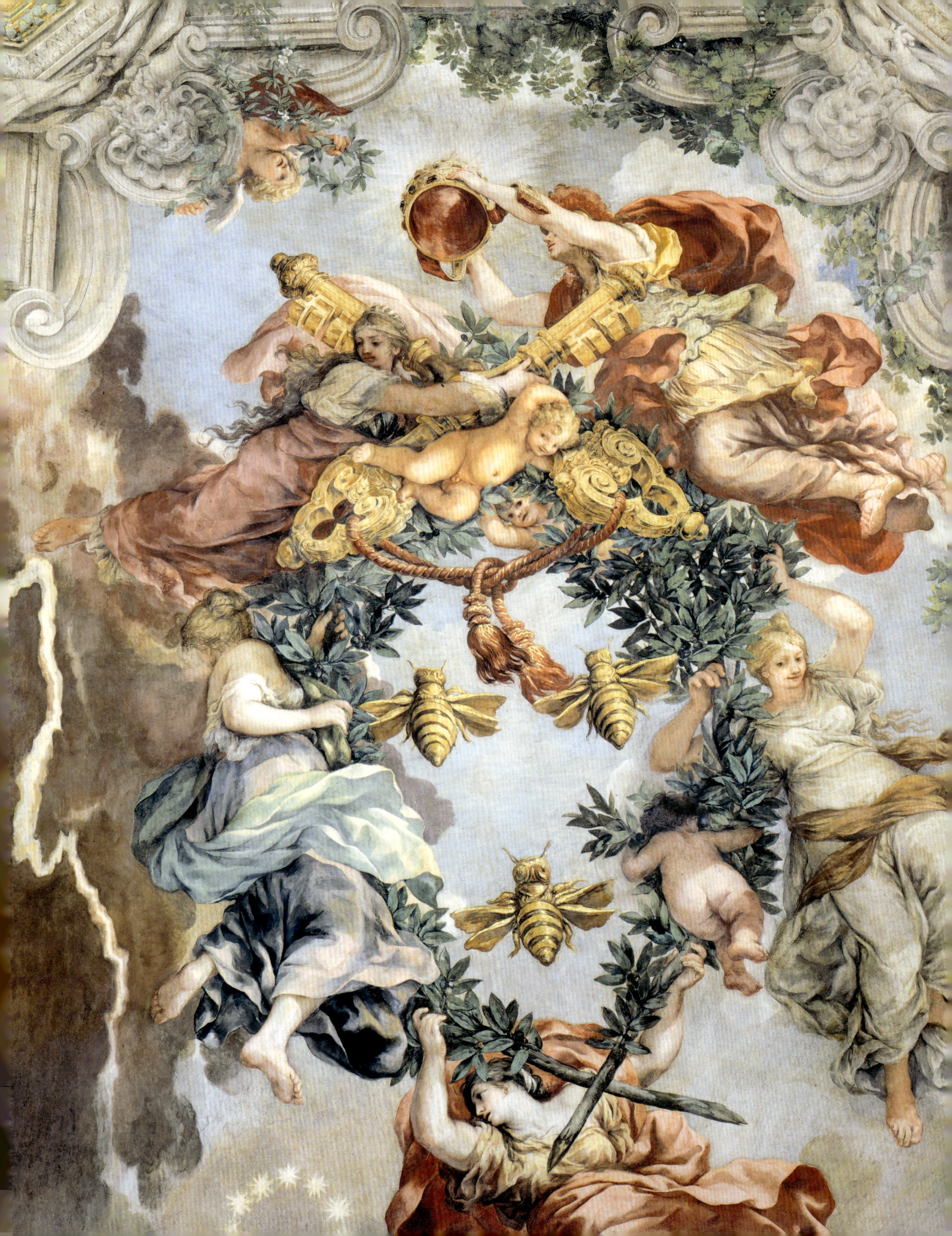

3

Power

The easiest way to overwhelm is from above, as this is the vantage point from which all authority tends to descend. And so it follows that, in spaces of power, such as at the palaces of royalty, autocracy and rulership, the ceiling becomes an exercise in communicating that domination. This is achieved through the incorporation of various messages signalling such things as immense wealth and immortality. Portrayed with sentiments ranging from intimidation to whimsy, they are realized in ways that range from painterly ingenuity in composition to the use of beetles and bees. For example, ceilings such as the *Allegory of Divine Providence* at Palazzo Barberini in Rome or the Sala dei Giganti in Palazzo del Te, Mantua, employ a *sotto in su* technique. Literally meaning 'from below to above', this involves the extreme foreshortening of figures and objects in order to create the effect that they are suspended in the air, at times bearing down and entering into the space of the beholder beneath (who duly flinches in anticipation). A similar interrogation and sense of the patron's presence can be felt on the North Portico of Blenheim Palace, Oxfordshire, in the form of a sequence of disembodied eyes.

While the ceilings featured in the following pages range from medieval Granada to Rajasthan and Turkey, there is one age that dominates: the age of absolutist authority in Europe, of prince-bishops, popes and kings. It is no coincidence that the Würzburg Residence, Banqueting House in Whitehall Palace and Palazzo Barberini all share the common theme of apotheosis – the elevation of the princely individual to sit with the gods in an imagined kingdom of immortality, as performed across these grandiose ceilings with blousy pomp, conceit and vainglory.

However, not all ceilings in the palaces of the powerful are so baldly egotistical. By contrast, the Muslim palaces of the Alhambra in Granada, Topkapı in Istanbul and Bundi Palace in Rajasthan, strike a more humble chord. While no less visually impressive and sensually rich, they reference the spirituality of creation and the flow of life without recourse to mythologizing self-aggrandizement. With power, there is also the luxury of time to indulge in pleasure, leisure and comedy, examples of which range from the elegant confines of Catherine the Great's Chinese Palace at Oranienbaum, St Petersburg, to the witty and unexpected view from below in Vicenza's Palazzo Chiericati's Sala del Firmamento.

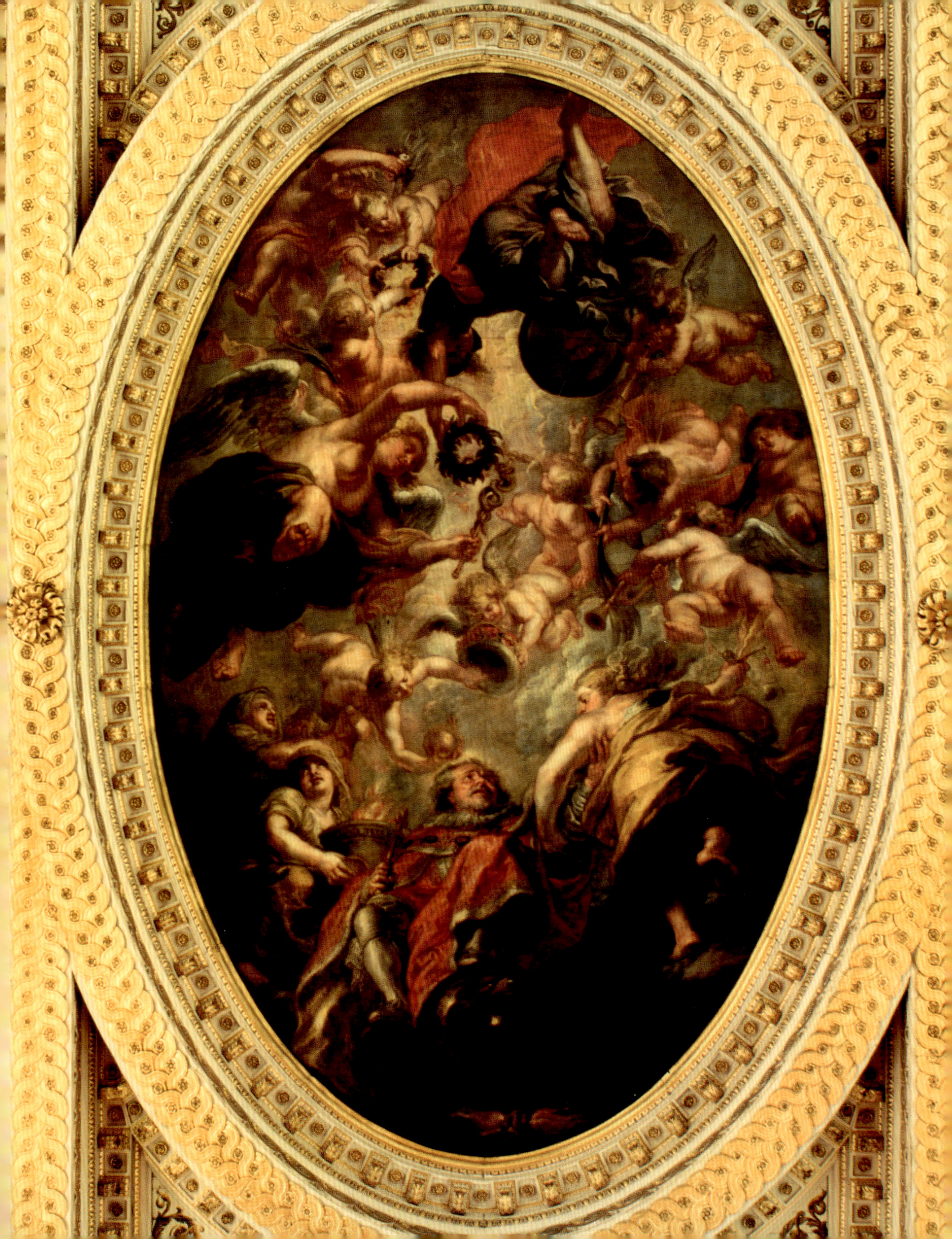

Peter Paul Rubens

Ceiling at the Banqueting House

1629

Whitehall Palace, London,

United Kingdom

Left: The central panel, *The Apotheosis of James I*, by Peter Paul Rubens.

Banqueting House, United Kingdom

On his walk from his bedchamber to the execution scaffold in 1649, one of the last things King Charles I would have seen is the painted ceiling of the Banqueting House in his residence at Whitehall Palace. Who knows, perhaps the central image of his father James I ascending into heaven was a comforting sight for Charles as he contemplated his own impending death. After all, his father had proclaimed that the king was 'God's lieutenant on Earth' and answerable only to a higher power and not the people. If the depiction of his father's triumphant immortality was anything to go by, then Charles had little to fear.

The Banqueting House is the only surviving part of the royal residence at Whitehall, otherwise destroyed by fire in 1698. Decorated and developed by Charles I and his father James I, the room draws on the prevailing styles in continental European art and architecture and seeks to reflect the elegance and power of a new Great Britain. The reign of James I, king of England and of Scotland, brought the two hostile nations together and saw the first significant expansion of art and culture in the newly formed United Kingdom. The Banqueting House was designed by Inigo Jones between 1619 and 1622, the first homegrown talent to produce classically inspired buildings in Britain; buildings that would borrow from the language of ancient Roman and Italian Renaissance architecture to reflect Britain's membership of a cultural elite, one that could draw comparisons with the powerful civilized nations of the past.

As a nation, England had been reliant on outsourced European skill to craft the art and architecture that served the British Crown, and on this occasion the task of painting the ceiling fell to Sir Peter Paul Rubens. Unfazed by the daunting prospect of producing the 225 sq m (2,400 sq ft) of painted canvas required for the Banqueting House commission, Rubens boasted: 'My talent is such that no undertaking, however vast in scope or diversified in subject, has ever surpassed my courage.'

Commissioned in 1629 and completed in 1636, the narrative cycle is a historical allegory to glorify the reign of English King James I, who had died in 1625. The Stuart monarch had succeeded to the thrones of Scotland (as James VI in 1567) and England (as James I in 1603) when the last Tudor monarch Elizabeth I died without an heir. James I's greatest political achievement was the unification of England and Scotland after centuries of hostile relations. The decorative scheme in the Banqueting House ceiling was intended to be a microcosm of the new united power, as well as a representation of the divine nature of kingship. Drawing on the visual language of choice in European art, Rubens delivers his message through a mixture of allegorical, biblical and mythological figures.

At the north end, the first of the three major panels is titled *The Union of the Crowns*. Scotland and England appear as female personifications – Scotland in a white gown, the colour of Scottish patron saint St Andrew, and England in red, the colour of St George's cross. Both hold a crown over an infant Charles I, who is depicted here as the offspring of the two countries united by his father, who presides over the scene holding his sceptre, while a helmeted figure who is either Britain or the figure of Minerva, goddess of wisdom, ties the two nation's crowns together.

The central panel, *The Apotheosis of James I*, sees the king raised

Below left: Peter Paul Rubens, *The Union of the Crowns*. The countries of Scotland and England appear as female personifications dressed in red (England) and white (Scotland).

Below right: Peter Paul Rubens, *The Peaceful Reign of James I*.

Opposite: A full view of the nine canvases of Rubens' ceiling at the Banqueting House.

to the status of a deity. He is accompanied by an eagle, symbol of Jupiter, king of the mythological pagan gods, and is coaxed gently into the realms of immortality by a young woman in yellow who is the figure of Justice. Other female personifications of Piety, Zeal and Religion represent the king's virtues, and Minerva, with a figure of Victory, carries the triumphal crown. Longer rectangular panels on either side of the ceiling celebrate the peace and prosperity of the Jacobean reign. Cornucopia and chariots groaning with fruit suggest abundance, while frolicking putti convince the viewer of the sort of leisure that only comes with stable rulership.

At the south end, another panel, *The Peaceful Reign of James I*, is fitted above where the monarch would sit. The relationship between peace, stability and prosperity is credited to the wisdom of the monarch in multiple ways. Here, James I appears as an echo of King Solomon, the Old Testament king of Israel known for his wisdom, and in case we missed the point, Minerva, the helmeted goddess of wisdom, slays Mars, the god of war in his red cape. In the foreground this is reiterated again with the figure of Mercury holding a caduceus entwined with two snakes, which is another symbol of peace. Two lovely women embrace – they are presumably figures of Peace and Plenty – and gave Rubens a chance to exploit his reputation as a painter of voluptuous quivering female flesh.

Charles I and his father's belief in their God-given right to rule, celebrated here, led ultimately to the temporary fall of the monarchy, when citizens no longer wanted to believe in the unswerving virtues of their arrogant Stuart rulers. In light of this, Rubens' ceiling was never going to save the king.

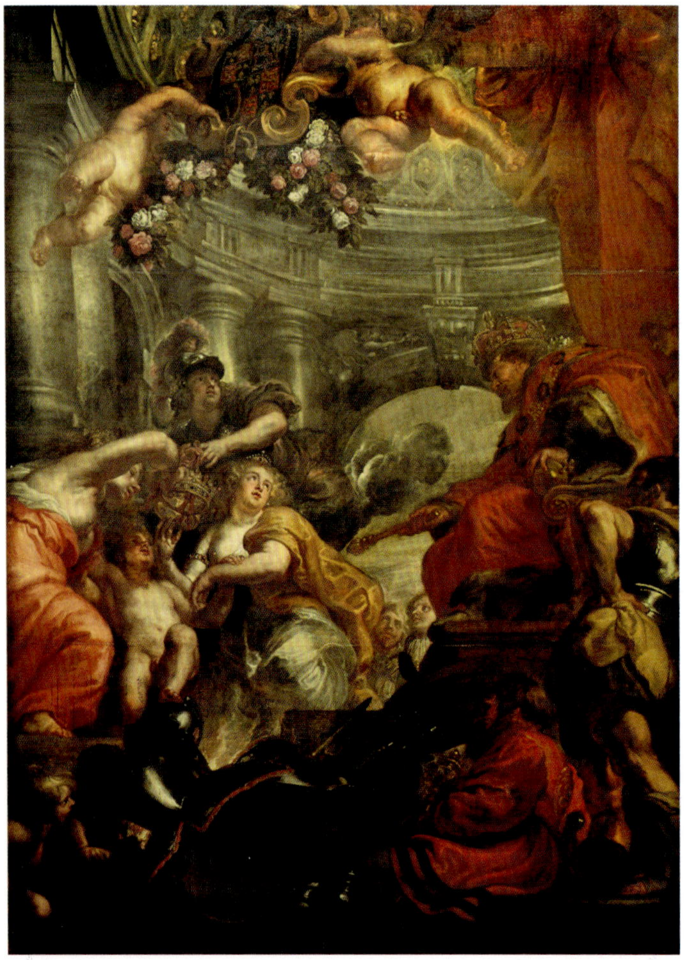

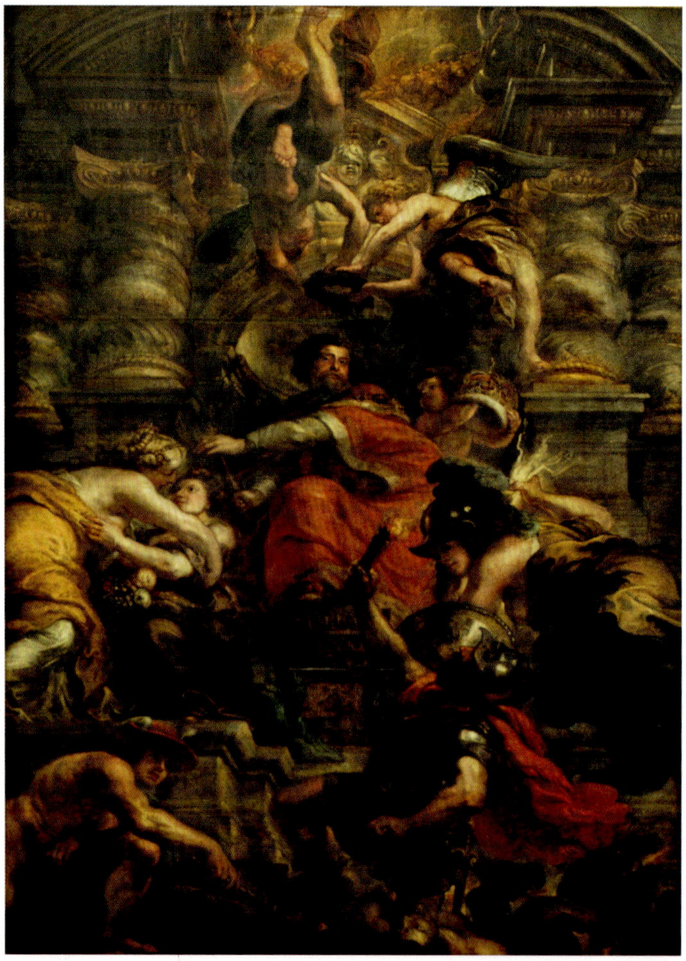

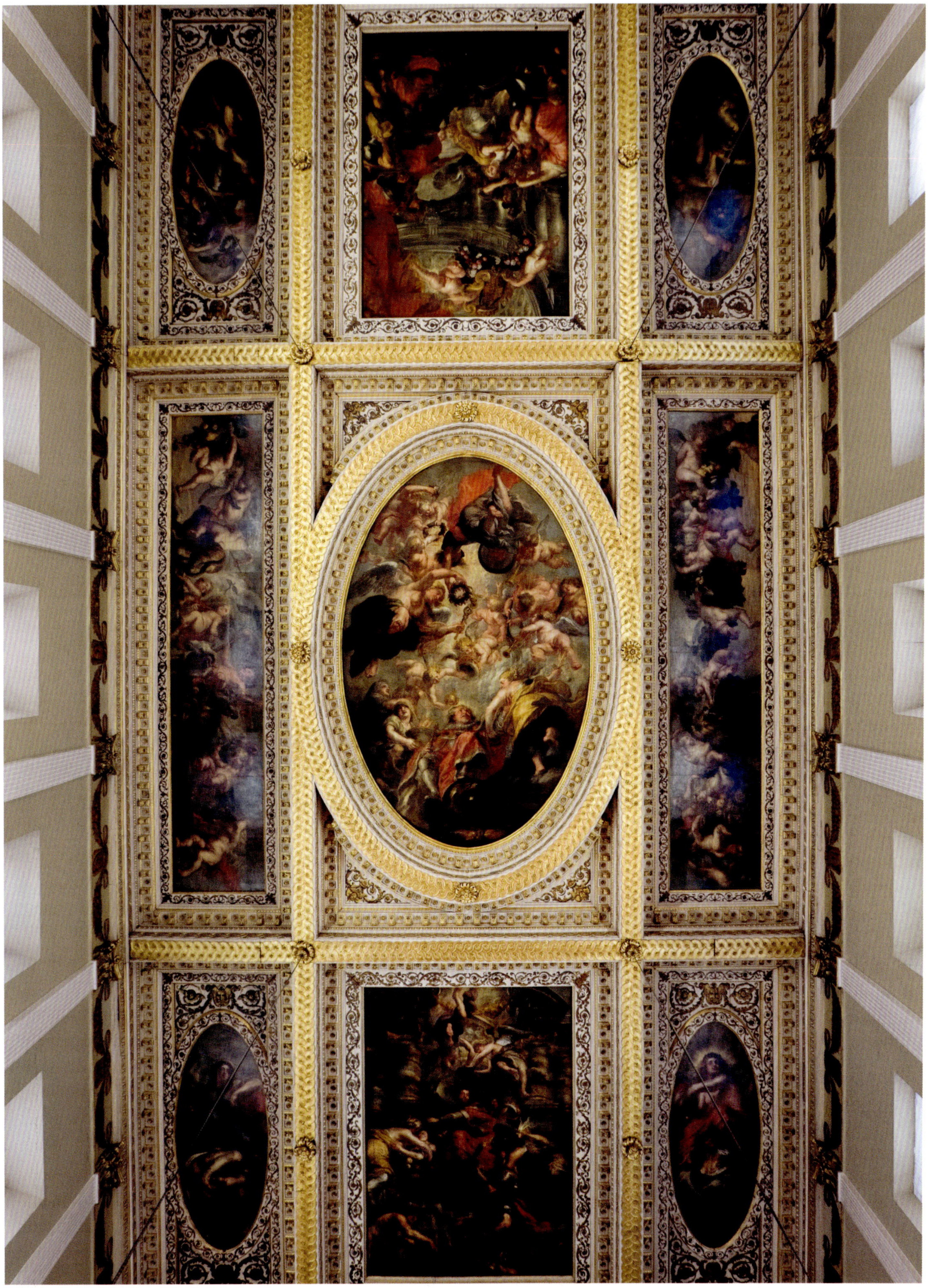

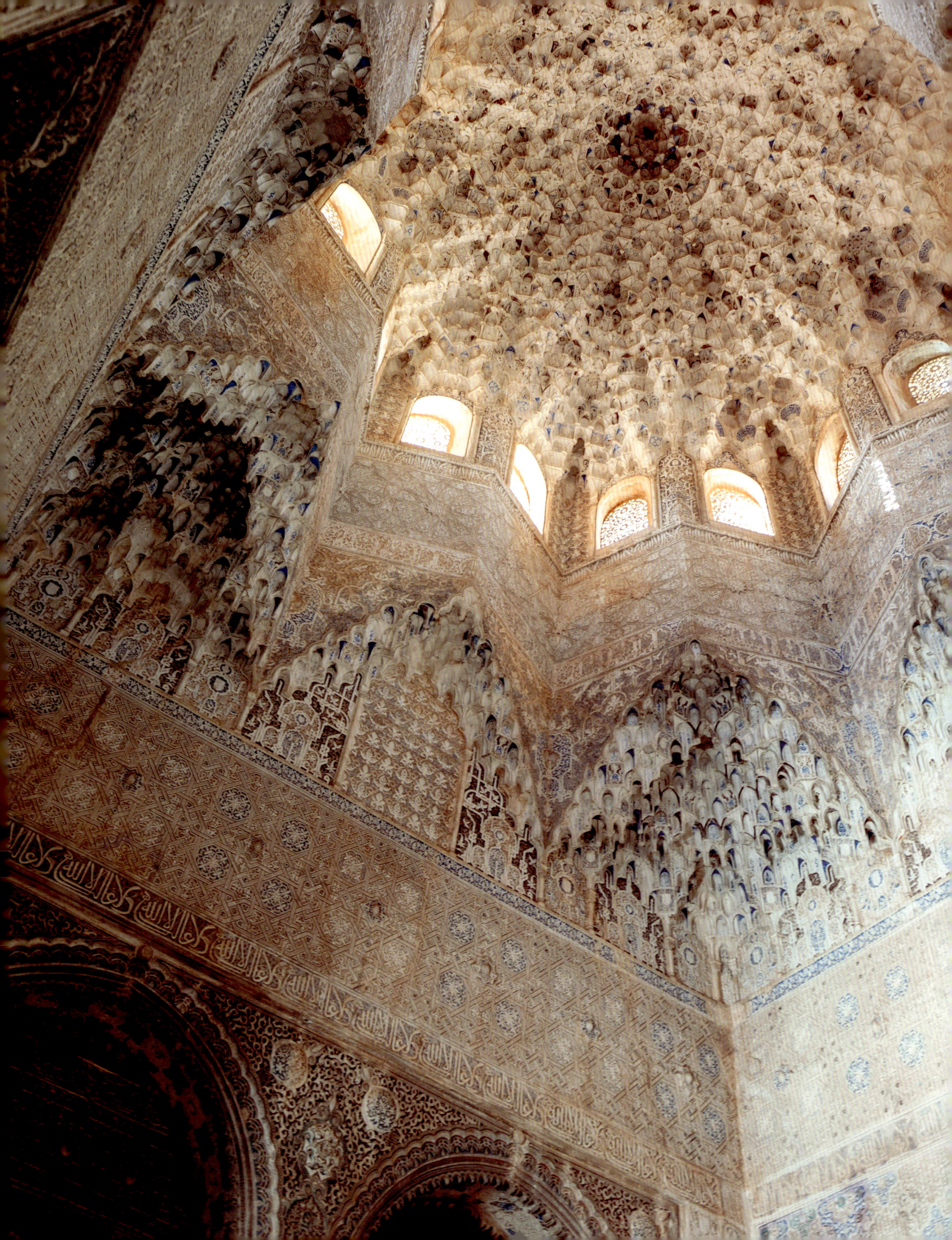

Hall of the Abencerrajes

14th Century

Alhambra Palace, Granada, Spain

Left: The dome of the Alhambra Palace, a thirteenth-century Moorish palace complex built on Roman ruins in Granada, Spain.

Overleaf: Hall of the Abencerrajes at Alhambra Palace.

Alhambra Palace, Spain

In tales of power, extreme beauty and extreme violence are rarely absent. So, the golden honeycombed ceiling of the Sala de los Abencerrajes in the Alhambra Palace bears silent witness to a glorious and gory past and the Nasrid caliphate that occupied the palace as its seat from 1334–91. Nestled in the Assabica Hills of Granada in Andalusia, Spain, the grandiose complex is the oldest Muslim palace to have survived from the Middle Ages. Described by Moorish poets as a 'pearl among emeralds' in allusion to the green space of the forests that surround it, the palace's prevailing design aesthetic was to replicate a sense of paradise on Earth. To do this without images, which were – and continue to be – a graven taboo in Muslim culture, the decoration and aesthetic experience of the Alhambra relies on the effects of the forces of nature at play with the architecture and manipulation of materials such as stucco and stone.

For example, the palace is designed around quadrangles, allowing the inter-penetration of exterior courtyards open to the dazzling sunlight, while creating shadowy interior spaces. Furthermore, the movement of water is sensed everywhere, from fountains whose flow is stemmed to arrive in pools contained within marble basins that reflect the colours, inscriptions and textured surfaces of the interiors. To mark the transition between such spaces, Islamic architecture uses the characteristic feature of the muqarnas. This elaborate structure resembles the naturally occurring phenomena of honeycomb and stalactite formations and was typically applied to the undersides of domes, pendentives, cornices, squinches, arches and vaults to differentiate and transition between smooth planes of architecture.

In the Hall of the Abencerrajes, a glorious octagonal golden starburst of muqarnas forms a canopy above the room. In a world without images, the splendour and complexity of universal creation needed to be celebrated in different, more metaphysical ways, and the elaborate technical design of the muqarnas, with their numerous distinct units, conveyed the many atomic particles of existence – all in connection with God. Contemplated in this way, the muqarnas marked a transitory space between the finite living world and the eternal spirit world, the entry point to which was represented by the dome extending up towards an imagined heavenly sphere.

Historians have suggested that the relatively closed nature of the Hall of the Abencerrajes denotes its former function as a winter music room. Here, sound and vision could intermingle, with the vibrating chords of plucked instruments and flutes heard through shafts of coloured light from the many stained-glass windows beneath the muqarnas. Just as in Christian churches, the effect was to stimulate the senses into perceiving God in the material world.

However, this paradisiacal serenity is interrupted by the legend that gives the hall its name. According to this tale, the Abencerrajes family (Arabic for 'saddler's sons') was a powerful faction in fifteenth-century Granada. One of the clan was so consumed with unquenchable passion for the daughter of the royal family that he was caught climbing up to her bedroom window. Enraged by this assault, the sultan ordered that all of the family be locked in one of the rooms of the palace and slaughtered. Other versions suggest that the last sultan of

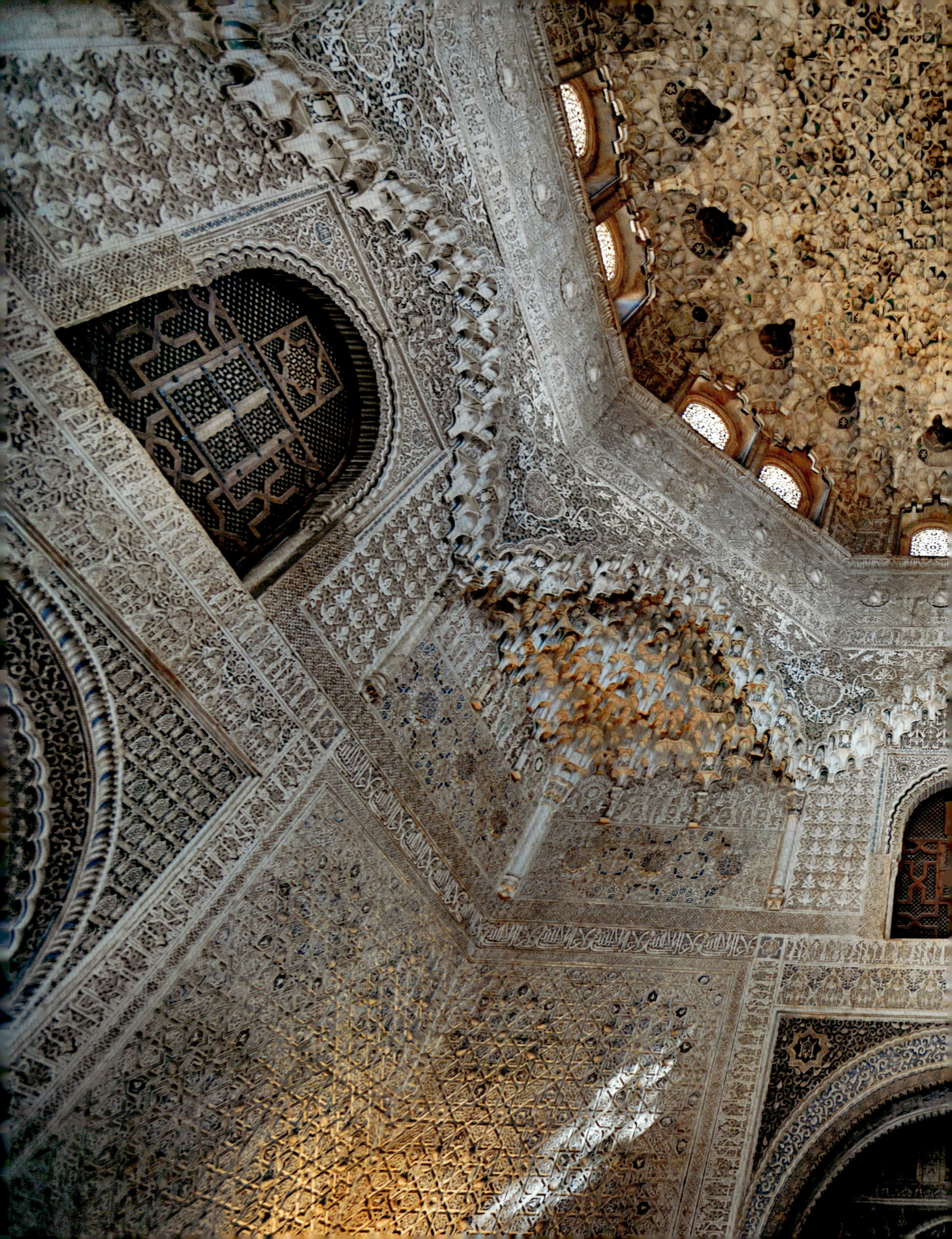

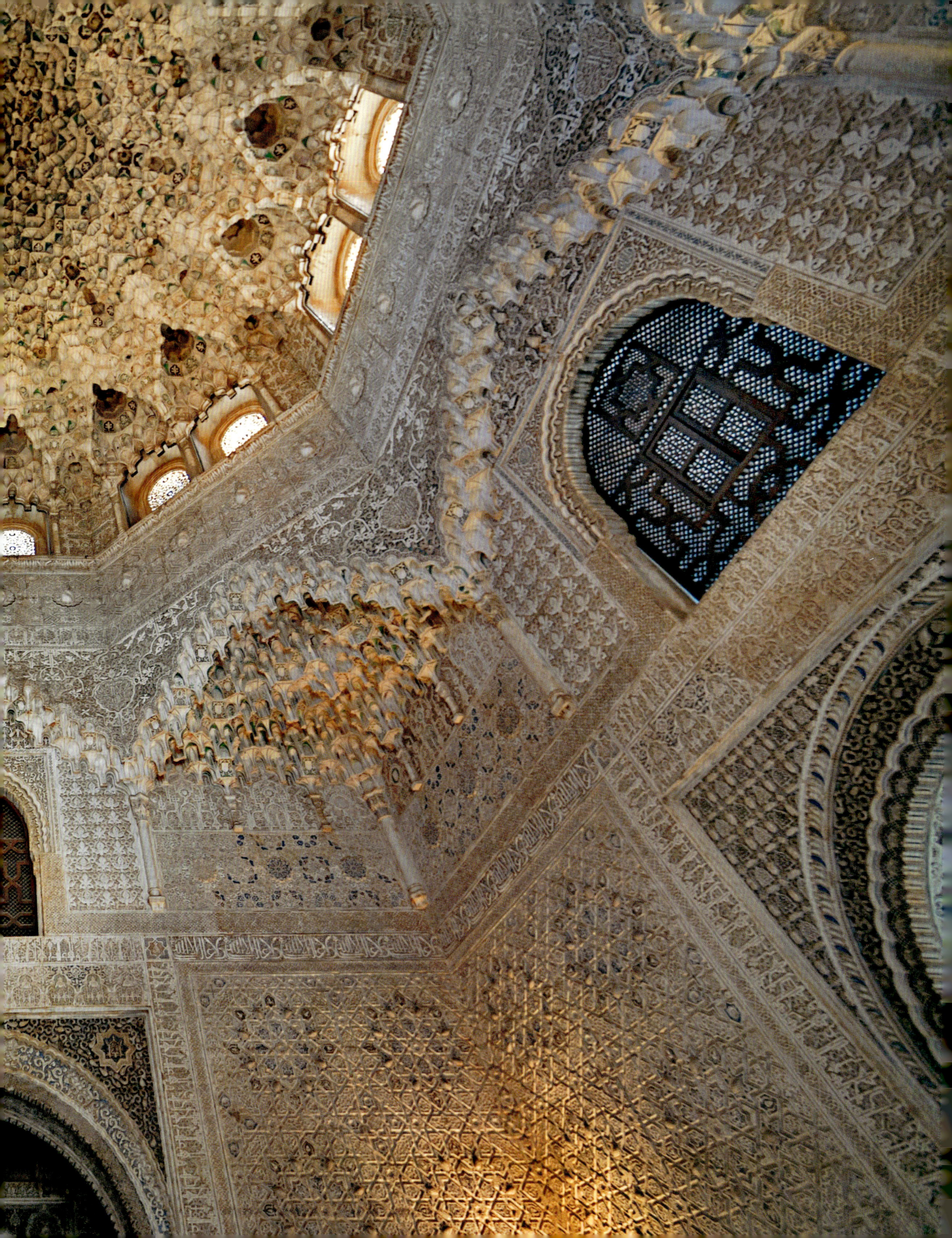

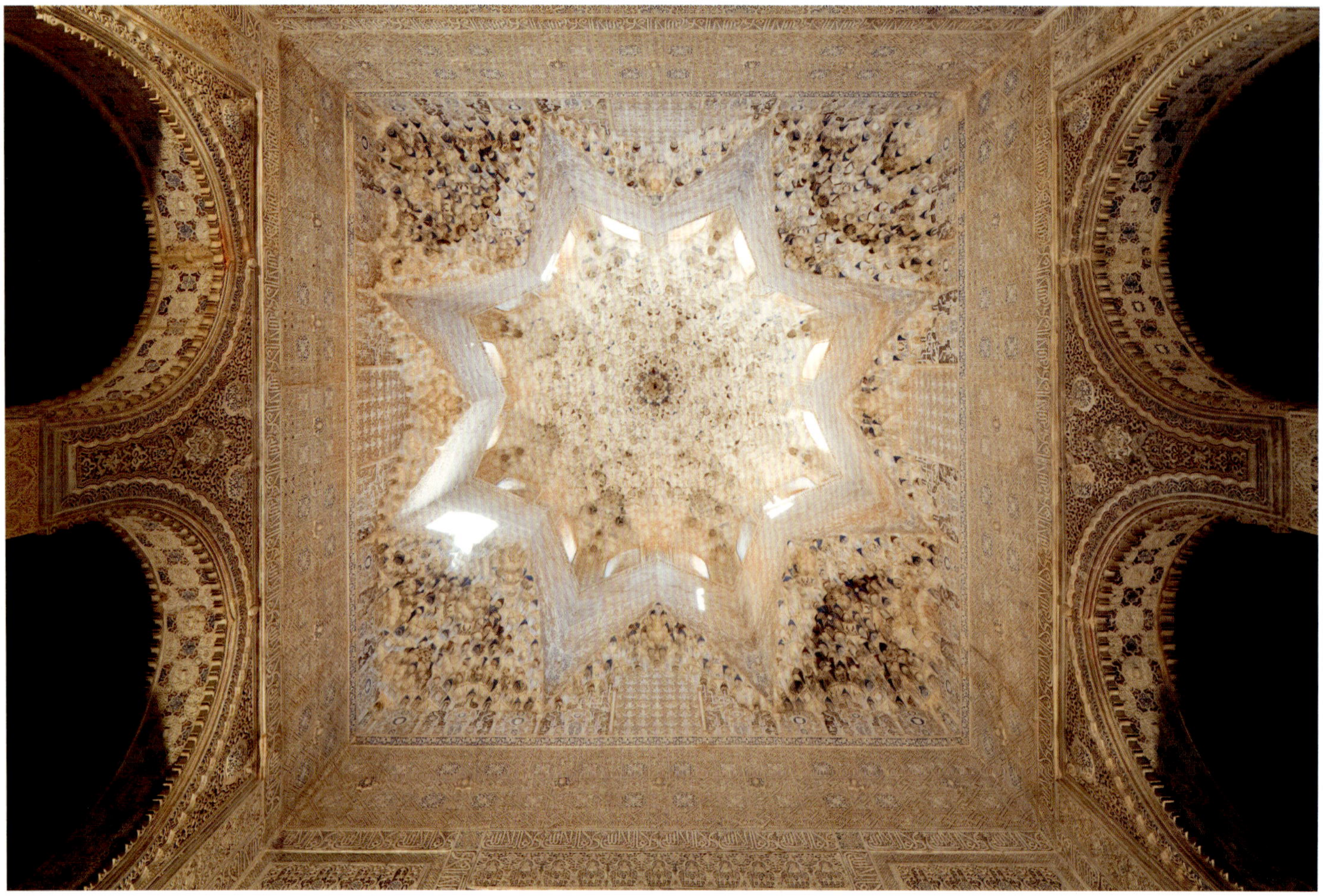

Granada invited the chiefs of the Abencerrajes to a banquet inside the hall, before summarily murdering them. Supposed evidence of this massacre lies in the ferruginous stains around the marble basin on the floor, said to be the indelible reminder of spilled blood that stills haunts the space. It is a brutal tale to consider amid such artistry of design and spirituality, which is perhaps why this narrative seized the romantic imagination and has been perpetuated across art and literature and even inspired two operas.

Above: A view of the dome at Alhambra Palace.

Below: Detail of the ornate walls and ceiling of the Hall of the Abencerrajes of the Alhambra Palace. The mocarabes honeycomb work and stalactite design may be a symbolic representation of the cave where Mohammed received the Koran.

Opposite: Detail of the vaulted ceiling in the Hall of the Abencerrajes.

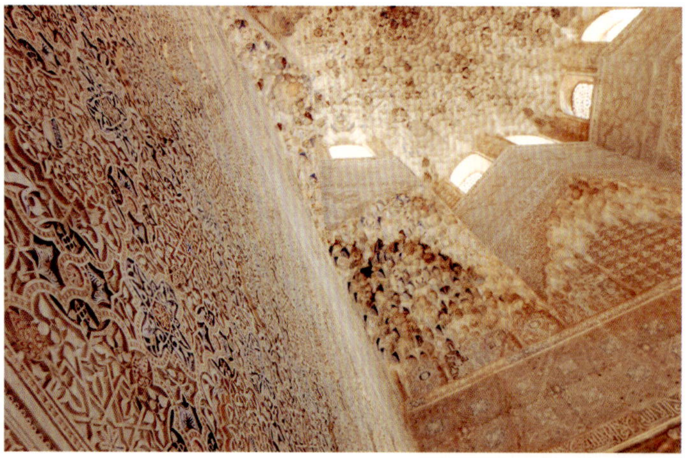

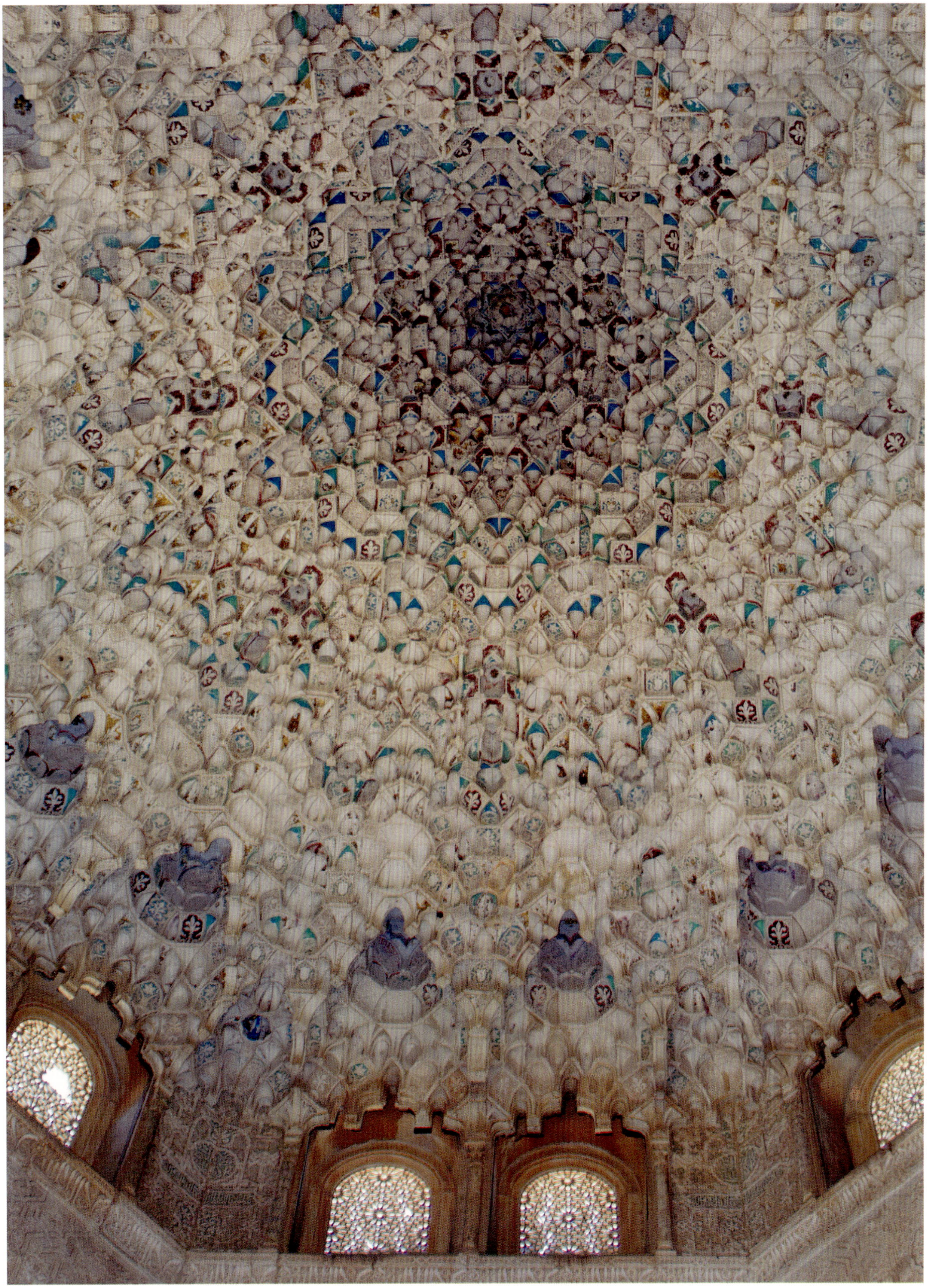

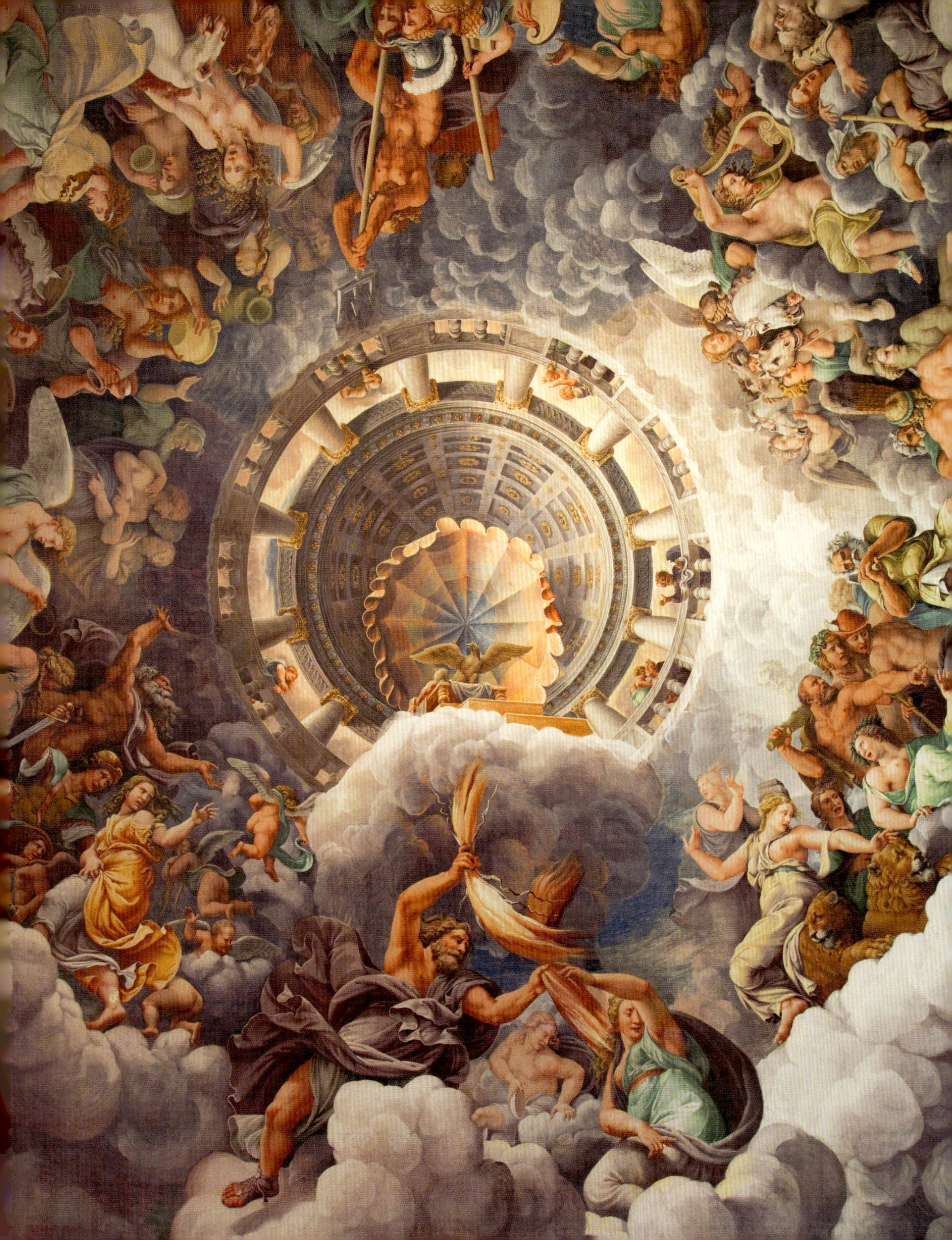

Giulio Romano
Sala dei Giganti
1532–35
Palazzo del Te, Mantua, Italy

Left and overleaf: In the illusionistically painted, Jupiter, king of the gods, throws lightning down to defeat the giants that are painted lower down in the same room.

Palazzo del Te, Italy

What happens when you take on the mythological gods of Mount Olympus? A vortex of destruction in which rocks and thunderbolts rain from the sky, buildings collapse and your senses are choked. That's the feeling of walking into the *Sala dei Giganti*, or the Room of the Giants in Palazzo del Te. The story is a cautionary tale from Greek mythology, often known as the 'Gigantomachy', when the giants of the earth moved mountains to try and scale Mount Olympus, the mythological home of the pagan gods, and overthrow them. Jupiter, king of the gods, reacted by harnessing all the bellicose power of the sky to slay these contenders for supremacy, hurting them horribly and suppressing them under the earth where they lay pulsing in pain, only to resurface as erupting volcanoes and tremoring earthquakes.

The work was painted by Giulio Romano, artist in residence for the Gonzaga court at Mantua. He had been summoned from Rome by Federico II Gonzaga to design and decorate Palazzo del Te, the pleasure villa of the Gonzaga court just outside Mantua. Romano, a protégé of the artist Raphael, had grown up in Rome at the foot of the Capitoline Hill, surrounded by the rubble and ruins of antiquity, echoes of which resonate here in both the reference to classical buildings and the close observation of broken masonry. The vertigo-inducing ceiling corkscrews upwards into an illusionistically painted dome within a temple that is similar to both the dome of the Pantheon and the emperor Nero's Golden House, both in Rome. Here we see a billowing canopy under which Jupiter's throne is perched, along with his accompanying imperial eagle. These imperial allusions were intentional; Federico Gonzaga had received the imperial investiture from his ally and protector, the Holy Roman Emperor Charles V.

Beneath Jupiter, who hurls a bolt of lightning at the insubordinate giants, the residents of Mount Olympus survey the destruction and mutilation. A one-eyed giant Cyclops releases a silent agonized howl as his head is crushed between tumbling rocks. On the north wall, the apparent supporting architecture of the room gives way, holding us in horrible suspension, as we wait for the crash. At the part where the vaulting rises, four personifications of the wind blast gusts of air and blow the hornpipes of war. The painting, from ceiling to floor, is seamless and cycloramic, the effect of which makes it both claustrophobic and vertiginous. Moreover, once inside the room, one is also inside the painting and it seems as if there is no way out.

The effect of Romano's painting was equally profound on Renaissance contemporaries. The biographer and art theorist Giorgio Vasari suggested that there was nothing more horrible and terrifying in paint than the *Sala dei Giganti*. On the whole, Renaissance painting cycles were designed to privilege the viewer, giving them a unique vantage point that suggested that all the action was playing out for them at a safe distance. Here these expectations are reversed; the painted ceiling fuses seamlessly with the walls of the room, so there is no clear distinction between the real space of the room's architecture and the artificial space of the image. A bearded giant dressed in green turns to snarl into the space at the centre of the room, with an accusatory stare that suggests that the action above is playing out not for the spectators' viewing pleasure but because of them.

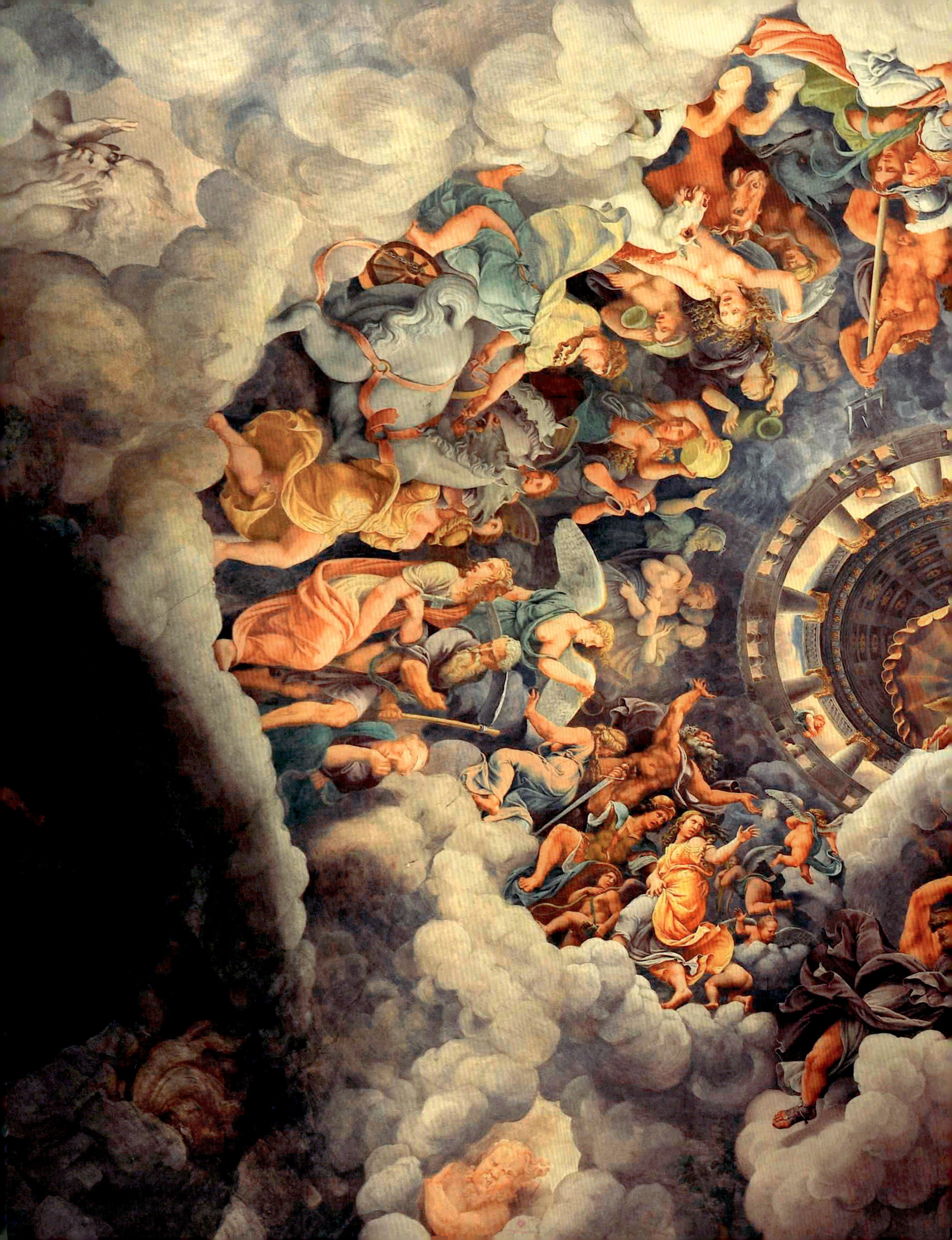

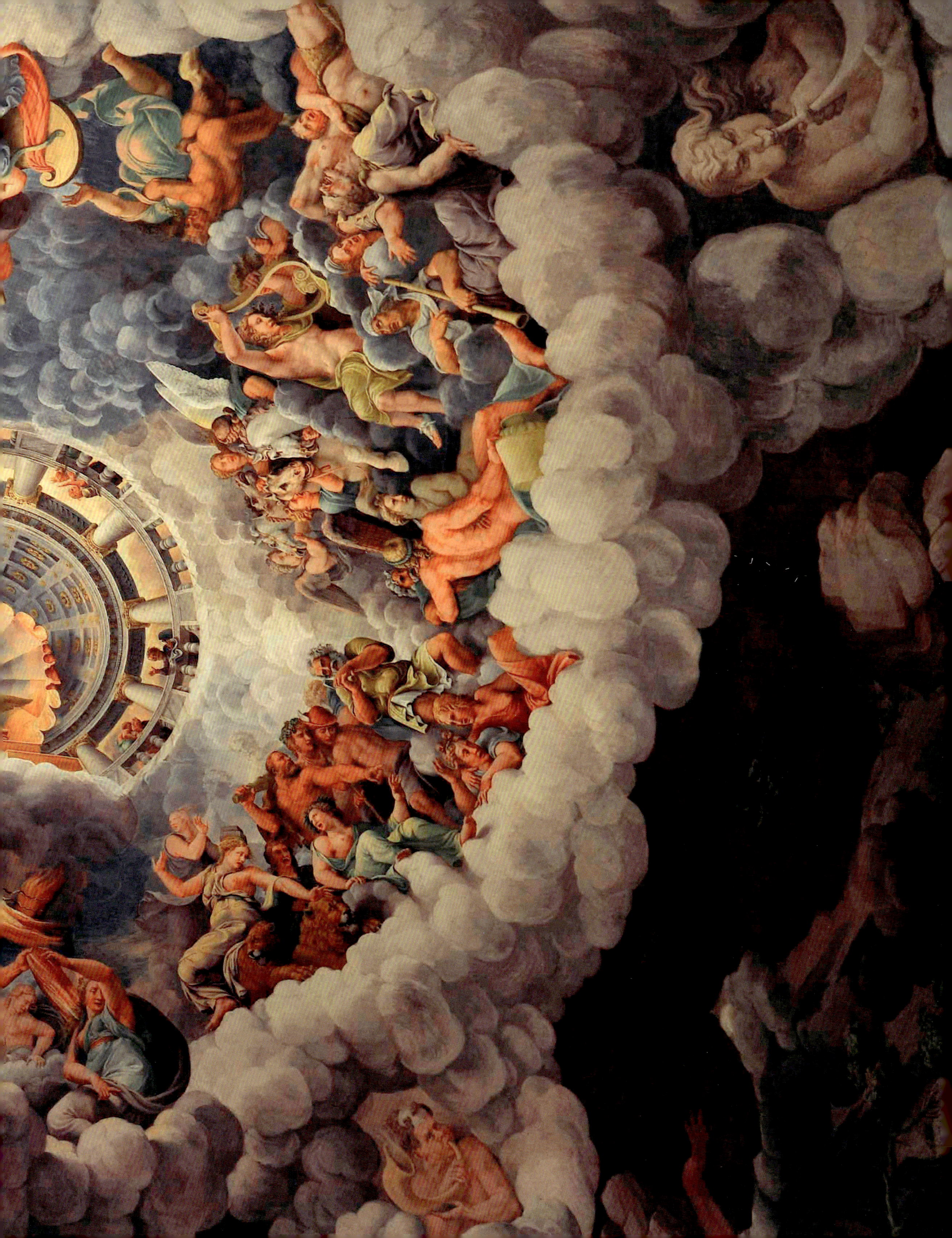

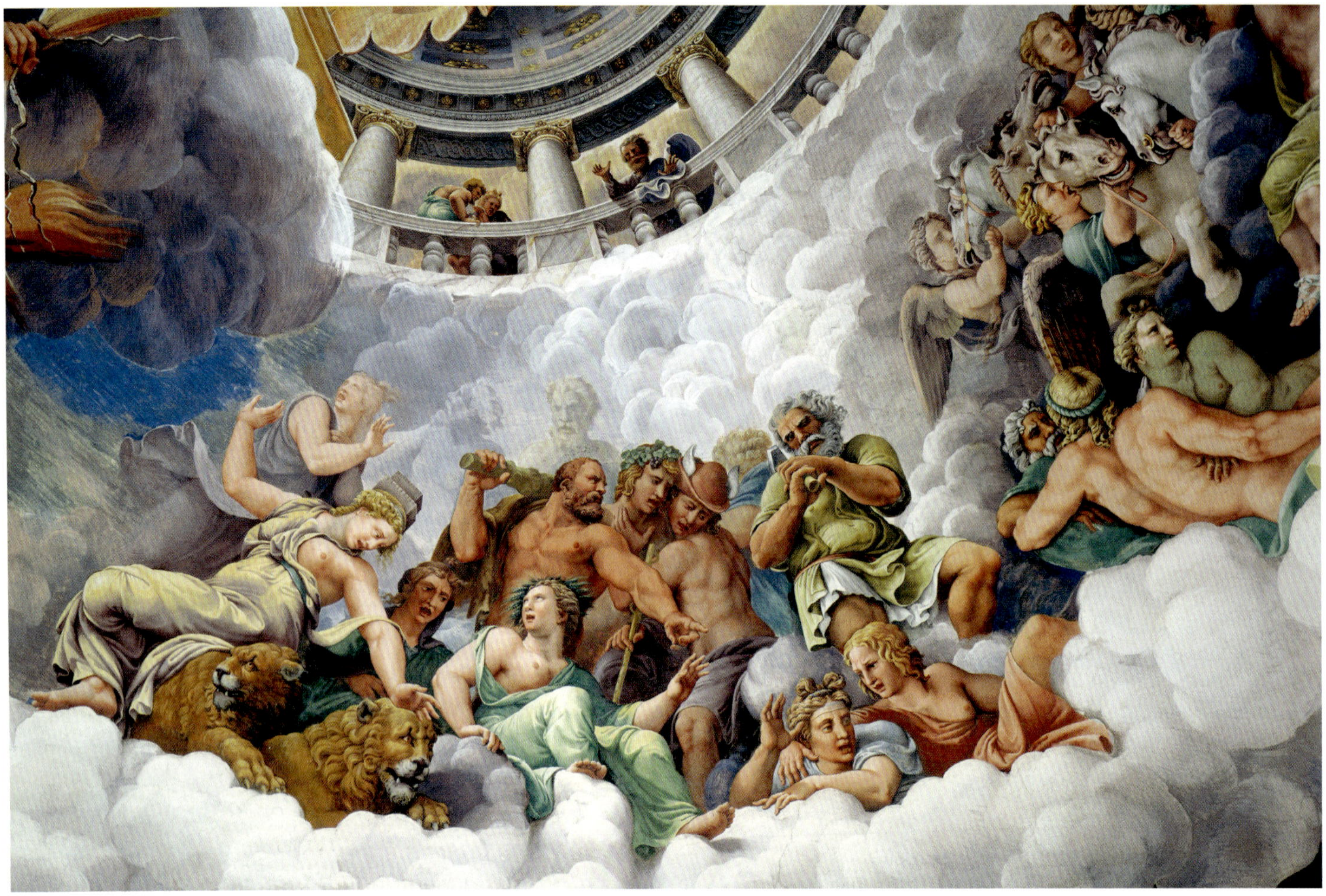

Above: The gods of Mount Olympus exchange concerns over the assault by the giants from below. These include Hercules standing with his club and Mercury with winged helmet.

Below: On the north wall, rebel giants are knocked down by the collapse of a building.

Opposite: In the middle of the image, a personification of the wind blasts gusts of air and blows the hornpipes of war.

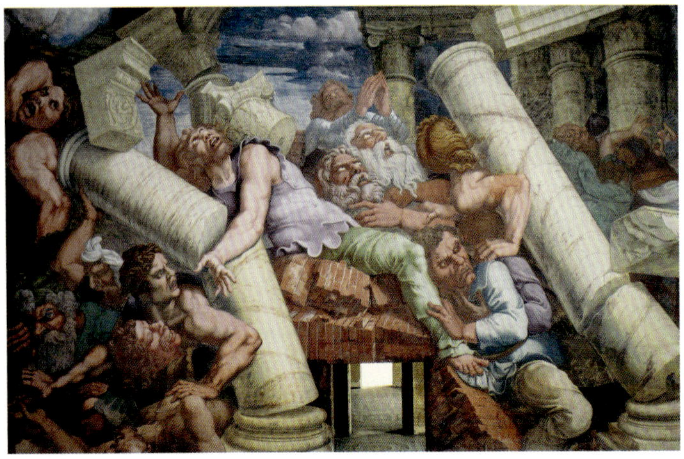

The experience was also about what was underneath as much as looking up. Originally the floor was covered in rocks and stones that denied any secure footing for the visitor and added to the feeling of disorientation. This sense of drama and extreme sensation was in keeping with Palazzo del Te's function as a place for Federico II Gonzaga to carry out his passionate affair with his mistress Isabella Boschetti, away from the judicious watch of her husband and from the duke's disapproving mother Isabella d'Este.

It is, however, much more than just a metaphor of raw and inclement fury in the face of insurgency or a tortured lover's whimsy. The gigantomachy was also a metaphorical battle between the sky and earth. Between the idealized residents of Mount Olympus who represented the intellect, and their primordial counterparts, the giants, who were traditionally thought of as the offspring of Gaia, the ancient deity of the earth and primitive chaos. Romano's room represents the constantly evolving struggle between order and discord, between earth and sky, between body and mind.

The painting's theme of destruction was eerily prescient; less than one hundred years later, in 1630, the palace was looted from top to bottom, when 36,000 mercenary soldiers sacked Mantua, bringing with them a devastating plague that wiped out much of the local population. The giants of Romano's painting were left frozen in time as the earth shook around them and nothing but eerie echoes filled the silent rooms for centuries.

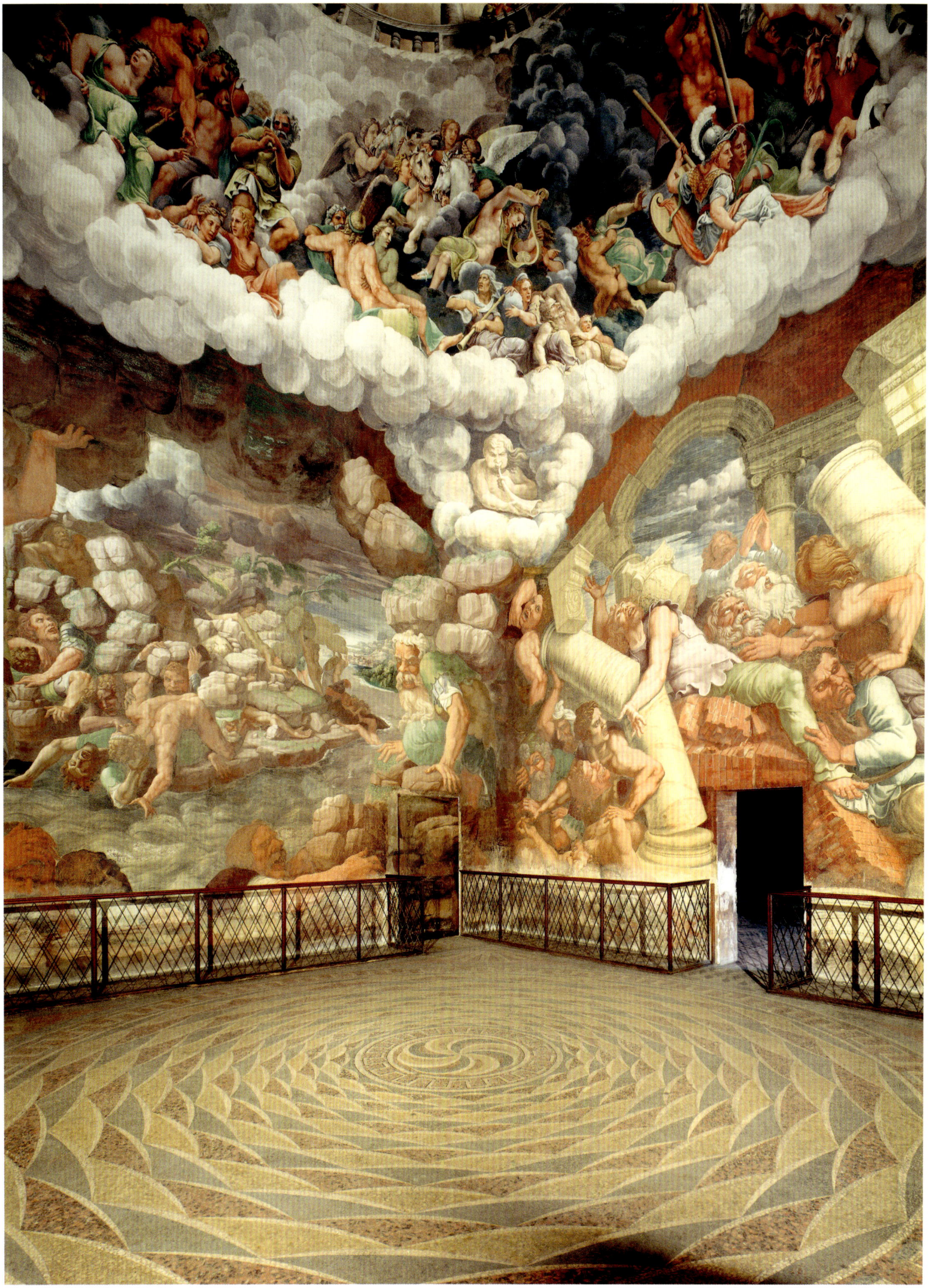

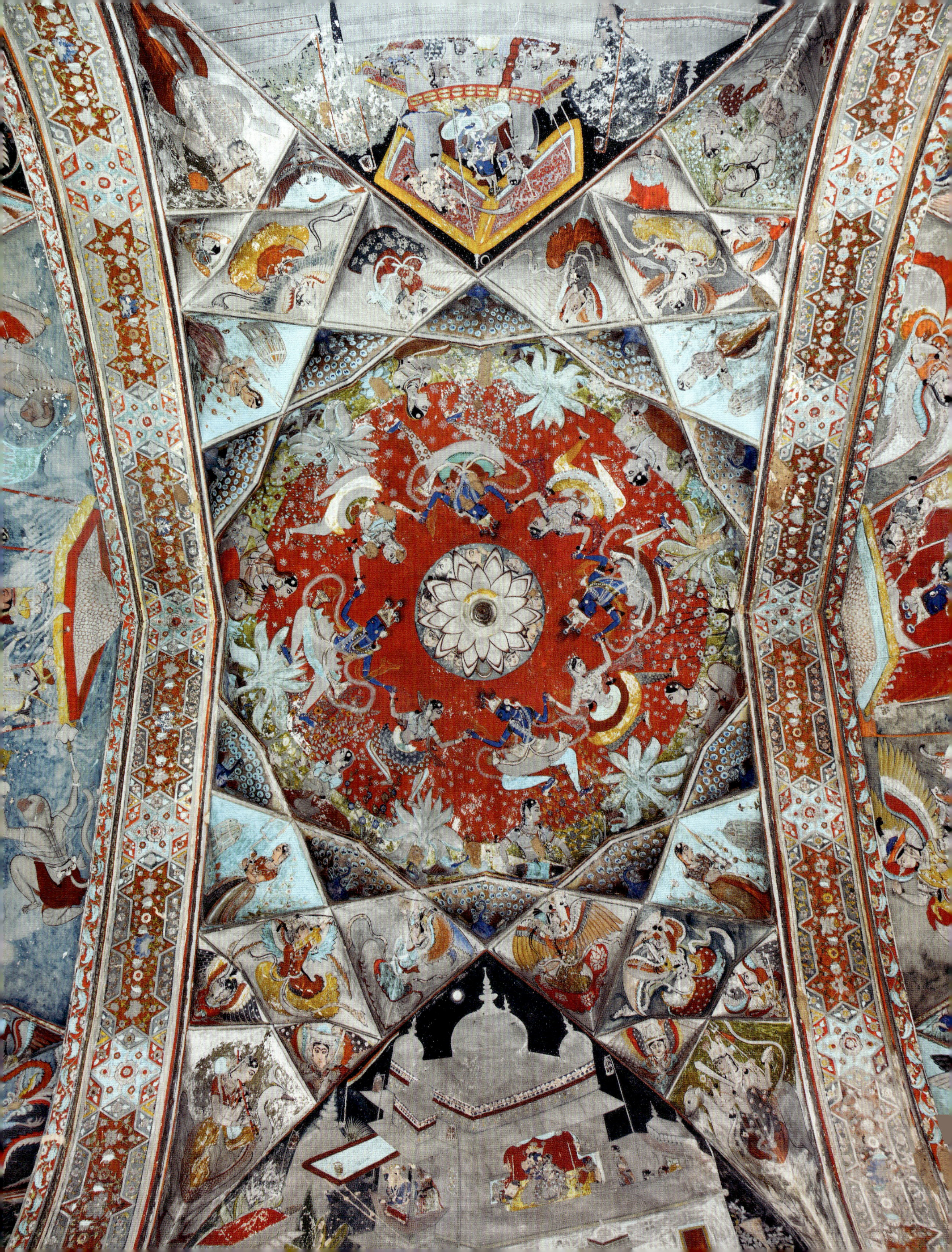

1605

Badal Mahal, Bundi Palace, Rajasthan, India

Left: The beautiful murals lining the walls and ceiling of the Badal Mahal, also known as the Cloud Palace.

Badal Mahal, India

Nestled like a jewellery box within the sprawling rooms of the Bundi Palace in Rajasthan, is the interior hall of the Badal Mahal, or Cloud Palace. A heady and sensual jamboree of Hindu figures and animals cavort and dance across the crimson ceiling in this room, which some say served as the queen's quarters, while others claim it provided a domestic enclosure for Rao Ratan Singh's fifteen wives.

Described by English journalist, poet and novelist Rudyard Kipling as made by goblins not by men, the Bundi Palace lies in the southeastern corner of the modern Indian state of Rajasthan. Prior to Indian independence this had been a semi-independent kingdom ruled by members of a Rajput warrior clan and was still partly occupied up until 1948. Bundi was ruled by the Singh dynasty from 1554, when the palace and fortress was developed, but it was Bhoj Singh, who reigned from 1585–1607, and his son Ratan Singh, reigning from 1607–1631, who were responsible for the painting cycles that decorate the ceilings and walls of the complex. They enlisted the services of artists trained in the imperial manner from Chunar, who had an interest in depicting vibrant individualized portraits and in painting actual events, and who initiated a revolutionary development in local painting styles.

The ceiling design radiates like the petals of a flower from the central image of a silver disc of a moon on which a lotus flower dipped in crimson is encircled with the heads of nine deities. These include four-headed Brahma and Shiva the Destroyer, the principal Hindu gods of creation and destruction. This configuration is echoed and enlarged as the central design expands to form the shape of a mandala – a spiritual and ritual symbol in Hinduism and Buddhism that is a microcosmic representation of the universe.

A field of fiery red sees male figures with blue skin jive energetically with bejewelled maidens on a backdrop of delicate floral motifs. This tells the story of the Hindu deity of compassion and tenderness known as Krishna, whose flute playing proved irresistible to the *gopis* (milkmaids). Together they danced the world into existence with their rasa lila dance during the course of one night that lasted 4.32 billion years. The blue figures are all repetitions of Krishna, whose skin colour represents space and infinity. According to the story of rasa lila, Krishna made each *gopi* feel like the total focus of his divine attention, and this represents the Hindu belief in a love that is both universal and individual. The painting pulses with the sound of clogs, jangle of bangles and the rhythm of drums beaten by the seated female figures at the dance. The esoteric rasa lila of Krishna seems to suggest that the world started with a dance of male and female energies, and not with a big bang.

Moving outwards into the splayed segments of the mandala are images of squabbling monkeys, dancing ladies with tambourines, warriors clashing shields and winged deities dripping with necklaces. Amid this cacophony of sensuality, a central scene depicts the blue-skinned Krishna on a chariot drawn by Ganesh, the elephant-headed god of fortune, attended to by women and bookended by winged figures. This is possibly an aspirational projection of the patron Rao Ratan Singh himself, elevated to the status of divine Krishna. Court life plays out around the hunting

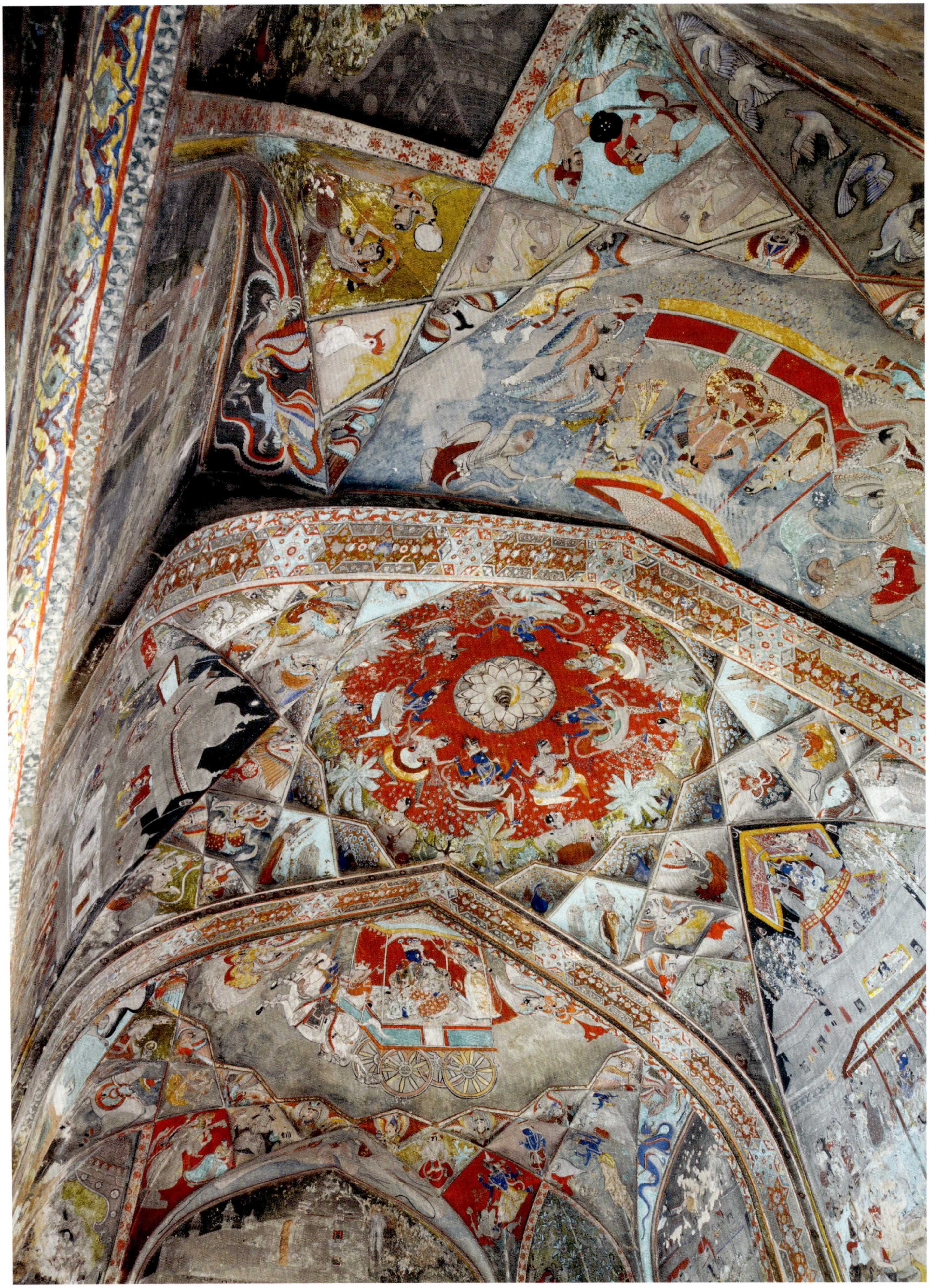

frieze teeming with elephants and small figures of the Singh court that runs underneath the squinches supporting the half domes of the ceiling. Rao Ratan Singh appears here on the western wall, admiring a miniature painting of an elephant, and is very similar to an image in the Museum of Islamic Art in Berlin dated to a similar period, as well as a harem alluded to behind a screen. Underneath this a ragamala unfolds – a series of scenes amalgamating art, music and poetry. They express nuanced emotional states in the love life of the deity Shiva and fertility goddess Parvati, and are peopled with celestial musicians who further animate the room with life.

Opposite: The ceiling design radiates like the petals of a flower from the central image of a silver disc of a moon on which a lotus flower dipped in crimson is encircled with the heads of nine deities.

Below: Detail of the painted ceiling in the Badal Mahal. The esoteric rasa lila of Krishna seems to suggest that the world started with a dance of male and female energies, and not with a big bang.

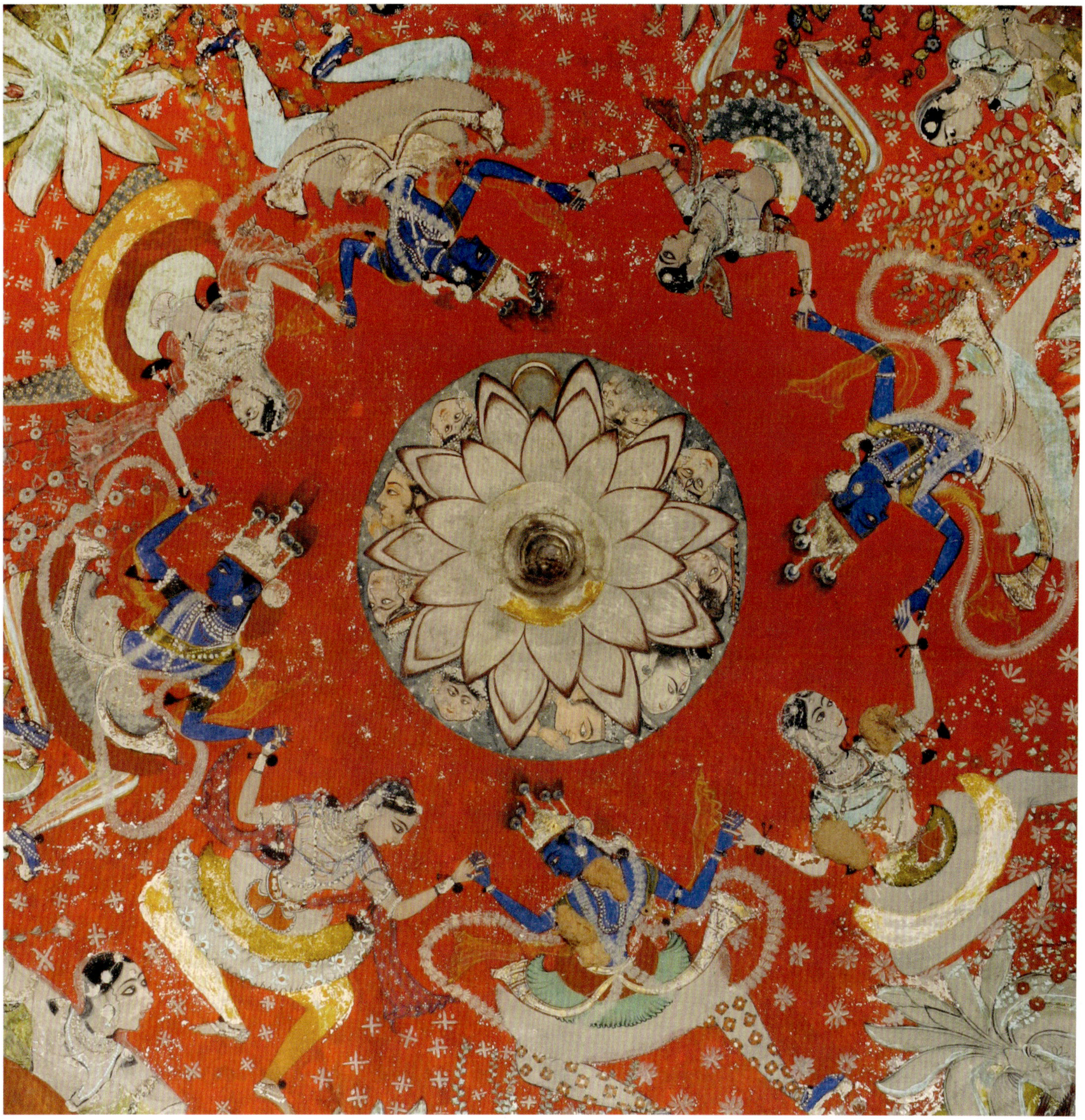

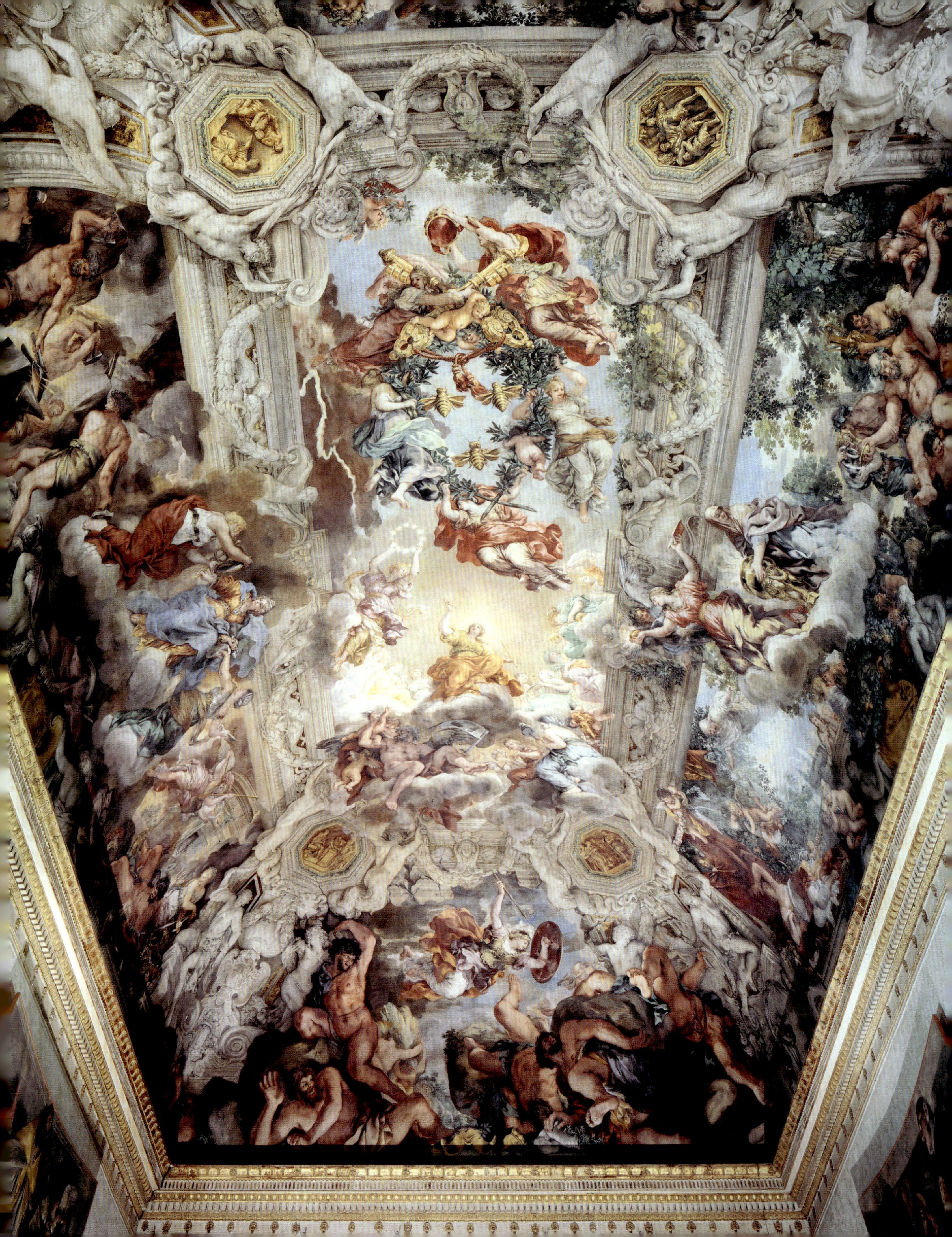

Pietro da Cortona

Allegory of Divine Providence

1633–39

Palazzo Barberini, Rome, Italy

Left and overleaf: *Allegory of Divine Providence*, by Pietro da Cortona, the frescoed ceiling of the Grand Salone on the first floor of the Palazzo Barberini.

Palazzo Barberini, Italy

Rome, among many other things, is a city owned by bees. Look up and you'll notice them perched on masonry, on the tops of fountains, on the exterior of palaces, even in St Peter's basilica. Representing the city of the popes and centre of the Catholic Church, the bee was deemed a suitable symbol for religious endeavour and Christian values. Why? The bee works tirelessly to make honey for the hive, always dedicated to its place in the order of things. The worker bee is also a paragon of chastity; never mating, always toiling and the product of its labours was the sweet honey nectar, comparable to the mellifluous word of God.

So when Maffeo Barberini became Pope Urban VIII in 1623, he knew that the bee and what it stood for would be useful to him and his dynastic ambitions. He added three honeybees to the Barberini coat of arms, and through his artistic patronage of painters, sculptors and architects, decorated the city with these winged labourers. You'll also see them centre stage in the vaulted ceiling of the grandiose reception room of the Palazzo Barberini in Rome, painted by Pietro da Cortona, the illustrious painter and architect of the seventeenth-century European baroque, who crafted the quintessential image of aristocratic self-aggrandizement.

The title of the work refers to the papal signature *Divina Providentia Pontifex Maximus* (Supreme Pontiff by Divine Providence), and the figure of Divine Providence herself appears resplendent in gold, seated on clouds in the central panel and surrounded by figures of Time and the Fates. The bees, at the heart of the image, are framed by a giant laurel wreath held up by personifications of Faith, Charity and Hope. A figure of Rome is crowning the family insignia with a papal tiara, while a personification of Religion holds a pair of golden keys to tie the whole garland together. These keys are the enduring symbol of papal authority on Earth and refer to the first pope, St Peter, who represented the Church and the only route into heaven. Below the garland is another crown in the form of an illuminated diadem of stars, this time held by a figure of Immortality.

In this composition, the whole cosmos comes together to glorify the reign of Urban VIII. Perhaps this was a necessary move; critics of the pope and his nepotism were keen to draw another analogy – that Barberini and his many kin flocked to Rome like a swarm of bees to drain the Church of its spiritual honey.

Maffeo Barberini leaves us in no doubt as to his status as the judiciously appointed temporal and spiritual leader of the Church, with God, the immortals and the antique heritage of the city of Rome all in agreement on his suitability for the role of pope, an office he held between 1623 and 1644. But this was not the extent of the honours bestowed on the pompous Barberini. Look again, and a third crown – this time made of laurel leaves – is extended by a putto in the top left-hand corner. This was for Maffeo Barberini's accomplishments as a poet in a tradition perpetuated by the medieval and Renaissance world, in particular for the writer Dante, who adopted the laurel crown in emulation of his poetic hero, an analogy that Barberini wanted to claim also for himself.

In a departure from the *quadro riportato* composition for ceiling painting (the effect of framed pictures resting against architectural fixtures), da Cortona embraced the compositional

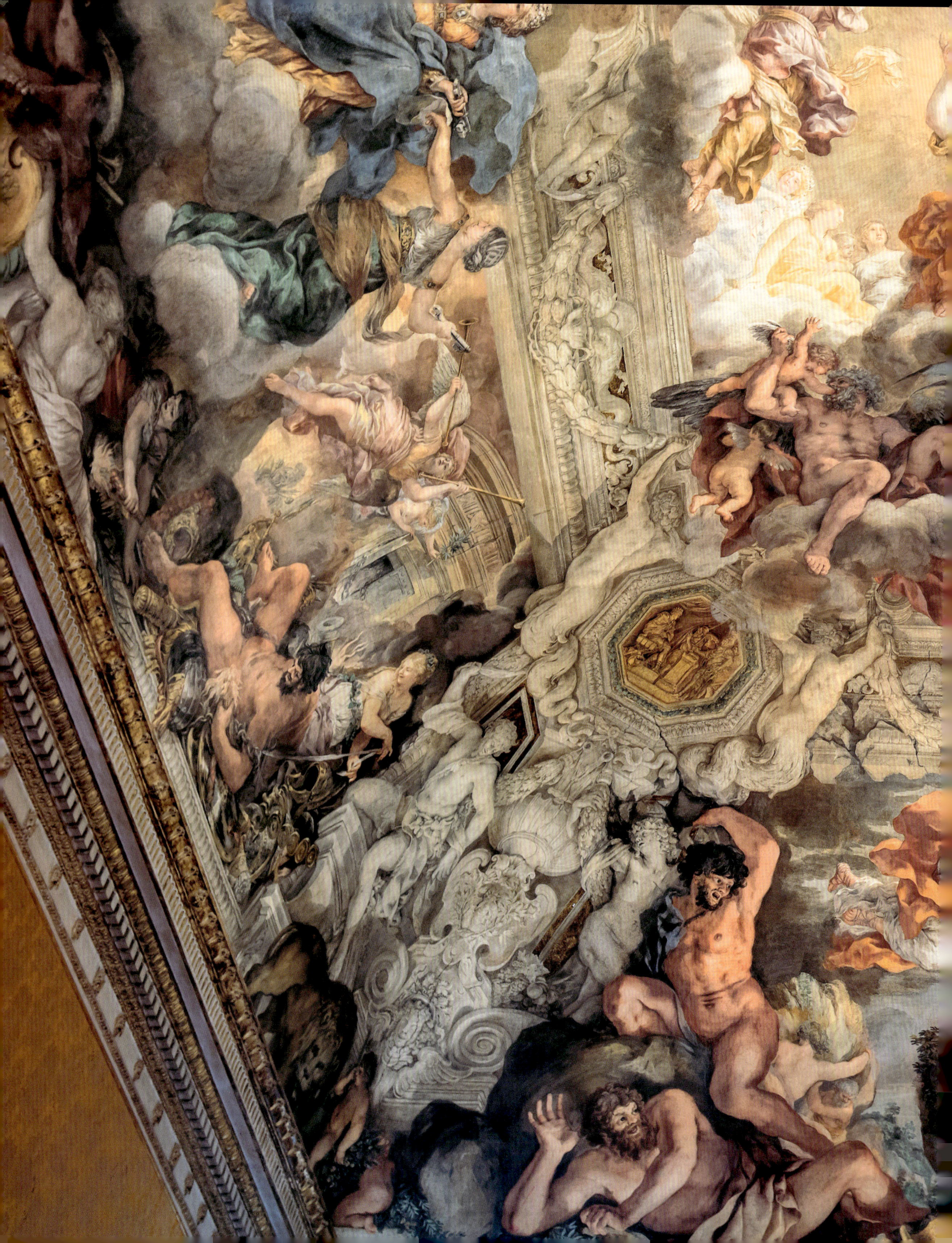

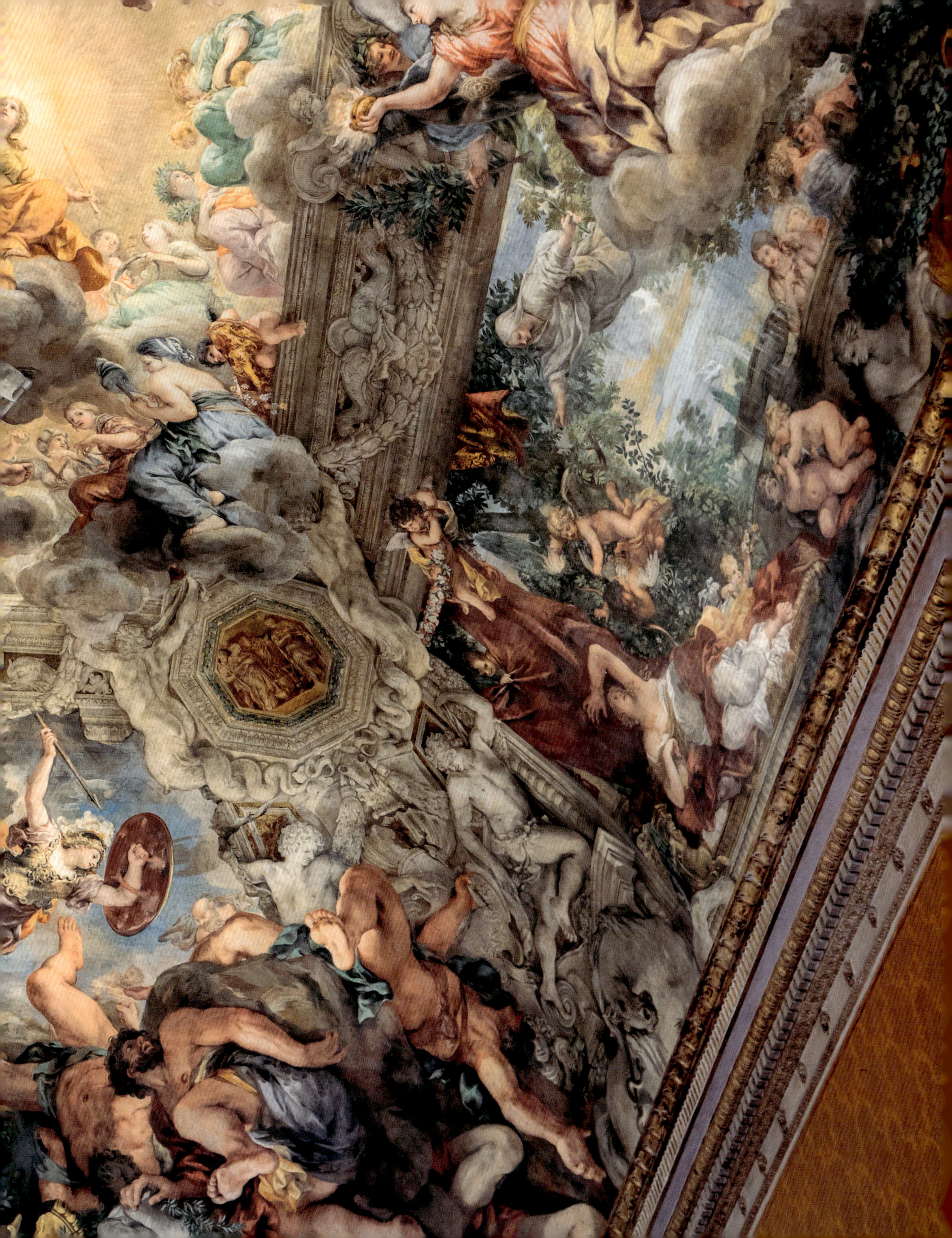

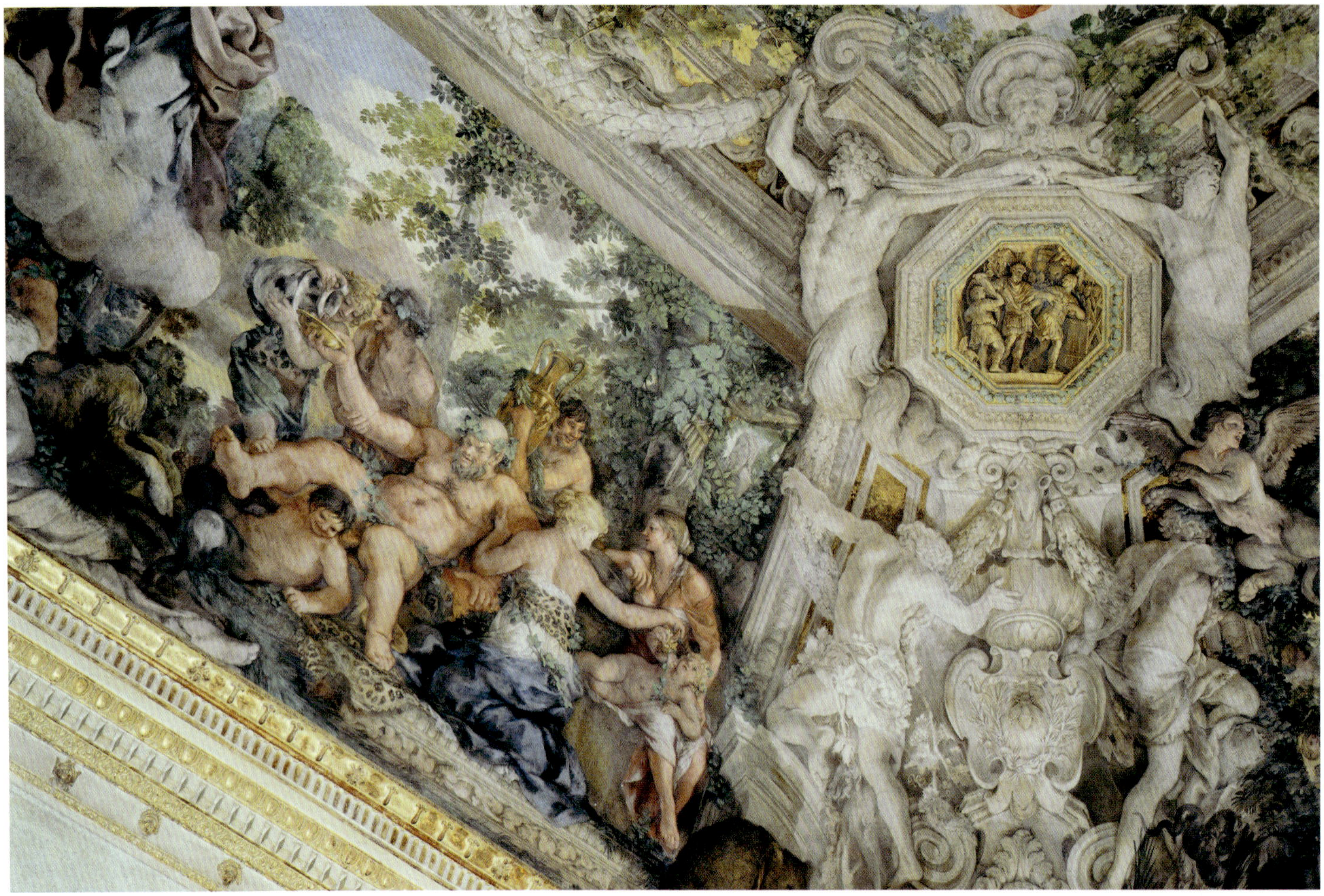

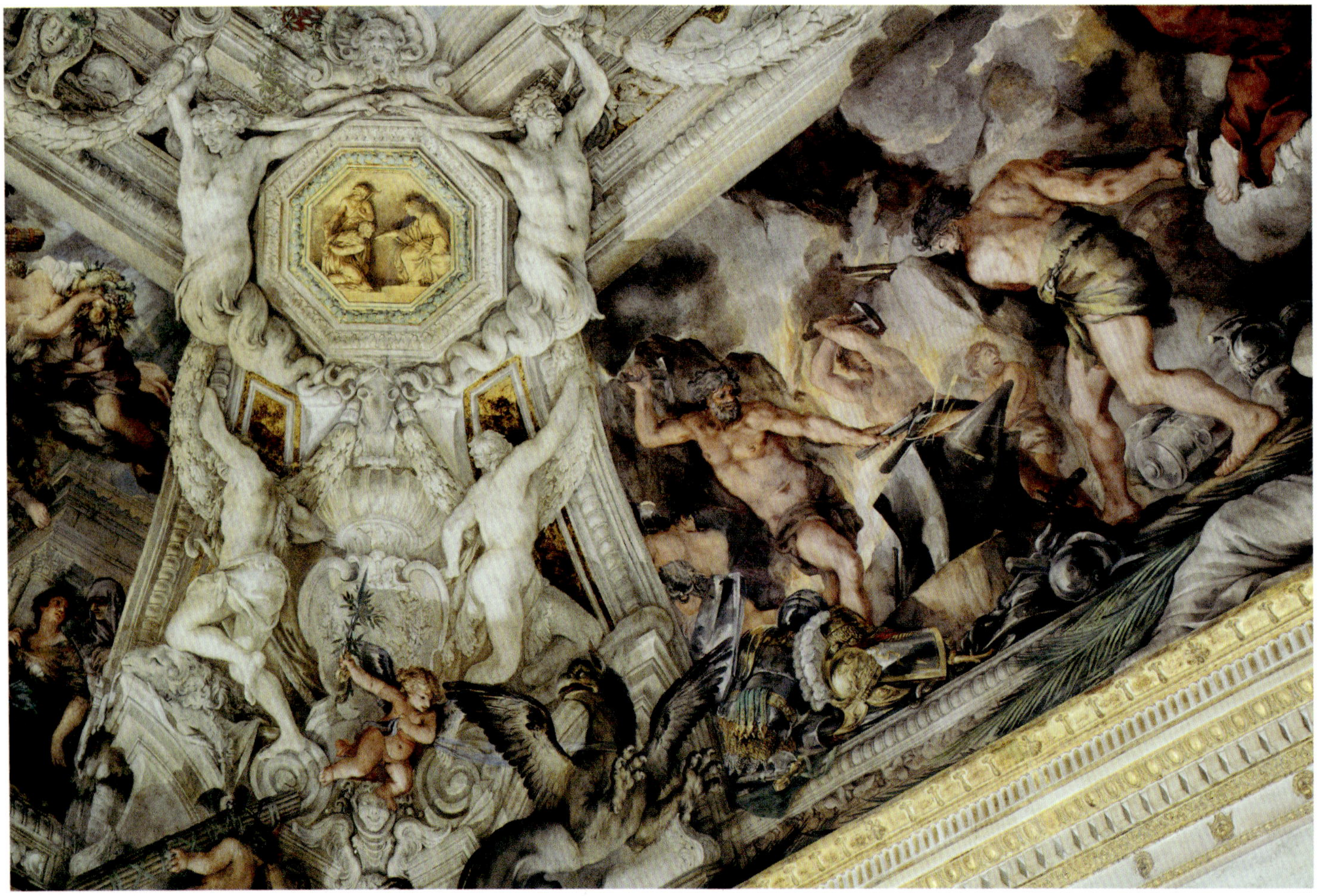

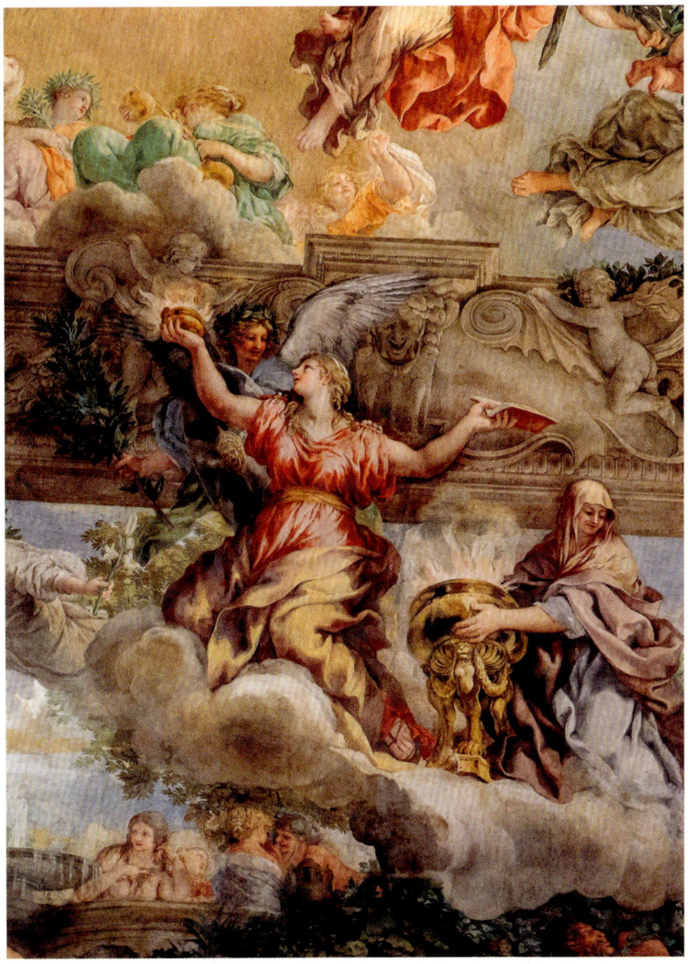

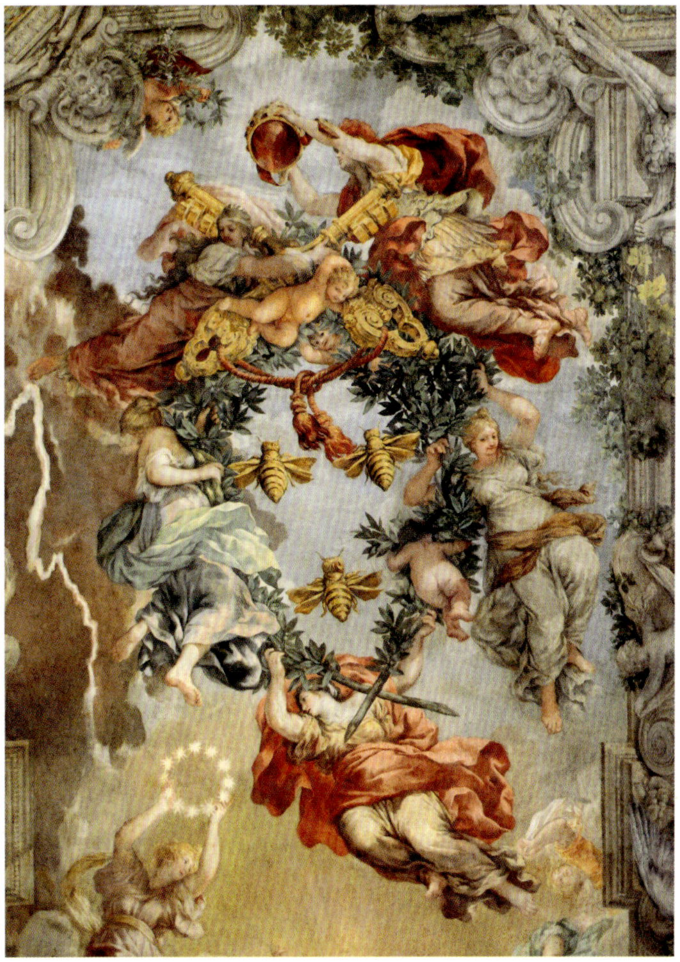

Opposite top: Detail of *Drunken Silenus*, a mythological story which is employed here to illustrate the virtue of Maffeo Barberini's temperance.

Opposite bottom: Illusionistic *trompe l'oeil* painting gives the effect of stucco carving framing the vault. To the right, an image of *Vulcan's Forge*.

Above left: Detail of the *Allegory of Divine Providence*.

Above right: The bees, at the heart of the image, are framed by a giant laurel wreath held up by personifications of Faith, Charity and Hope. A figure of Rome is crowning the family insignia with a papal tiara, while a personification of Religion holds a pair of golden keys to tie the whole garland together.

technique of *quadratura* by opening the illusory space to an imaginary sky, creating the effect of a heavenly vision across 336 sq m (3,600 sq ft), crowded with figures and garlands, fictitious stucco cornices, relief sculpture and bronze medallions, all painted in fresco on the two-tiered vaulted ceiling.

Four octagons, one in each corner of the vault, depict the four Virtues with figures of Justice, Fortitude, Temperance and Prudence, each accompanied with motifs pillaged from classical mythology and ancient history. For example, Minerva in her helmet slaying the Giants expresses Fortitude. These examples, often obscure, depict parables from mythology and ancient history, not only to reflect the interests of the age in which Barberini lived, but also to showcase his learnedness, erudition and ambition as a means of intellectual superiority over those less highly educated than himself.

However, while Maffeo Barberini was happy to have the world and the Gods revolve on the Palazzo Barberini ceiling, in a spiralling freneticism that literally raises the roof on his achievements, he was less tolerant of actual theories that sought to explain the movement of celestial bodies in our solar system. The pontiff was famously steadfast in seeing to the arrest, trial and conviction of the scientist Galileo Galilei who promoted the theories of Copernicus, suggesting that Earth revolved around the sun. More palatable was the promotional propaganda that the bees revolved around the pope, and not just during Maffeo Barberini's temporal reign; bees would become synonymous with the identity of the pontiff well into the nineteenth century and long after his demise.

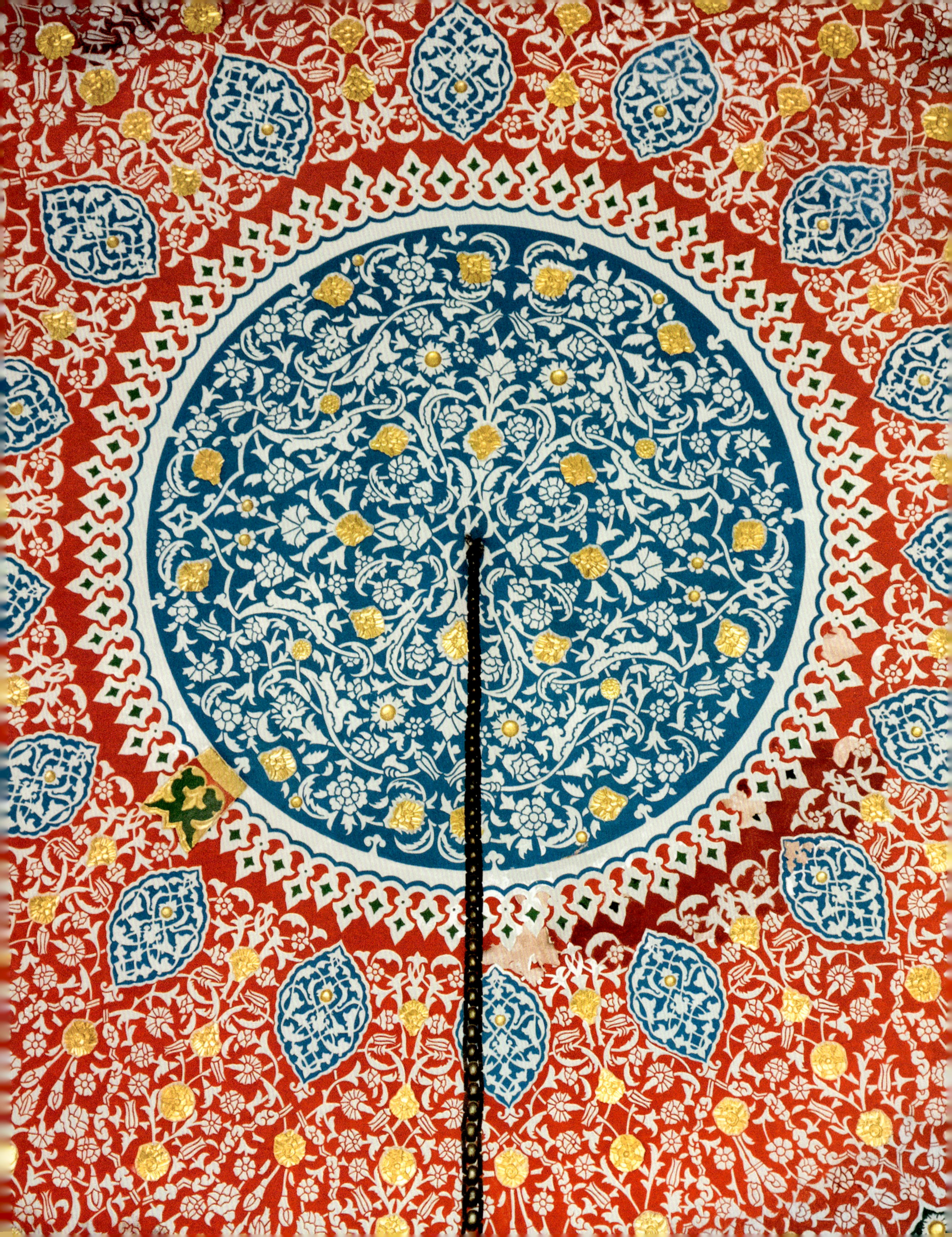

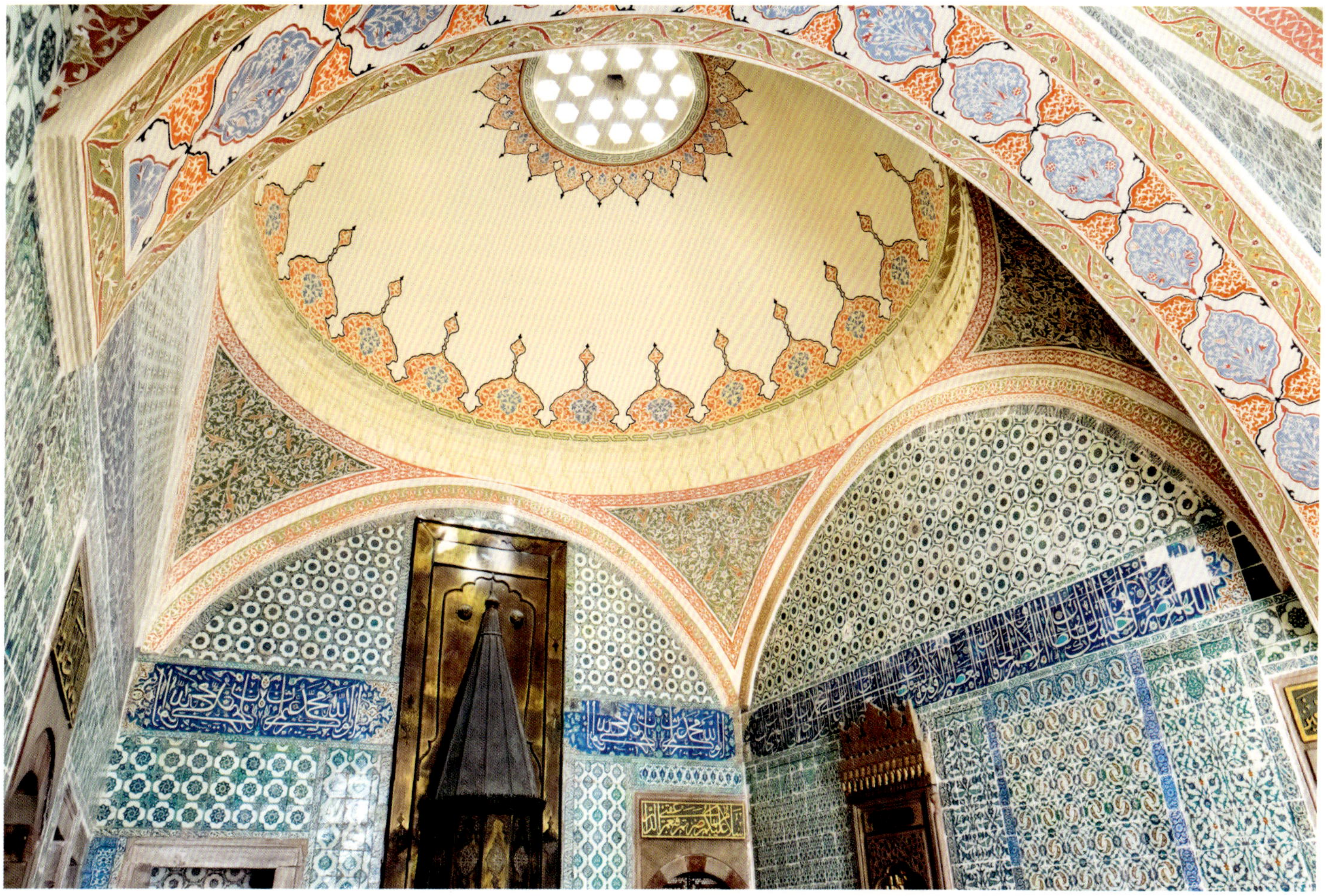

textiles alongside the extravagant tilework. The kiosk was built to commemorate the Baghdad Campaign of Murad IV after 1638. Here, the sultan and his associates could listen to music or sleep off their meals to the babbling lull of a fountain, looking up at lofty domes that blurred the separation between inside and outside – and this mortal life and another – with their delicate vegetal floral designs.

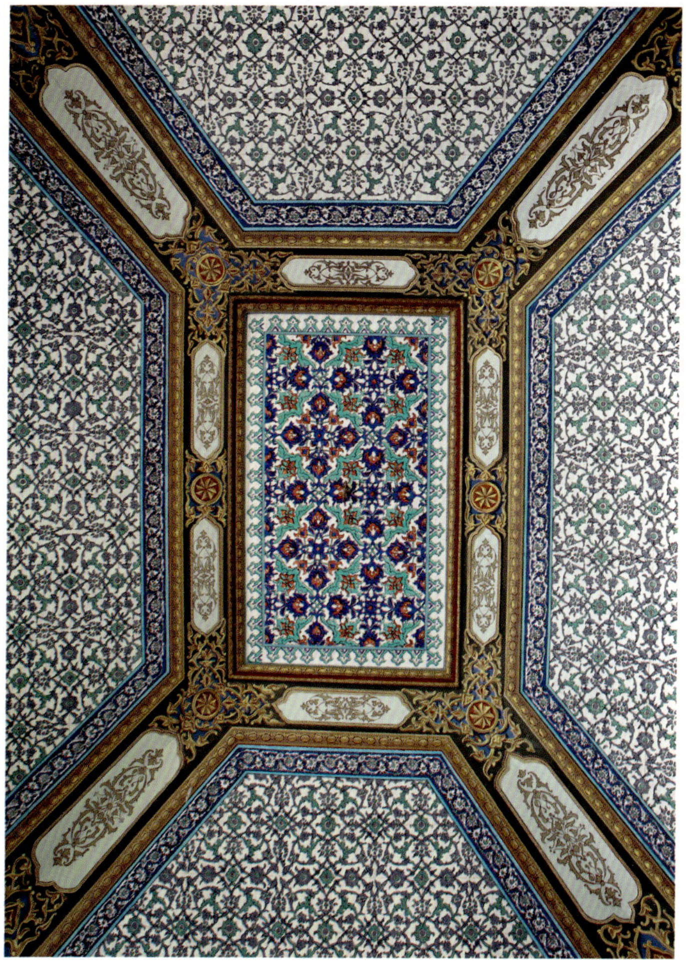

Above: Room in the Harem of Topkapı Palace.

Right: Tiled ceiling decoration in Topkapı Palace.

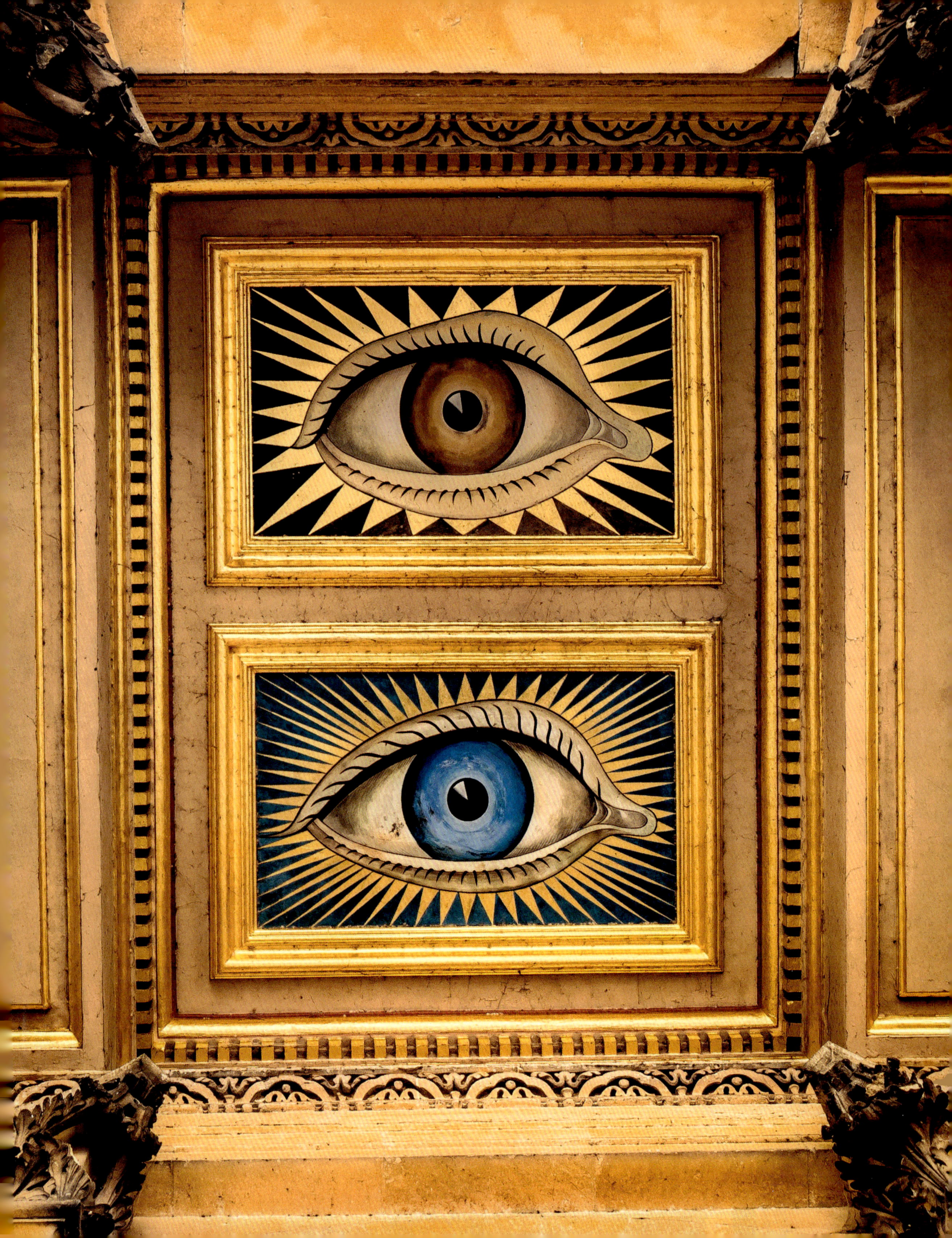

Colin Gill

North Portico

1928

Blenheim Palace, Oxfordshire,

United Kingdom

Left and overleaf: The all-seeing eyes of Colin Gill's North Portico ceiling at Blenheim Palace bear down on the visitors below.

Blenheim Palace, United Kingdom

Six unblinking, disembodied eyes bear down on all those who arrive at the principal entrance to the palatial setting of Blenheim Palace, the ancestral home of Sir Winston Churchill. Three eyes are brown, the remaining three a cerulean blue, all of them encased in enigmatic starbursts. It is a peculiar welcome to one of England's largest and most prestigious stately homes, the only secular and non-royal building in the country to be known as a 'palace'. But Blenheim has always been a place of controversy. The house was built between 1705 and 1722, as a gift from Queen Anne to the 1st Duke of Marlborough for his valiant victory at the Battle of Blenheim in 1704. Planning and development fell to the duke and his wife. They disagreed over who should be entrusted with the design and the job was handed to the English dramatist and sometime architect Sir John Vanbrugh who had worked with Nicholas Hawksmoor on the baroque behemoth of Castle Howard in Yorkshire. The building is idiosyncratic in all respects. Part mausoleum, part monument and part domestic family home, it was criticized by the public as a flamboyantly excessive drain on public funds. After completion it became known as an architectural failure that was too severe and grandiose – so much so that Vanbrugh never worked again.

While the palace is known for its tapestries, old master paintings, antiques and furniture, the North Portico tells the story of one of the building's more eccentric inhabitants. The decoration of the portico dates to 1928 and the patronage of Gladys Deacon, the second wife of the 9th Duke of Marlborough, who commissioned British war artist Colin Gill to paint the eyes of her and her husband in 1928. The duchess allegedly scaled Gill's ladder waving a silk scarf so that he might perfect the exact shade of her famously disarming eyes. Having studied at London's Slade School of Fine Art, Gill was dispatched to the Western Front in France during the First World War, where he employed his artistic training working as a camouflage officer. On his return, he was commissioned to paint a contemporary history painting commemorating the dead for a memorial project known as the Hall of Remembrance, a commemorative building that was never completed. His observations of trench warfare can be seen in the work *Heavy Artillery* (1919) in the Imperial War Museum, London.

Celebrated for her meteoric beauty and famed for her intellect and wit, the duchess beguiled Europe, capturing the admiration of Marcel Proust, Auguste Rodin (who gifted her a sculpture), Claude Monet and the Crown Prince of Prussia, among many others. Born in Paris to American parents, she spent most of her early years in France, including an education in a convent to which she was sent after her father murdered her mother's lover.

Deacon arrived in England in the late 1890s and befriended the Duke of Marlborough's first wife Consuelo. Unsurprisingly she acted as muse for a number of modernist artists who captured her in portrait form. They included Italian futurist artist Giovanni Boldini, John Singer Sargent and the sculptor Jacob Epstein. Soon after her arrival in England, Deacon became the Duke of Marlborough's mistress ensconced at Blenheim, although the pair did not marry until 1921 when his first marriage ended. The second duchess was committed to her pursuit of a perfectly formed Grecian profile, and soon after her marriage she underwent cosmetic surgery to inject paraffin wax into the bridge

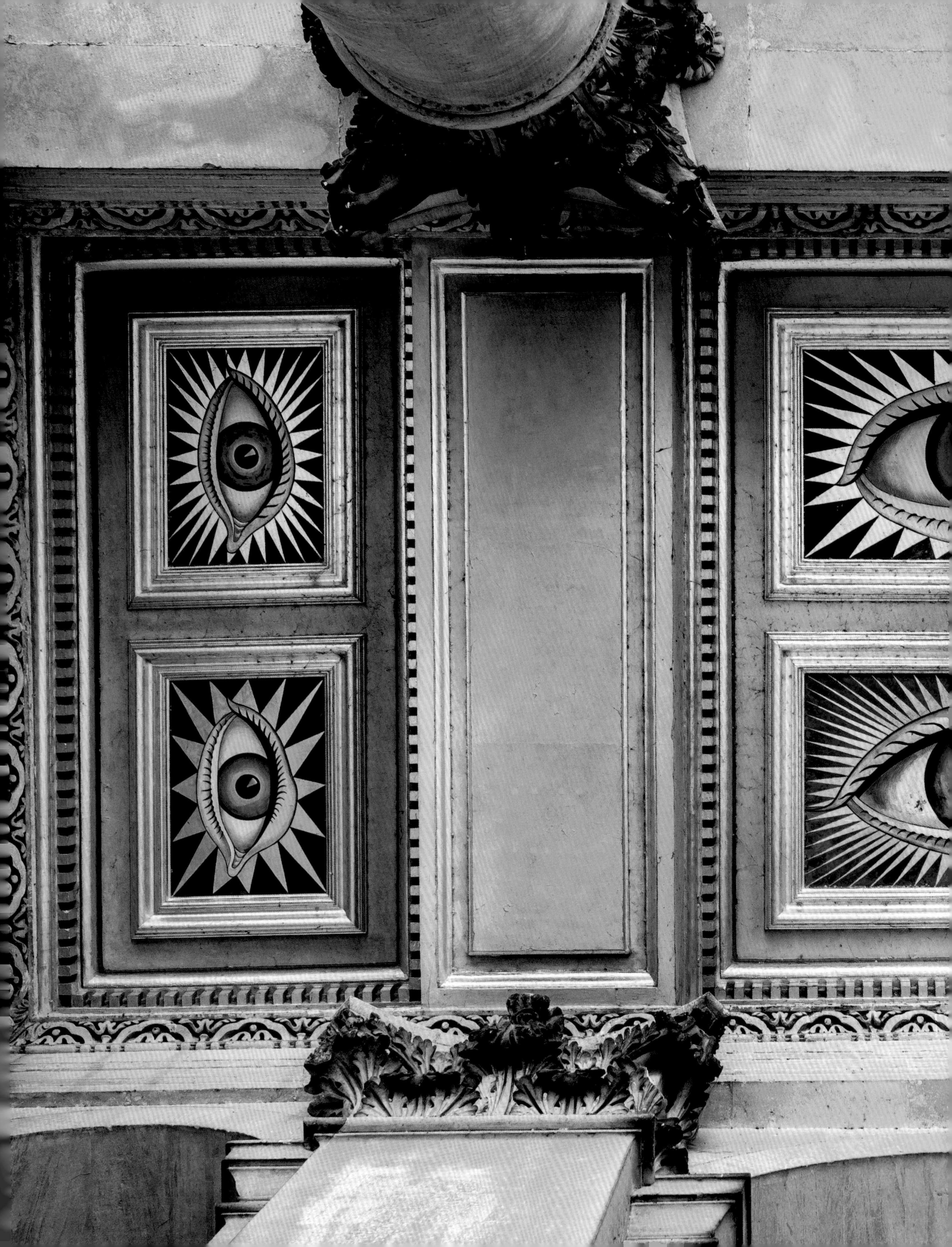

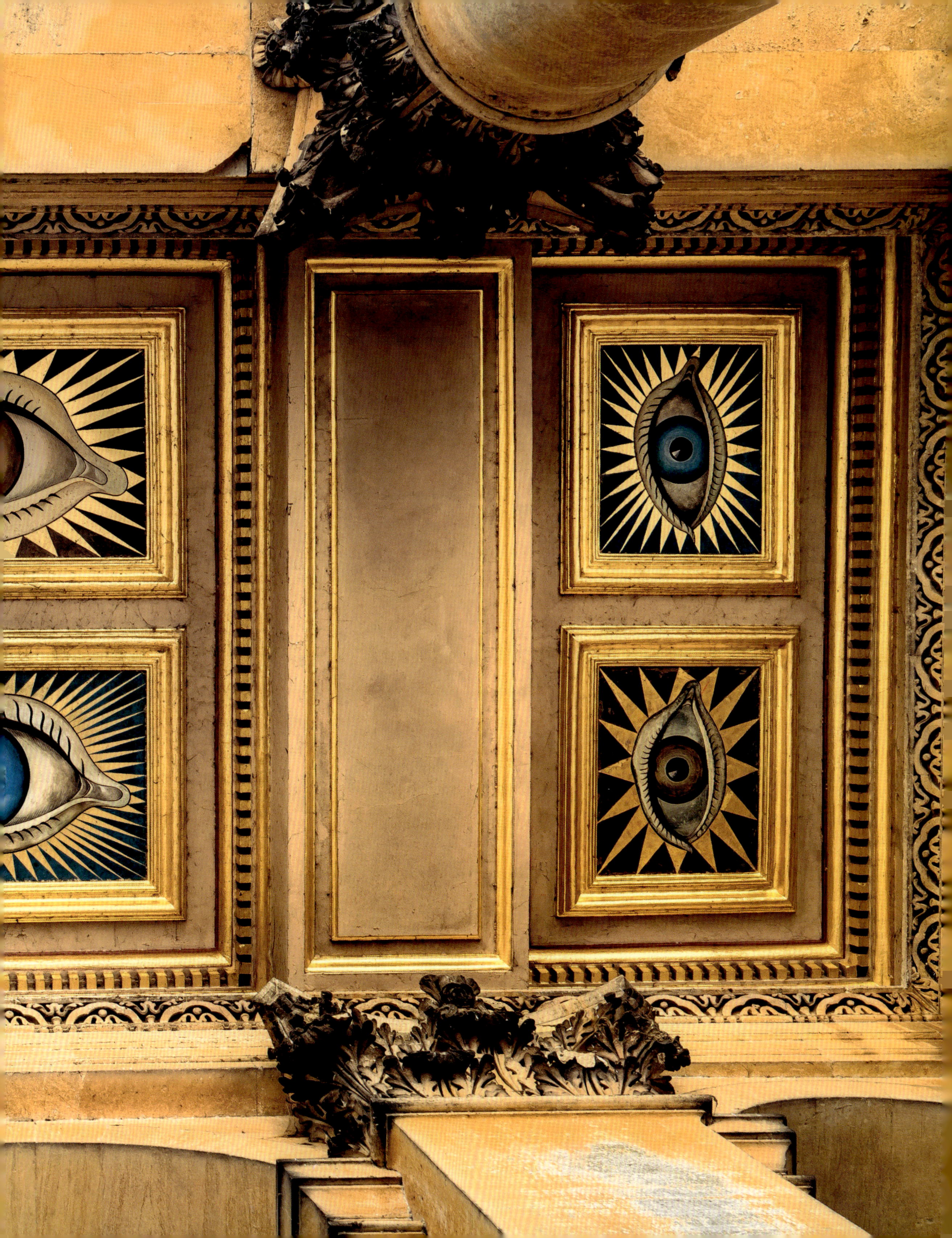

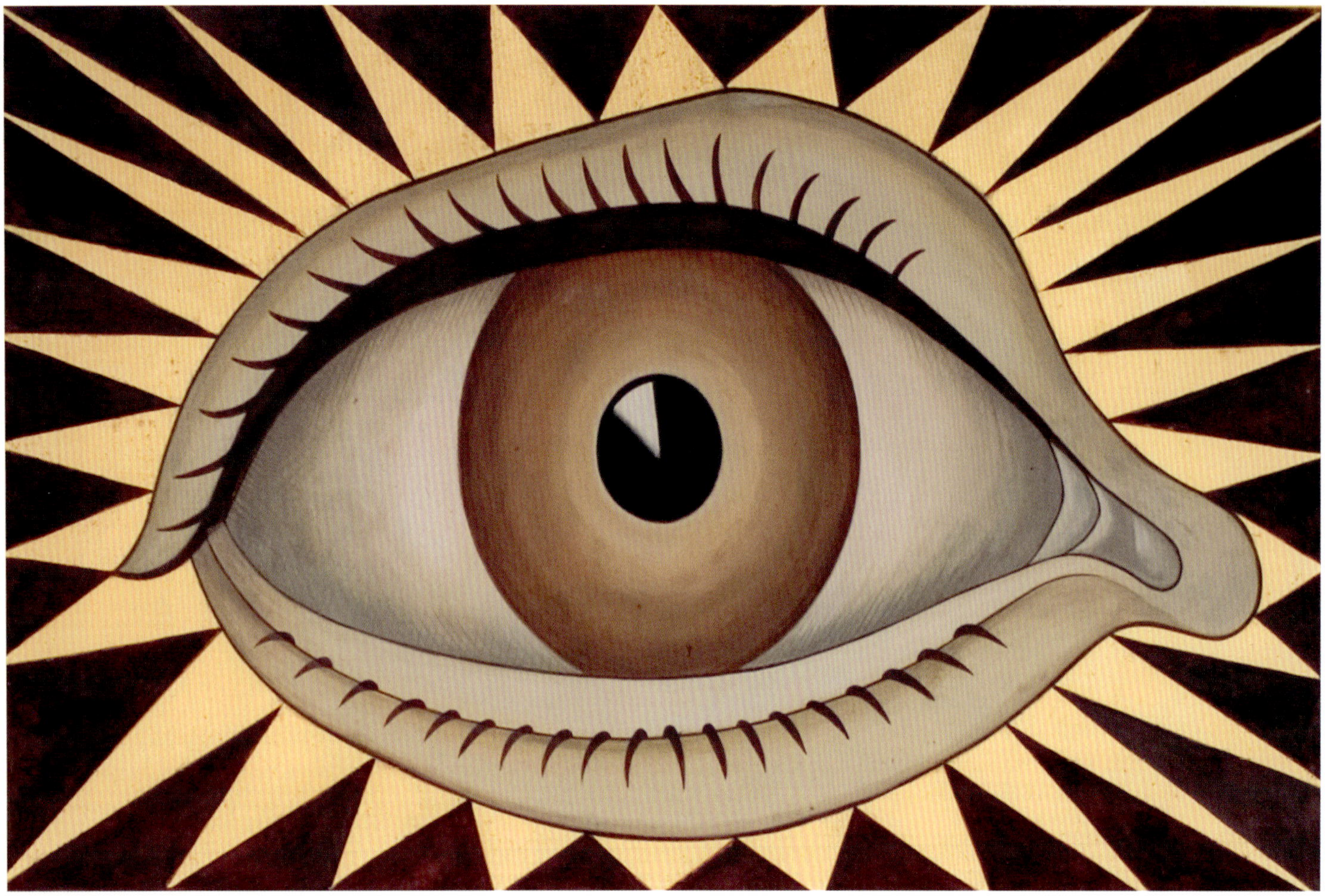

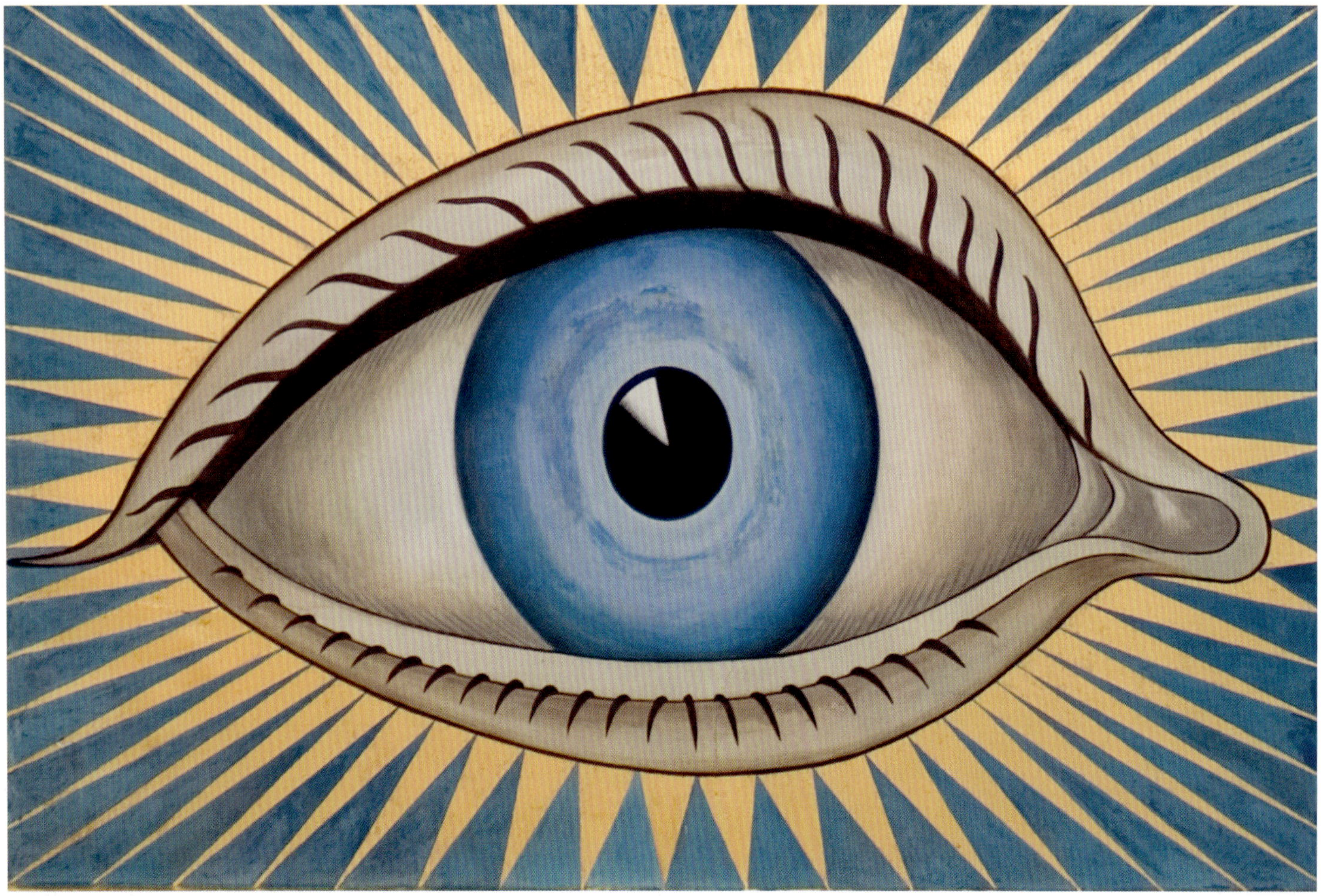

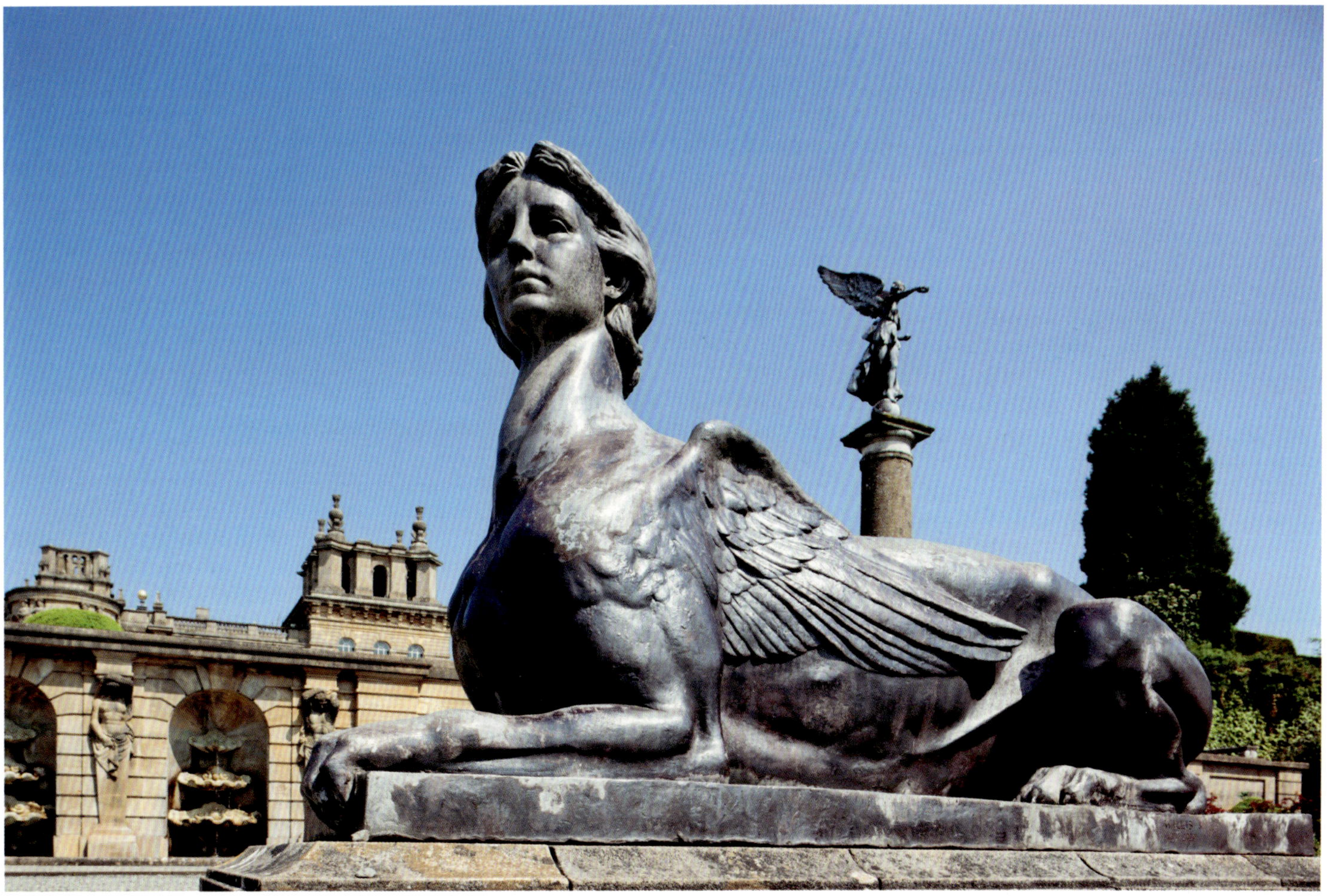

of her nose. However, the wax became displaced and collected in hard lumps around her chin, disfiguring her famous beauty.

Gill's painting of eyes may be something of a window onto a troubled soul who lived a life of colourful experiences, but any intended meaning remains oblique and lies buried with the enigmatic duchess, who died a nocturnal recluse, surrounded by cats. Having said this, the eye as a visual symbol has a significant history and has appeared on churches, temples and even on banknotes. For example, the Eye of Horus was a popular motif in ancient Egyptian mythology and represented good health, protection and royal power. In Europe in the medieval period the eye symbol was often surrounded by a triangle that symbolized the Holy Trinity of Father, Son and Holy Spirit and represented the omniscient eye of God keeping watch on humanity, and was later taken up by the Freemasons as a reflection of their belief in this all-seeing power who saw and judged everything.

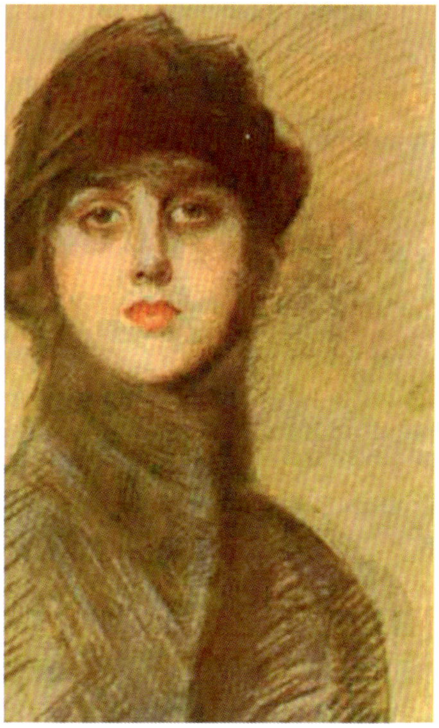

Opposite: The painted eyes of Gladys Deacon and the 9th Duke of Marlborough.

Above: One of two sphinx statues at Blenheim Palace that bear the features of Gladys Deacon.

Right: Portrait of Gladys Deacon by John Singer Sargent.

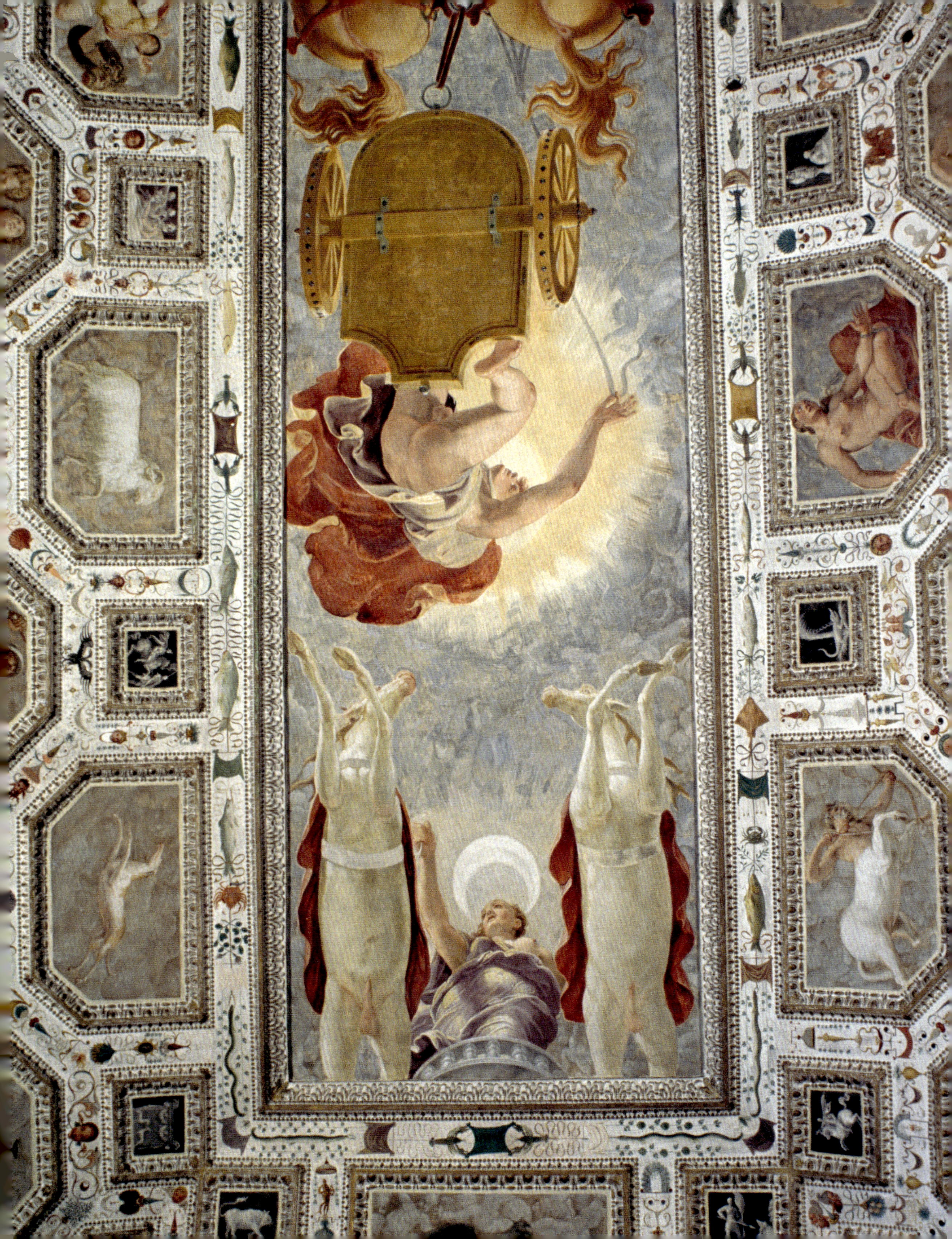

Domenico Brusasorci

Room of the Firmamento

1550s

Palazzo Chiericati, Vicenza, Italy

Left and overleaf: The ceiling in the Palazzo Chiericati. In the central panel, against a powdery grey sky, a pair of bare buttocks and testicles eclipse the watery light of the sun.

Palazzo Chiericati, Italy

Looking up at the ceiling of the reception room in Vicenza's Palazzo Chiericati gives a whole new perspective to the concept of the divine firmament. The usual symbols and images depicting astrological constellations and zodiac signs are embedded in stucco coffering, but in the central panel, against a powdery grey sky, a pair of bare buttocks and testicles eclipse the watery light of the sun. This unexpectedly explicit view is of the god Apollo, mythological deity of art, music, poetry and the sun, depicted here in his chariot as he makes his daily passage across the sky. This narrative from classical mythology explained the movement of the sun and daybreak. Apollo's twin sister Diana, goddess of the moon, hunting and fertility, stands crowned with a silver crescent at the edge of the panel, poised in her chariot to repeat her nightly voyage across the same sky, under the mantle of the moon.

Painted by Domenico Brusasorci, the frescoed panel pays homage to a similar depiction of Apollo and Diana from 1526, painted by Giulio Romano, and which can be found in the Stanza del Sole in the Palazzo del Te, Mantua. It could be that the affluent Girolamo Chiericati sought to emulate the esteemed Duke of Mantua's claims to cultural sophistication. The subject matter was also dear to an erudite Renaissance audience, as it stimulated a philosophical consideration of the incessant and cyclical nature of time passing, and humankind's powerless fate beneath the movement of the gods and the sky.

But beyond this veneer of lofty and cultured speculation there is a bawdy joke, and, like all the most popular jokes it is concerned with scatological themes of nude body parts and defecation. Look closer, and it is not just Apollo who exposes his undercarriage, but all of the four horses stationed on the ceiling as well. It is a ribald twist on the *sotto in su* technique beloved of Italian painters from the sixteenth to eighteenth centuries, which creates the illusion of objects and figures, free-falling or on a precipice, seemingly about to enter the space of the viewer. For example, whereas guests to the Palazzo del Te's Sala dei Giganti cowered from the anticipated blows of Jupiter's thunderbolts and showers of toppling masonry (see p. 134), here in the reception room of the Palazzo Chiericati, directly beneath the bottoms of Apollo and four strapping stallions, a different sort of precipitation is implied.

The palace was designed by Andrea Palladio, the popular sixteenth-century architect who reinvigorated the tenets of classical Roman architecture and who dominated the civic commissions in Vicenza, from the Teatro Olimpico to the Basilica Palladiana and a number of villas embedded in the surrounding hills of the city, all of which were constructed under the influence of the principles of classical architecture.

The subject matter of Brusasorci's ceiling with Apollo and Diana also reflects sixteenth-century Italy's continuing reverence for the classical world and mythological stories. Within this cultural climate, images of nude bodies reminiscent of the sculptures of heroes, gods and immortals were so ubiquitous that their nudity has almost become invisible. Such nudity is worn like an external carapace of impossibly perfect muscle. However, the nudes of art history are not always a meditation on classical civilization derived from the aesthetic and philosophical ideal of ancient Greece. This Apollo is naked under his voluminous cape, revealing a more mortal masculinity.

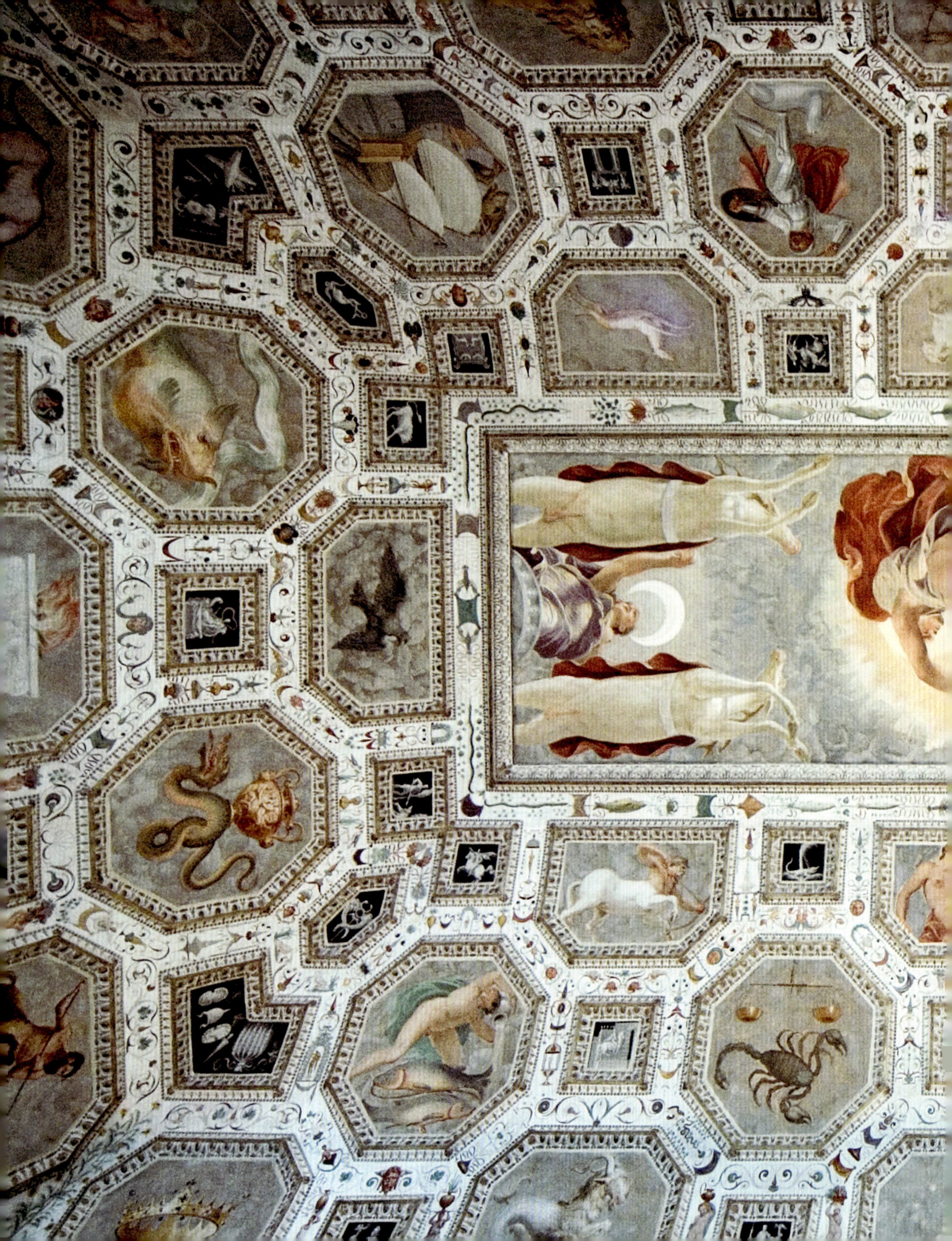

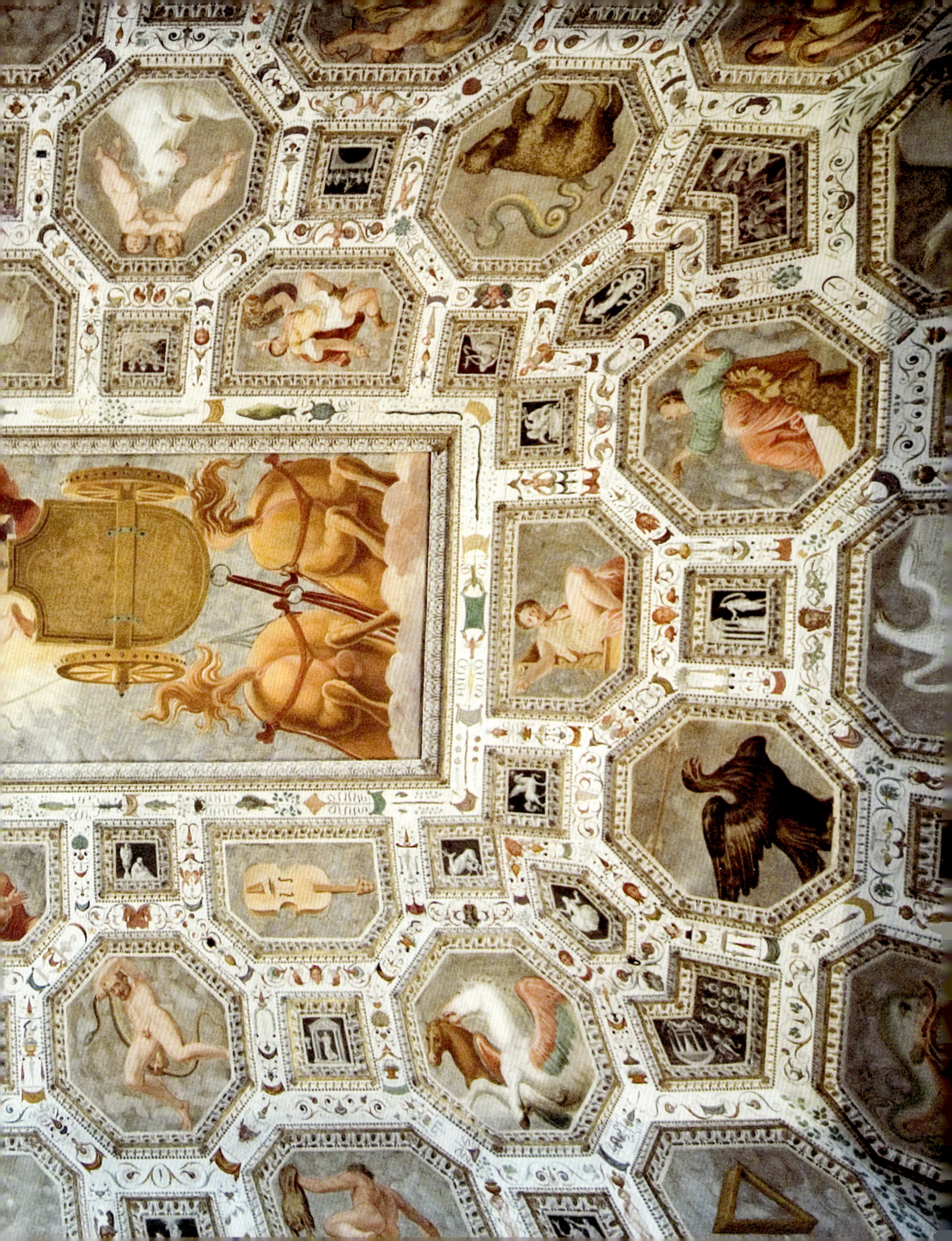

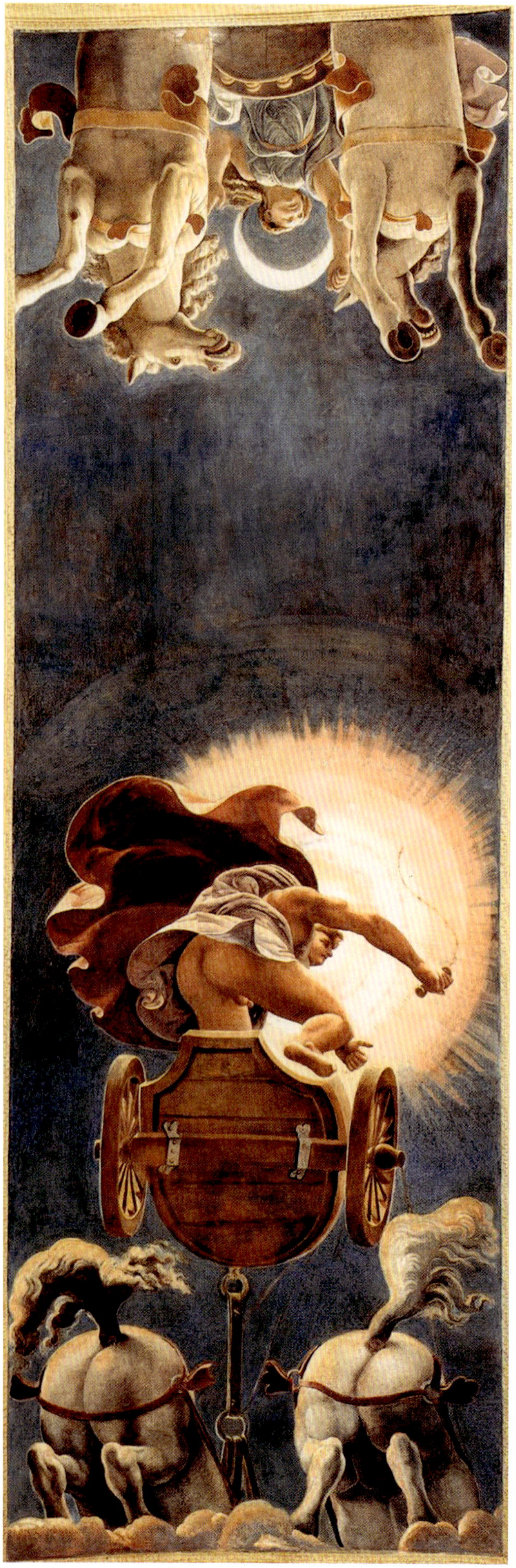

In recent years, scholars such as Patricia Rubin have turned their attention to images of the Renaissance rear, developing a host of ideas about bottoms and cultural history. Male buttocks that seized the imagination and artistic appreciation of contemporaries in Renaissance Italy include the gargantuan sculpture of Hercules that was exhibited in the courtyard of the Palazzo Farnese in Rome, and the continued appreciation of the tremulously sensual bronze androgyne David, sculpted in Florence by Donatello in the mid-fifteenth century, whose inner thigh is tickled by the feathered plume of the helmet of Goliath, recently slain by the hero.

Beyond the distracting view of Brusasorci's central panel, the ceiling is made up of stucco mouldings by Bartolomeo Ridolfi, on which Eliodoro Forbicini painted *grottesche* (grotesques). This term is used to describe the repeated garlands of curving foliage, masks and hybrid figures and is a stylistic interior decoration derived from the painted corridors of Emperor Nero's Domus Aurea in Rome, which dates to the first century [CE]. By the fifteenth century, the building was partly submerged under the soil of the city and the ruins were broken into from above, which lent them the names *grotte* meaning caves. The frescoed panels inserted into the stuccowork depict signs of the zodiac and also images of Roman monetary coins, reflecting an interest in the study of currency, collecting and connoisseurship. So, while the idiomatic phrase to *ragionare col culo*, or to think with one's backside (in other words, foolishly) would not be lost on the Renaissance viewer to the Palazzo Chiericati, who might chortle or blush when confronted with the bare bottom of Apollo from below, the erudite allusions to classical mythology and history would have more than tempered this, to promote the status of Girolamo Chiericati as an educated and cultured patron.

Left: Domenico Brusasorci's frescoed panel pays homage to a similar depiction of Apollo and Diana, titled *Chariot of the Sun*, painted by Giulio Romano in 1526.

Opposite: The frescoed panels inserted into the stuccowork depict signs of the zodiac and also images of Roman monetary coins, reflecting an interest in the study of currency, collecting and connoisseurship.

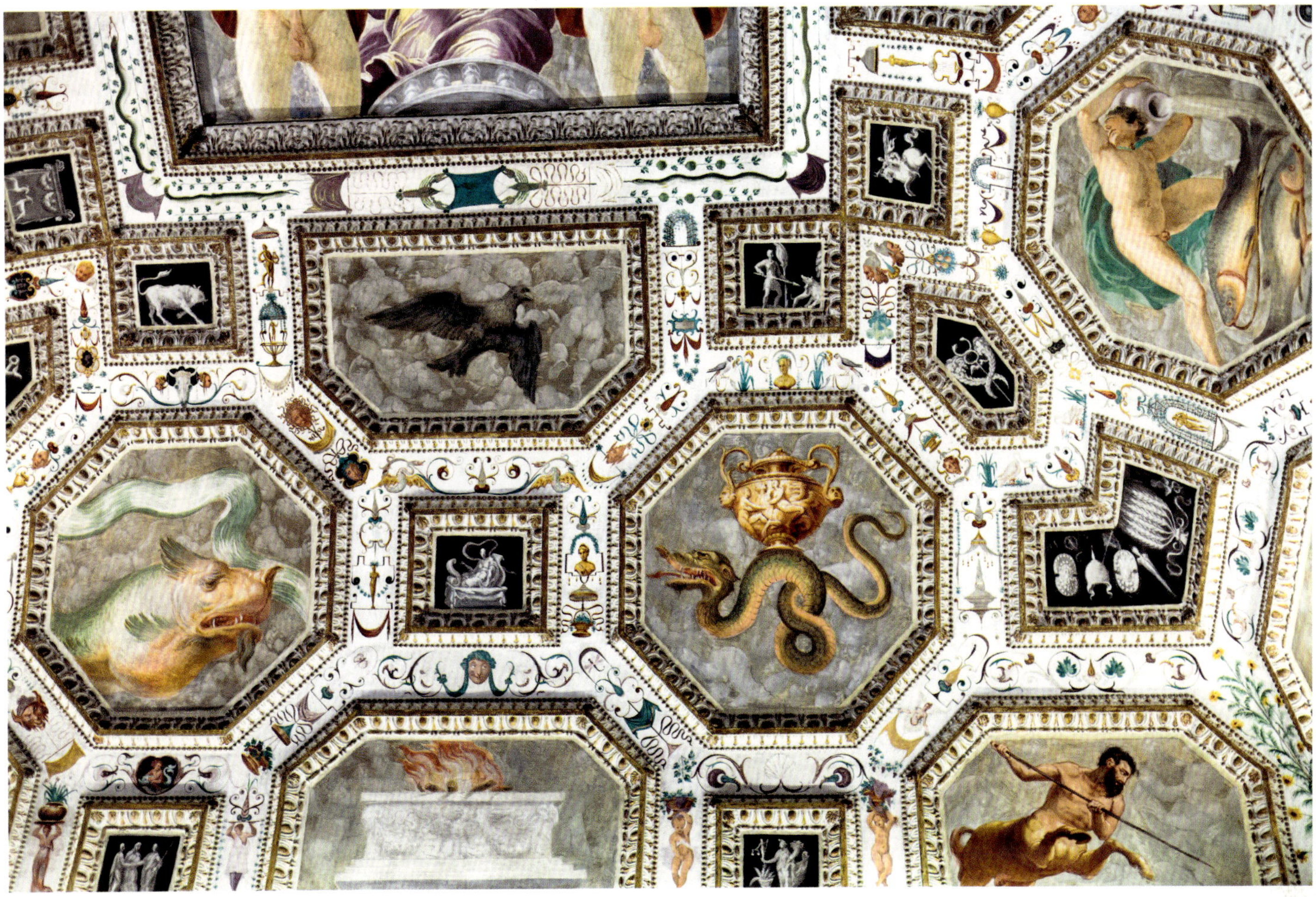

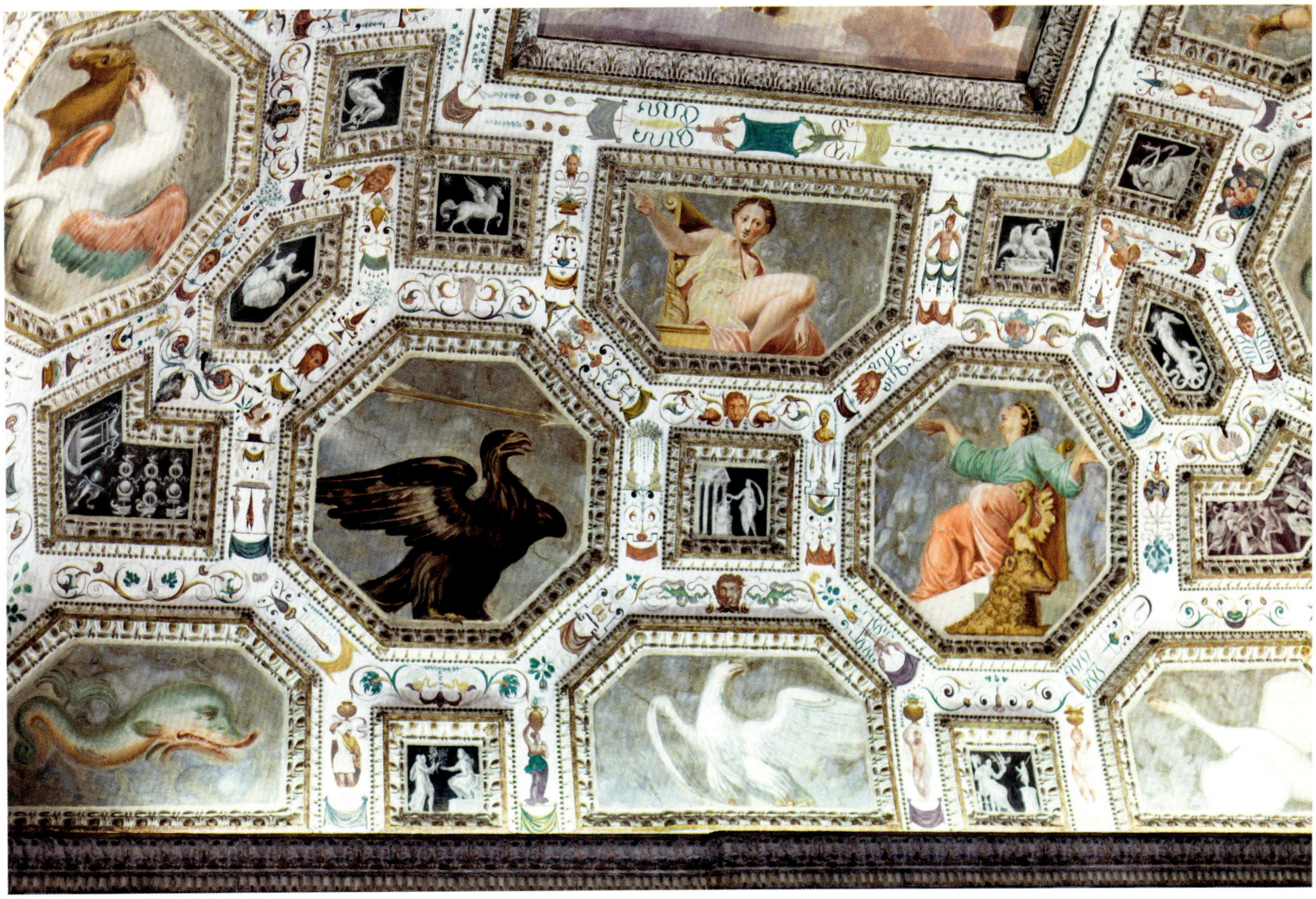

Jan Fabre

Heaven of Delight

2002

Royal Palace of Brussels, Brussels, Belgium

Left and overleaf: Jan Fabre's *Heaven of Delight*, occupying the ceiling of La Salle des Glaces in the Royal Palace of Brussels, is made up of jewelled scarab beetles. The wing cases extend down from their entrapment on the ceiling to encrust a grand chandelier.

Royal Palace of Brussels, Belgium

In 2002, the Italian-born Queen Paola, wife of Belgian King Albert, decided that she was tiring a little of the monotone decor in the interior of the Palais Royale in Brussels. She decided to revive the tradition of commissioning contemporary artists to install permanent artworks in the royal residence, a custom that had languished since Auguste Rodin decorated the throne room with bas reliefs in the early twentieth century. Queen Paola set about finding a twenty-first century update to La Salle des Glaces (the Hall of the Mirrors), a barrel-vaulted, stucco-panelled ceremonial room. She found her answer in the controversial Dutch artist Jan Fabre, who is known for his unconventional choice of materials and his recurrent obsession with insects, especially the jewel scarab beetle, whose iridescent green wing cases have been a favourite medium in his sculptures.

In restaurants in Malaysia, Thailand and Indonesia, the insects are considered to be a delicacy and are eaten for their high protein content. The glistening wing cases are usually discarded, but Fabre's team collected 1.6 million of them and, over the course of four months, created an alternative type of mosaic on the ceiling of the mirrored hall by gluing them in a predetermined pattern. Legs of giraffes, the wings of birds and the eyes of salamanders all emerge in the seemingly shifting surface. Due to the opalescent glossy surface of the wing cases, the view of the ceiling shifts and morphs in terms of colour and perceived texture depending on the viewpoint in the room. For example, the surface transmogrifies from emerald green to rich ochre shot through with blue and purple, and reflects a sheen that seems sometimes like feathers, sometimes like scales.

The work is called *Heaven of Delight* in homage to the fifteenth-century artist Hieronymus Bosch (Fabre's self-proclaimed master) and his arcane triptych of panel paintings known as the *Garden of Earthly Delights*. Also originating from the Netherlands, Bosch's work has bedevilled scholars' attempts at interpretation and features hybrid zoomorphic forms and dreamlike animal and human interactions.

For the human mind, the elusive alien beauty of the insect kingdom confronts us with elements of fear, threat and paranoia, making it a rich source of inspiration for contemporary art. Something of this mixture of fear and fascination lends Fabre's ceiling its power – after all it is an infestation of sorts in the grandiose order of the ceremonial palace. But there is a certain tension at play between the teeming surface area covered by the beetle wings and the way in which this is controlled by the strict ordering of the material into hermetically sealed panels; a tension that is, however, held in a slippery balance. The wing cases extend down from their entrapment on the ceiling to encrust a grand chandelier, and in doing so transform the ornamental light into something resembling a giant monstrous insect of the imagination. Nor is this the first time that beetle wings have been used in the decorative arts; John Singer Sargent's portrait of the English Victorian actress Ellen Terry as Lady Macbeth from 1889 captures the Shakespearean actress in her iconic stage costume made from thousands of similar beetle wings.

While many palace ceilings promote idealized stories of apotheosis and enduring temporal power, Fabre's *Heaven of Delight* projects another vision of immortality and history. For the scarab

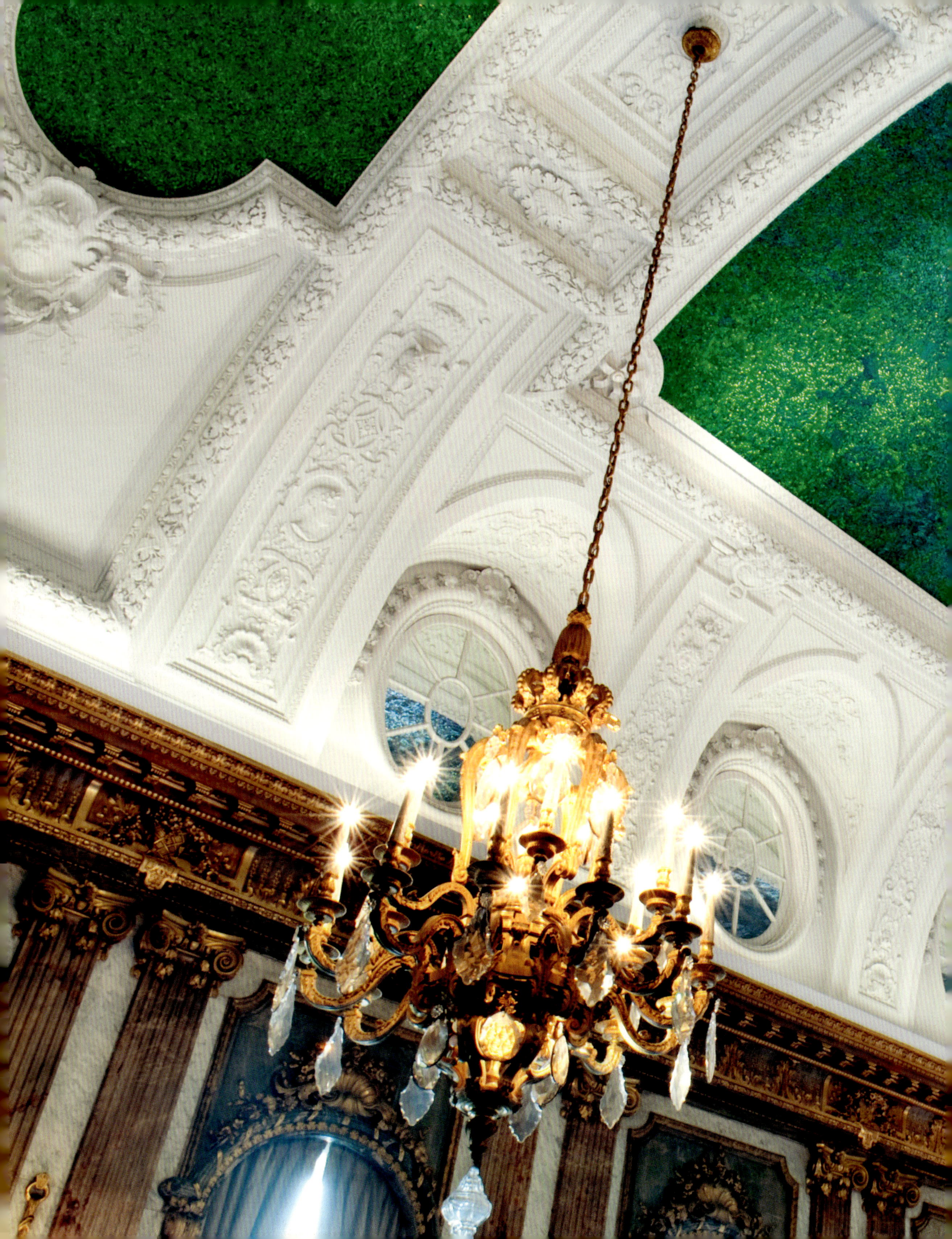

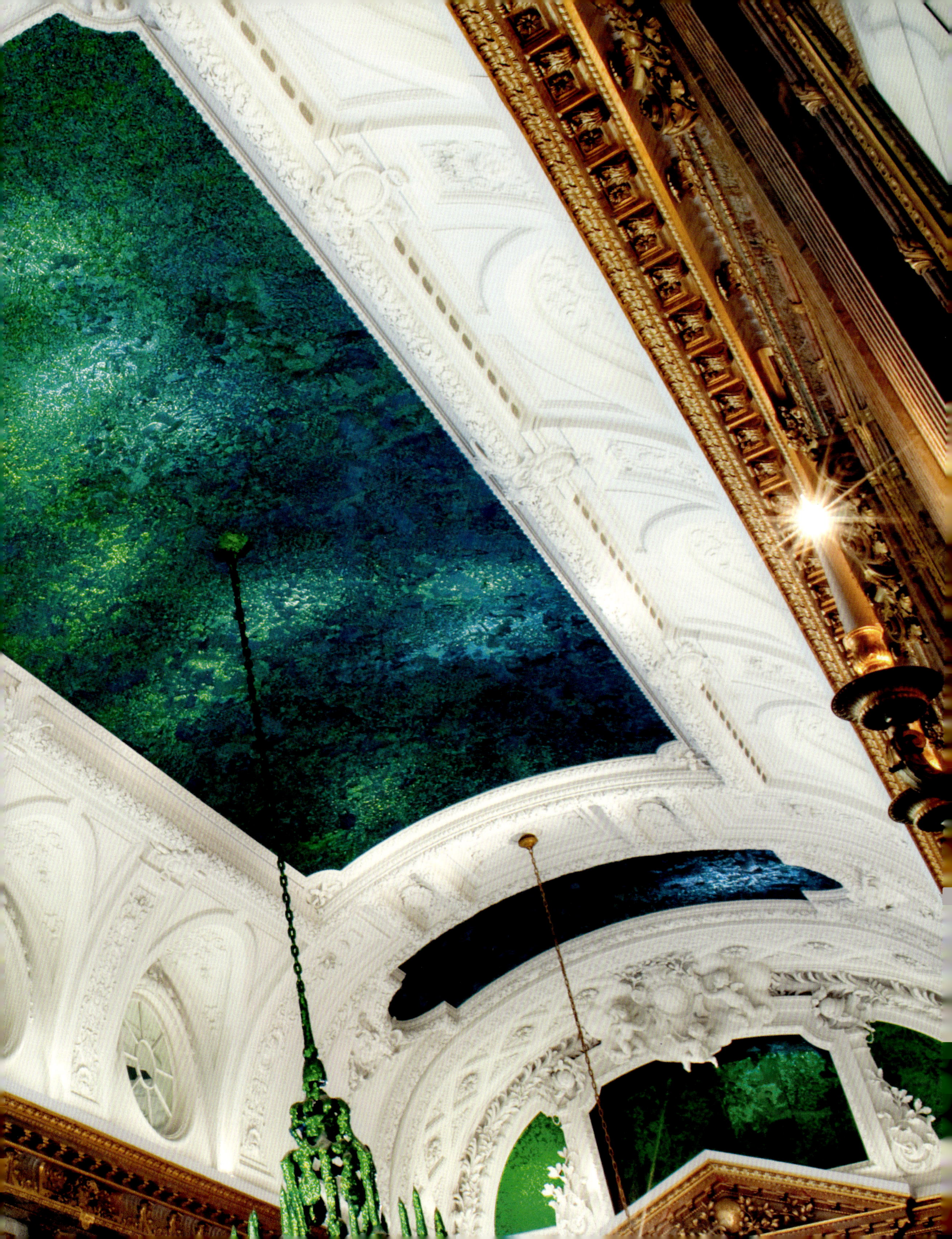

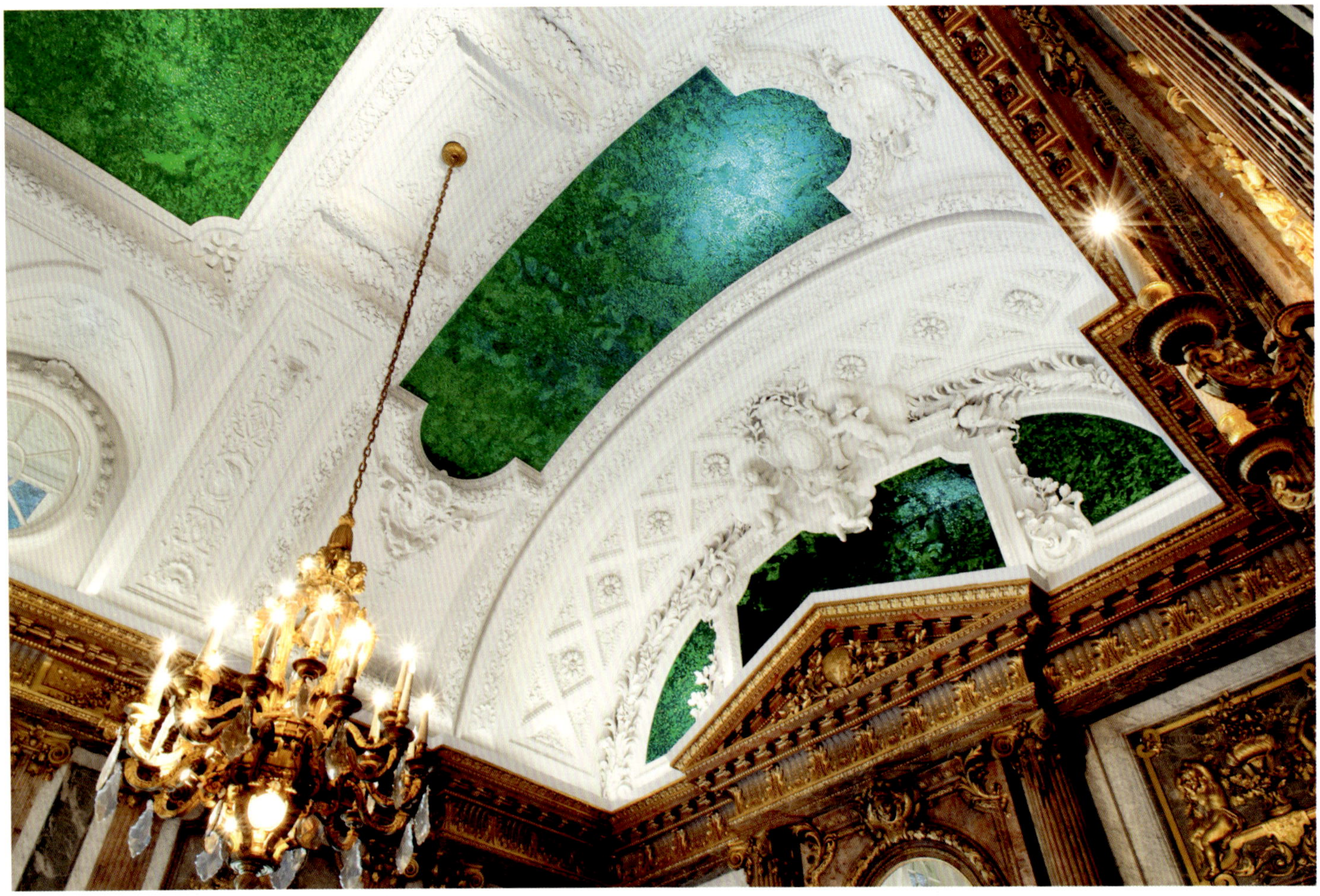

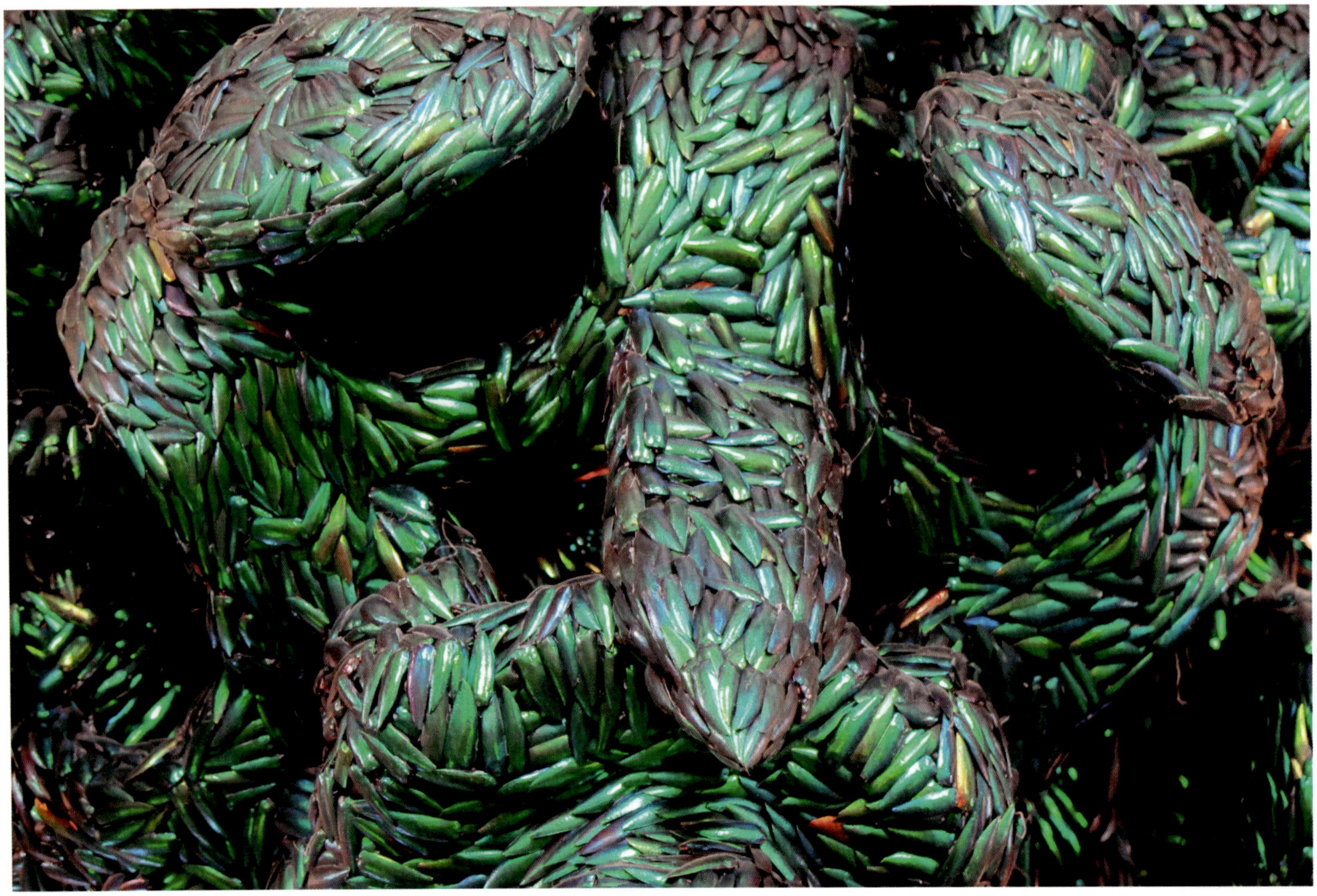

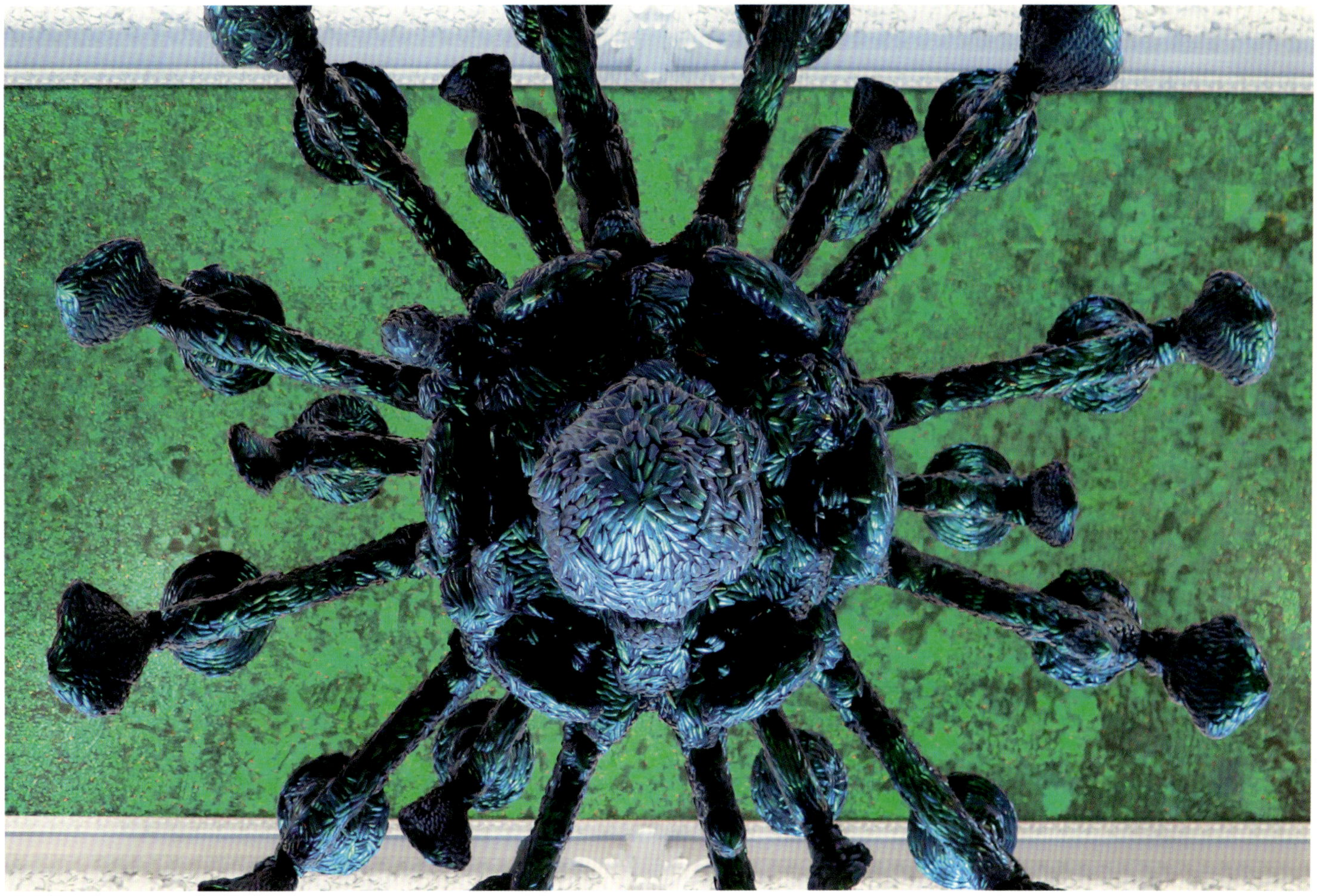

Above and opposite bottom: A lamp made of jewelled scarab beetles hanging from the ceiling of La Salle des Glaces in the Royal Palace of Brussels.

Opposite top: Interior of the Royal Palace of Brussels.

beetle is an ancient link in the evolutionary chain, little changed since it first roamed the earth 130 million years ago. As such, it provides us with a bridge to deep time as a carrier of ancient knowledge, orientating itself, for example, by the sun and the pattern of stars in the sky – practices that humans have forgotten or relinquished through evolution. In fact, the scarab beetle has long been revered across human history. Ancient Egyptian civilizations associated the insect with the god of the rising sun because of the way in which it rolls dung balls in microcosmic imitation of the passage of the sun. The scarab became a symbol of regeneration, and even in later millennia, an early Christian symbol of resurrection. They were also associated with miraculous transformative powers, as the seventeenth-century Jesuit and polymath Athanasius Kircher believed that the scarab was formed from *prima materia* – a primeval substance regarded as the original material of the universe.

Whereas the Latin aphorism *ars longa, vita brevis* was used to explain the ability of art to promote the glory of an individual in posterity even after their own death, the beetle wings outlive the immortalizing efforts of art, as they are composed of a substance called chitin, far stronger than any oil paint and inviolable to the elements. Long after the occupants of the palace are gone, the opalescent beauty of the installation will not fade.

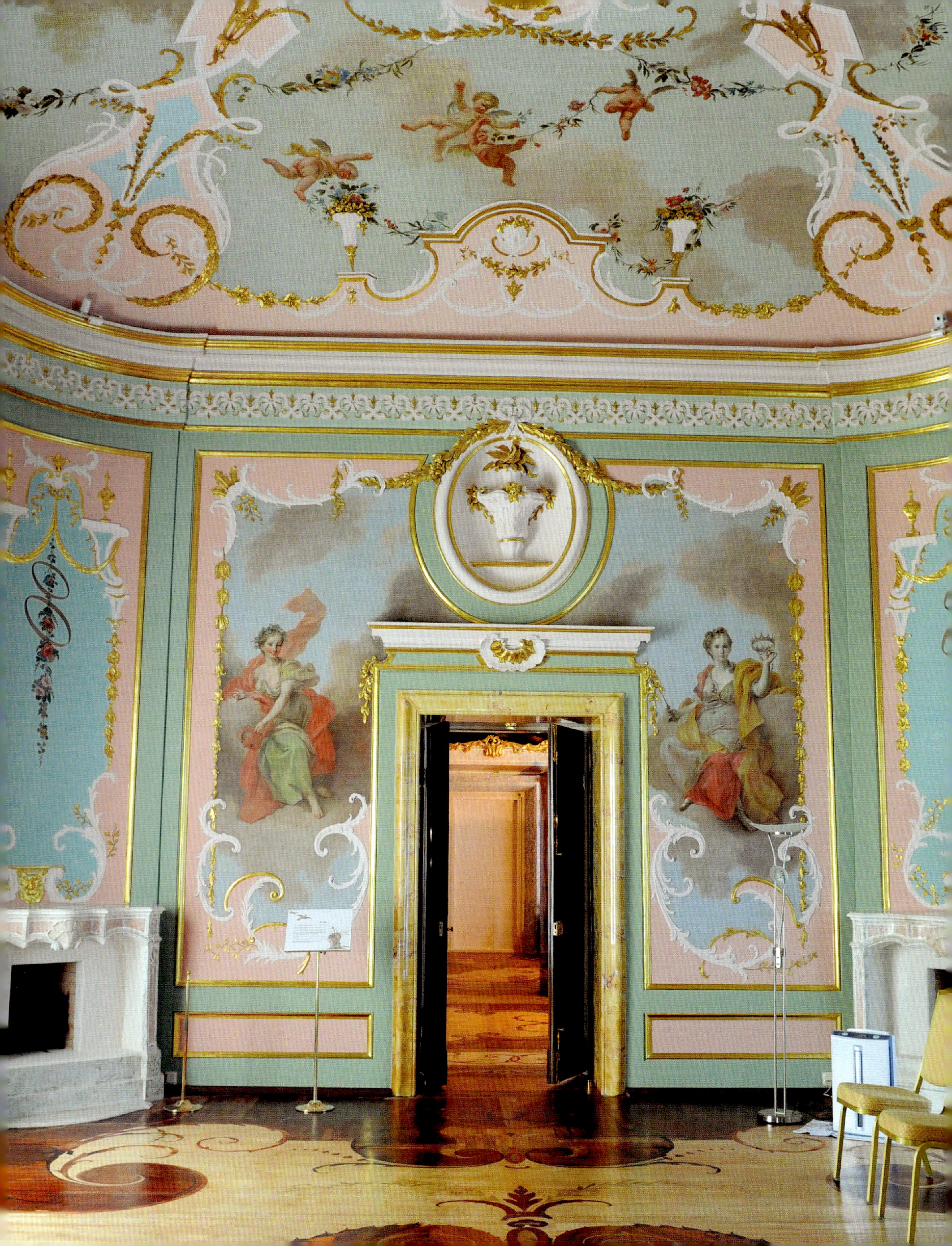

Stefano Torelli

Hall of Muses

1768

Chinese Palace, St Petersburg, Russia

Left: Hall of Muses in the Chinese Palace, St Petersburg, a private residence of Empress Catherine II built by the architect Antonio Rinaldi in the Rococo style.

Chinese Palace, Russia

Newly freed from her husband, and in possession of a lover who shared her passion for decorative arts and architecture, the politically brilliant and intellectually gifted Empress Catherine II of Russia built the Chinese Palace at Oranienbaum to be a place of her own. It lies to the west of St Petersburg, on the Gulf of Finland among other royal residencies. The estate was owned originally by Prince Alexander Menshikov, a favourite of Peter the Great who had a habit of building lavish palaces that rivalled the magnificence even of the tsar. Menshikov fell from grace in 1728 and was stripped of all his titles and estates. Oranienbaum was later given to Grand Duke Peter, the nephew of the Empress Elizabeth and future Emperor Peter III, husband to Catherine. He employed the architect Antonio Rinaldi to build a new, perfectly square, miniature version of the original, but in the fashionable Rococo style. After her husband's death it was Catherine's turn to make her mark on Oranienbaum and the new Chinese Palace was constructed (designed also by Rinaldi) and opened in 1768.

This residence was intended to be Catherine's private pleasure palace; a summer 'dacha' retreat for her and her intimates, including her lover Grigory Orlov, officer of the Praetorian Guard of St Petersburg. With the help of Grigory and his brother Alexei Orlov, Catherine had set in motion a coup d'état that had resulted in the arrest and murder of her husband Emperor Peter III. As the newly crowned Empress of Russia, and with the task of legitimizing her rulership, she set about crafting a cosmopolitan self-image of herself at the helm of a modernizing, outward-looking new Russia. The Chinese Palace was designed to fulfil some of these aspirations. Some of the groundwork had been laid already in the name of the estate alone – the name Oranienbaum is a version of the German term for 'orange tree' and referred to the exotic greenhouses that had been part of an earlier palace in the grounds. Originating in the East, the orange tree encapsulated everything luxurious, desirable and exclusive to the aspirational aristocracy.

The fashion for 'chinoiserie' in Europe in the eighteenth century was contagious among the wealthy and elite and was prompted by the arrival in Europe and Russia of Chinese exports of lacquerware, porcelain and silks. These inspired decorative motifs in interiors that appealed to Western curiosity and imagination with fantastical landscapes, dragons, pagodas and characters in Chinese dress all depicted in lush, vivid colours. However, these details were mostly drawn from a fantasy vision of the Orient as seen through a Western lens and rarely based on genuine fact. Despite this, the adoption of a Chinese style (however notional) for her Rococo palace was part of Catherine's wider interest as an enlightened ruler in understanding the shared humanity across the boundaries of different nationalities. Catherine modelled herself as an open-minded ruler who drew from the currents of western European politics, especially the philosophical ideas espoused by the Enlightenment. For example, she acted as patron and correspondent of Denis Diderot, the French philosopher who had sought refuge in Russia when he fell under criticism for the antireligious nature of his *Encyclopédie* project in his native France. In this manner she aligned herself with other rulers in Europe, such as her ally and rival Frederick the Great of Prussia, who had entertained the French philosopher

Voltaire for two years in his summer palace. Determined not to be outdone by him in the pursuit of either philosophy or luxury, Catherine commenced building of her Chinese Palace just as Frederick completed his Chinese Teahouse in 1764.

The conceptual design of the interior fuses the fascination for the Orient with the traditional tenets of the humanities and classical learning in Old Europe. Catherine enlisted the Italian-born Stefano Torelli, then professor at the Academy of Fine Arts in St Petersburg, to decorate the interior of the Hall of Muses, a place for contemplation and appreciation of the arts, and perhaps for listening to musical recitals. The concept was prevalent in palaces across Europe – from Vienna to the Vatican Palace in Rome. As was customary, the room invoked the nine muses of ancient Greek mythology who presided over the arts and sciences, lending divine inspiration to humans. Among these are Erato, muse of love poetry, Calliope, muse of heroic poetry and rhetoric, and Terpsichore, the muse of dance.

The Hall of Muses demonstrates the Rococo decorative characteristics of shell- and coral-like formations and arabesque curves known collectively as 'rocaille'. This style cultivated less grandiose interiors in favour of a more warm and intimate environment that was in harmony with the rural environment of Oranienbaum. Here in Catherine's palace the decorative painted tendrils and garlands bring the natural world inside and they creep like vines around the pastel pink, blue and eau de nil panelled walls of the Hall of Muses, fusing the natural with the manmade. As is often the case with natural beauty, Catherine's enjoyment of her palace was to be ultimately short-lived. Once finished, and with her love affair evaporated, she spent very little time here. By the end of the century, Oranienbaum had already been given over to use, rather incongruously, by a Naval Cadet College.

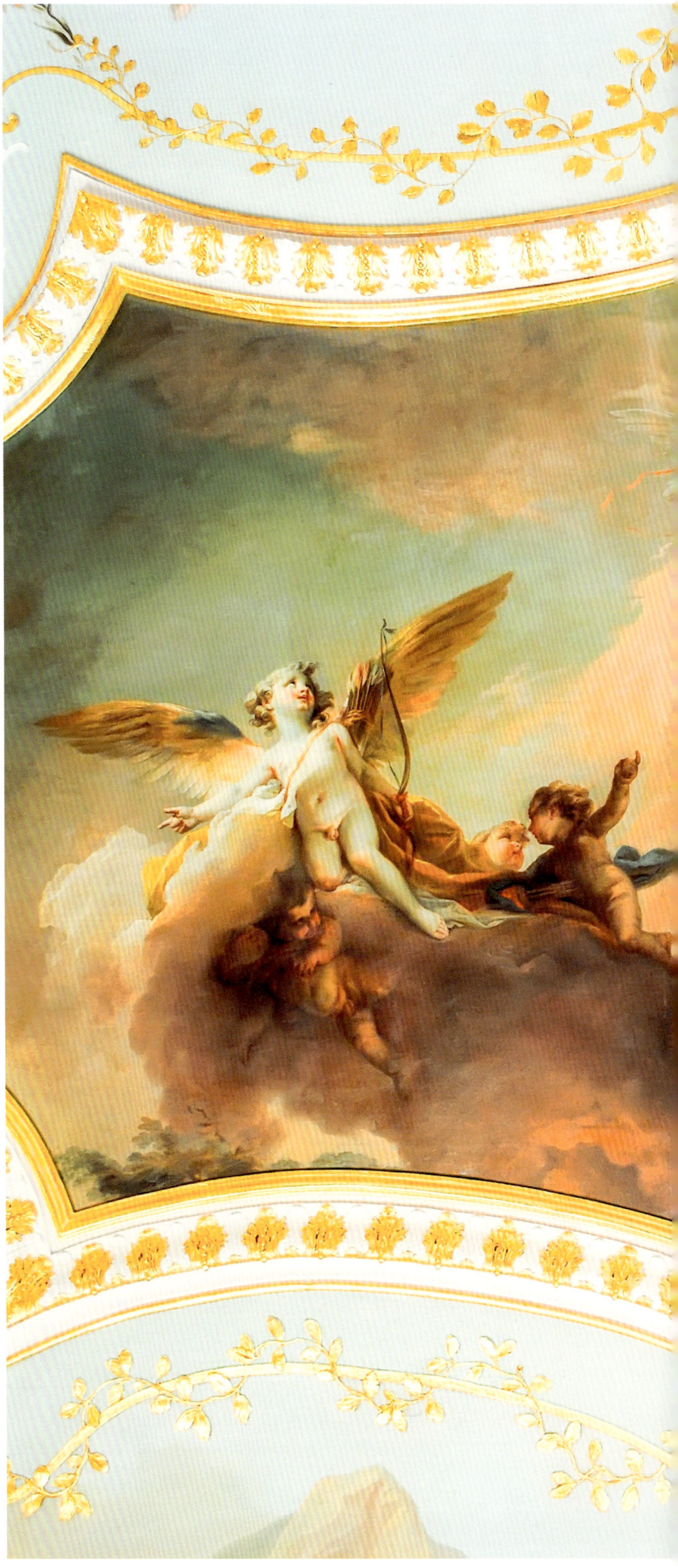

Opposite: Detail of one of the Hall of Muses' stuccos.

Right: *Portrait of Catherine II in Front of a Mirror* by Vigilius Eriksen.

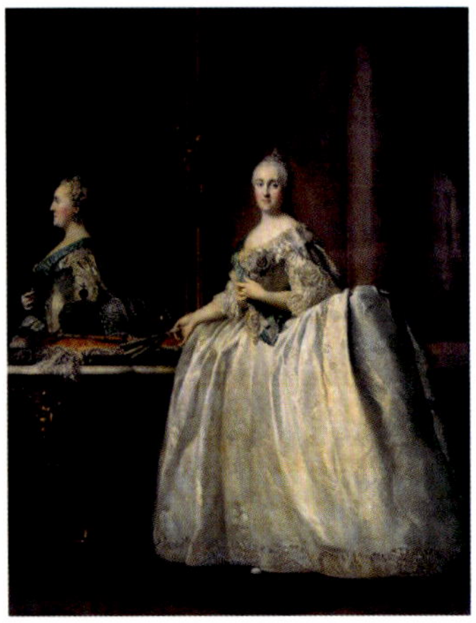

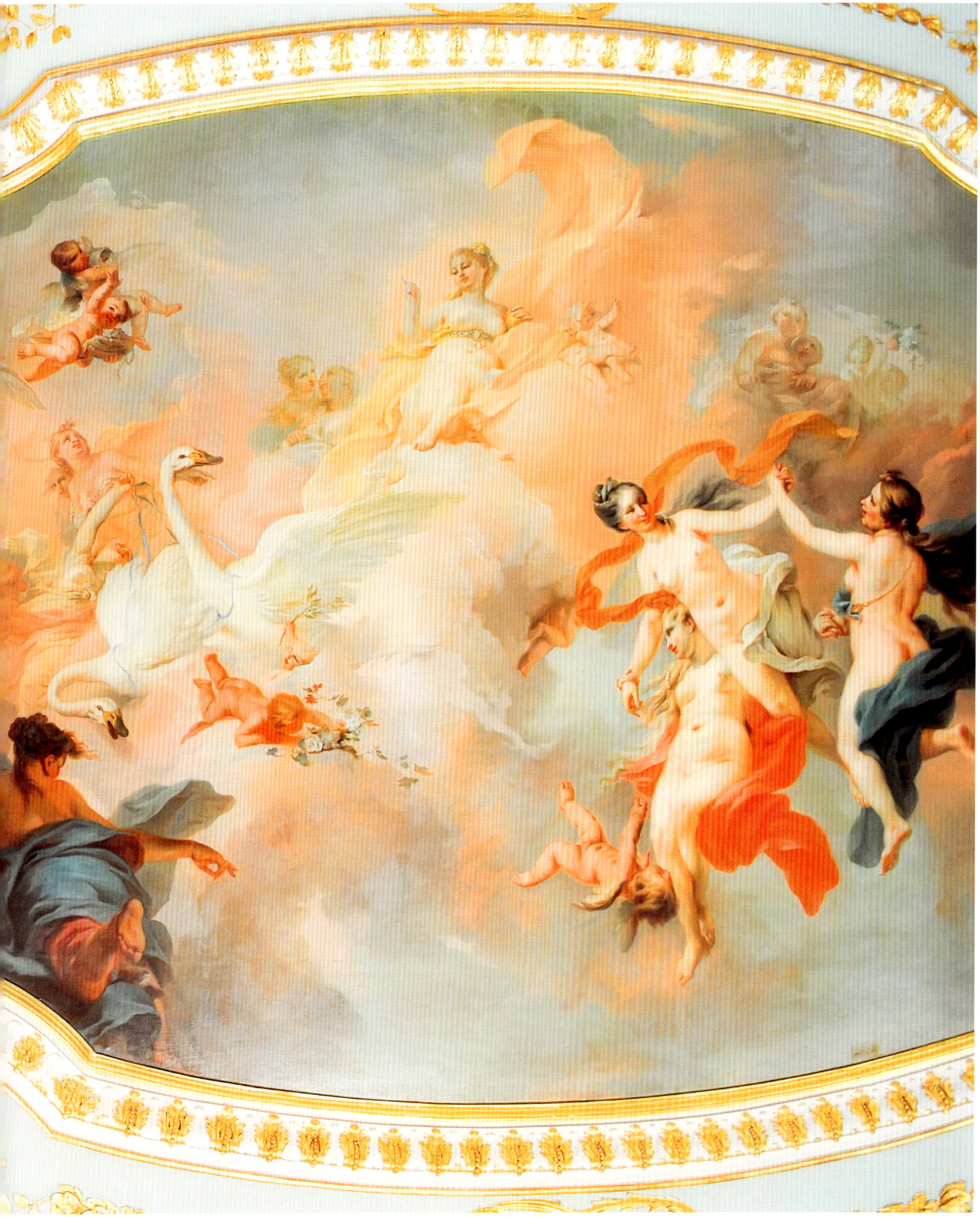

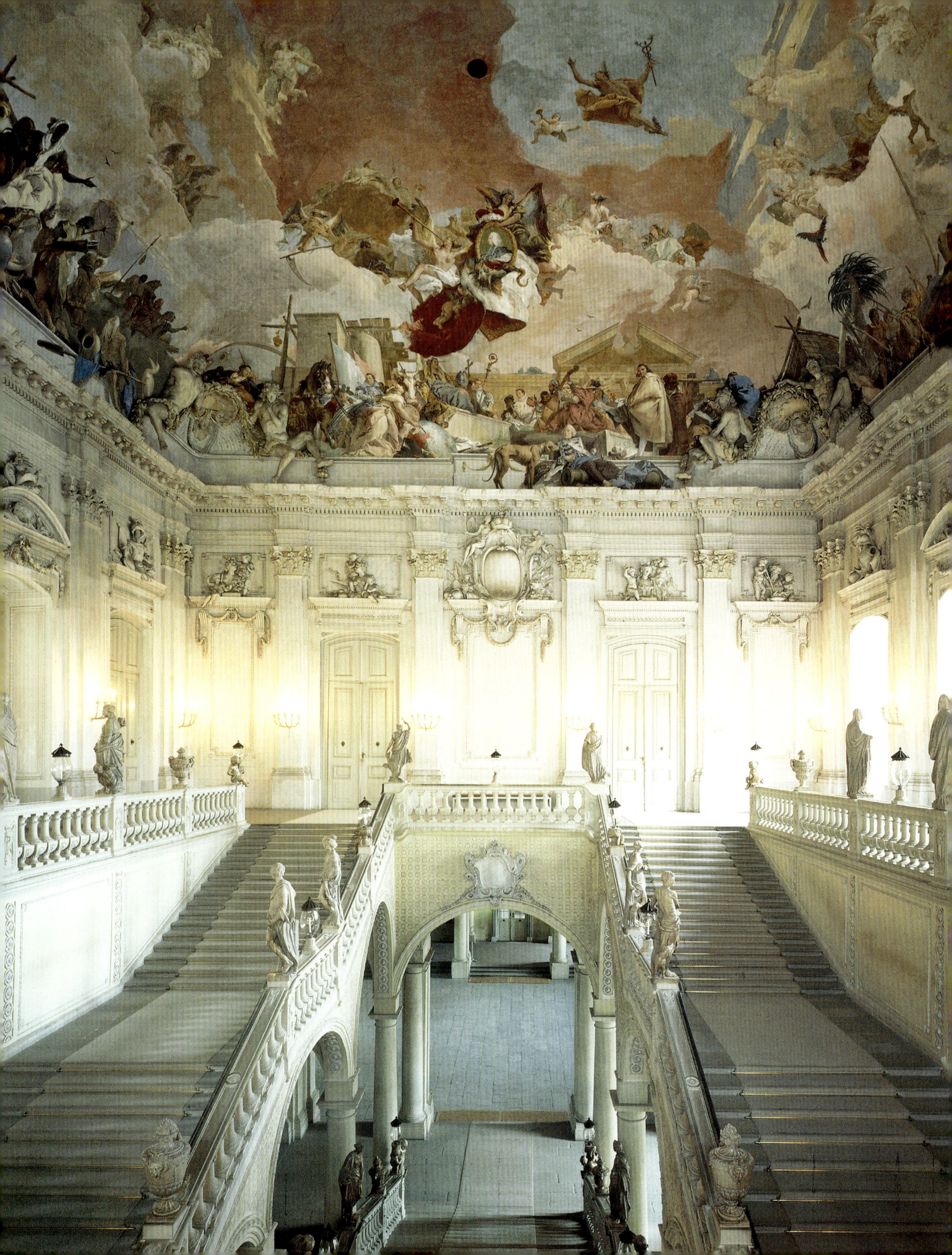

Giovanni Battista Tiepolo

Apollo and the Continents

1752–53

Würzburg Residence, Würzburg, Germany

Left: The grand staircase at the Würzburg Residence, with Giovanni Battista Tiepolo's frescoed vault above it.

Overleaf: Central image of Giovanni Battista Tiepolo's *Apollo and the Continents*.

Würzburg Residence, Germany

After his election in 1749, the priority for the Prince-Bishop Karl Philipp von Greiffenclau was decorating his palace of pomp and splendour known as the Würzburg Residence. Von Greiffenclau was an erudite ruler who spoke five languages and had spent an extended period in Rome on the Grand Tour. Besides his career in the Church, he held a doctorate in law and was appointed Rector of the University of Mainz and the University of Würzburg.

The decoration of the Residence had been an ongoing and grandiose project that no painter had yet satisfied, until Giovanni Battista Tiepolo took on the commission to paint the Kaisersaal (Imperial Hall). Its successful completion resulted in a further commission to paint the ceiling of the grand ceremonial staircase with an all-encompassing world view depicting the sun god Apollo and the four continents, with Europe at the heart of a microcosm that unfolds across 600 sq m (6,500 sq ft) of painted ceiling. A mellow glow radiates from the centre of the vault, pooling into a crisper violet light around the edges. Here is the influence of Tiepolo's native Venice, an endless laboratory of light reflecting on the water of the lagoon and its various atmospheric and aesthetic effects.

Tiepolo commenced the painting before the building work was even complete (under the design of principal architect Balthasar Neumann) and faced the vexing conundrum of devising a pictorial narrative for a vast ceiling for which there was no one viewpoint – for visitors ascending the stairs, the viewing angle constantly shifts and morphs.

Looking up from the staircase, a strange and exotic world unfurls before us. A bare-breasted figure of America with brightly coloured plumage in her hair sits astride a giant crocodile. A clutch of severed heads in the foreground suggests that these New World inhabitants are savages who practise cannibalism, while the lack of buildings reflects the contemporary belief in the primeval state of America, as yet untouched by civilization, let alone architecture or cultivation. America points to the right, gesturing towards a banner with the image of a mythical beast known as a 'gryphon', which serves as a reference to Prince-Bishop Greiffenclau's coat of arms. America and her retinue, like the spectator on the staircase, are on their way to pay respects to the Prince-Bishop with bountiful gifts made of silver and gold, and a cornucopia of fruits, accompanied by a page with a pot of chocolate and the gift of an alligator, belly up to the sky.

The upper wall to the right of this shows a group representing Africa, with one figure dismounting from a giant dromedary. She has reached Europe, where she looks up to see a medallion with a portrait of Prince-Bishop in the sky, for she, too, is on her way to pay homage to the great man and is accompanied by big-game hunters bearing ivory tusks as gifts. In the foreground, a monkey chases an ostrich as a nod to the demand for luxury commodities from Africa by wealthy European consumers – ostrich feathers being highly prized.

Asia, meanwhile, is seen riding haughtily on an elephant. The accompanying imagery portrays the continent as both a place of depraved violence and as the fountainhead of civilization. The former is represented by the slaying of a lactating tigress and a manacled slave in agony, while, on the right-hand side, is a block of stone with an indecipherable arrangement of words from the

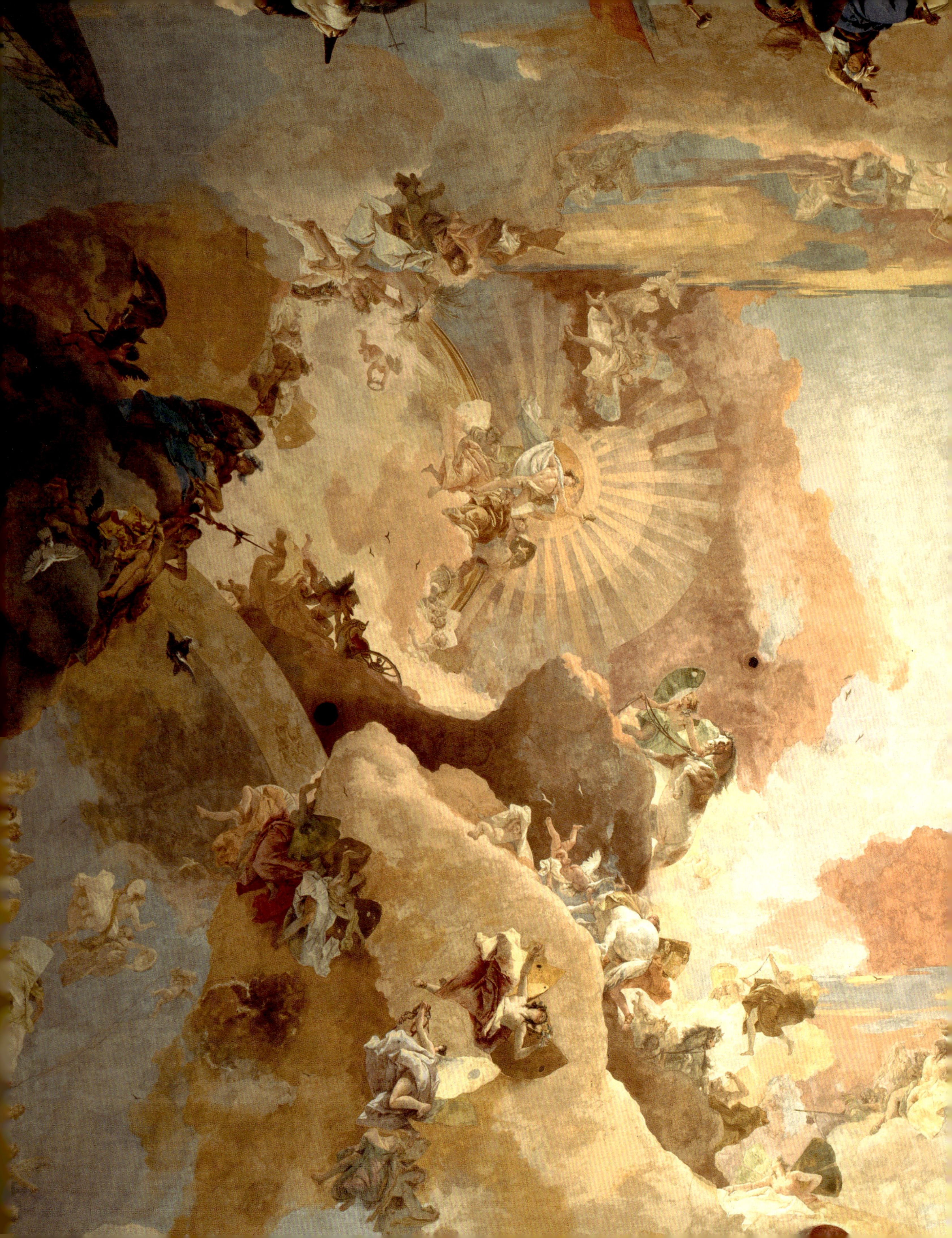

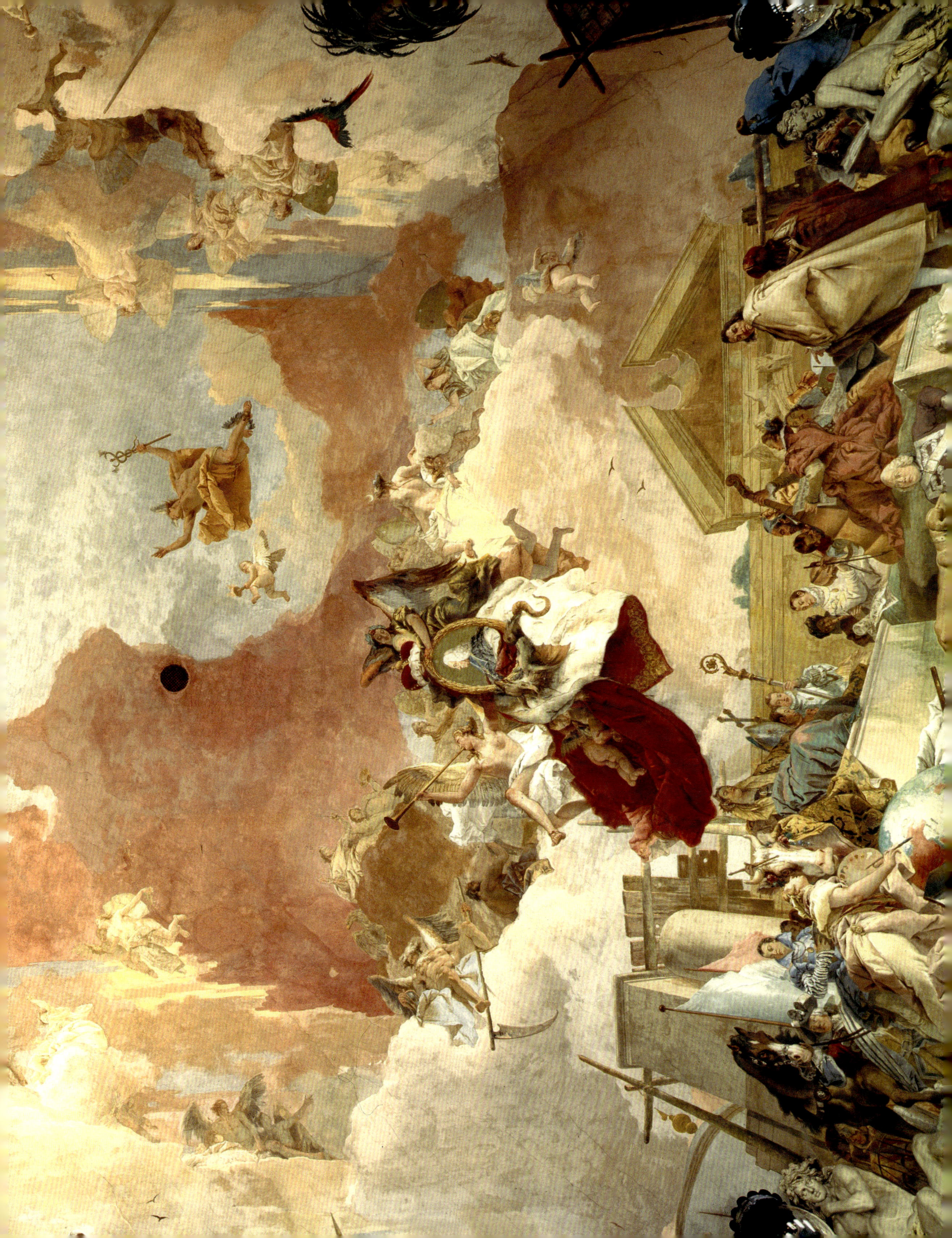

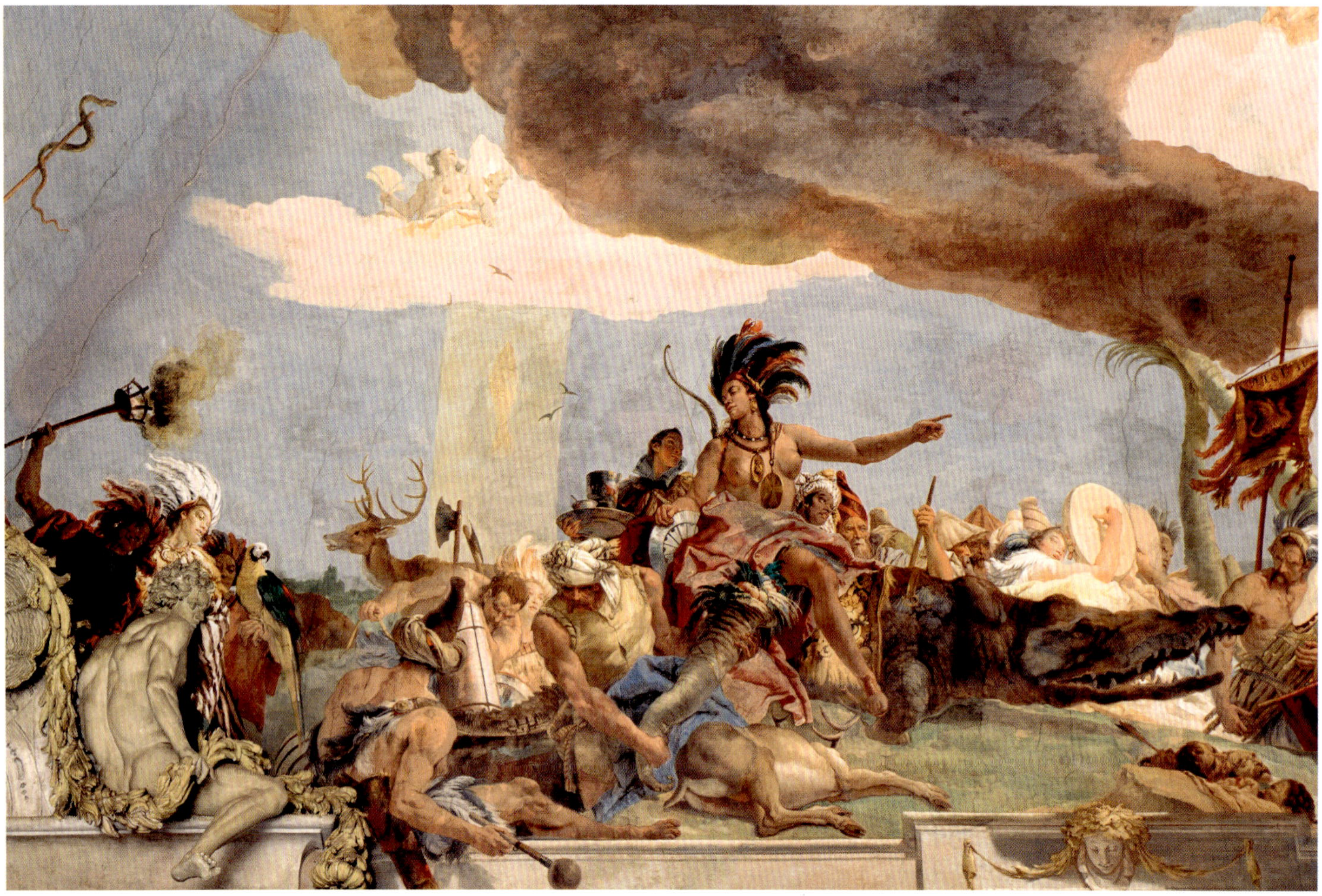

Above: A figure of America, personified by a bare-breasted figure with brightly coloured plumage in her hair.

Below: Depiction of Africa with one figure dismounting from a giant dromedary.

Opposite: Figures of Fame and Virtue carry a portrait of Prince-Bishop von Greiffenclau towards Mount Olympus and immortality, which acts as the centrepiece of the pictorial narrative.

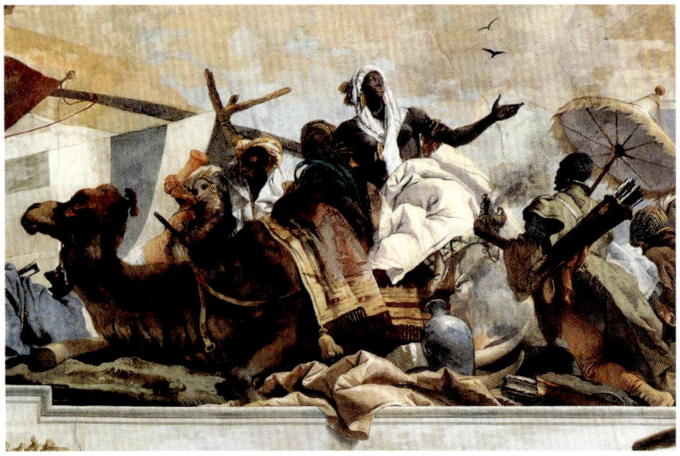

Greek and Palmyrene languages. This represents the birth of literacy and is accompanied by Athena, goddess of wisdom. In the background, primitive shelters of branches and planks symbolize the first rudimentary dwellings that evolved into the fine art of architecture. Meanwhile, a view of Mount Calvary where Christ was crucified is a reminder that Christianity started in this corner of Asia.

Europe is the centrepiece of the pictorial narrative, appearing on the south wall and visible only when the spectator climbs the staircase and turns to look backwards. She is presented here, with crown and sceptre, as the natural sovereign of the world who commands the respect of all other continents. A cast of illustrious residents line the foreground and include portraits of contemporary artists, architects and composers, including the architect of the Residenz Balthasar Neumann and Tiepolo himself. The patron Prince-Bishop von Greiffenclau appears in portrait form on a medallion suspended by personifications of Fame and Virtue, who sound a trumpet and bestow a crown above the painting. He is being carried upwards to Mount Olympus, where immortality and Zeus, king of the gods, awaits with thunderbolts, while Ganymede the cupbearer sits poised with wine.

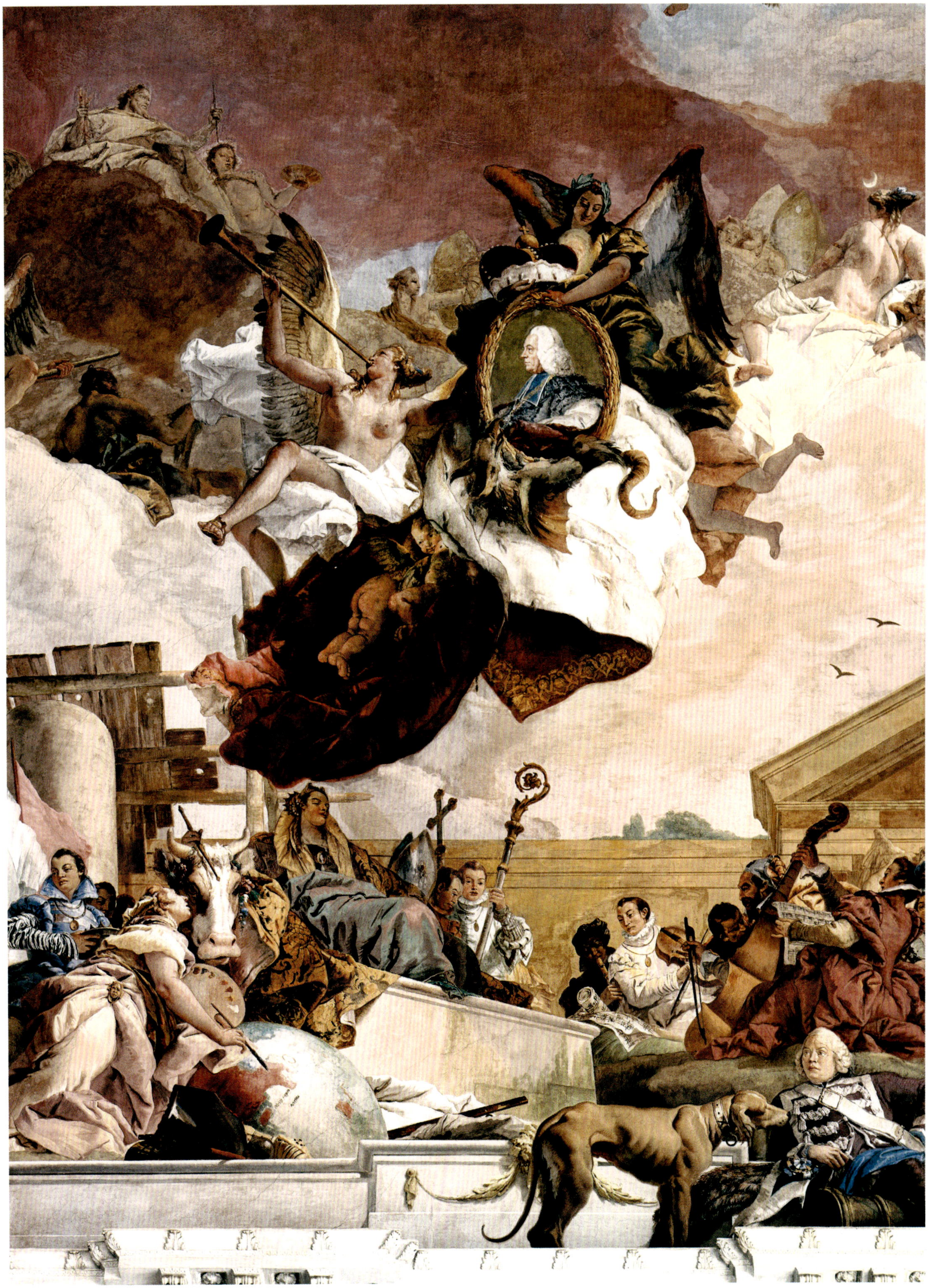

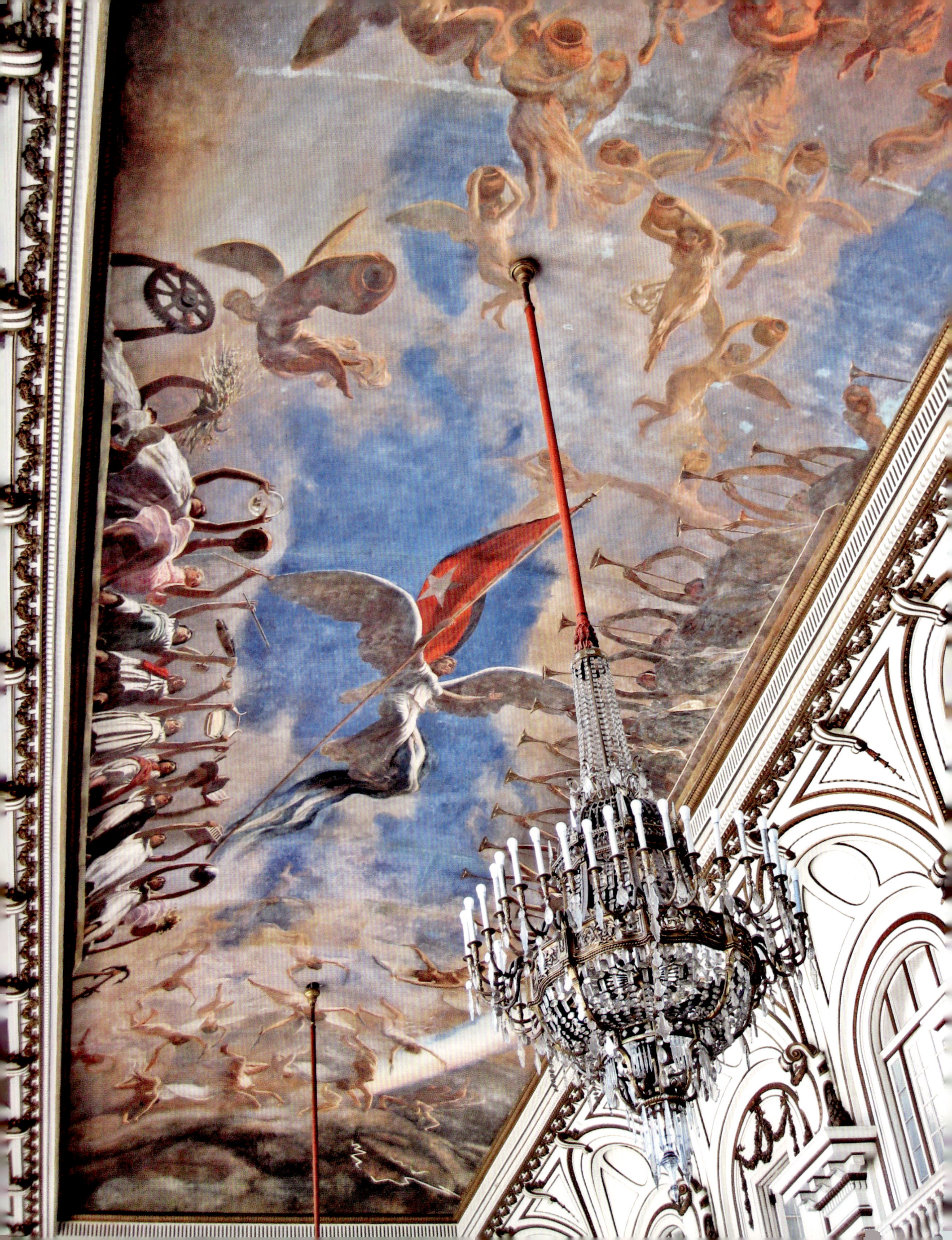

4

Politics

Behind the closed doors of political establishments, painted ceilings often represent an idealized projection of the affairs of state playing out in the rooms below. A ceiling is the perfect canvas on which to craft a self-styled civic and national identity, working in a certain sense as an extension of the body politic.

This form of connection between council and ceiling was important for the independent city-states featured in the following pages, such as the Golden Hall in the Augsburg Town Hall, Germany and the Hall of the Great Council of the Palazzo Ducale, in the most serene republic of Venice, Italy. In both of these, those in power emblazoned their central council halls with idealized images of temperate, fair and virtuous states, yet without losing a sense of richness and luxury as is evidenced by the overwhelming use of gilt in each example. Other political centres, such as the Hall of the Chronicles, City Hall, Barcelona, found dramatic ways in which to plough the annals of memory and victory to make for a more unsettling than reassuring visual experience.

Although, for the most part, a sense of splendour and drama unites the ceilings in this chapter, this is often finely balanced with subject matter that actively seeks to limit any critiques of absolutist despotism. For example, the ceiling of the Painted Hall in the Old Royal Naval College in Greenwich, London, promotes the values of the British Enlightenment. As such it champions the idea of a constitutional monarchy invested in the democratic rule of the people in the face of absolutism abroad. This was also a time in which science and enquiry began to challenge religious belief. That is not to say that the spiritual or absolutist aspect was ever absent in the political realm. The dome of Washington DC's Capitol Building draws strongly on past tropes of European absolutism to depict the apotheosis of the first US president, George Washington, who presides as an immortal in a pantheon of heaven where mythological gods mingle with innovators and engineers.

There is also an element of transience in the political arena, as one regime gives way to another over time, and this often leads to the repurposing of buildings associated with past political entities. So when it comes to the interior decoration it is not uncommon for somewhat ironic associations to arise. For example, the jubilant and titillating *The Loves of the Gods* in the Galleria Farnese, Rome, once entertained the papal Farnese family, but strikes an incongruous tone in a building now occupied by the French embassy. Or consider the former Cuban dictator Fulgencio Batista's Presidential Palace in Havana, which today functions as a celebration of the rebel armies that deposed him.

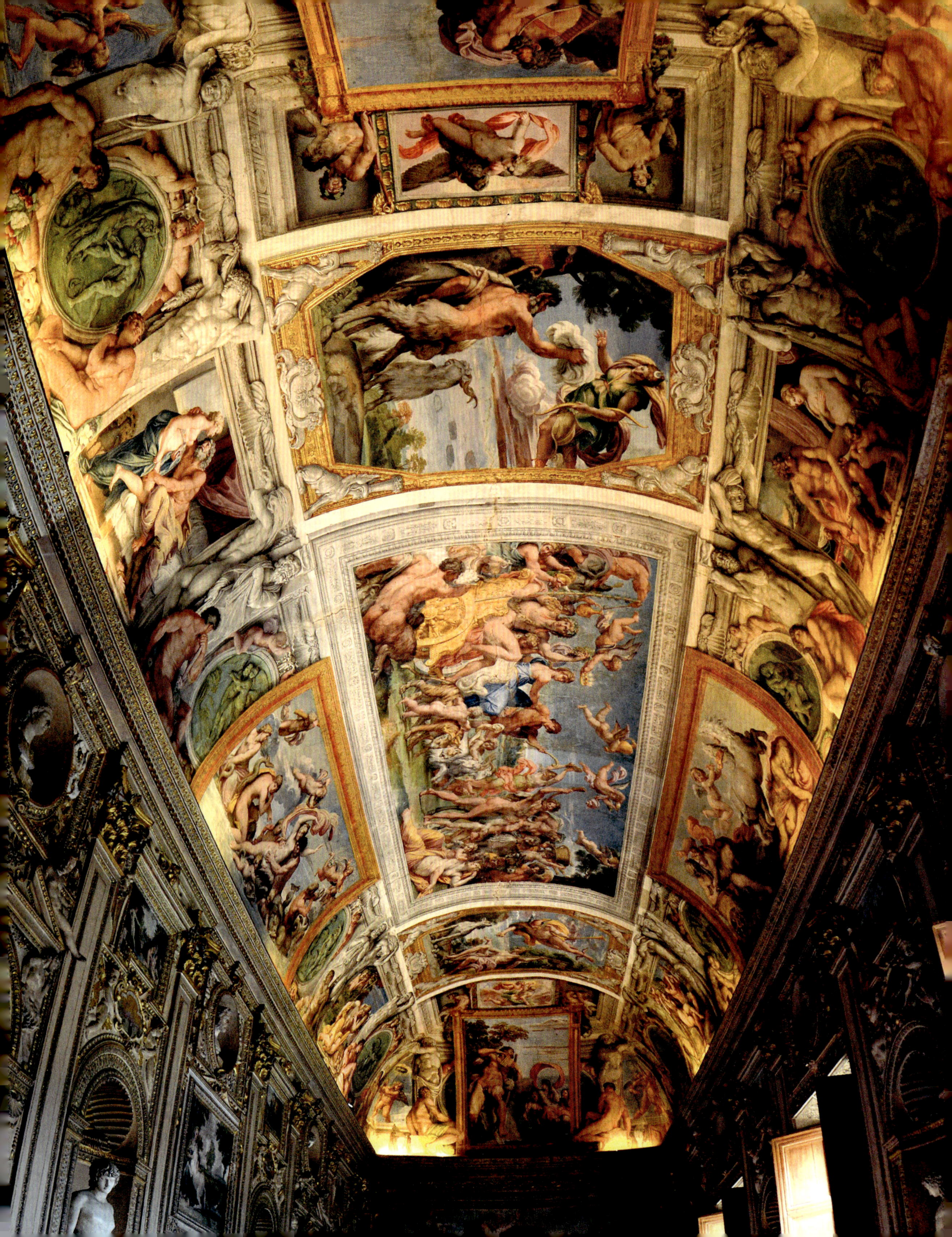

Annibale Carracci

The Loves of the Gods

1597–1607

Palazzo Farnese, Rome, Italy

Left and overleaf: View of the Galleria Farnese's vaulted ceiling in the Palazzo Farnese, Rome. The Palazzo Farnese, one of the most important high Renaissance palaces in Rome, is currently the French Embassy in Italy. Several main rooms were frescoed with elaborate allegorical programs, including *The Loves of the Gods* in the Galleria Farnese by the Bolognese painter Annibale Carracci.

Palazzo Farnese, Italy

Home to the French Embassy in Rome since 1936, the formidable stone exterior of the Palazzo Farnese shields a colourful secret. On balmy evenings, when the windows of the first-floor *piano nobile* are open to the Roman night, glimpses can be snatched of the lusciously frescoed ceiling of the Galleria Farnese. Gods and goddesses carouse in chariots to the smash of tambourines, drunks slip ungracefully off donkeys and languorously sensual male nudes hold up paintings, sculptures and garlands of fruit and vegetation. The painting cycle, known as *The Loves of the Gods*, was produced by Annibale Carracci between 1597 and 1608, with help from his brother Agostino and a band of Roman painters Giovanni Lanfranco, Francesco Albani and Domenichino and Sisto Badalocchio.

The work was commissioned by cardinal Odoardo Farnese, whose great uncle was Alessandro Farnese, otherwise known as Pope Paul III. As was the custom, Odoardo Farnese lived a princely lifestyle, and the decoration of his Roman palace reflected unequivocally his predilection for art collecting, wine and pleasures of the flesh.

The painting cycle is arranged in a compositional strategy known as *quadro riportato*, which is the presentation of painted images in fictitious painted frames. These depict the loves, mishaps and tragedies of the pagan gods and goddesses in episodes mostly derived from Ovid's *Metamorphoses*.

The ceiling is an entirely flat surface of a curved barrel, layered up with what looks like framed paintings and sculpted reliefs, bedecked with grimacing masks, handsome nude bodies, statues and bronze roundels and garlands of fruit and vegetables, all painted in illusionistic *trompe l'oeil* (trick of the eye). In the four corners of the room, the ceiling seems open to the sky, where putti frolic in azure spaces of an imagined beyond. Illusion is the theme here in more ways than one – not only in its *trompe l'oeil* effects that showcase a painting's ability to trick the eye, but also in lifting a veil on the mythological gods and goddesses of Mount Olympus, revealing them to suffer the same blows in affairs of love and sex that we mortals do.

Centre stage is the marriage procession of the pagan god Bacchus and his lover Ariadne, the daughter of King Minos. Goats and tigers pull the couple's chariot accompanied by a throng of satyrs, nymphs and putti bearing wine and food and playing instruments. This was a fitting tribute to Bacchus, who was the Roman deity associated with fruitfulness and ecstatic release. The procession leads the lovers to their bed and the subsequent union that will spawn the personification of wine. Chubby drunk Silenus – the inebriated yet wise tutor to the god Bacchus – brings up the rear carried on an ass.

Above this revelry a smaller, rectangular image depicts the story of Cephalus, the mortal who spurned the affections of Aurora, goddess of the dawn. Below, Thetis the sea nymph and Peleus the Greek prince – parents of the Greek hero Achilles – share a watery embrace on the waves. Both images are encased in what looks like a resplendent gold frame.

Beyond these, illusionistically placed behind the central band of images, is Galatea on her dolphin while a shell drifts by with the jealous one-eyed Cyclops playing the pipes. Elsewhere, enraged with jealousy, he throws a boulder at Galatea and her

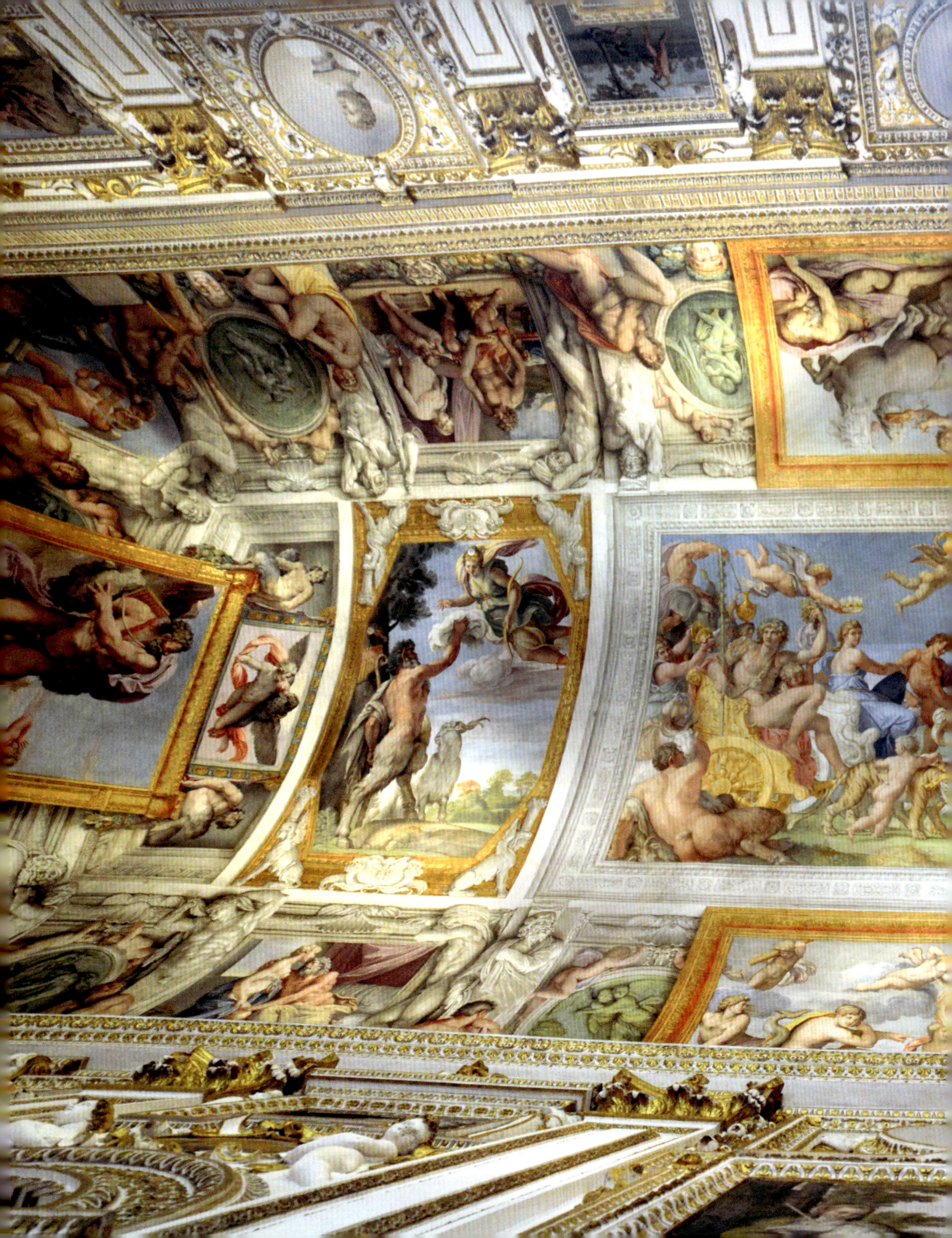

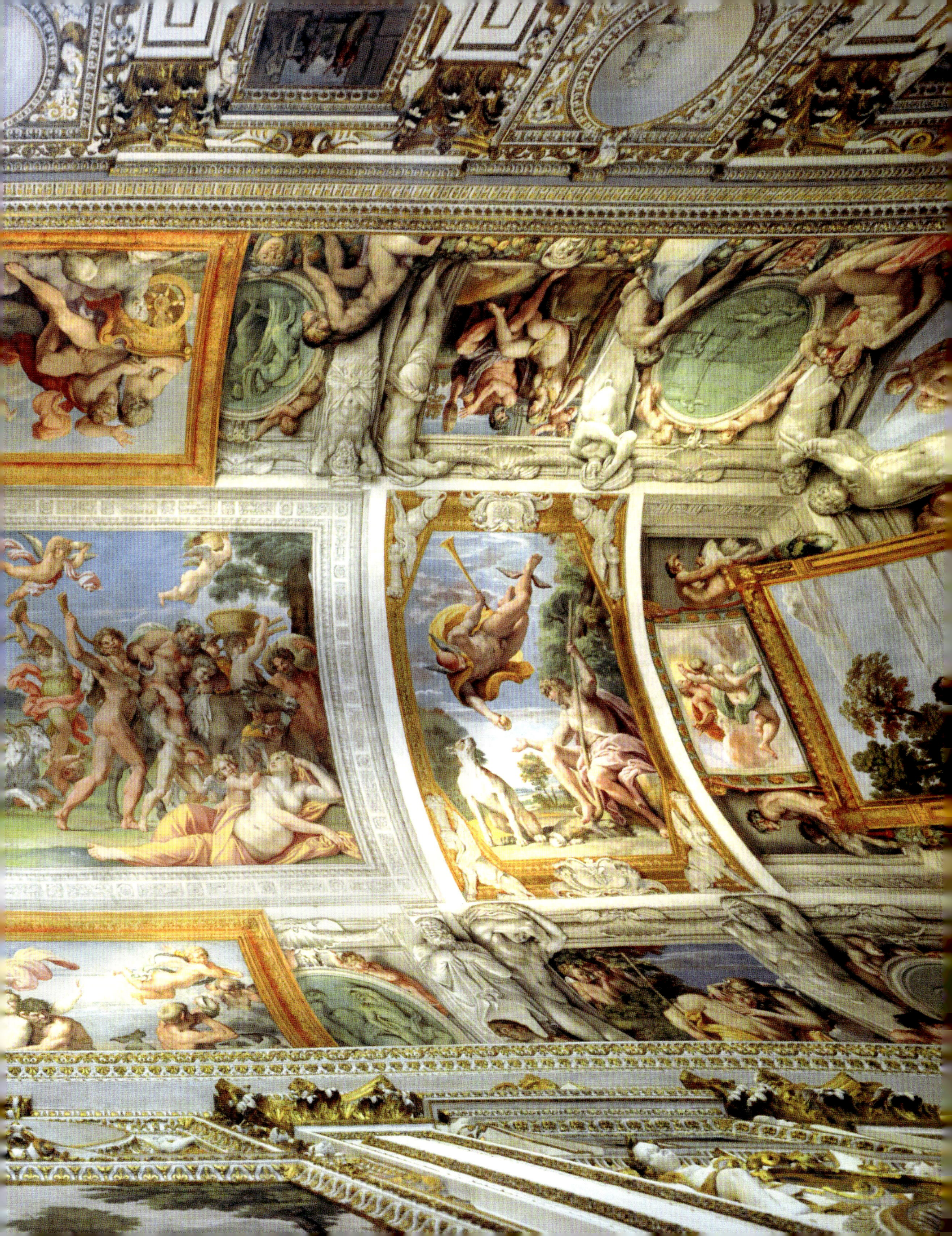

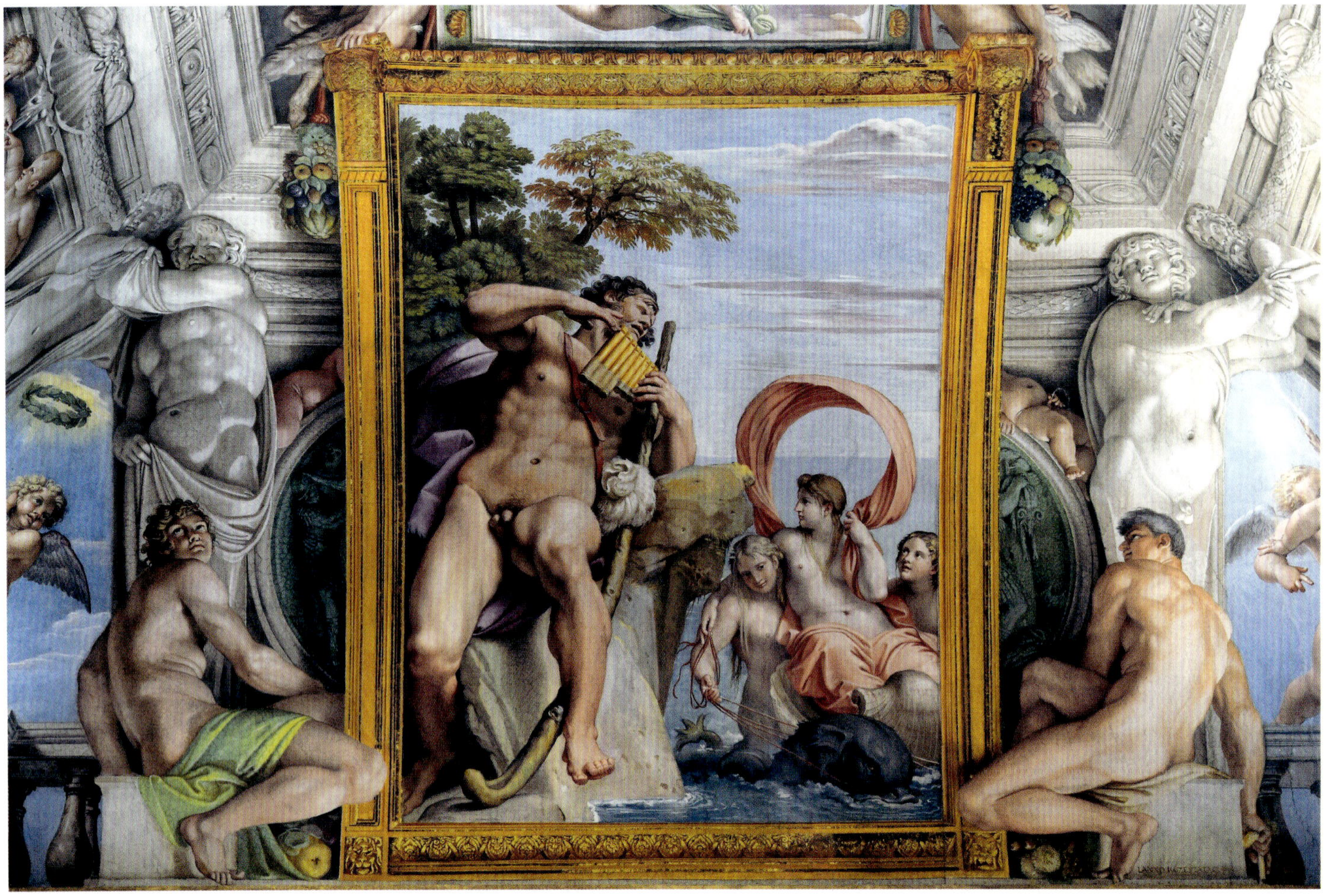

Above and opposite top: Galatea on her dolphin while a shell drifts by with the jealous one-eyed Cyclops playing the pipes.

Opposite top: Enraged with jealousy, Cyclops throws a boulder at Galatea and her Acis.

Right: The depiction of Jupiter, king of the pagan gods, and his long-suffering wife Juno.

Opposite bottom: *The Farnese Bull*, housed at the National Archaeological Museum in Naples.

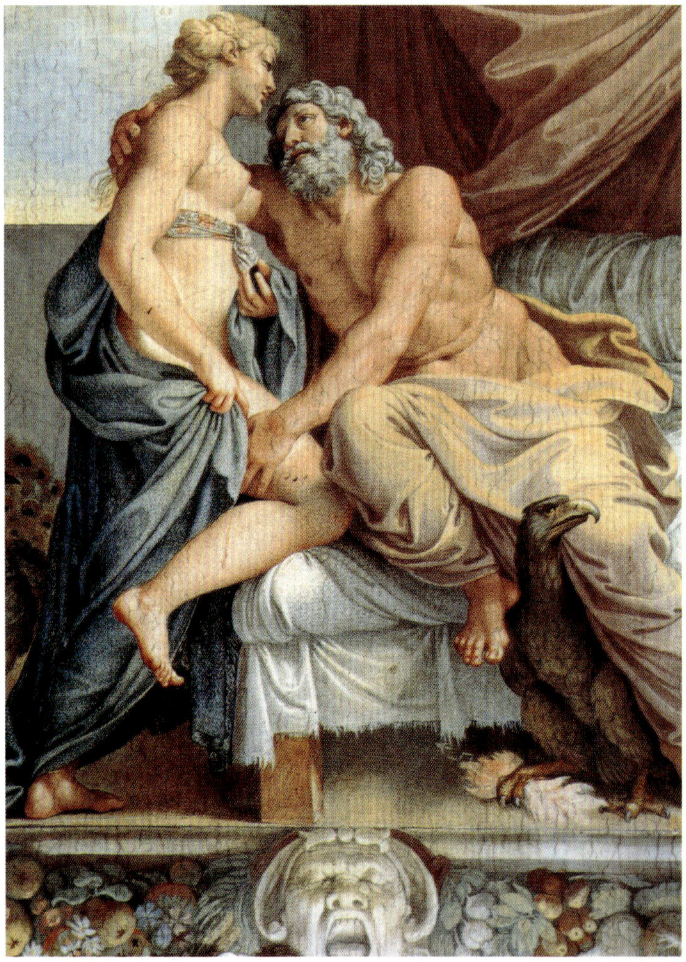

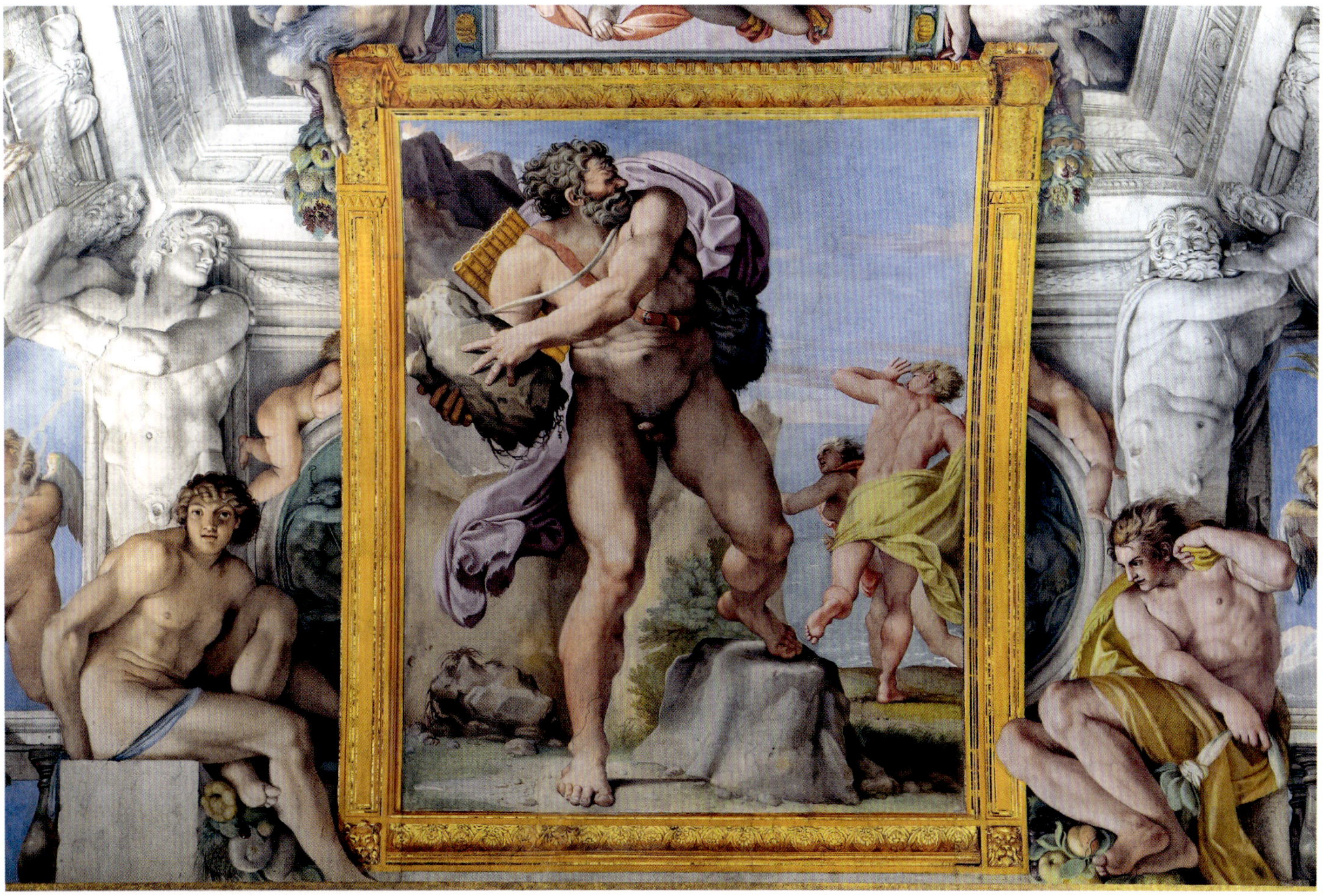

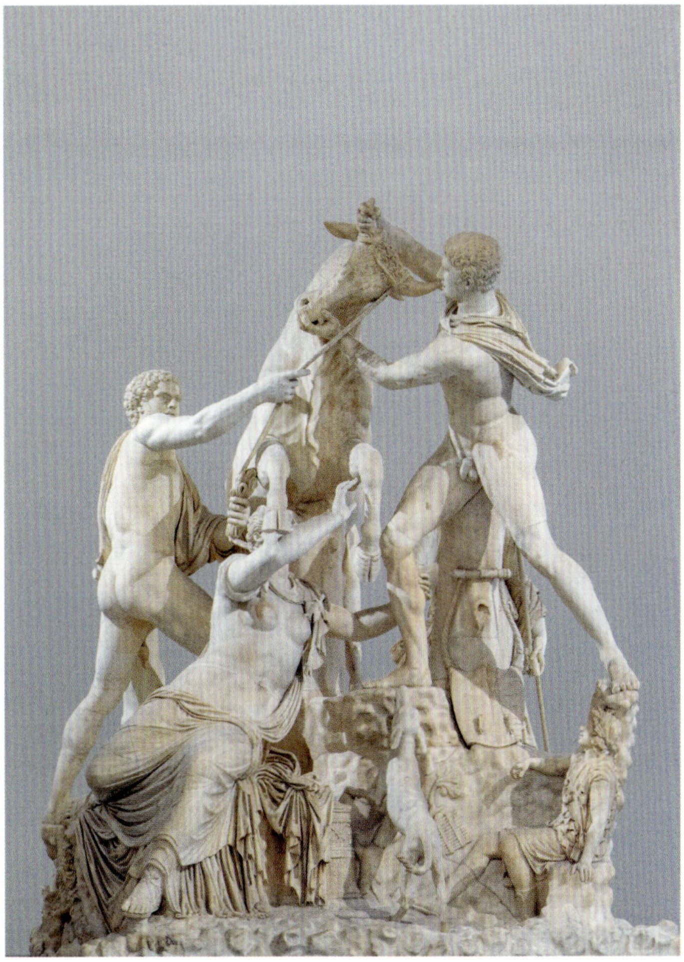

lover Acis. There are scenes of lovers in impossible technicolour such as Juno and Jupiter and Venus and Anchises, contrasted with painted illusory cornices and patinated bronze medallions to give a sense of different materials supported by one another in different strata of visual space.

The Loves of the Gods draws self-consciously on the legacy of Michelangelo's frescoed ceiling across the river in the Vatican Palace. Carracci, fuelled by competition with Caravaggio for dominance of the artistic landscape of Rome, was keen to insert himself into that lineage of great frescoed ceilings. Fresco was considered to be a manly art, more technically demanding than painting in oil, and a greater display of skill.

As a painter, Carracci was a stalwart of the classical style, which made a harmonious pairing with the collections of Greek and Roman antiquities that were part of the Farnese collection, much of which is in the Capodimonte Museum and the National Archaeological Museum (both in Naples).

The finished result exalts the painter as much as its patron, which is perhaps why Odoardo Farnese was embittered with the end result. He presented Annibale Carracci with five hundred scudi on a saucer, an embarrassingly pitiful sum for so much work, made the more lamentable by the fact that it was the artist's swansong, occupying him until a mere year before his death. However, the legacy of the work outstripped the short-changing of his fee. For the next two centuries, the ceiling became a blueprint for technical mastery in fresco and the preparatory drawings were consulted as the paragon of the classical academic tradition for subsequent artists' history paintings across Europe.

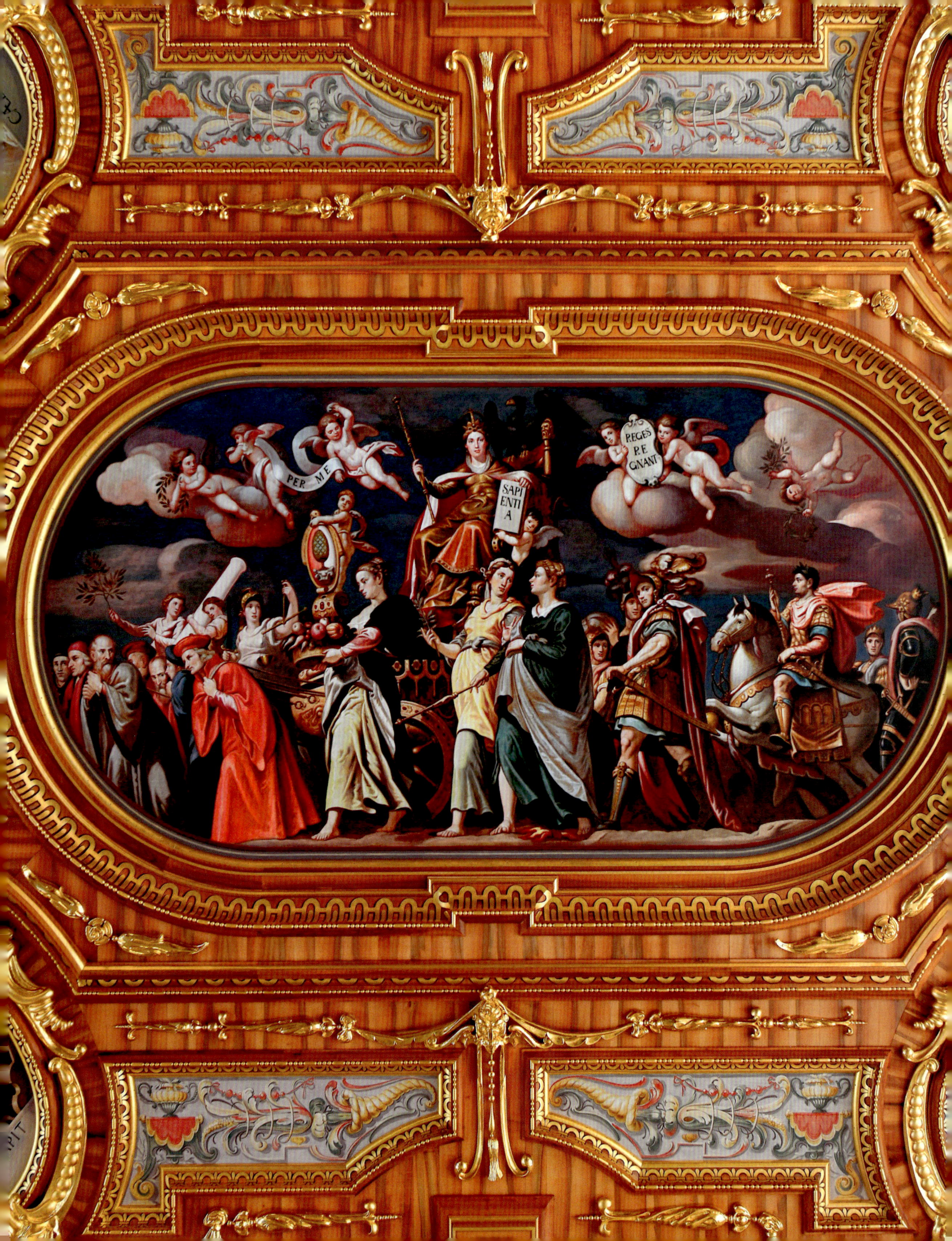
PER ME
SAPI ENTI A
REGES P.E GNANT

Peter de Witte and Matthaus Raders

Golden Hall

1624

Augsburg Town Hall, Augsburg, Germany

Left and overleaf: At the centre of the Golden Hall's ceiling is a personification of knowledge and wisdom, flanked on one side by a depiction of the construction of Augsburg.

Augsburg Town Hall, Germany

The Bavarian city of Augsburg was founded by the Romans in 15 [BCE], making it Germany's third-oldest city. Precisely 1,600 years later, it reached its zenith as a wealthy, self-governing imperial city of the Holy Roman Empire. Although there had been an administrative centre or town hall since 1385, in 1615 it was renovated as part of a grandiose rebuilding plan to reflect Augsburg's importance as the seat of the Imperial Reichstag (government). The city was also significant in respect of the religious political currents of the early modern period. In particular, it witnessed the tensions and negotiations between the Catholic Church and the new rival Protestant Church founded by Martin Luther, who himself came to Augsburg to meet a representative of the pope. It was in this same town hall that the Peace of Augsburg had been signed in 1555, marking the full agreement between Catholic and Protestant patricians and making the city the only place where the two faiths governed side by side.

The fact that this was the first building of its time to have more than six storeys is testimony to the idea that big is always considered better, especially when aiming to dominate the skyline. But the building's height became disadvantageous in the twentieth century, proving an easy target for Allied air raids. The damage extended to the double-height Golden Hall at the heart of the building, later restored in 1985 to coincide with the city's two-thousand-year anniversary.

The hall's coffered walnut ceiling is decorated sumptuously with gold leaf and depicts the riches of the city through a sequence of restrained allegorical images of the ideal city and the supremacy of wisdom. The main painting is a figure of knowledge or wisdom (known in Latin as Sapientia) with a banner emblazoned with the Latin *per me reges regnant* (I rule the rulers). In other words, the only king to be found in this town hall is one of knowledge and good judgment. By using Sapientia rather than a figure of victory or the apotheosis of an individual, the key visual imagery diplomatically sidesteps any potential criticism for using imagery to promote vainglorious corruption – something that was of key concern to the Protestant community.

The central image is flanked on one side by a depiction of the construction of the city, featuring a portrait of the Stadtbaumeister Elias Holl, who laid the building's foundation stone in 1615. Another Latin banner proclaims 'cities are founded'. Surrounding this ode to urban development are four smaller ovals, each one depicting an allegory: knowledge, fertility, diligence and piety – the key attributes behind the successful genesis of an autonomous self-governing city-state.

On the other side of Sapientia is an image depicting the fortification of Augsburg. Here, the Latin banner incants 'enemies are repelled', presumably through the virtues that are represented in allegorical female form in four smaller ovals. These are Healing, Justice, Honesty and Prosperity, the last envisioned as a stout woman in a well-equipped kitchen that glistens with pots and pans and tankards.

The painting work was carried out by the Flemish-born artist Peter de Witte, known in Italy as Pietro Candido (and Peter Candid in Bavaria). Born in Bruges, Belgium, de Witte moved to Florence, Italy, as a child and became an artist at the Medici court and a member of the Accademia delle Arti del Disegno, along with

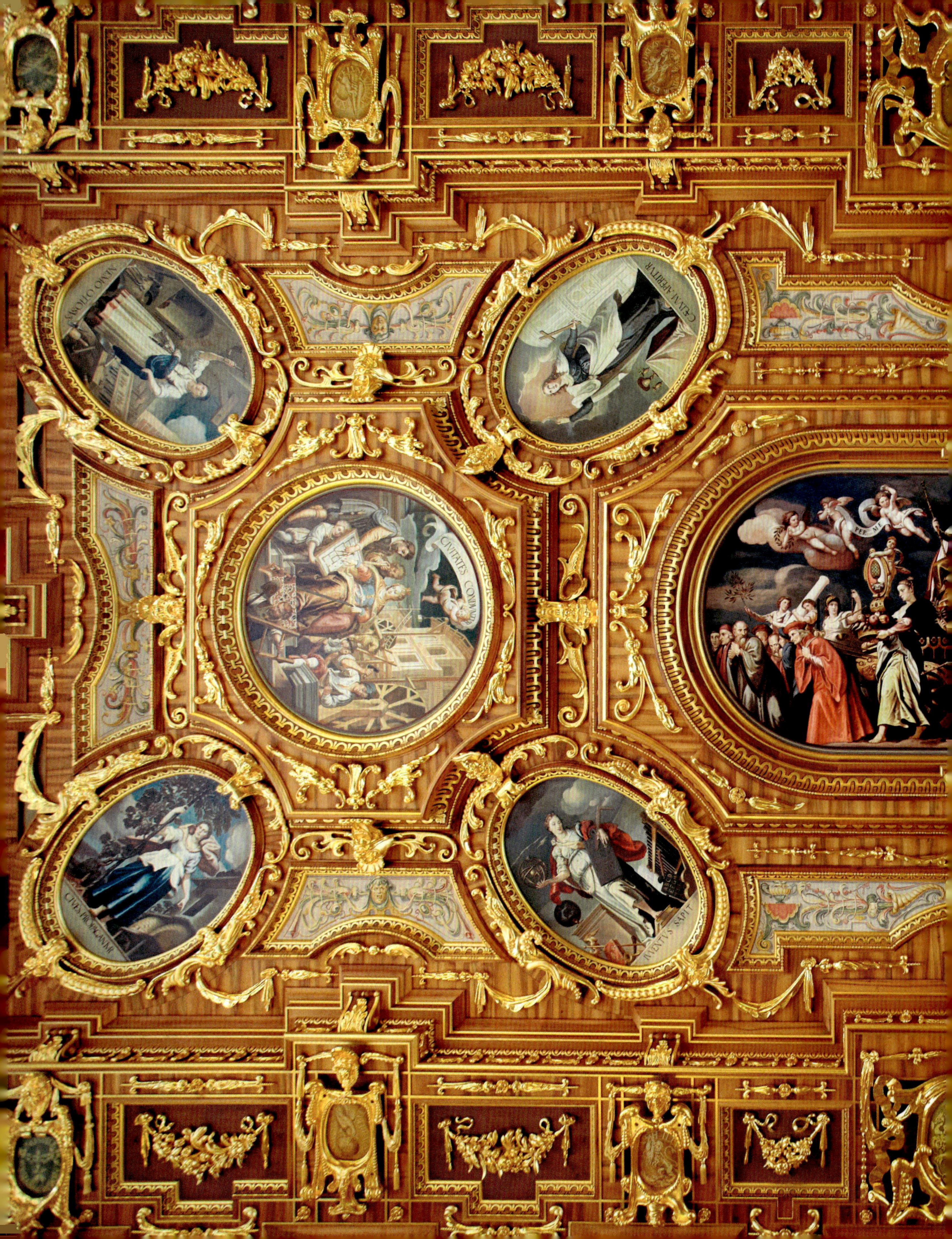
PER ME

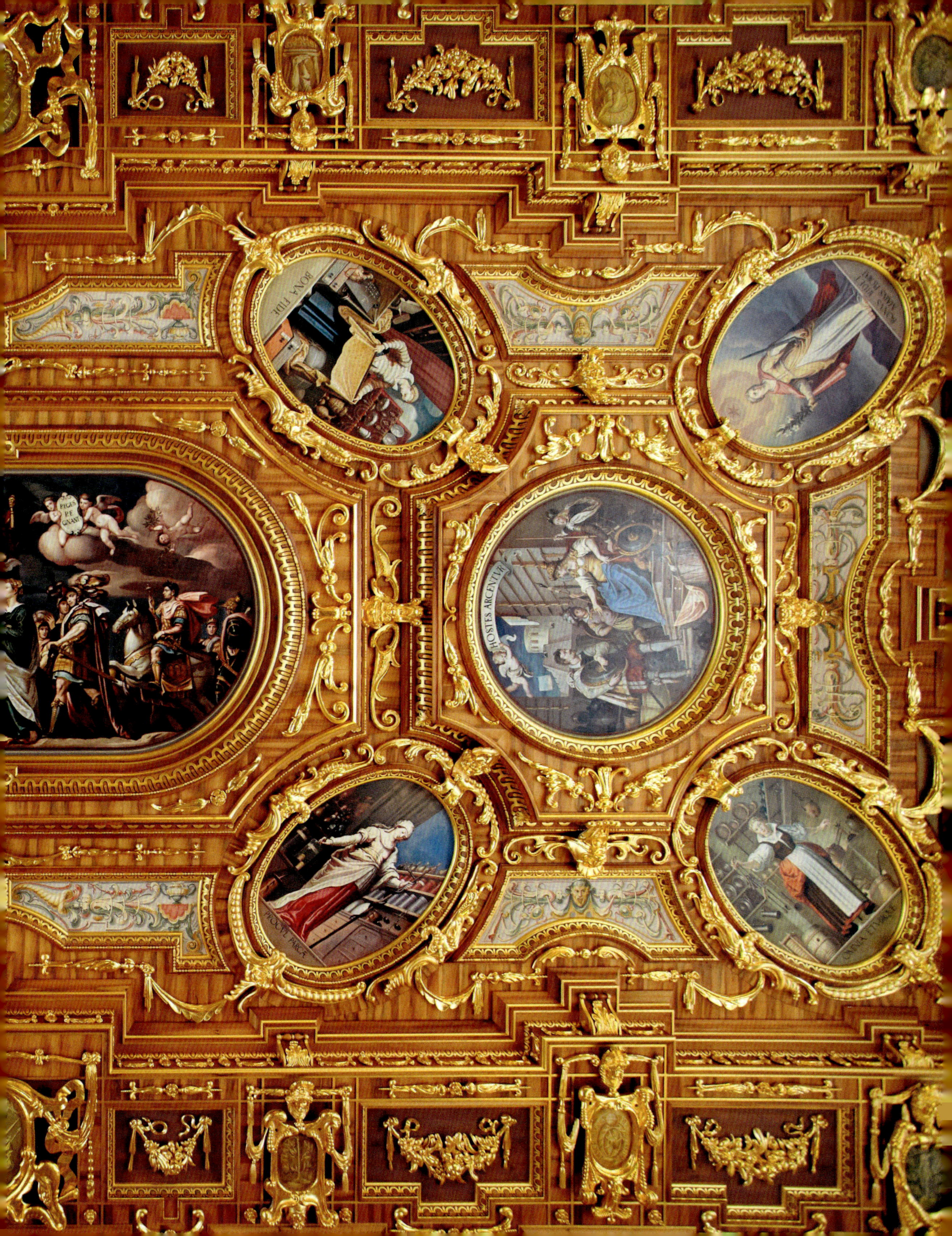
BONA FIDE
HOSTES ARCENTVR

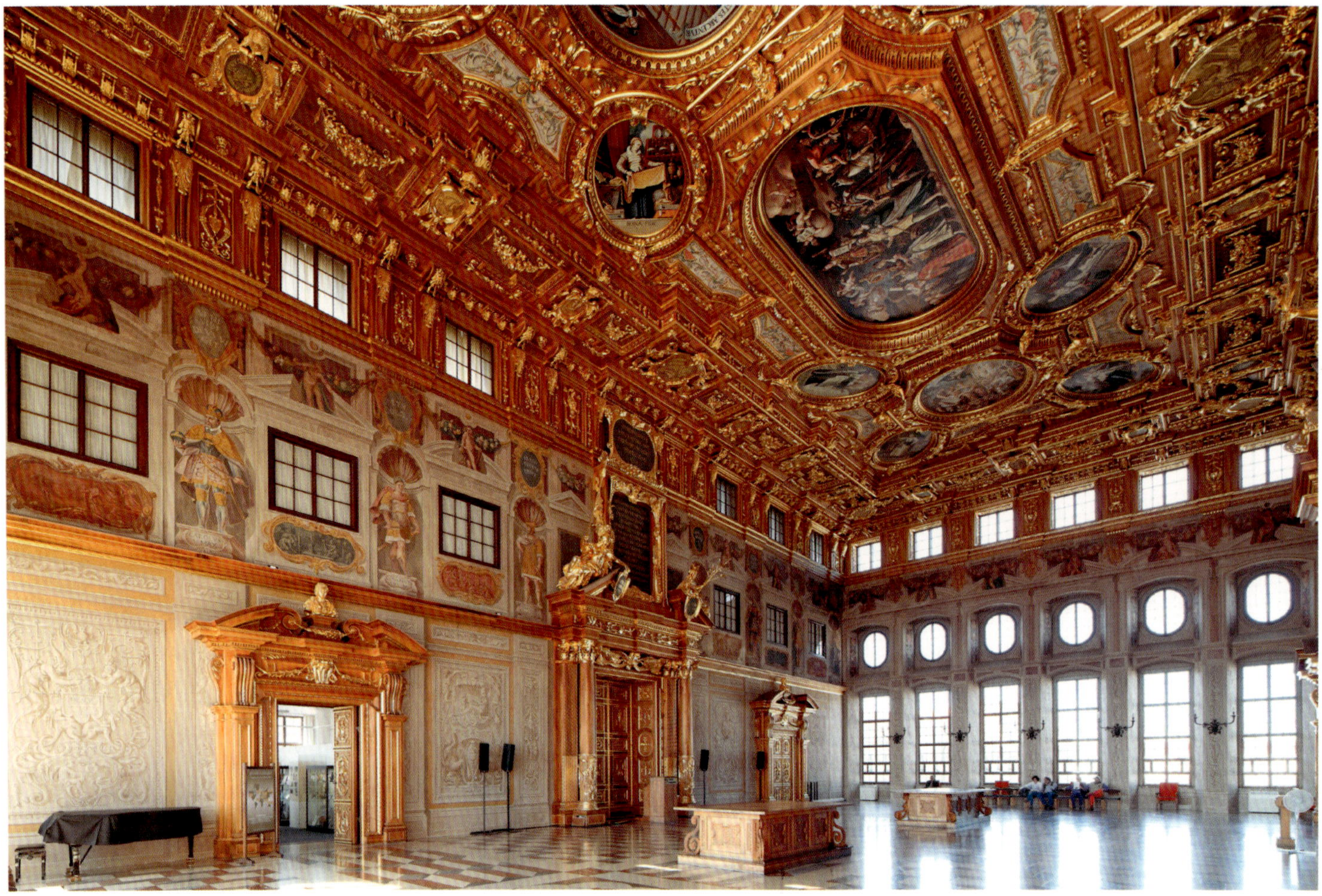

Michelangelo Buonarroti. He is credited with introducing Italian fresco painting into Bavaria.

The choice of de Witte to paint the defining imagery for Augsburg's carefully crafted civic identity was an ideological one. In employing a painter who brought with him the prestige of the Florentine Medici court, Augsburg could emphasize its parallels with the Italian city, which also had accumulated its wealth and prosperity through banking and trade. Furthermore, Augsburg (like Florence) benefitted from networks of merchant guilds, and a favourable position at the intersection of European trade routes. This provided a fertile ecosystem for artists and artisans who were in demand for commissions from both state and individuals. But this arcadian time of plenty was ultimately short-lived; by 1634 the population of Augsburg had almost halved as a result of plague epidemics, and the grand aspirations of the city as promoted through its Golden Hall had temporarily lost some of their burnish.

Above: The interior of the Golden Hall, Augsburg Town Hall.

Right: A portrait of the Stadtbaumeister Elias Holl, who laid the building's foundation stone in 1615.

Opposite: Ceiling detail showing the ornate carving and painted panels in the Golden Hall.

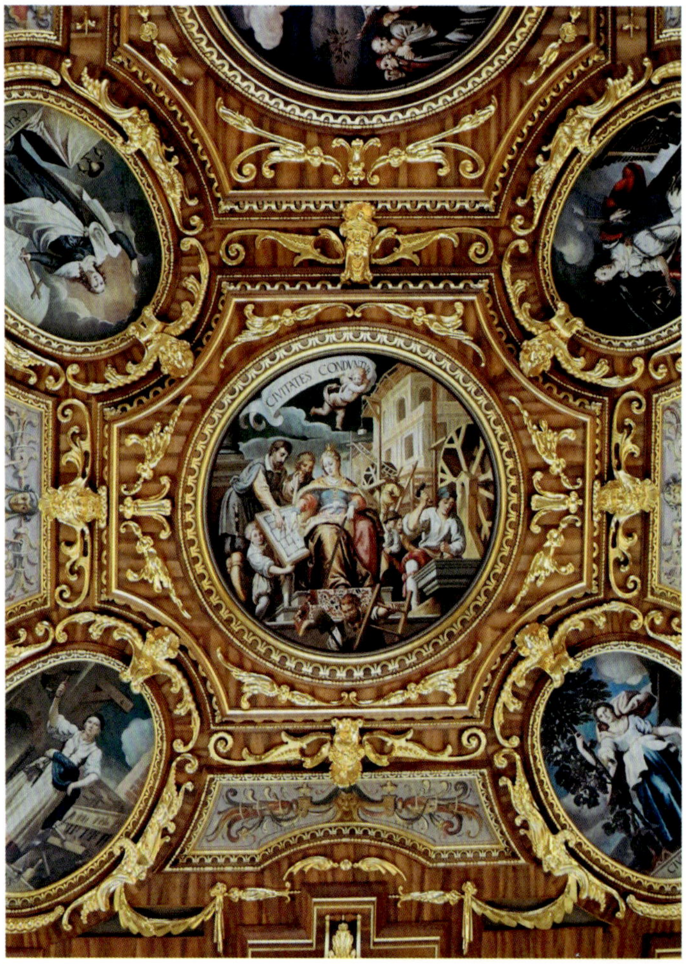

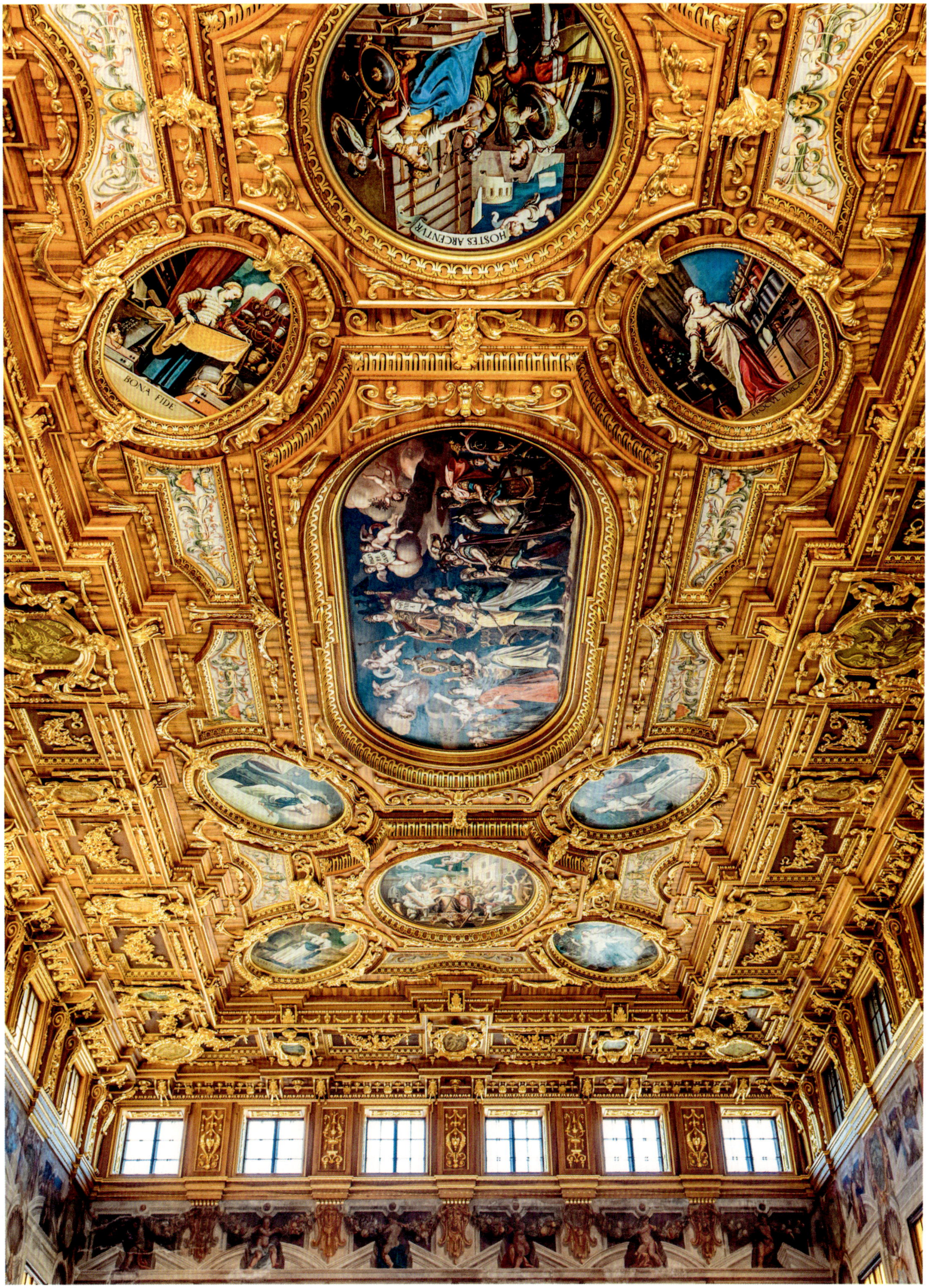

197 Augsburg Town Hall

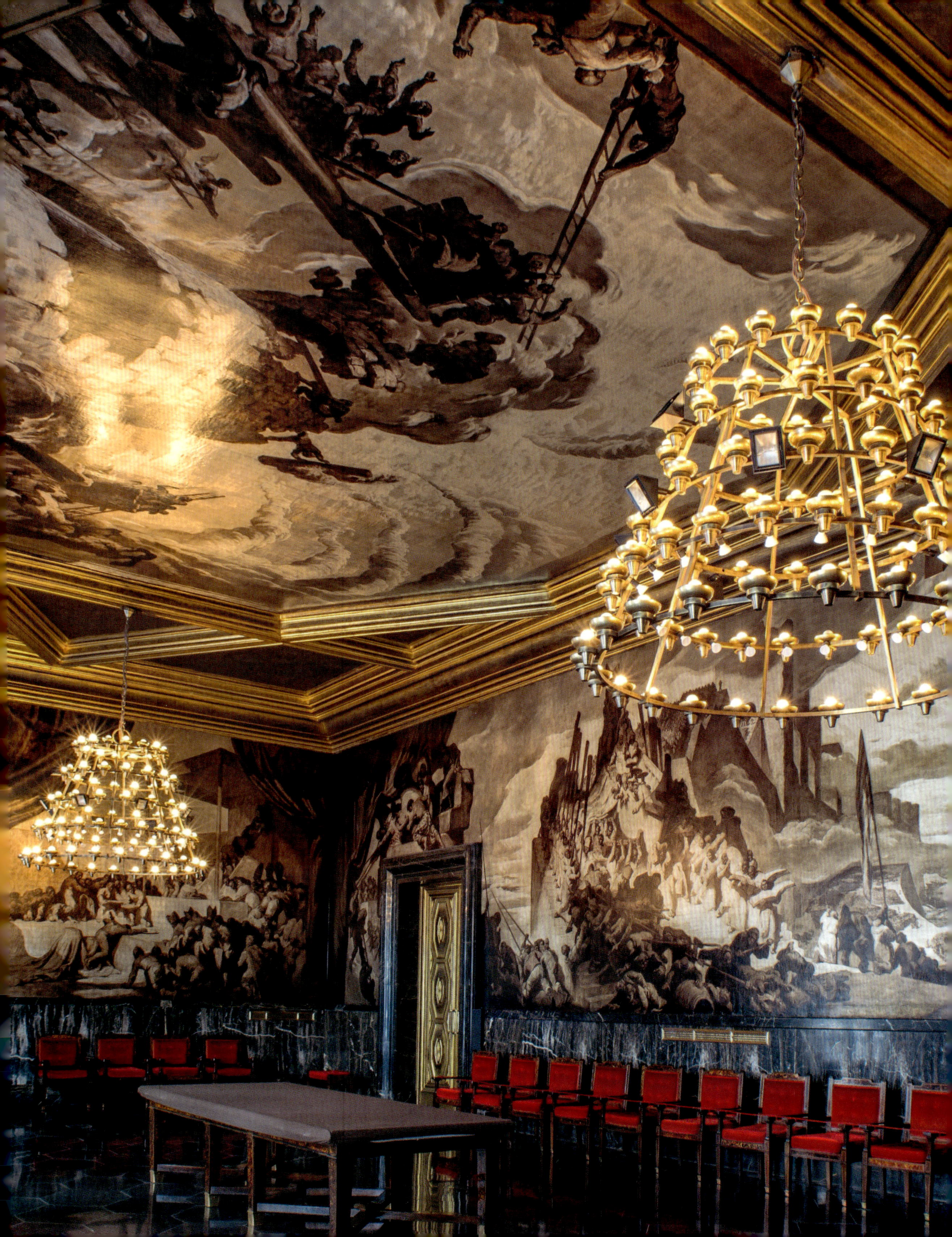

Josep Maria Sert

Hall of the Chronicles

1929

City Hall, Barcelona, Spain

Left and overleaf: Hall of the Chronicles with Josep Maria Sert's mural paintings.

City Hall, Barcelona

Art history is a mercurial chronicler. Those artists who are widely celebrated and go on to be revered in posterity, and those who remain forgotten in the dust of the archives are often subject to the prevailing political attitudes of their age. This might explain why the Catalonian artist Josep Maria Sert, who was a key figure among the cultural luminaries of twentieth-century Europe, fell into obscurity after his death in 1945. Sert has been largely overlooked and understudied by art historical scholarship, despite being friends with Marcel Proust, Paul Valéry and Coco Chanel and boasting painting commissions that include the Council Chamber of the League of Nations in Geneva, Switzerland, the Rothschild family mansion and mural paintings at the Waldorf Astoria in New York.

But even the most feted can be ousted if their personal political allegiances are perceived as intolerable. Sert, in particular, became known for his outspoken support of fascist leader General Francisco Franco during the Spanish Civil War, and continued to maintain a friendship with him once the general had become dictator of Spain in 1939. Even Sert's work in salvaging many of the paintings in the Prado collection in Madrid, for safekeeping during the civil war, did not work to secure his reputation. Left-leaning politics were not unusual among twentieth-century mural artists, and extended all the way to Marxism if you were Diego Rivera, who was Sert's contemporary. But while Rivera's name has echoed through the annals of art history as the Mexican mural painter of industry and modernity, Sert garners little recognition, despite having picked up one of Rivera's rejected commissions for the mural of American Progress in the lobby of New York's Rockefeller Center (Rivera is said to have refused to remove a portrait of Lenin at the centre of the fresco).

That history should have forgotten Sert is ironic, judging by the subject matter of his paintings in the Casa de la Ciutat (Barcelona's city hall), in a room known as the Hall of the Chronicles. Here, the walls and ceiling crawl with Sert's dramatically descriptive paintings in black, grey and burnished gold, as they unravel in a cinematic panorama around the room. The commission came from the town mayor in 1929, as the world's gaze settled on Barcelona as the host of the World Exhibition. The subject matter looks to an earlier period of Catalan swashbuckling imperialism and also to the traditions of Catalan literature, drawing as it does on the historical chronicles of the medieval writers Ramon Muntaner and Bernard Desclot. Both wrote about the life of the mercenary soldier and pirate Roger de Flor, the Sicilian commander of the Great Catalan Company of the 'Almogavars', mercenary fighters who defended Constantinople (now Istanbul) from siege by Ottoman Turks in an early-fourteenth-century campaign. De Flor was adopted into the imperial Byzantine family of Andronicus II Palaeologus. Made Caesar in 1304, he was assassinated in 1305 at Adrianople, by the hand of the same imperial dynasty who had honoured him. One whole wall is dedicated to the simple pathos of this murder, as Roger de Flor lays slumped in front of an imperial altar, with a blade in his back. All around, scenes of plunder and devastation cascade down the walls and from the ceiling, reliving what is known as the Catalan Vengeance. This was a two-year campaign of plundering across Thrace and Macedonia

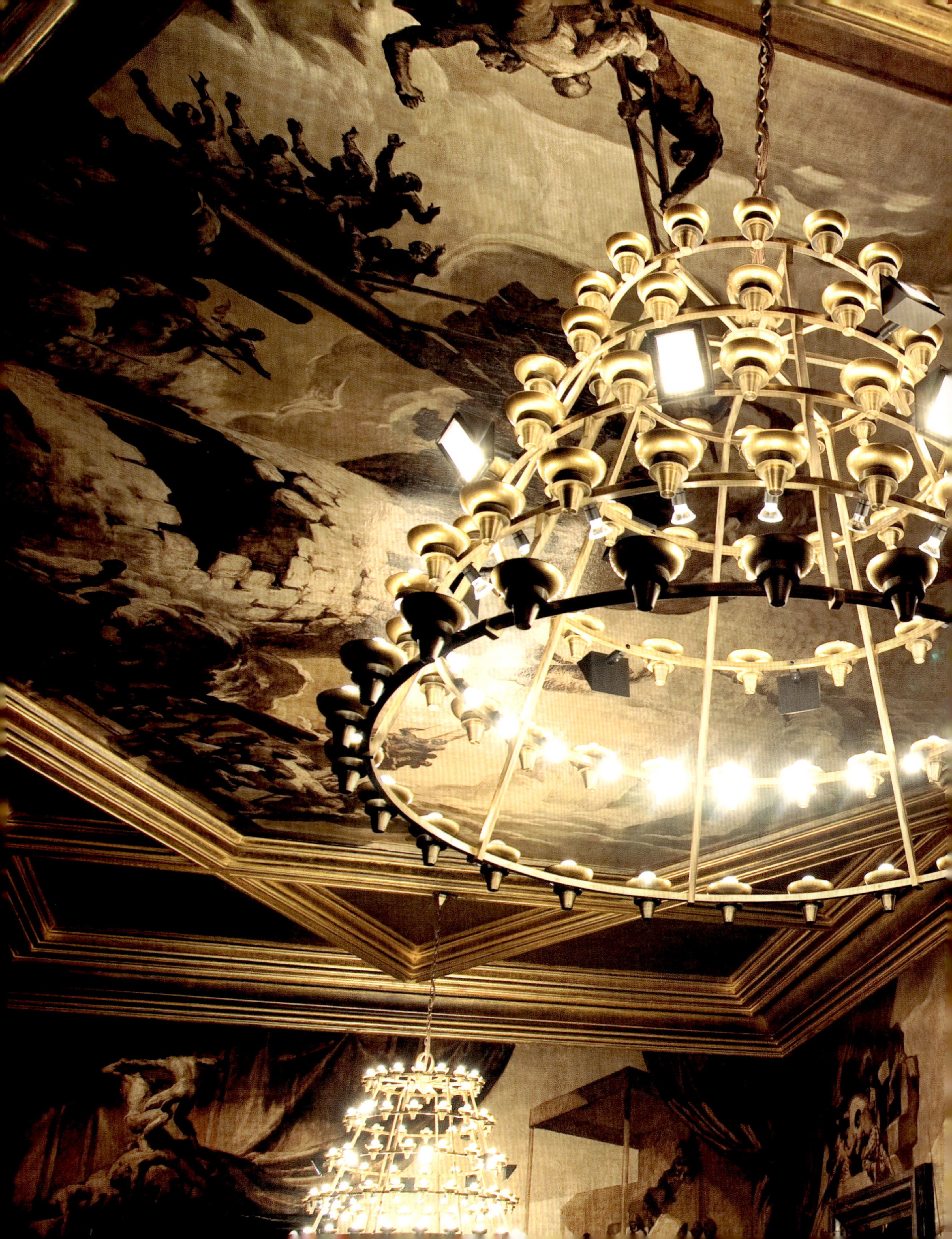

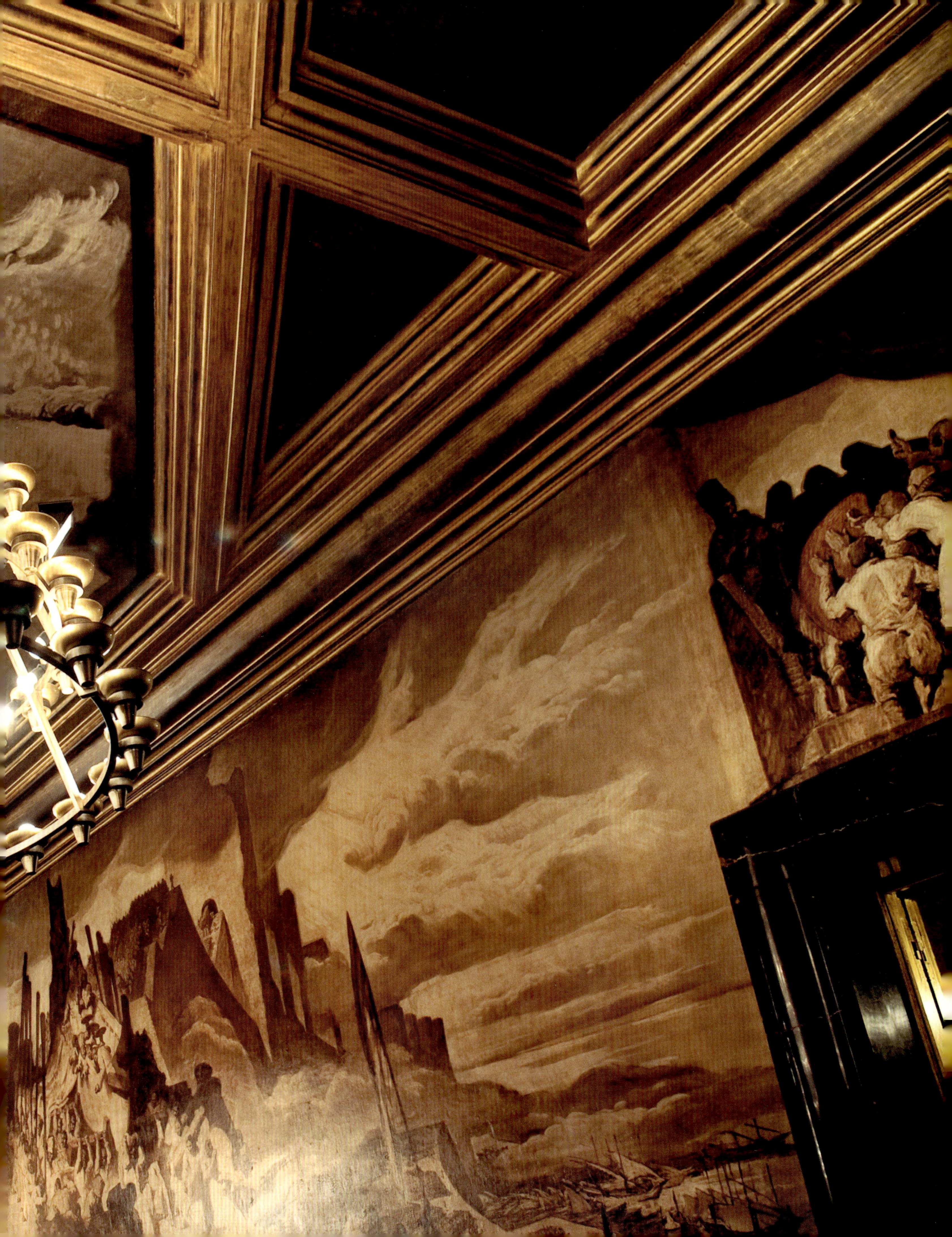

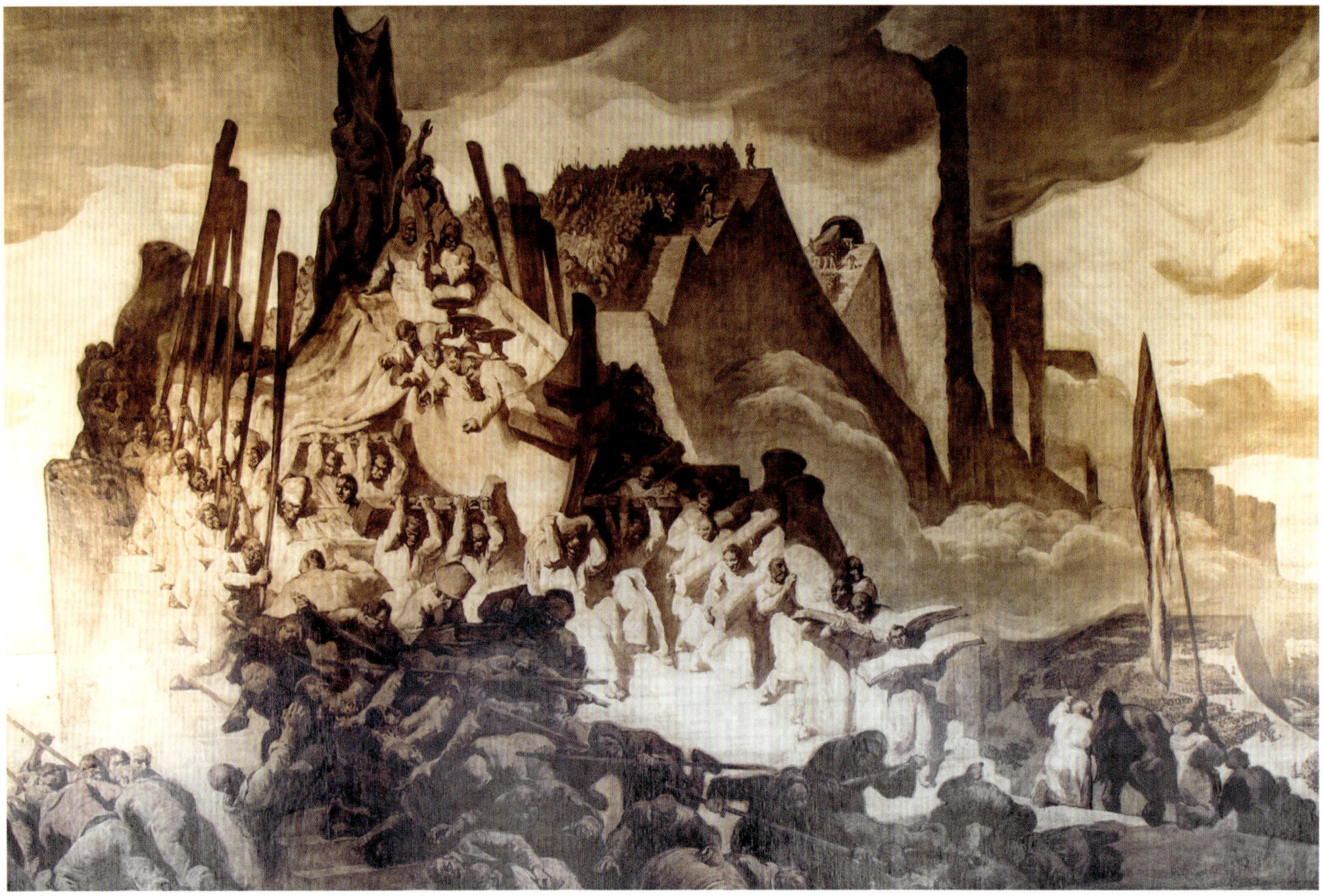

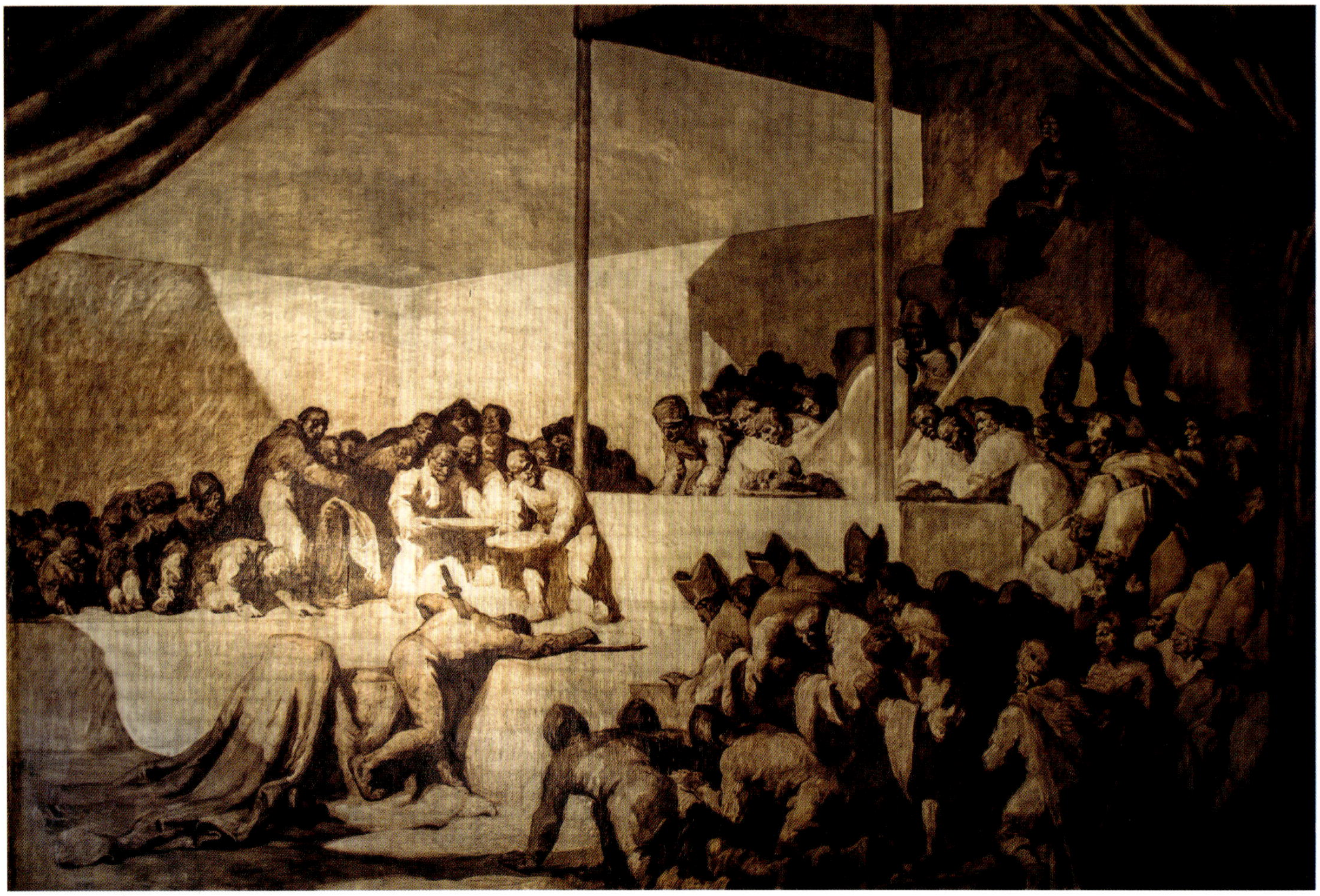

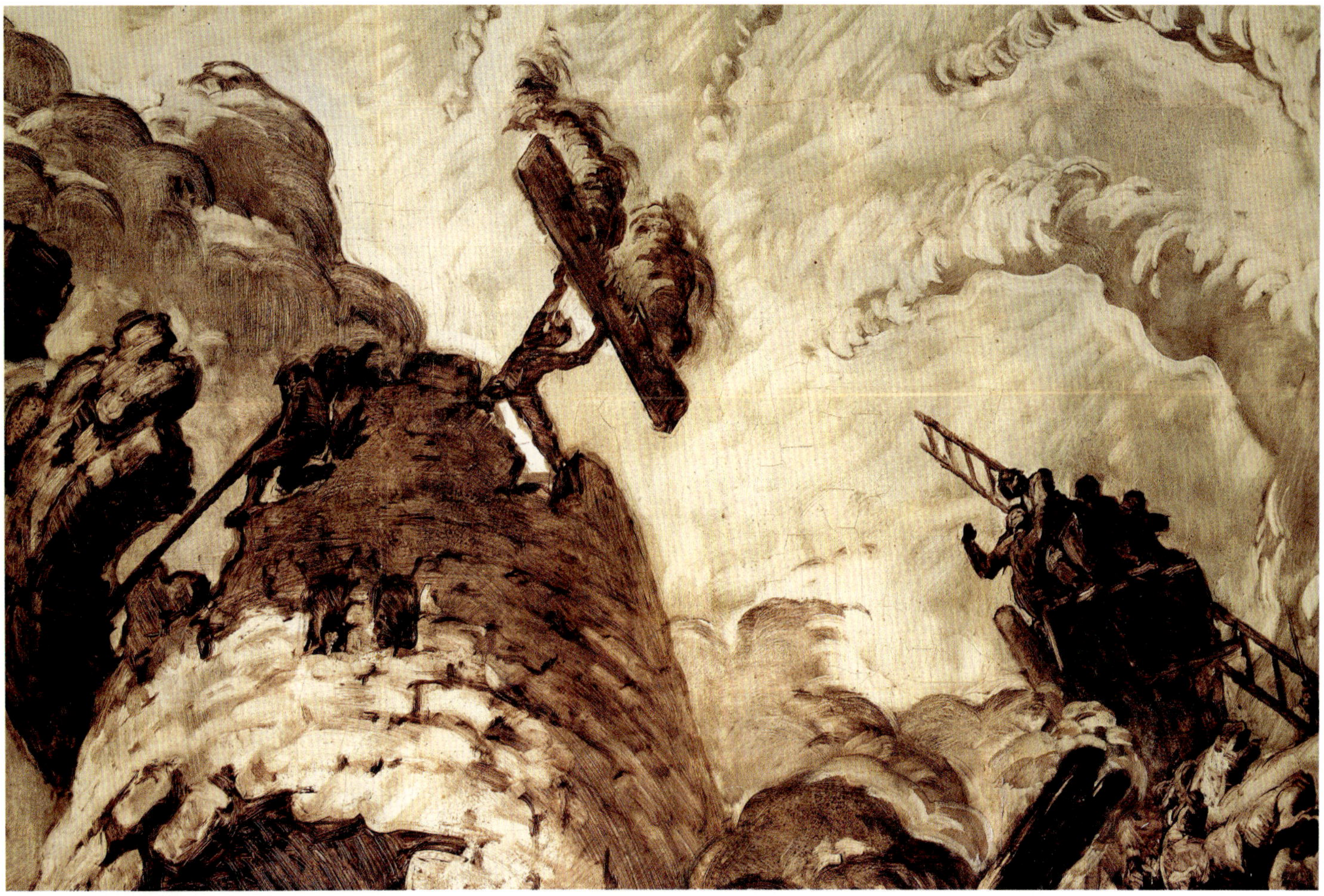

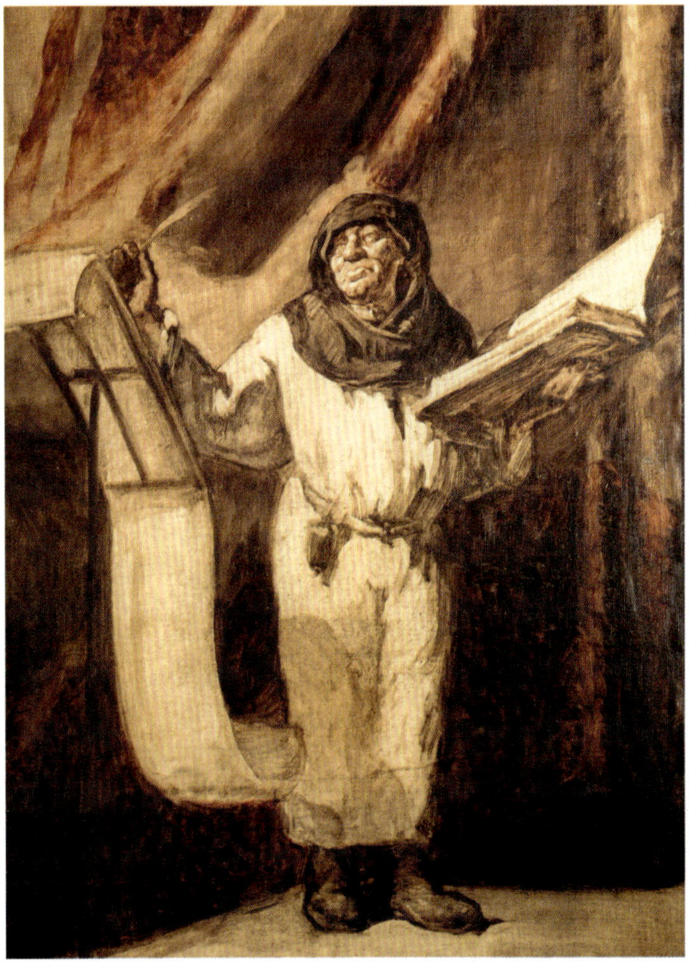

by angry Almogavars demanding payment after the death of their commander.

The central canvas on the ceiling freeze-frames the dramatic tension of one such engagement. Here bricks and burning timber rain from a grey sky that is stippled with swirls of smoky cloud, while figures brandishing ladders swarm like ants around the precarious building. In fact, the tower is not at all stable – neither in the fictive space of the drama unfolding above, nor in the viewing of it in real time in the Hall of the Chronicles. On entering the room and looking up while walking across to the other side, the tower appears to elongate and reorientate in an artful display of painted optical illusion.

Opposite top and bottom: All around, scenes of plunder and devastation cascade down the walls and from the ceiling, reliving what is known as the Catalan Vengeance.

Above: The central canvas, depicting the two-year campaign of plundering across Thrace and Macedonia.

Left: Detail from the Hall of Chronicles.

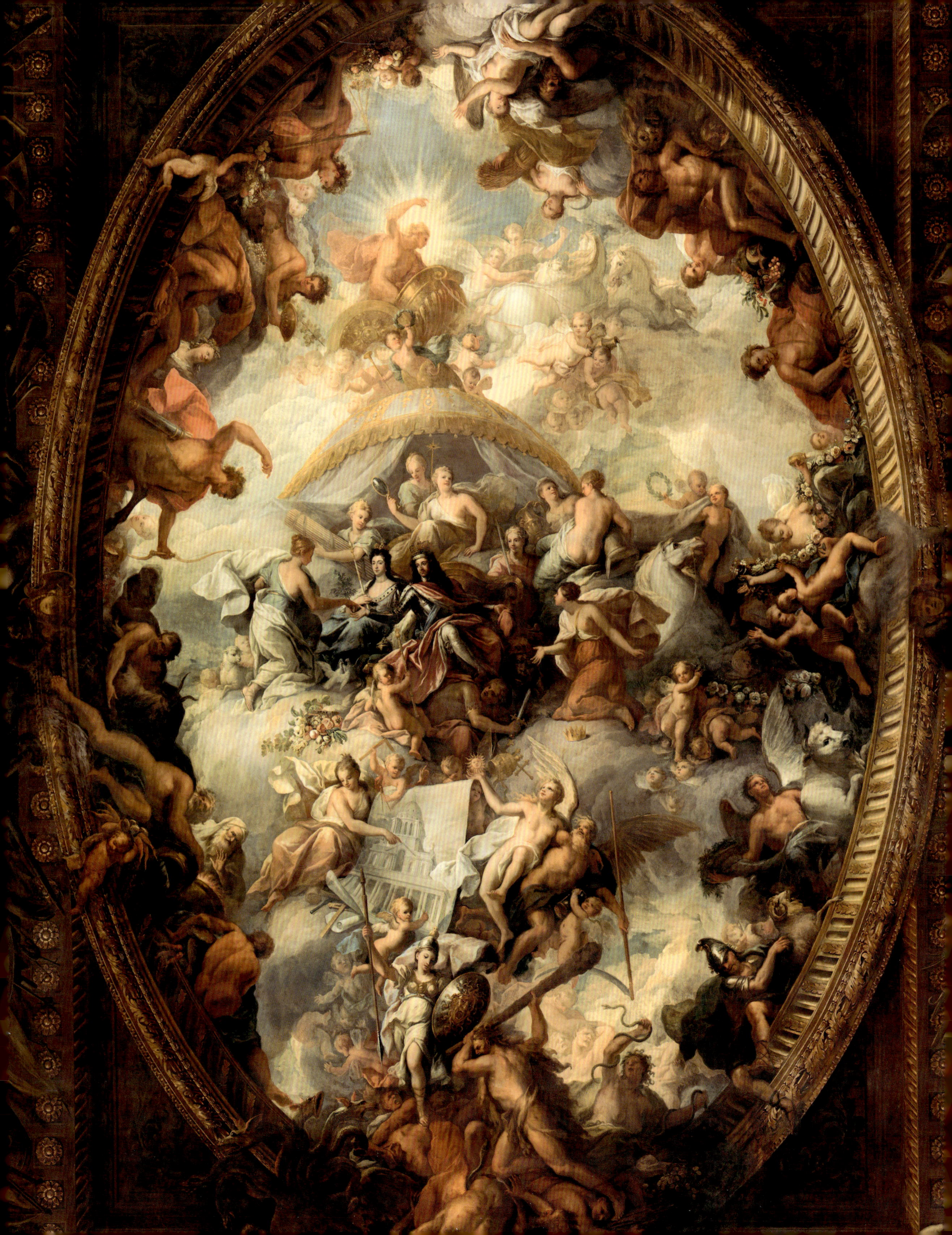

James Thornhill

Ceiling of the Painted Hall

1707

Old Royal Naval College, London, United Kingdom

Left and overleaf: A view of the ceiling of the Painted Hall, displaying the central oval, titled the *Triumph of Peace and Liberty Over Tyranny*, which depicts King William and Queen Mary enthroned in heaven.

Old Royal Naval College, United Kingdom

James Thornhill's epic work covers 3,700 sq m (40,000 sq ft) and employs a cast of close to two hundred characters to depict a microcosm of Britain's place in the world at the start of the eighteenth century, a time when Britannia proudly ruled the waves. Starting life as a finely decorated dining hall for veteran seamen, the Painted Hall at what was originally called the Royal Hospital in Greenwich quickly became one of London's first tourist attractions when completed in 1727, earning the artist a knighthood – the first ever given to an English painter.

Designed by leading English architects Christopher Wren and Nicholas Hawksmoor, to house and care for wounded servicemen returning to Britain, the Royal Hospital was instigated by Queen Mary II in 1694. It subsequently became known as the Old Royal Naval College, a training establishment for the Royal Navy. Over the course of nineteen years, Thornhill painted the lower and upper halls and a vestibule.

The ceiling promotes the British Royal Navy in maintaining the good fortunes of the country, overseen by the custodians of the new constitutional monarchy of Great Britain, the monarchs King William and Queen Mary. Thornhill began work in 1708 and was under instruction to include as many references as possible to the importance of the British Navy in steering Britain's political fortunes. The central oval is titled the *Triumph of Peace and Liberty Over Tyranny*. Enthroned in heaven are King William and Queen Mary. The sun god Apollo sheds light over the couple while a figure of peace hands an olive branch to the king. He in turn hands a red cap of liberty to the kneeling figure of Europe. The work borrows from Italian baroque ceiling paintings, in particular the work of the Italian painter Antonio Verrio, who worked at Windsor Castle and is credited with bringing the illusionistic style of Roman ceiling painting to the United Kingdom. As such, Thornhill's ceiling draws certain comparisons with Pietro da Cortona's *Allegory of Divine Providence* (1633–39) in the Palazzo Barberini (see p. 144). Any similarities are in style alone, however, as the underpinning message of Thornhill's work expresses the very opposite of the sorts of god-given justifications for rulership that aggrandized the papal Barberini family. Despite the majestic fanfare and triumphalism, the Painted Hall at Greenwich is really a painting espousing the ideals of the British Enlightenment.

Inspired by seventeenth-century political writers such as Thomas Hobbes and John Locke, and the Bill of Rights of 1689 – an act that limited the powers of the monarchy and protected freedom of speech – Britain proudly self-identified with an enlightened approach to governance and rulership. There was a new conviction that kings gain authority not from God, but from the democratic will of the people, through their elected representatives in parliament. This is central to the identity of the monarchs William and Mary, and the king's foot sits on the head of a recognizable portrait of the French king Louis XIV, the Enlightenment's enduring symbol of unjustified and despotic autocratic rule. Beneath them, figures of Wisdom and Virtue destroy the vices of Calumny, Detraction and Envy, casting them out of this British version of heaven. Lower still, are foreshortened figures of the twelve signs of the zodiac, and the four seasons. These signify the passage of time, but also the movement of the sky, which, through the mapping of stars,

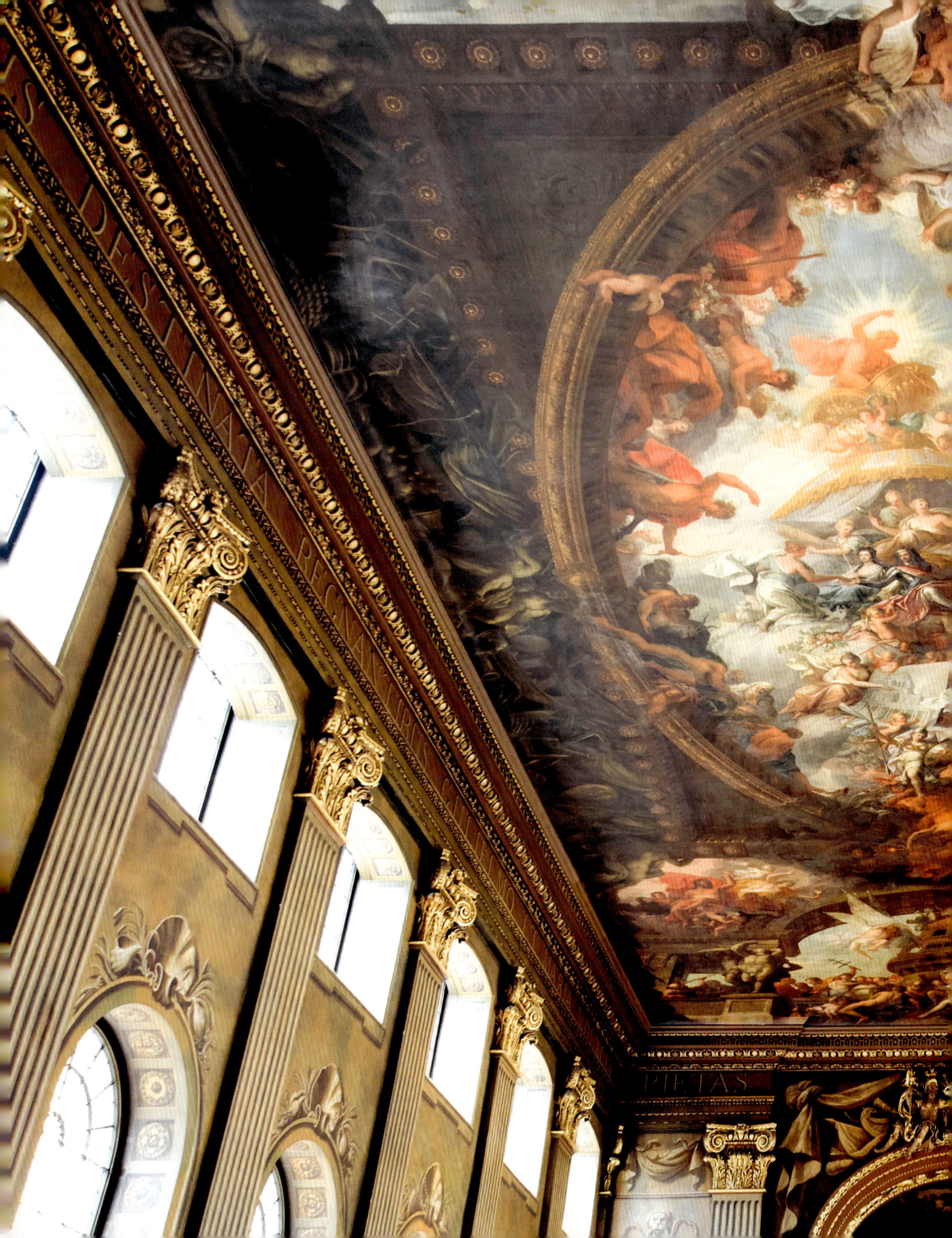
PIETAS

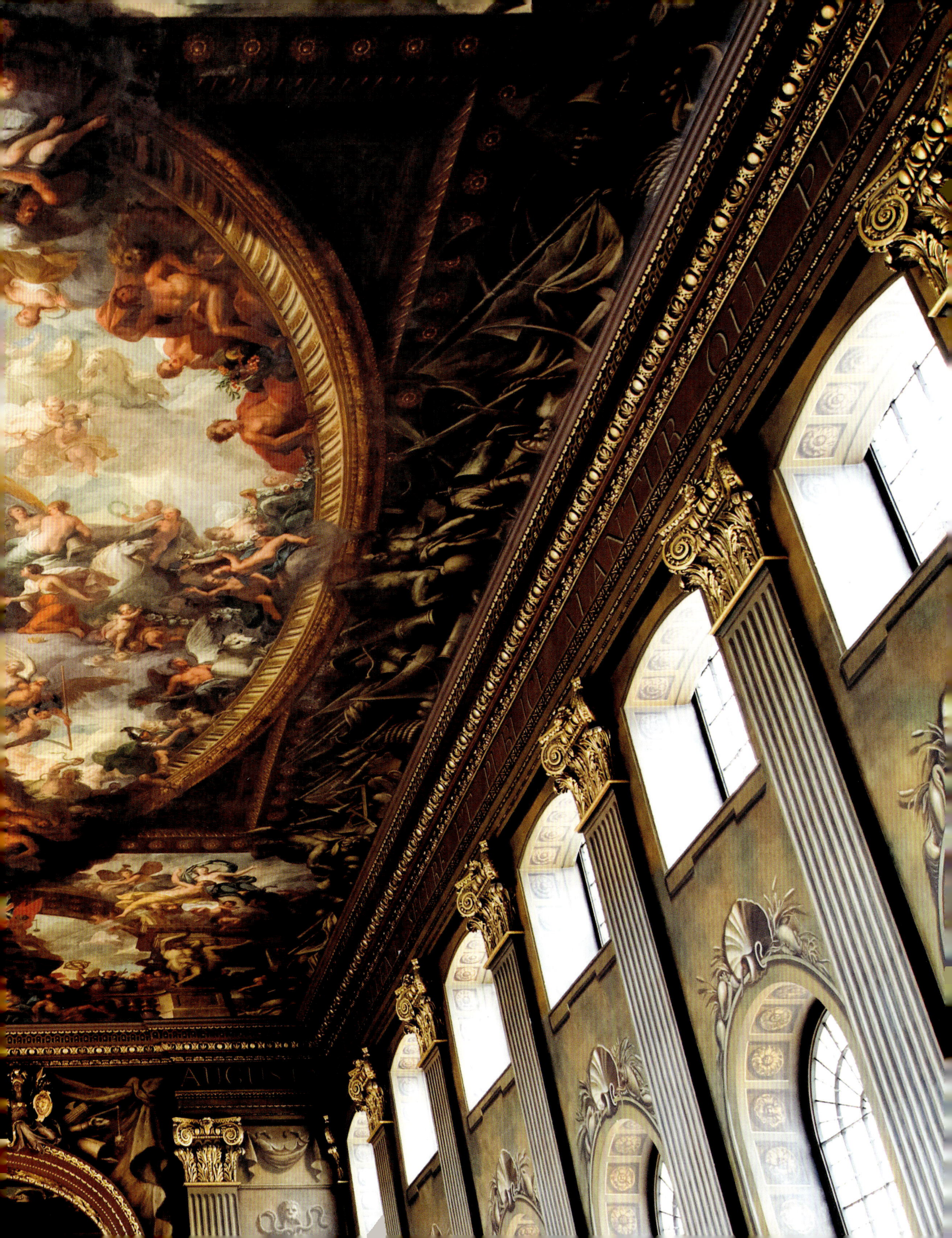

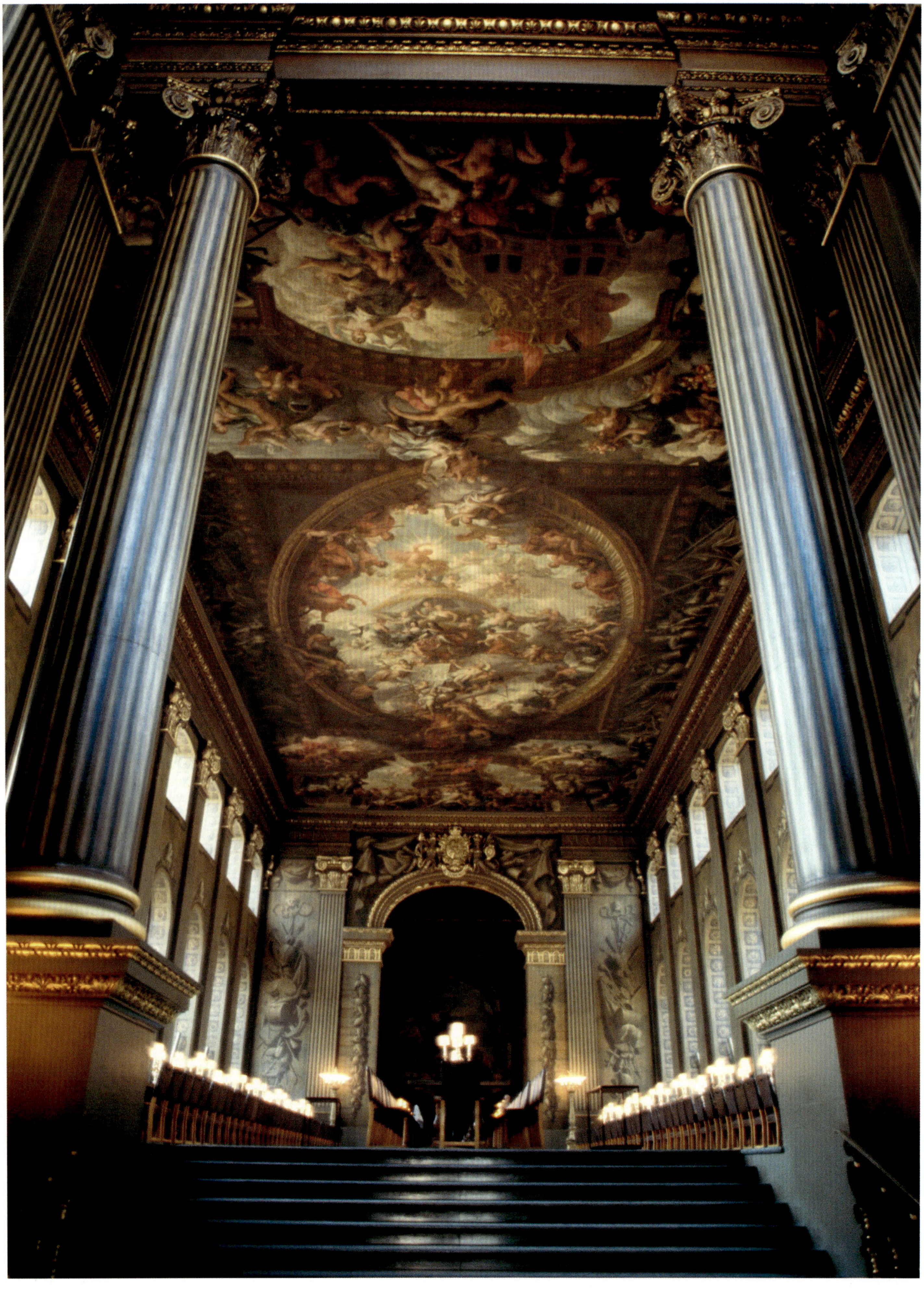

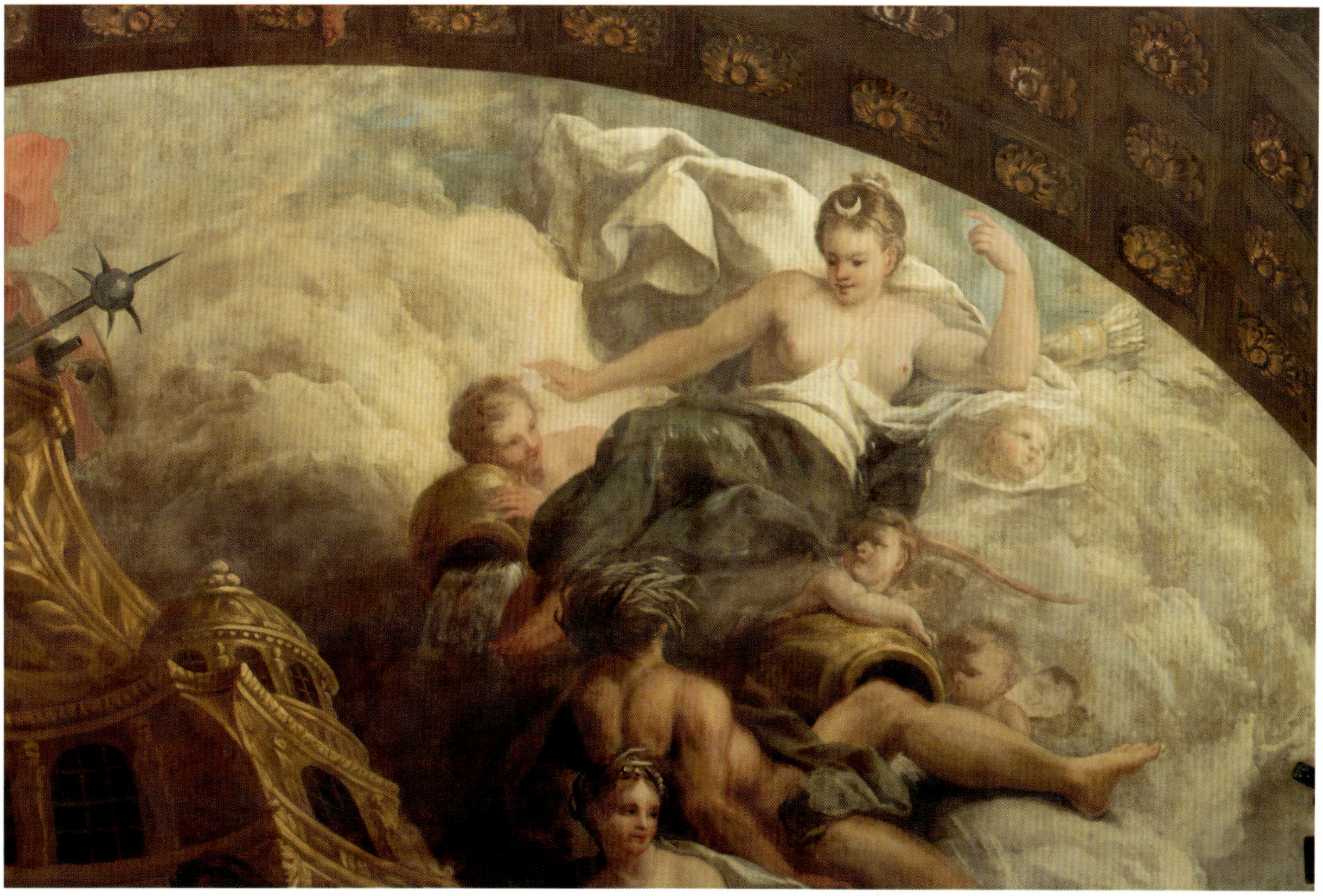

was the basis of all navigation at sea, and a vital component of the Royal Navy's success.

The early eighteenth century was a time when the laws of science began to challenge the fixed belief systems of religion. This development made a significant impact on practices such as astronomy and spatial physics, an understanding of which guided Britain at sea. In 1687, leading English scientist Isaac Newton had published his theory on gravitational pull and the subsequent relationship between the moon and the tides. This accounts for the figure of the mythological moon goddess, Diana, on the ceiling, identified by her crescent-shaped hairband and bare breasts.

Leading scientists share equal space with the monarchs in this work. At the east end is Sir John Flamsteed, the first Astronomer Royal, with his assistant Thomas Weston. They point a stargazing instrument known as a mural arc at the goddess Diana who in turn gazes down at a personification of the River Severn, a female figure dressed in green. Thanks to James Thornhill's explanatory notes, we know that this alludes to the understanding of the tidal system of the River Severn, which became perilous when the moon was closest to the earth. Portraits of Danish astronomer Tycho Brahe, a pivotal figure in understanding the night sky, and Copernicus, the Renaissance astronomer, also feature.

Too grand to be a sailor's mess, the Painted Hall took on a state and ceremonial function and between 1824 and 1936, also served as the National Gallery of Naval Art. In October 1805, three months after the Battle of Trafalgar, Lord Nelson's body was brought to the Painted Hall to lie in state for three days, during which more than 30,000 visitors came to pay their respects to the naval hero.

Opposite: Interior of the Painted Hall, Royal Naval College.

Below: A depiction of Sir John Flamsteed (right), the first Astronomer Royal, with his assistant Thomas Weston.

Above: The figure of the mythological moon goddess, Diana.

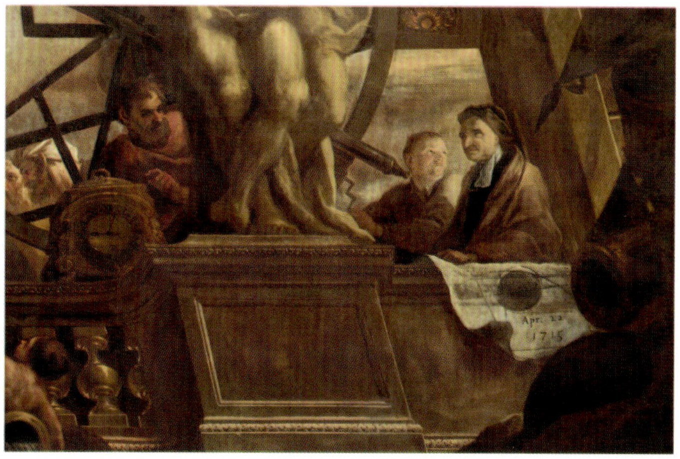

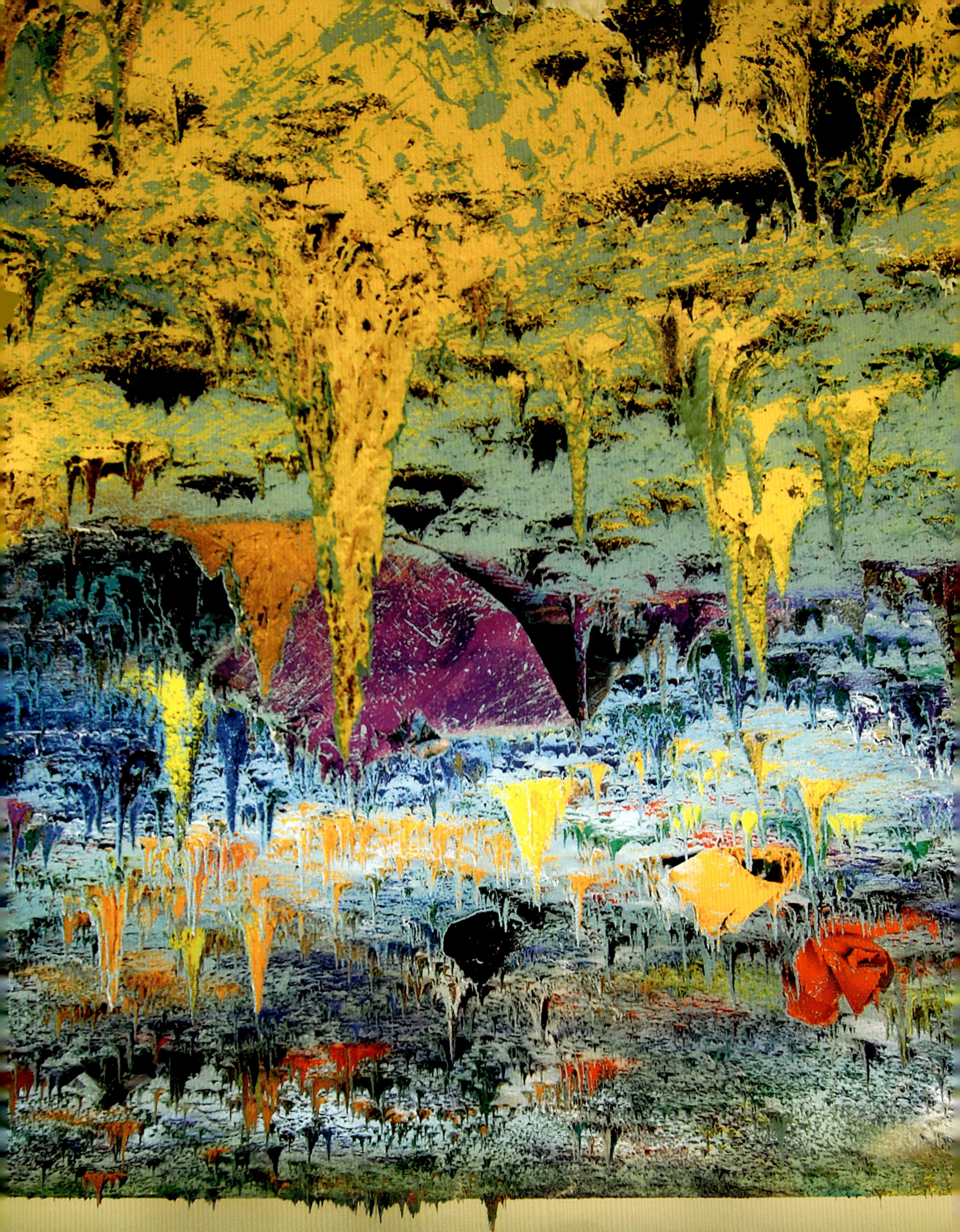

Miquel Barceló

Ceiling of the Human Rights and Alliance of Civilizations Room

2008

United Nations Office, Geneva, Switzerland

Left: Ceiling sculpture by Miquel Barceló in the Human Rights and Alliance of Civilizations Room, United Nations Office, Geneva, Switzerland.

United Nations Office, Switzerland

Miquel Barceló's ceiling of painted stalactites slips in peaks and crests across the dome of the Human Rights and Alliance of Civilizations Room at the United Nations headquarters in Geneva. At first glance, this could be a grotto, dripping with millennia's worth of mineral formations, or the subaquatic blossoms of an ocean reef. Or perhaps it is what the surface of the moon would look like if it were sprayed with cannon jets of paint.

In fact, it is the geography of Earth's nations in thirty-five tonnes of paint, comprising pigments gleaned from earth and rocks from around the globe. This disparate, elemental matter comes together in a miasmic polychromatic flow irrespective of the borders, racial differences or colours of their origins, to express the utopian political ideal of harmonious international relations.

The concept was inspired by the artist's experience of a mirage in the heat of the Sahel desert in Africa, where Barceló describes witnessing a vision of the world flowing drop by drop towards the sky. This topsy-turvy fantasy is characteristic of Barceló's work, which takes inspiration from the natural world, in particular the flux of environmental elements, such as the sea, and geological phenomena. This sense of organic, organized chaos unites the composition of the ceiling here at the Palais des Nations with points of reference in the natural world ranging from the cave as the meeting place for early humans, to the sea as the primordial cradle of all life, and the 'big African tree' as a place to sit under and talk. Stalactites up to 1 m (3 ft) long hover over the delegates in the chamber, and are supported by an aluminium honeycomb structure attached to the dome.

Barceló's work also references the twentieth-century painterly style of abstract expressionism, in which constellations of colour were created by the movement of the artist working on impulses from his own subconsciousness, propelled by the forces of creativity. In this way, Barceló's ceiling can be thought of as something reflective of the landscape of both the internal and external worlds and of many overlapping environmental terrains. Likewise, the piece evades artistic categorization, as it is at once flowing and sculptural, painterly and three-dimensional.

Barceló's ceiling was the first project realized with the support of the Fundación Onuart, a Spanish organization devoted to promoting dialogue in human rights conversations through the arts, while the Alliance of Civilizations project for which the chamber was constructed was launched by former Spanish prime minister José Luis Rodríguez Zapatero and his Turkish counterpart Recep Tayyip Erdo an to improve dialogue between the West and the Muslim world in 2006.

As such, it aims to change the conversation around art in the service of politics. The abstract nature of the artwork, and the absence of figures or references to moralizing or self-aggrandizing histories drawn from the perspective of one civilization, makes its message more universal and democratic. Furthermore, it promotes a different sort of aspirational approach in international relations, which is the pursuit of creativity as a model for problem-solving.

However, in the face of all of this eulogizing, the work was not unveiled without controversy over the twenty-three million euro price tag, with critics lamenting the siphoning of funds from international aid and vaccines to a project that seemed primarily to serve the ego of the Mallorcan superstar artist.

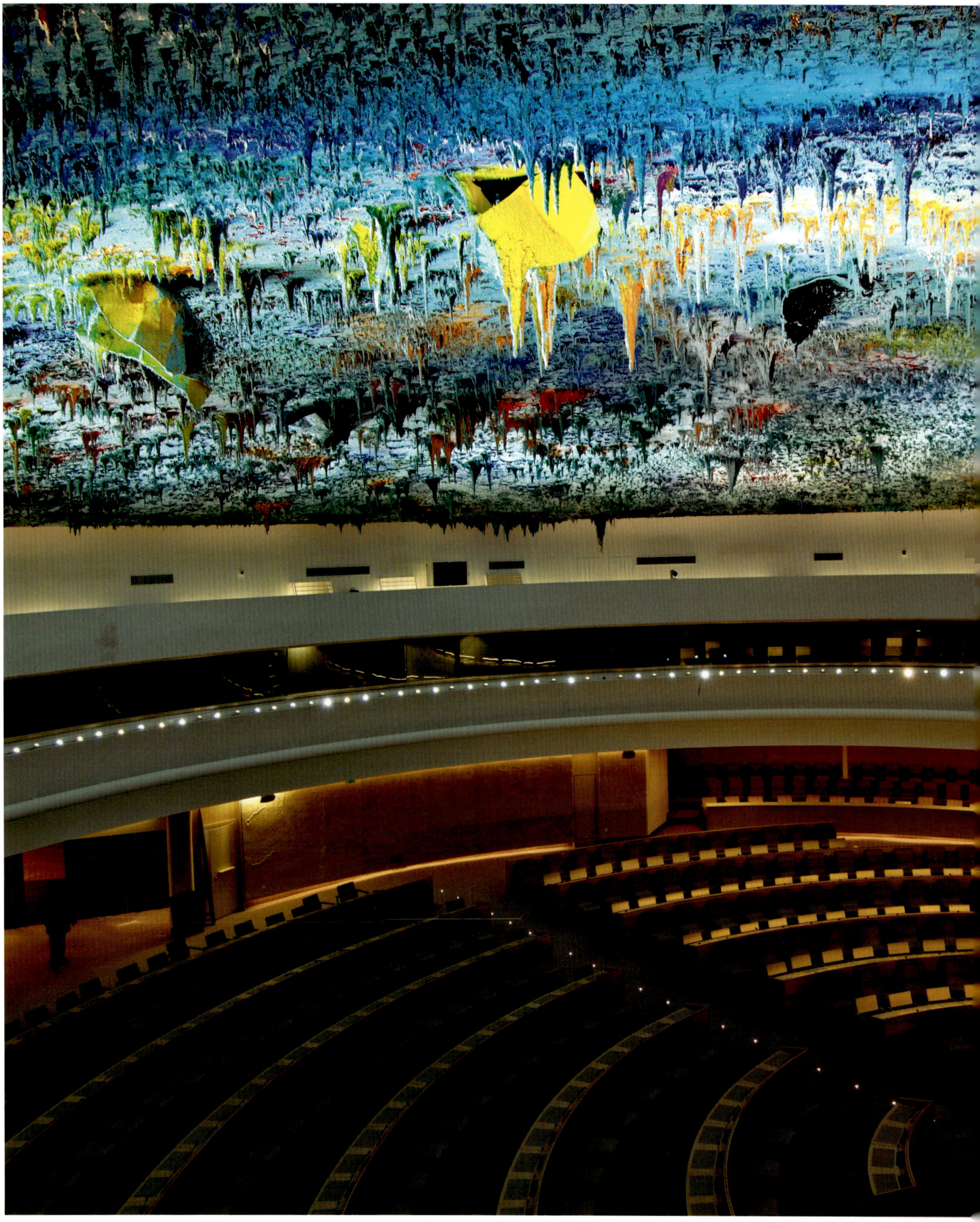

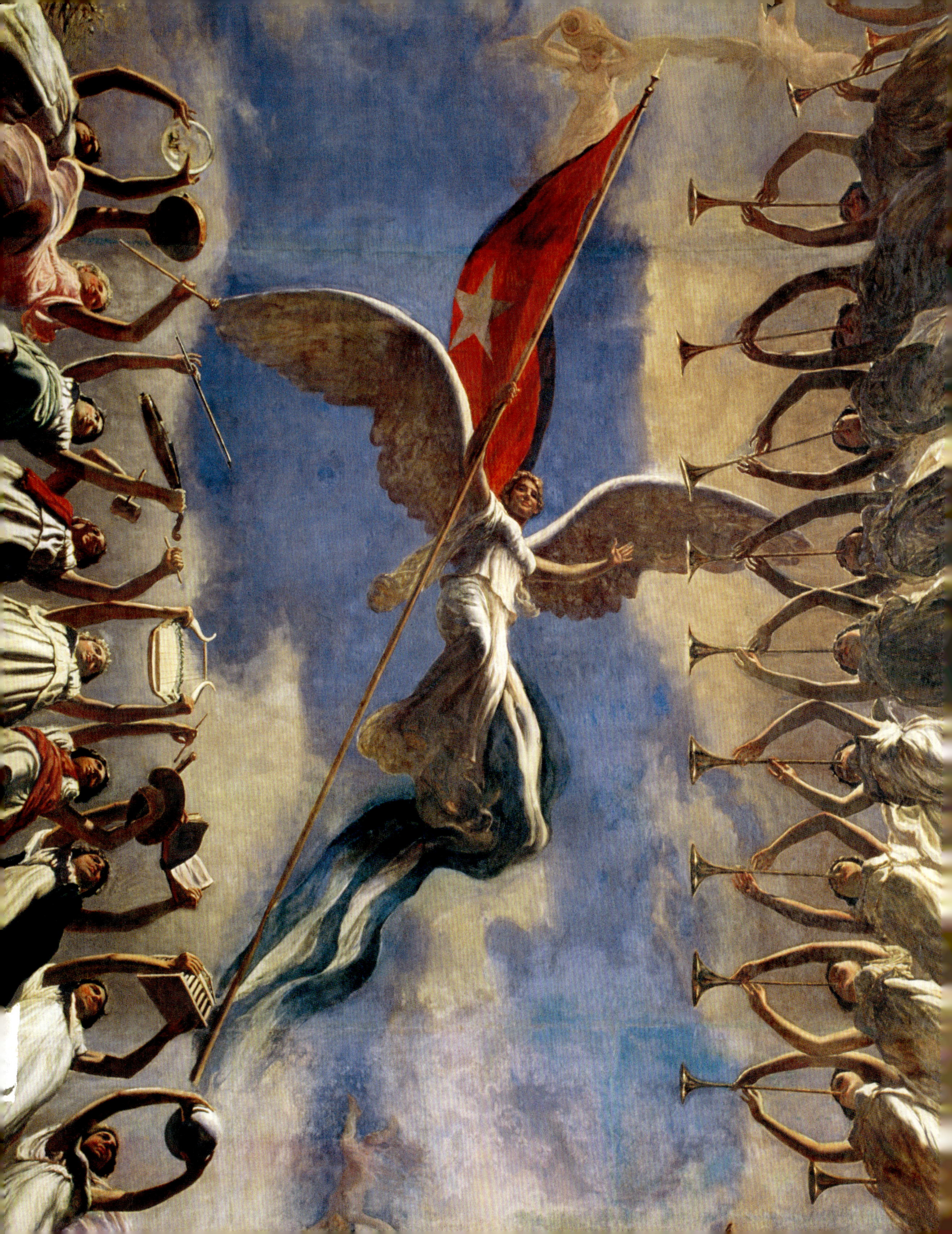

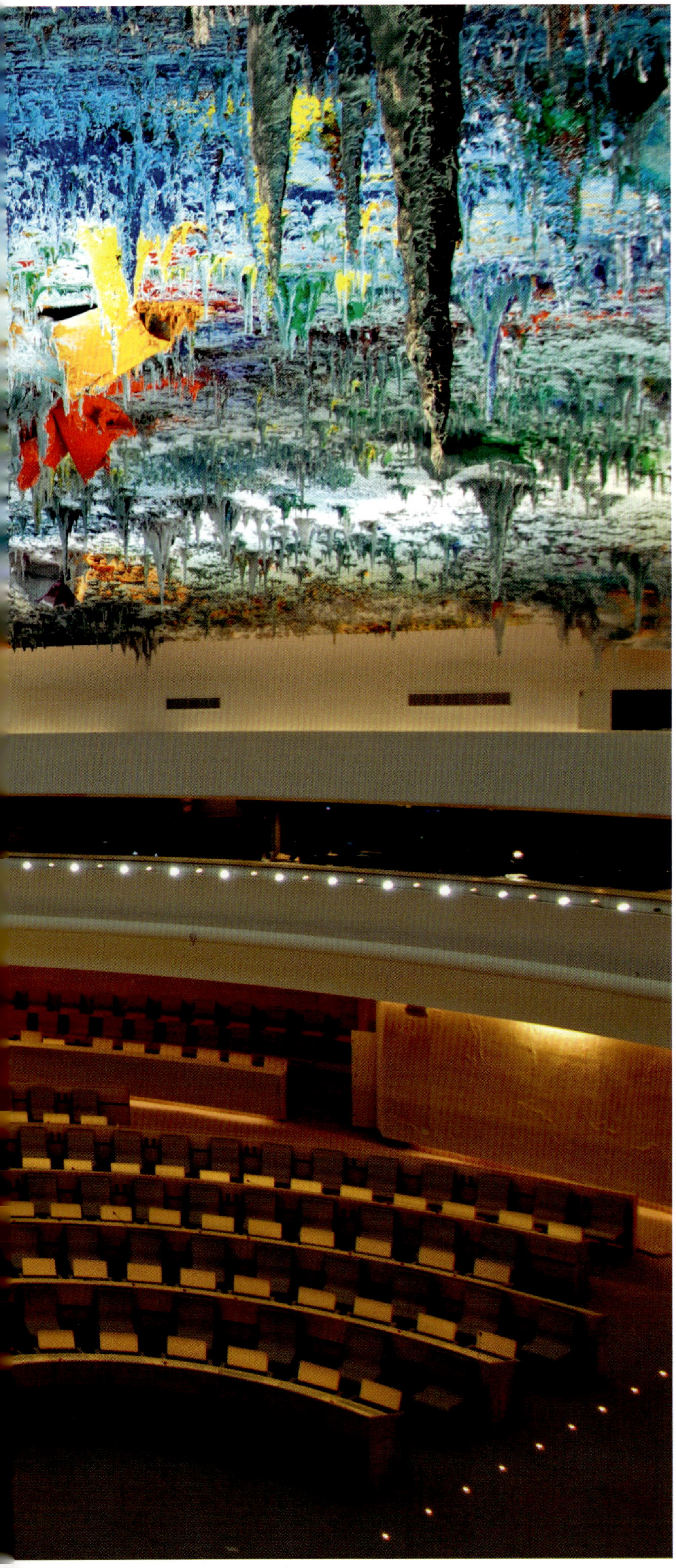

Left: The ceiling represents the geography of Earth's nations in thirty-five tonnes of paint, comprising pigments gleaned from earth and rocks from around the globe.

Below: Delegates read documents beneath Miquel Barceló's ceiling.

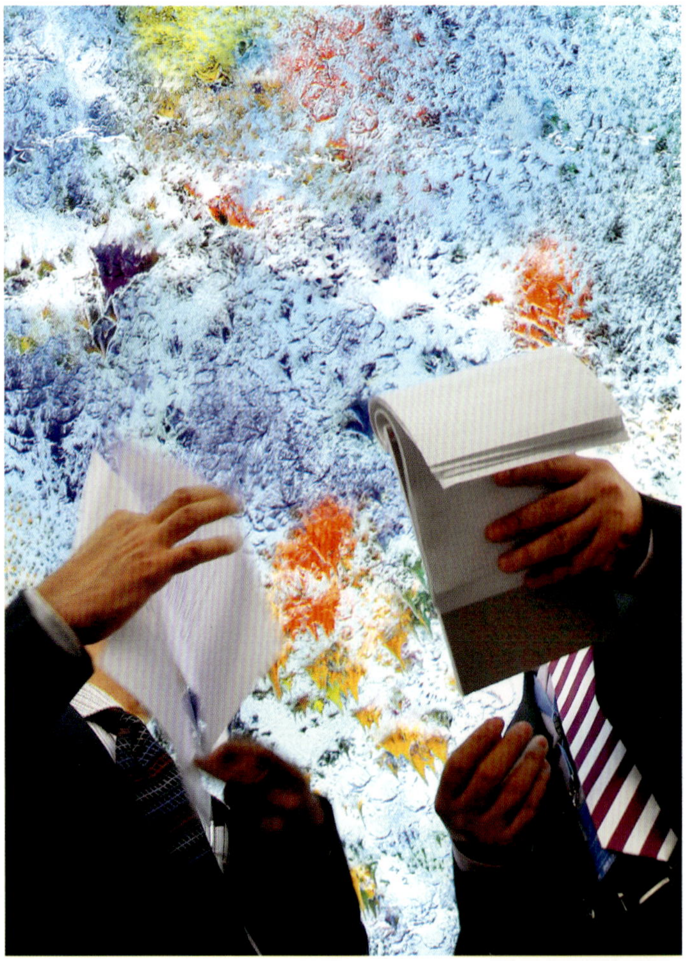

Paolo Veronese, Jacopo Tintoretto, Palma il Giovane
Hall of the Great Council
1575-78
Palazzo Ducale, Venice, Italy

Left: The central canvas depicting the *Apotheosis of Venice.*

Overleaf: The Hall of the Great Council in the Palazzo Ducale, Venice.

Palazzo Ducale, Italy

The throng of bodies often reached two thousand, each one an element in the great machine of the Venetian Republic. They met every Sunday, for the ritual business of running the affairs of state, a process that was as sanctified and essential to the health of the republic as attending church. As members of the Grand Council, they representated the patrician families of Venice whose names were listed in the Golden Book, and were the font from which all legislative and executive power was subsequently elected. Here on the *piano nobile* of the Palazzo Ducale (Doge's Palace; the official residence of the ruler of the republic and political heart of the city), the Grand Council were preoccupied with the legislative affairs of the state. They were also encased in a painting cycle spanning the walls and ceiling that was so complex it required a 128-page booklet to explain it. The booklet was written by Girolamo Bardi, a historian who was part of a specialist team enlisted with overseeing the production and design of the triumphalist decoration of the meeting room after a fire all but destroyed it in 1577. The decorative programme is a colourful and complex marriage between art and politics in which the iconography and narrative elements revolve around the glory and divinely appointed rulership of the republic of Venice.

An immense flat ceiling replaced the medieval barrelled original and was decorated with gilded cornices in which a series of paintings are installed. Premier painters of the period were employed, such as Paolo Veronese, who painted the central canvas depicting the *Apotheosis of Venice*, a scene of universal jubilation celebrating abundance and contentment across all sections of Venetian society. Poor, but happy, Venetians crowd around soldiers on horses in the foreground, while the noble classes jostle between a black slave and two turbaned Asians on the balustrade. They crane their necks to look up at the figure of Venice being crowned by a winged figure of victory, while another figure of victory sounds a trumpet horn. Venice is personified as a snooty blonde, dressed in the ducal robes of white and gold brocade with an ermine cape. She is modelled on figures of the goddess Roma from classical antique medals. This draws parallels between Venice and the cultural and military achievements of ancient Rome. Spiralling columns on either side of the image reference the Temple of Solomon in Jerusalem and envisage Venice as the new Christian capital of the world. Within these, two smaller towers flank the figure of Venice and recall the medieval gateway to the Venetian arsenal, the hub of Venice's naval power and her seemingly invincible maritime empire. A celestial court lies at Venice's feet on a semicircular cloud. They are all personifications of virtuous ideals that characterize the state. There is Honour with an olive branch and laurel crown next to Peace, also with an olive branch. Security appears with caduceus and crown, while a reclining seminude woman with exposed breast and her back to us represents Felicity or Good Fortune. Another blonde nude with wheat in her hair is a figure of Abundance, and Liberty in a red Phrygian cap completes the group.

Aside from her glorious virtues and centrality in the Christian, military and civilized world, Venice is also represented as a queenly and indisputable ruler of provinces. Palma il Giovane's *Venice Crowned by Victory Gathers her Subject Provinces* sees a crowned personification of the republic seated in profile and enswathed in

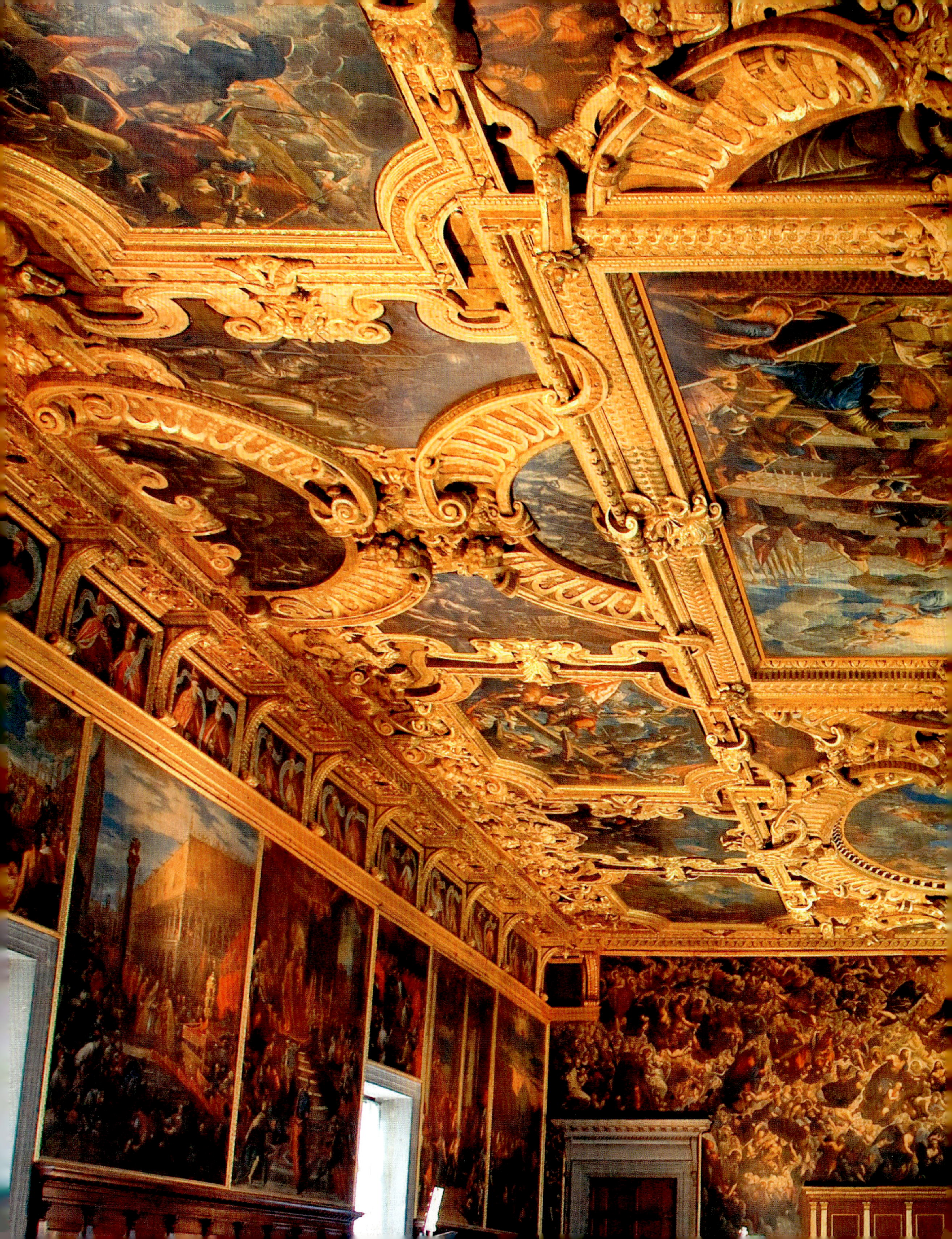

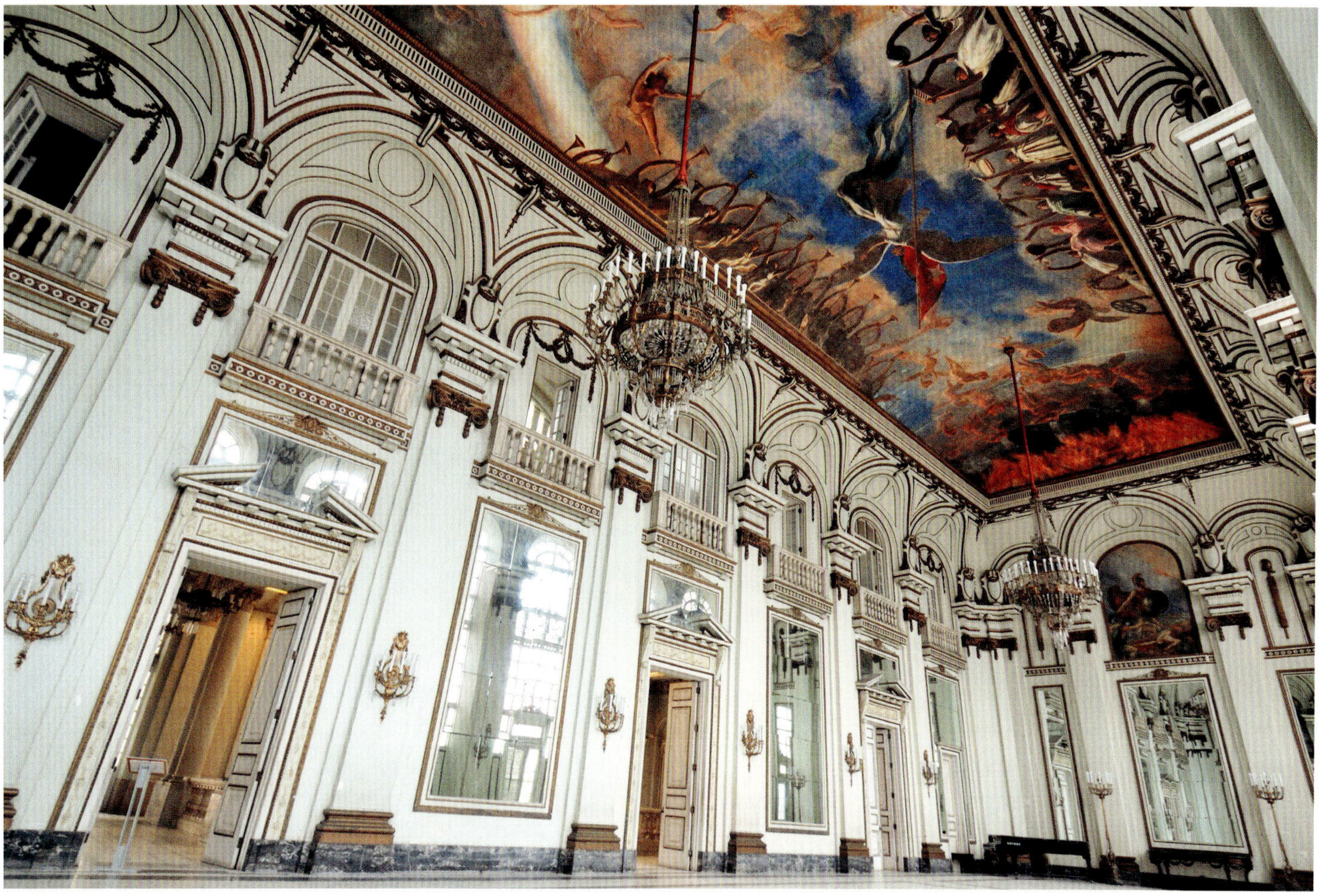

liberty, equality and fraternity borrowed from the ideology of the French Revolution, as well as being symbolic of the blood shed in the pursuit of freedom. The star was also an aspirational motif to draw associations with the stars and stripes on the Star-Spangled Banner, as Cuba had intended to join the United States in response to the USA's efforts in liberating the island. The rest of the design of the national flag is obscured in the image but consists of three blue stripes referring to the three political departments of the colonial island, and two white stripes signifying purity and strength. Flanking one side of the personification of Victory is a chorus of trumpets sounding out the chords of eternal glory, and on the other side, nine allegorical figures – potentially the Muses – offer symbols of music, architecture, painting and poetry, alongside the fruits of an abundant and blessed harvest.

The image is, therefore, a marriage of modern political and classical literary tropes, suggesting a mutual dependence between political victory and national pride on the one hand and the development of a country's arts, industry and knowledge on the other. As such, the glories of independence in 1902 continue conveniently to be relived through the revolution of 1959 in triumphalist fashion in the building's new role in celebrating just that.

Opposite: A chorus of trumpets flanks one side of the personification of Victory.

Above: Interior of the Museum of the Revolution.

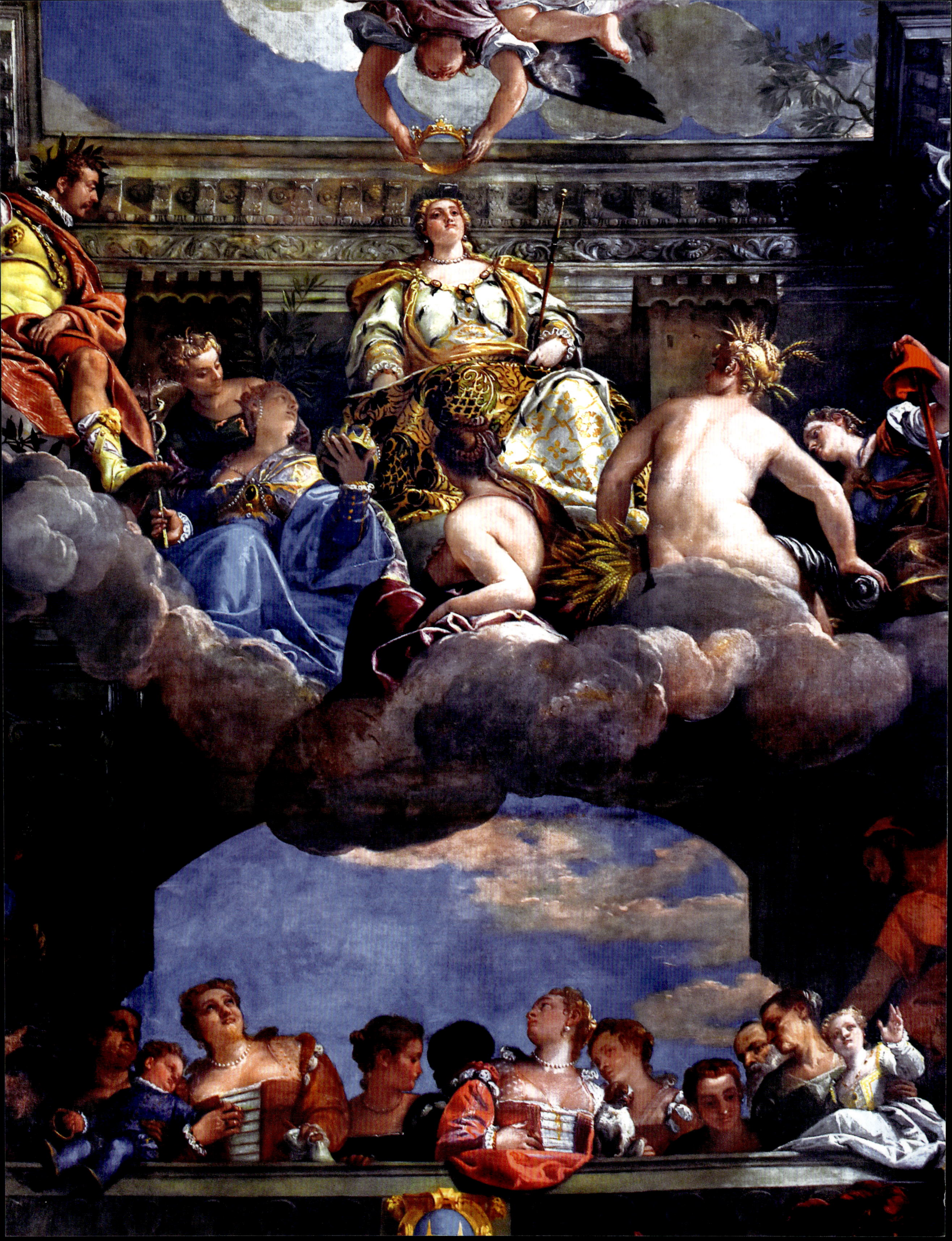

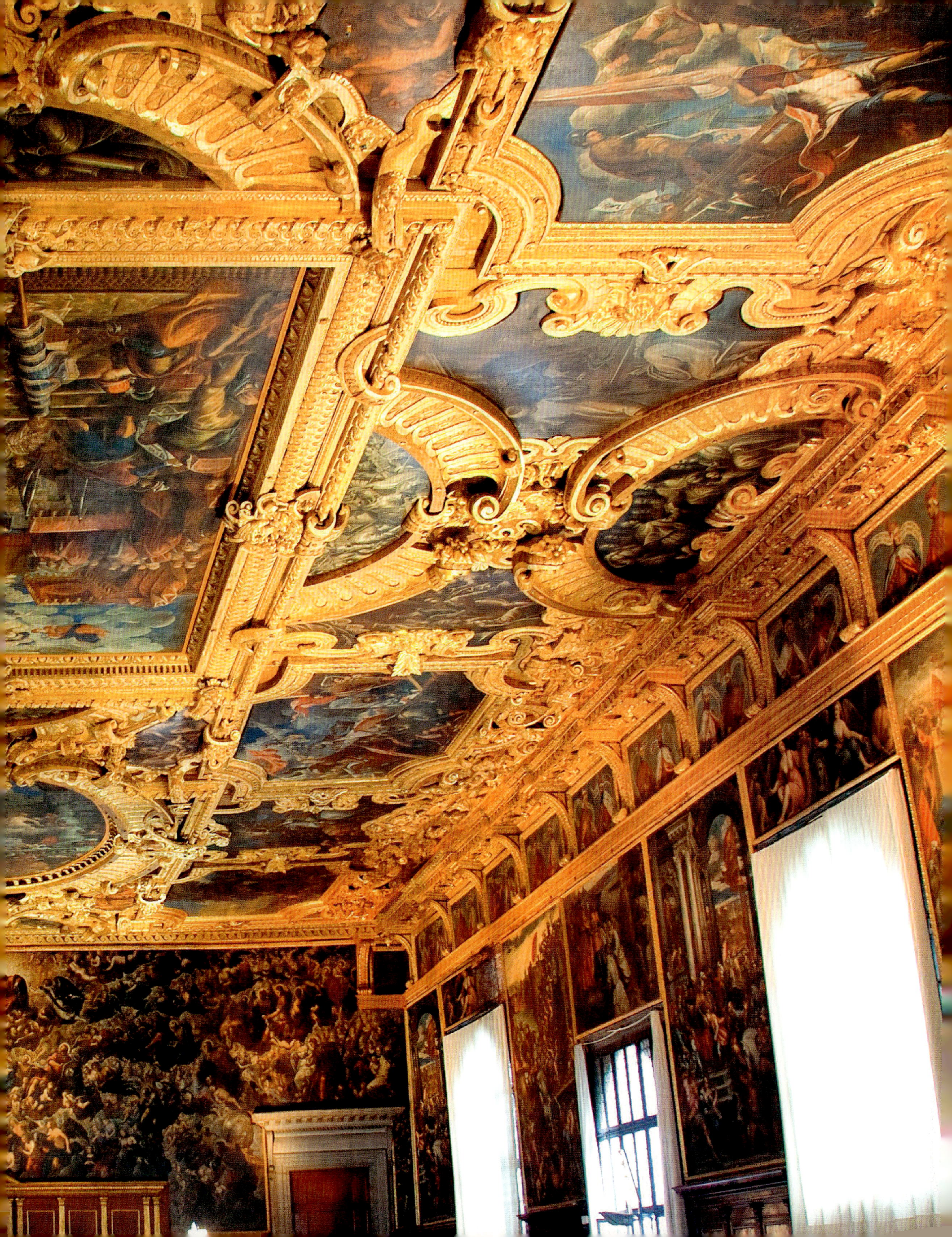

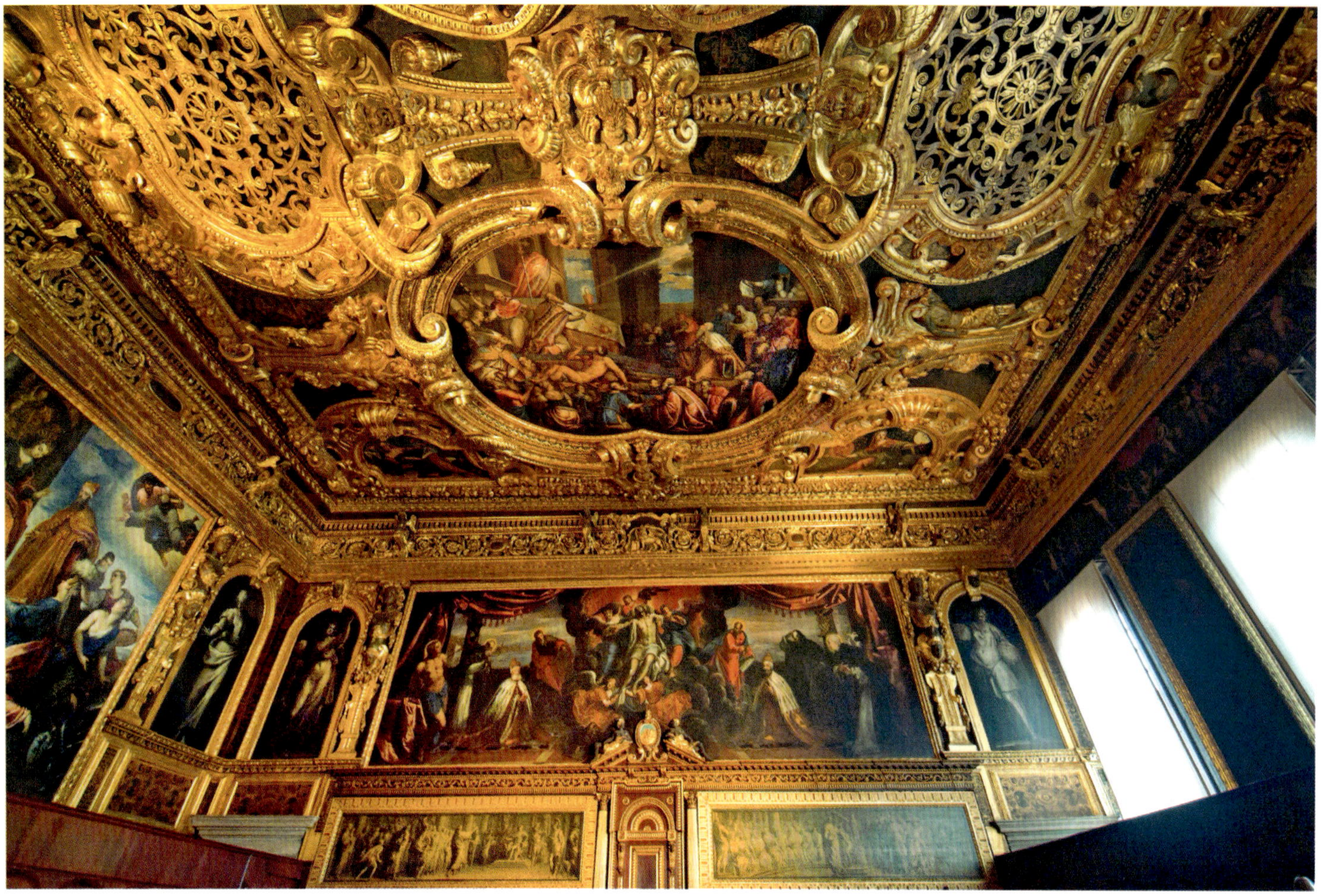

Above and opposite: The ceiling is decorated with personifications of the Virtues, as well as individual illustrations of Venetian bravery and courage.

Below: Palma il Giovane's *Venice Crowned by Victory Gathers her Subject Provinces*.

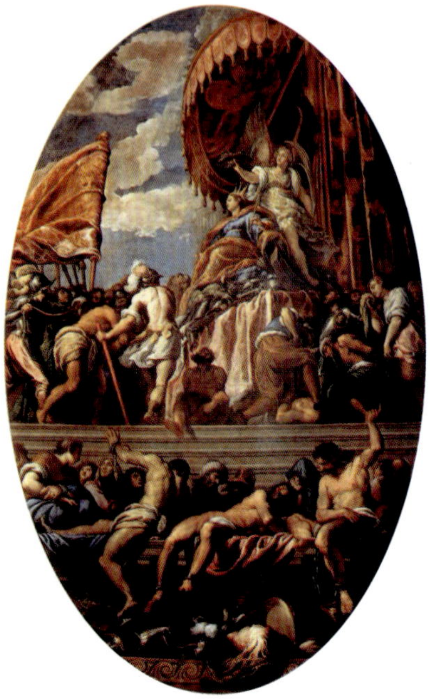

oceans of fabric under a scarlet baldachin. She sneers down over a parade of military commanders, who offer captive prisoners of war in chains who will make up the eventually peaceful provinces of ever-victorious Venice. This theme is continued in Jacopo Tintoretto's *Doge Niccolò da Ponte Receives Subject Cities and Provinces* in the centre of the ceiling. The facade of the Basilica of San Marco provides the backdrop, while representatives from conquered cities carry booty, standards and the keys of their dominions up a flight of stairs in offering to the doge who accepts them with outstretched arms. A crowned Venice bends down to offer a victory wreath to the doge and promotes the idea that divine justice supports the militaristic ambitions of the Venetian government, while reminding the council of the necessary cooperation of the provinces and territories to the health and stability of La Serenissima – the most serene republic.

Amid this extendedly vainglorious portrait, there are some tempering elements. Only personifications of Venice bear the symbols of power such as the sceptre, and never the princely ruler, the doge. This suggests that the investiture of power lies not in the autocratic individual, but abstractly in the ideal of the republic. There is also a reminder of the importance of sacrifice and humility – for example, Palma il Giovane's *Venetian Women Offer Their Jewels to the Republic* immortalizes the generosity of Venetian women in financing the war chest for the republic's wars against Genoa in 1378 and 1380.

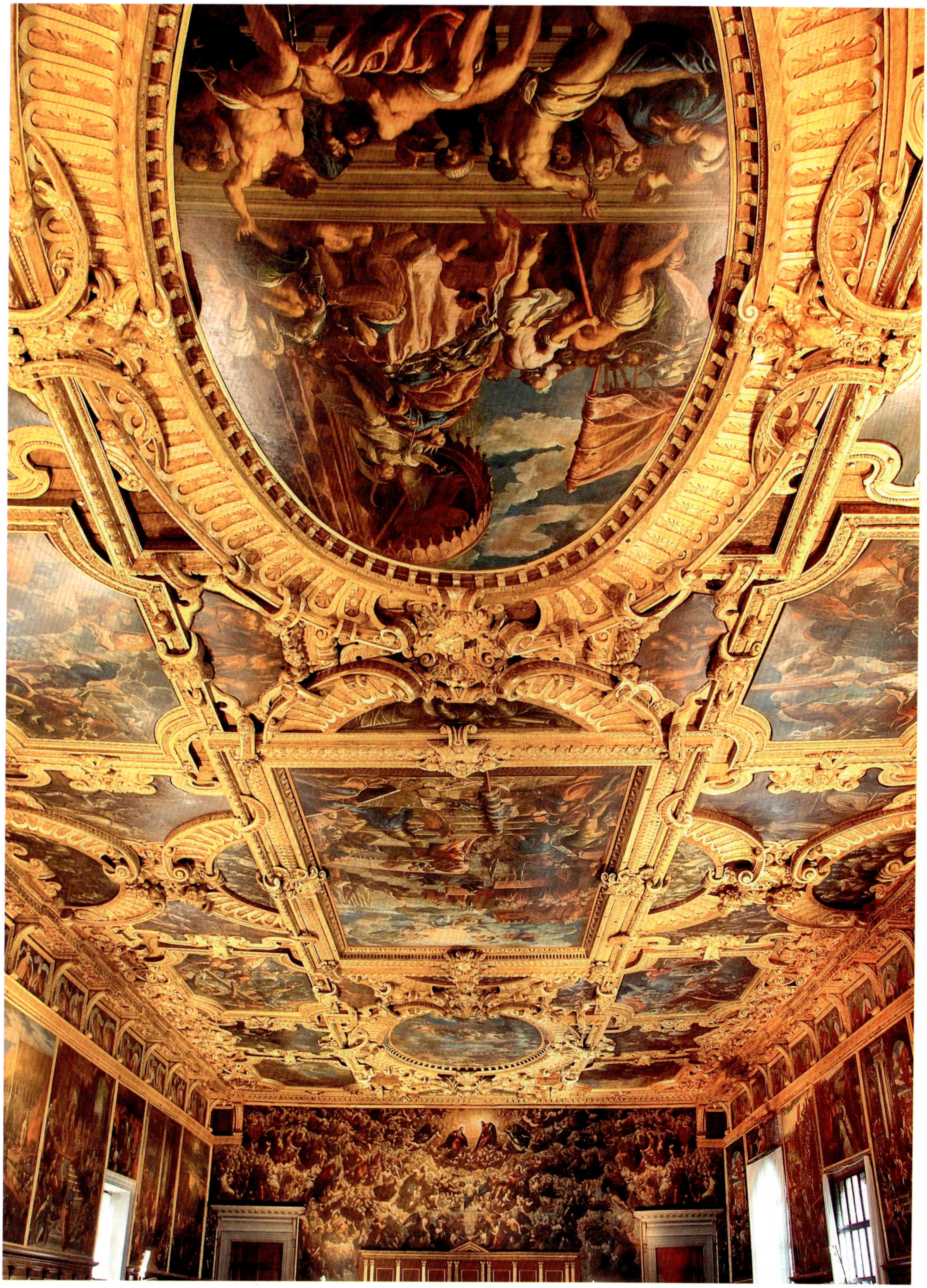

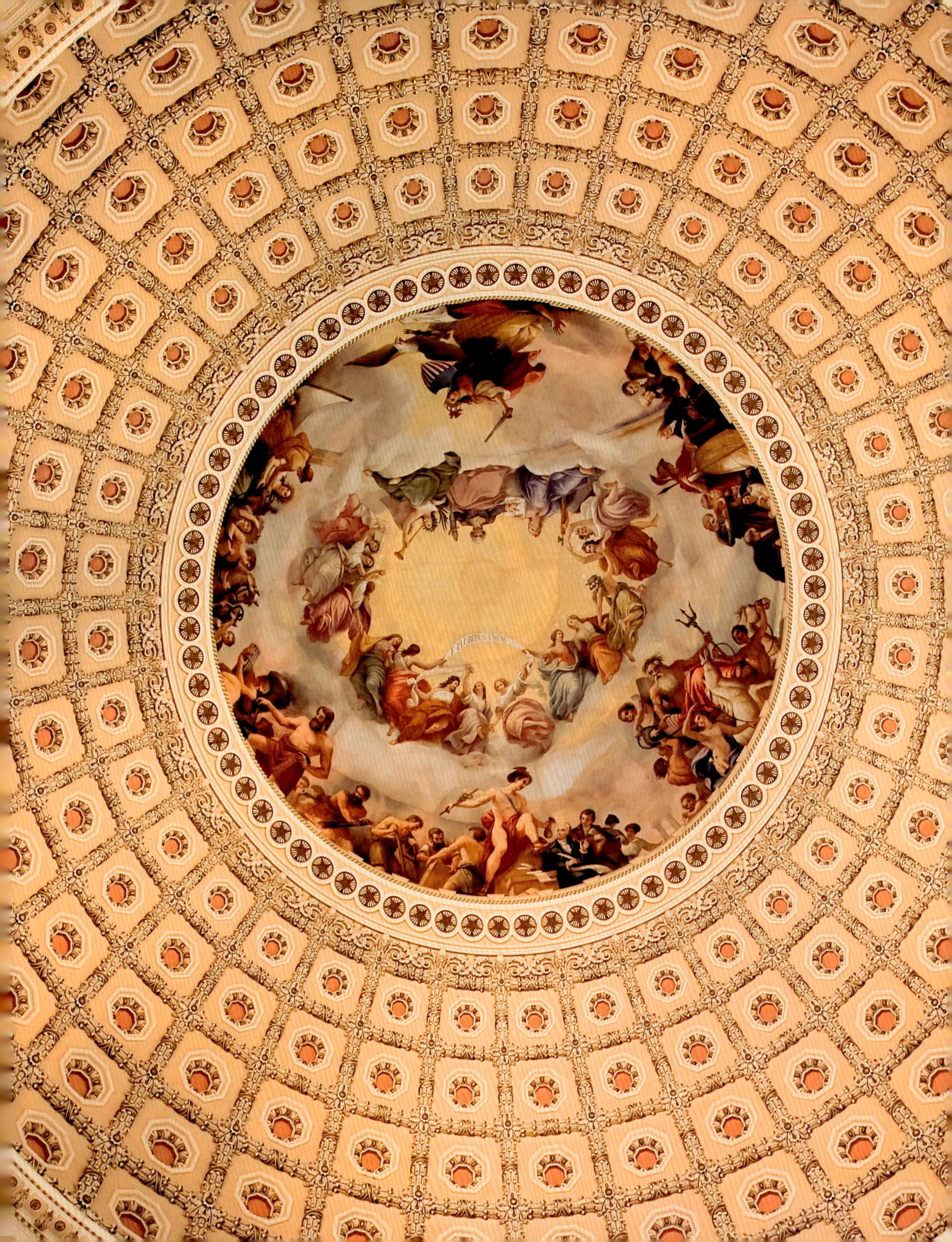
E PLURIBUS UNUM

Constantino Brumidi

The Apotheosis of Washington

1865

Capitol Building, Washington DC,
United States

Left and overleaf: Constantino Brumidi's *The Apotheosis of Washington* in the centre of the domed rotunda at the Capitol Building, Washington DC.

Capitol Building, USA

The process of nation-building is fraught with many decisions, not least how to craft a visual identity. Sometimes, the best place to start is through association and imitation of those you admire. So, if an apotheosis on a dome was good enough for the saints of the Catholic Church, and the palace ceilings of the popes and princes of Europe, why not take the same approach to immortalize the first president of the United States of America, commander-in-chief of the Continental Army George Washington? Also, to really make sure you hit the mark, you might want to do what other nations, such as Britain, did before they had a homegrown school of artists to fulfil public commissions, and call in the Italians.

The artist Constantino Brumidi was an immigrant to the United States, with a proven track record of prestigious commissions in his native Italy, including the interiors of Roman palaces and three years in the service of Pope Gregory XVI. The frescoed dome of the United States Capitol building draws richly on these visual sources and is an example of the ubiquitous neoclassical style that characterized the ideology and aesthetics of nineteenth-century America. Neoclassicism appropriated the visual motifs of the art and architecture of ancient Greece and ancient Rome as a way of emulating the politics, law-making and military supremacy of the classical past, at the time perceived to be the cultural pinnacle of civilization. Brumidi's spectacular canopy over the seat of US federal government looks to this classical past in its depiction of the birth of the United States' political and cultural identity as supported by a host of figures from classical mythology.

A portrait of the deceased President Washington looks down from his heavenly court in a limpid, pastel sky. Dressed in imperial purple, he is enthroned among virtuous personifications that promote a glorious tale of the United States of America in the nineteenth century. Directly beneath the gruff-looking president is a figure of war in the service of freedom. She gloats over figures of tyranny and kingly power (the most vilified privilege of the Enlightenment era) like the handmaiden of the president, who became an international symbol for liberation and nationalism as the leader of the first successful revolution against a colonial empire in the American War of Independence. War is accompanied by a far more bellicose-looking eagle carrying thunderbolts. Chosen for its attributes of long life and majestic appearance, the symbol of the bald eagle became synonymous with the United States after it was emblazoned on the Great Seal from 1782. However, it also draws parallels with the regal eagle that accompanied Jupiter, king of the pagan gods.

To the left of Washington, a winged figure of Victory draped in green sounds a horn, while to his right sits a figure of Liberty in a red Phrygian cap brandishing the glinting blade of the fasces, the symbol of authority from ancient Rome. Making a circle on either side of this central trio are thirteen women in flowing, classically inspired robes, each with a star above her head. These represent the thirteen colonies on the Atlantic coast of America who declared independence from British rule in 1776 to form the United States. Opposite the president, the women hold a banner with the Latin words *E Pluribus Unum*, meaning From one, many.

Around the outer circle of the image, mythological gods mingle with captains of industry and acts of invention. For example, Minerva, goddess of wisdom, appears with helmet and

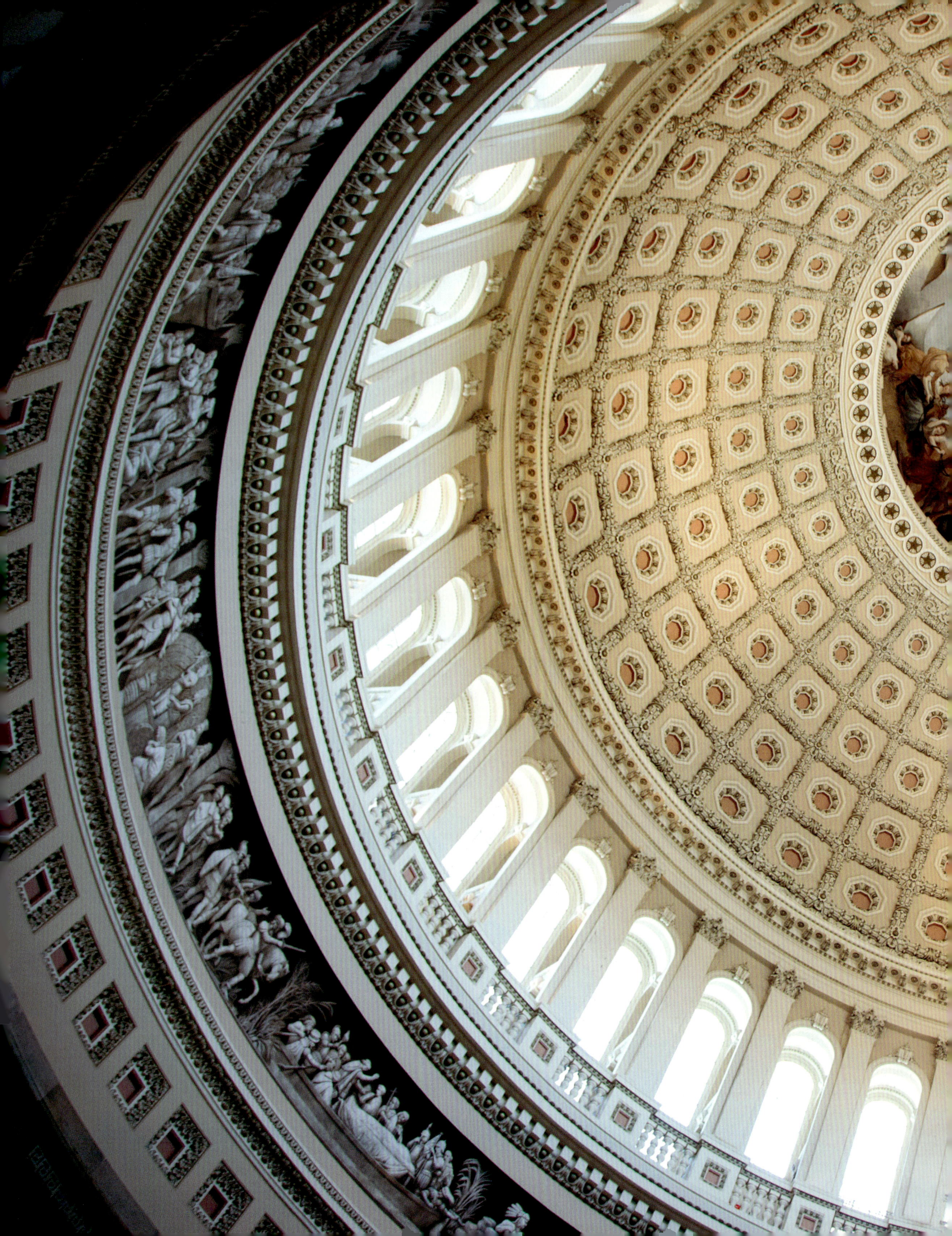

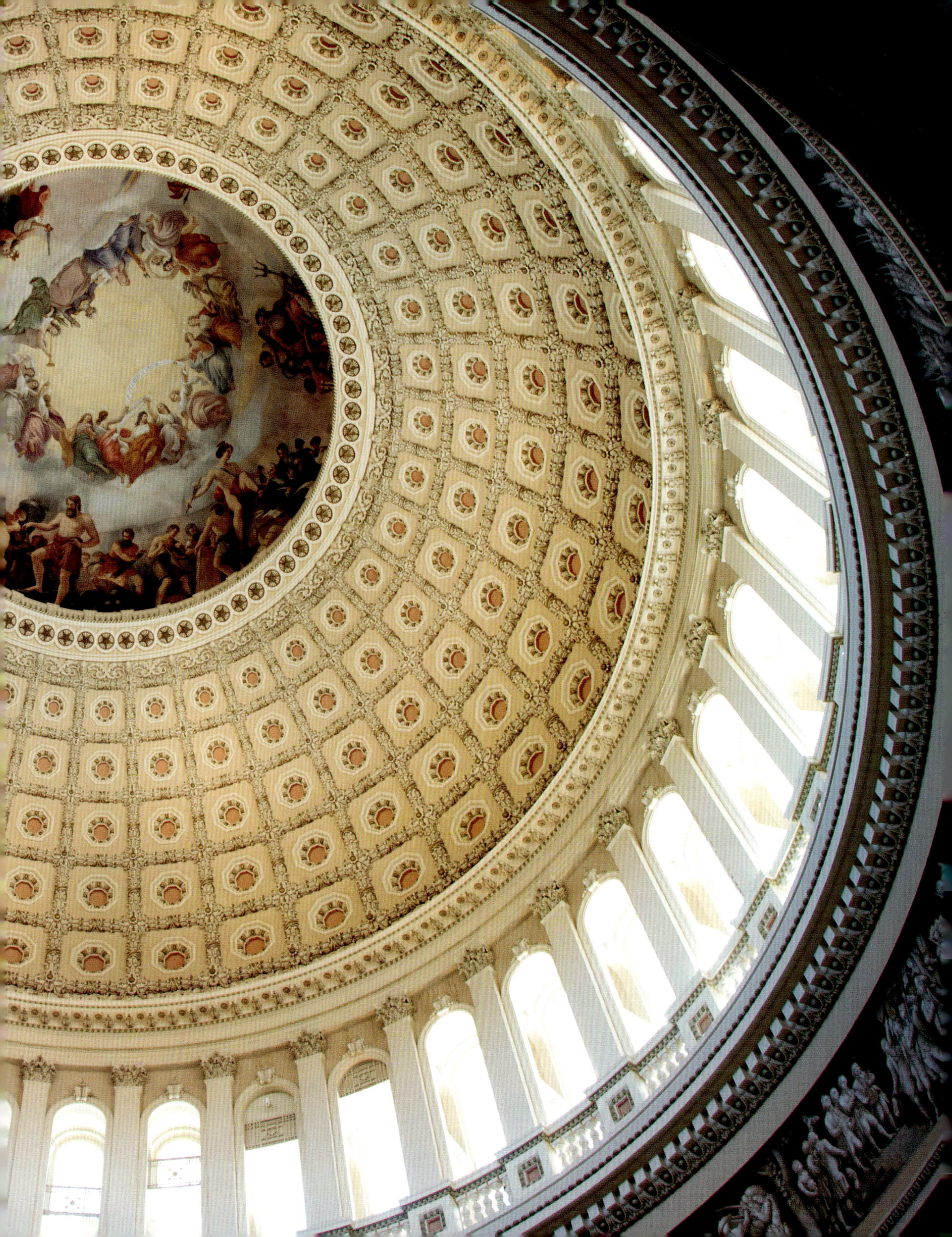

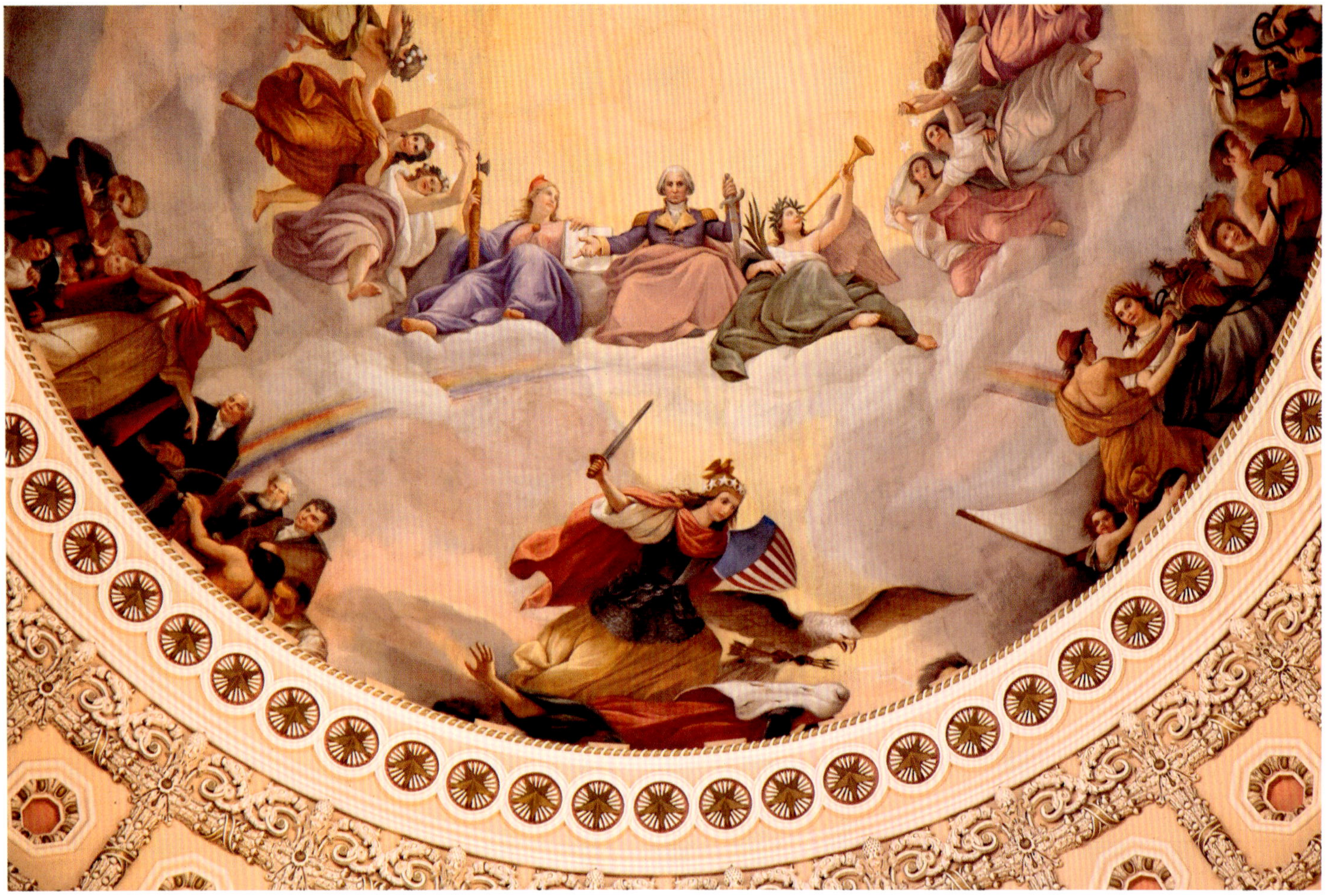

spear and points (in a gesture of anachronistic artistic licence) to an electrical generator for powering batteries. This represents American nineteenth-century invention while American scientists Benjamin Franklin, Samuel F. B. Morse and Robert Fulton watch on. Elsewhere, the marine god Neptune with his white beard and trident oversees the laying of the undersea transatlantic telegraph by the goddess Venus, an invention that reduced the communication time between America and Europe that had taken up to ten days with unreliable sea crossings, to a matter of minutes.

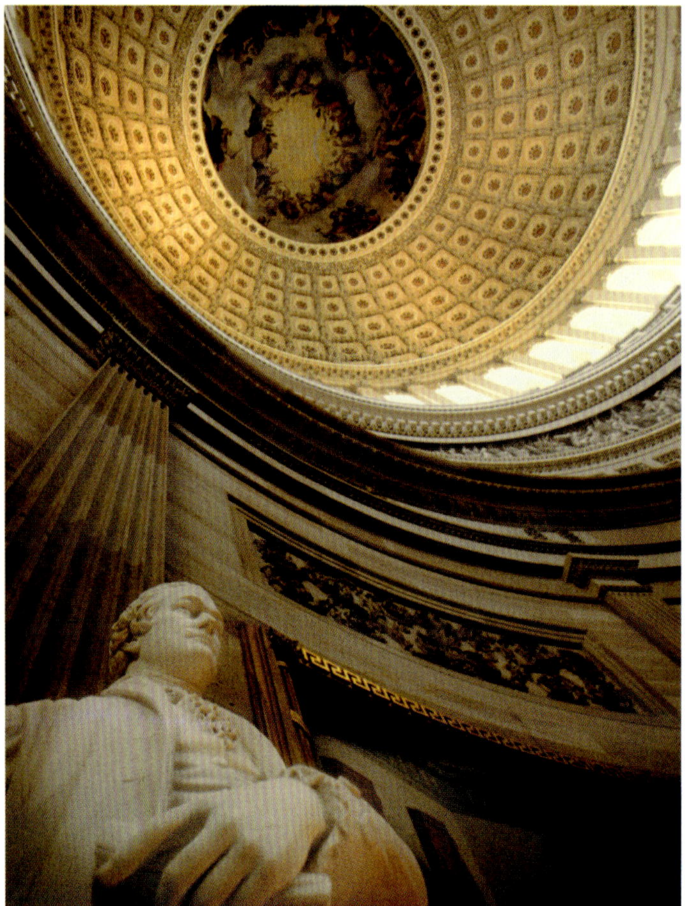

Above: A figure of war in the service of freedom, complete with a shield bearing the red, white and blue of the American flag, gloats over figures of tyranny. Accompanying her is a bald eagle, chosen for its attributes of long life and majestic appearance.

Right: A statue of Alexander Hamilton beneath *The Apotheosis of Washington.*

Opposite: At the centre of the work, President Washington looks down from his heavenly court, dressed in imperial purple.

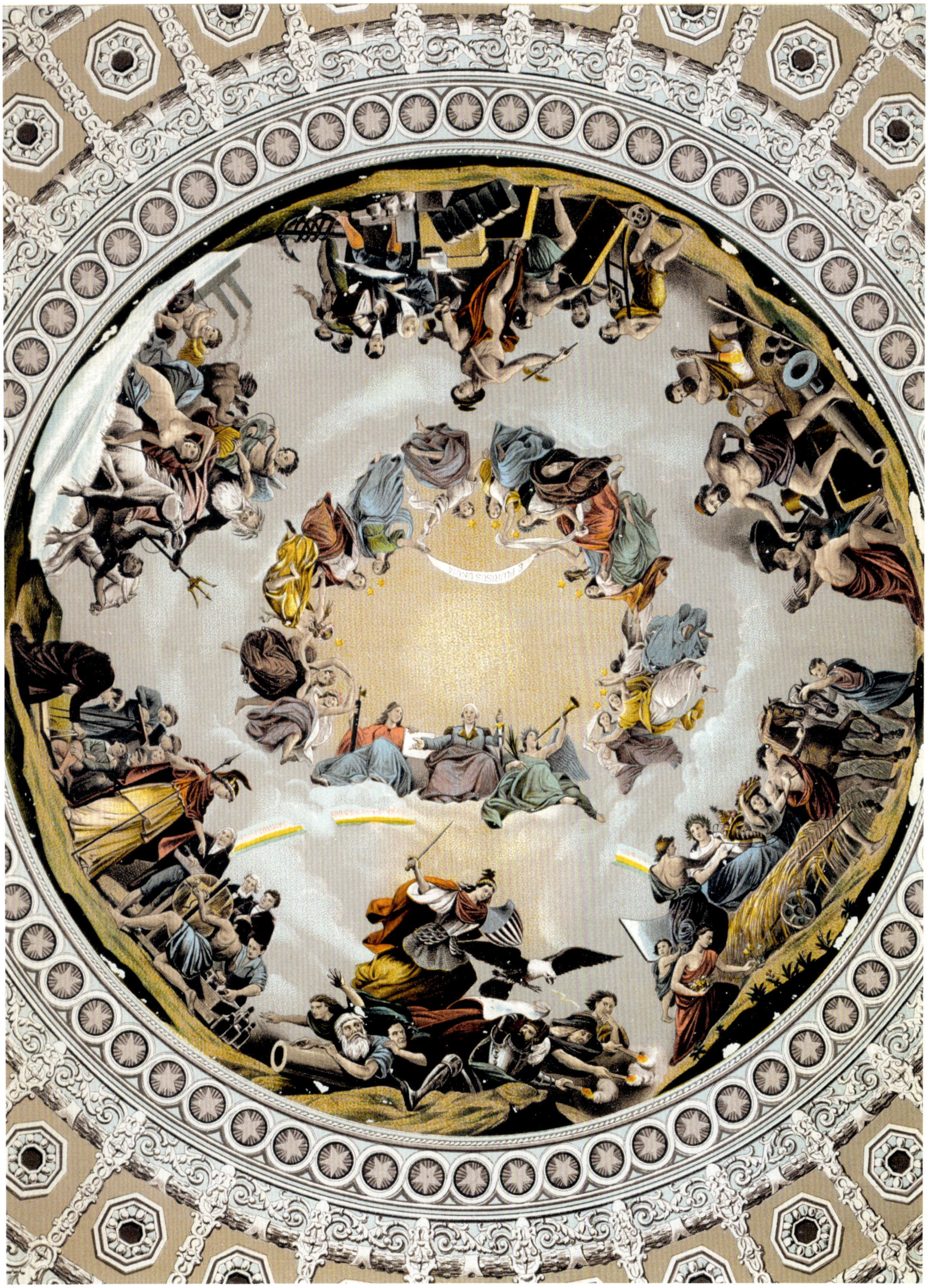

Further reading

Alpers, Svetlana and Baxandall, Michael, *Tiepolo and the Pictorial Intelligence* (London and New Haven: Yale University Press, 1994)

Auclair, Mathias and Provoyeur, Pierre, *The Chagall Ceiling at the Opera Garnier* (New York and Paris: Editions d'Art Gourcuff Gradenigo, 2013)

Babaie, Sussan, *Isfahan and Its Palaces: Statecraft, Shi`ism and the Architecture of Conviviality in Early Modern Iran* (Edinburgh: Edinburgh University Press, 2018)

Barkan, Leonard, *Unearthing the Past: Archaeology and Aesthetics in the Making of Renaissance Culture* (New Haven and London: Yale University Press, 1999)

Bazzotti, Ugo, *Palazzo Te: Giulio Romano's Masterwork in Mantua* (London: Thames and Hudson, 2013)

Bernadac, Marie-Laure, *Cy Twombly, The Ceiling: Un plafond pour le Louvre* (Paris: Editions du Regard, 2010)

Bikaner, Rajyashree Kumari, *Palace of Clouds: A Memoir* (New Delhi: Bloomsbury, 2018)

Cheney, Liana De Girolami, ed., *Radiance and Symbolism in Modern Stained Glass: European and American Innovations and Aesthetic Interrelations in Material Culture* (Newcastle: Cambridge Scholars Publishing, 2016)

Christiansen, Keith and Mann, Judith W., *Orazio and Artemisia Gentileschi* (London and New Haven: Yale University Press, 2001)

Dempsey, Charles, *Annibale Carracci: The Farnese Gallery, Rome* (New York: George Brazillier, 1995)

Donovan, Fiona, *Rubens and England* (London and New Haven: Yale University Press, 2004)

Gillgren, Peter and Snickare, Mårten, ed., *Performativity and Performance in Baroque Rome* (Abingdon: Routledge, 2017)

Hur, Nam-lin, *Prayer and Play in Late Tokugawa Japan: Asakusa Sensō-ji and Edo Society* (Cambridge, MA: Harvard University Press, 2000)

Irwin, Robert, *The Alhambra* (London: Profile Books, 2011)

Jensen, Robin, *Living Water: Images, Symbols, and Settings of Early Christian Baptism* (Leiden and Boston: Brill, 2010)

King, Ross, *Michelangelo and the Pope's Ceiling* (London: Random House, 2012)

Lucas, Anya and others, *The Painted Hall: Sir James Thornhill's Masterpiece at Greenwich* (London: Merrell Publishers, 2019)

Ortayli, Ilber, *Topkapi Palace: Milestones in Ottoman History* (Clifton, New Jersey: Blue Dome Publishing, 2008)

Schulz, Juergen, *Venetian Painted Ceilings of the Renaissance* (California: University of California Press, 1968)

van Hensbergen, Gij, *The Sagrada Familia: Gaudí's Heaven on Earth* (London: Bloomsbury, 2017)

Index

Page numbers in *italics* refer to illustrations

Index

Index

Picture credits

The publishers would like to thank the institutions, picture libraries and photographers for their kind permission to reproduce the works featured in this book. Every effort has been made to trace all copyright holders but if any have been inadvertently overlooked, the publishers would be pleased to make the necessary arrangements at the first opportunity.

4 Scott J. Ferrell/Getty 6 Brian Jannsen/Alamy 8 Royal Academy of Arts, London (Photographer: John Hammond) 9 Royal Collection Trust/© Her Majesty Queen Elizabeth II 2019 10-11 A. Astes/Alamy 12 Cultura RM/Alamy 14 Tuul and Bruno Morandi/Alamy 16-17 Riccardo Sala/Alamy 18 JIPEN/Alamy 19 RnDmS/Getty 20 Richard Maschmeyer/Alamy 22-23 Quentin Bargate/Alamy 24tl Hemis/Alamy 24tr Sarah Crake/Alamy 24b Melvyn Longhurst/Alamy 25t Hemis/Alamy 25b Sue Martin/Alamy 26 EThamPhoto/Alamy 28-29 Rob Whitworth/Alamy 30l Factofoto/Alamy 30r Cultura RM/Alamy 31t dsounak07/Alamy 31b Nathaniel Noir/Alamy 32 Aliaksandr Mazurkevich/Alamy 34-36 imageBROKER/Alamy 37t Jakob Fischer/Alamy 37b robertharding/Alamy 38 Creative Lab/Shutterstock 40 Creative Lab/Shutterstock 40-41 (Gatefold) akg-images/WHA/World History Archive 41t Vatican2008/Alamy 41b Mondadori Portfolio/Getty 42t Alessandra Benedetti - Corbis/Getty 42b funkyfood London - Paul Williams/Alamy 43tl Granger Historical Picture Archive/Alamy 43tr Christa Knijff/Alamy 43b Peter Barritt/Alamy 44 robertharding/Alamy 46-47 imageBROKER/Alamy 48t dbimages/Alamy 48b PRISMA ARCHIVO/Alamy 49 robertharding/Alamy 50 Hemis/Alamy 52 isogood/Alamy 53 Marco Varrone/Alamy 54 Roberto Fumagalli/Alamy 56t Martin Lindsay/Alamy 56b robertharding/Alamy 57t Novarc Images/Alamy 57b imageBROKER/Alamy 58 KHALED KASSEM/Alamy 60-61 age fotostock/Alamy 62 Tooykrub/Shutterstock 63t DutchMen/Shutterstock 63m KHALED KASSEM/Alamy 63b Crystite RF/Alamy 64 Kerrick James/Alamy 66 Didier Baverel/Getty 68-69 JOHN KELLERMAN/Alamy 70 Hemis/Alamy 71t GAUTIER Stephane/Alamy 71bl Phillip Minnis/Alamy 71br imageBROKER/Alamy 72 Neil Farrin/Getty 74-77t Azoor Photo/Alamy 77b Pictures Now/Alamy 78-80t A. Astes/Alamy 80b Hemis/Alamy 81 robertharding/Alamy 82 Leonid Serebrennikov/Alamy 84-85 Howard Sayer/Alamy 86 JOHN KELLERMAN/Alamy 88 JOHN KELLERMAN/Alamy 88-89 (Gatefold) Hemis/Alamy 89 Andrew Duke/Alamy 90 Stefano Politi Markovina/Alamy 91 B.O'Kane/Alamy 92 David BERTHO/Alamy 94t JONATHAN NACKSTRAND/Getty 94b David BERTHO/Alamy 95t David Kleyn/Alamy 95m Isaac Mok/Shutterstocker 95b David Kleyn/Alamy 96-97 Svetlana Day/Alamy 98 Carlos Soto 100-101 Bildagentur-online/Schickert/Alamy 102t Michael Miller/therealsanjose.com 102b DEA/A. DAGLI ORTI/Getty 103 The Artchives/Alamy 104 Kristina Blokhin/Alamy 106-107 Exotica/Alamy 108t Alessio Catelli/Shutterstock 108b Peter Ptschelinzew/Alamy 109 Alexandre Rotenberg/Alamy 110 erlucho/Shutterstock 112-113 ap-photo/Alamy 114 Danita Delimont/Alamy 115t ap-photo/Alamy 115b Gerardo C. Lerner/Shutterstock 116 Kumar Sriskandan/Alamy 118-119 Craig Lovell/Eagle Visions Photography/Alamy 120t Kerrick James/Alamy 120b Olena Buyskykh/Alamy 121 Paul Maguire/Alamy 122 DEA/G. NIMATALLAH/Getty 124 Rolf Richardson/Alamy 126 Royal Collection Trust/© Her Majesty Queen Elizabeth II 2019 127 image/Alamy 128 Leisa Taylor/Alamy 130-131 Images & Stories/Alamy 132t B.O'Kane/Alamy 132b Luis Dafos/Alamy 133 Hilary Morgan/Alamy 134 Walter Bibikow/Getty 136-137 Heritage Image Partnership Ltd/Alamy 138t De Agostini/M. Carrieri/Getty 138b DEA/M. CARRIERI/Getty 139 Photo Scala, Florence 140-141 Kimberley Coole/Getty 142 Tom Allwood/Alamy 144 DEA/G. NIMATALLAH/Getty 146-147 Ivan Vdovin/Alamy 148 DEA/G. NIMATALLAH/Getty 149l Ivan Vdovin/Alamy 149r Artexplorer/Alamy 150 Philipp Zechner/Alamy 152 Gaertner/Alamy 152-153 (Gatefold) Samuel Magal, Sites & Photos Ltd./Bridgeman Images 153 Endless Travel/Alamy 154 imageBROKER/Alamy 155t Ian Dagnall/Alamy 155b Ihsan Gercelman/Alamy 156-159 Anthony P. Morris, Farmoor/Alamy 160 Rolf Richardson/Alamy 161t RGB Ventures/SuperStock/Alamy 161b The Picture Art Collection/Alamy 162 DEA/C. GEROLIMETTO/Getty 164-165 Stefano Valentini/MiBAC 166 The Picture Art Collection/Alamy 167 Valery Voennyy/Alamy 168 jesuspereira/Shutterstock 170-172t Christophe Ketels/Alamy 172b-173 jesuspereira/Shutterstock 174 ITAR-TASS News Agency/Alamy 176 Hermitage/Wikimedia Commons 176-177 Sergey Lyashenko/Shutterstock 178-181 DEA/G. DALGI ORTI/Getty 182t Bildarchiv Monheim GmbH/Alamy 182b The Picture Art Collection/Alamy 183 INTERFOTO/Alamy 184 Tenreiro/Shutterstock 186 GABRIEL BOUYS/Getty 188-189 Agf/REX/Shutterstock 190t Eric VANDEVILLE/GAMMA-RAPHO/Getty 190b PD-Art/Wikimedia Commons 191t Eric VANDEVILLE/GAMMA-RAPHO/Getty 191b adam eastland/Alamy 192-196t imageBROKER/Alamy 196b Pierre André/Wikimedia Commons 197 DEZAIN_Junkie/Alamy 198 akg-images/Album/Ramon Manent 200-201 Cultura RM Exclusive/Quim Roser 202 akg-images/Album/Ramon Manent 203t akg-images/Album/Kurwenal/Prisma 203b akg-images/Album/Ramon Manent 204 Sam Whittaker/Opus Conservation 206-207 Alex Segre/Alamy 208 Arcaid Images/Alamy 209 Sam Whittaker/Opus Conservation 210 GFC Collection/Alamy 212-213 imageBROKER/Alamy 213 FABRICE COFFRINI/Getty 214 DEA/P. BAUDRY/Getty 216 age fotostock/Alamy 216-217 (Gatefold) Anne-Marie Palmer/Alamy 217-218 age fotostock/Alamy 219 adam eastland/Alamy 220 Peter Horree/Alamy 222-223 Hemis/Alamy 224t dominic dibbs/Alamy 224b Web Gallery of Art/Wikimedia Commons 225 Hemis/Alamy 226 Wiliam Perry/Alamy 228-229 National Geographic Image Collection/Alamy 230t Danita Delimont/Alamy 230b Randy Duchaine/Alamy 231 Photo 12/Getty

First published in 2019 by White Lion Publishing,
an imprint of The Quarto Group.

The Old Brewery, 6 Blundell Street
London, N7 9BH,
United Kingdom
T (0)20 7700 6700
www.QuartoKnows.com

A catalogue record for this book is available from the British Library.

ISBN 978 0 71124 217 3
Ebook ISBN 978 0 71124 846 5

10 9 8 7 6 5 4 3

Design by Glenn Howard
Printed in China

FSC
MIX
Paper from responsible sources
FSC® C124385

Quarto Knows